THE ECONOMIC PROCESS

T0290532

THE ECONOMIC PROCESS

An Instantaneous Non-Newtonian Picture

EXPANDED EDITION

Carmine Gorga

University Press of America,® Inc.
Lanham · Boulder · New York · Toronto · Plymouth, UK

University Press of America,® Inc.
4501 Forbes Boulevard
Suite 200
Lanham, Maryland 20706
UPA Acquisitions Department (301) 459-3366

Estover Road
Plymouth PL6 7PY
United Kingdom

Library of Congress Control Number: 2009938687
ISBN: 978-0-7618-4953-7 (paperback : alk. paper)
eISBN: 978-0-7618-4954-4

Illustrators: Carmine Gorga, Richard W. Tarr, and Barry Rower

Dedicated to

Franco Modigliani

for lending his enormous intellectual and moral assistance
in the application of new modes of thinking
to the difficult field of economic theory

Contents

PROLEGOMENA
(Preliminaries)

PART I
Overall Analysis of Keynes' Model

PART II
Analysis of the Component Elements of Keynes' Model

List of Illustrations

A Synopsis

This work...

- makes the economic discourse again intelligible to the layman

- transforms economics from a linear to a dynamic and organic discipline

- provides the framework for truly productive and just economic policies

Acknowledgments

A WORK LIKE THIS IS THE PRODUCT of many influences. The direct ones are acknowledged in the text. But no less important are the indirect ones, which—with certain incompleteness—can only briefly be mentioned here. Special thanks go to Professoressa Rosalia Scarlata from the Liceo Classico Sannazaro in Naples, Italy, who taught more than philosophy—she taught her class how to think; and to Professors Catello Cosenza, Vittorio de Caprariis, and Esposito De Falco: all three from the University of Naples. The first for guiding the initial steps through microeconomics; the second for firmly directing this writer's studies in that delicate area which lies between politics and political economy; and the third for visibly demonstrating some of the difficulties which lie in a purely mathematical approach to the study of economics.

An inestimable debt is owed to the 1999 Nobel laureate in economics, Professor Robert A. Mundell for instructing this writer, while at the Bologna Center of the Johns Hopkins' School of Advanced International Studies, in macroeconomic theory and policy; and to Professor John Powelson at the same School in Washington, D.C., for letting him utter the first words "in economics."

Two informal teachers, Mr. Mitchell S. Lurio and Mr. Norman G. Kurland, have dispelled many a cobweb in the field of economic policy; considering the relationships between economic policy and economic theory, their efforts could not but—however pallidly—be reflected here. Specific contributions are, of course, duly acknowledged in the text. And no less important has been the opportunity provided by Dr. Marco De Gasperi, Mr. John D. Atwood, and Mr. L. Denton Crews (together with their associates and superiors) to let this writer practice economics respectively in the fields of marketing and economic analysis, city planning, and community economic development from the perspective of President Johnson's War on Poverty.

Professors Harry G. Johnson of the Chicago and London School of Economics, John K. Shank of the Harvard Business School, and Raymond G. Torto of the University of Massachusetts were kind enough to submit themselves not only to a verbal presentation but even to the reading of a bare outline of the revision of Keynes' model. Passing those tests proved encouragement enough to further analysis.

And how to thank Dr. Franco Modigliani, Institute Professor at MIT, 1976 president of the American Economic Association, and 1985 Nobel laureate in economics? In long and intense series of conferences, he has not only dispelled remaining gray areas from the mind of the writer and compelled him to think more and harder.

Professor Modigliani has also contributed specific, crucial, clarifications to this work. Those that are of such magnitude as to be clearly identifiable have, of course, been duly acknowledged in the text. It is unfortunately impossible to mention the many subtle ones that have a running influence throughout the body of the work. He has been for me a true maestro of Socrates' school, the *maieutica*.

The composition of this book has been strangely bracketed by the *absence* of Professor M. L. Burstein. On the recommendation of Alan Reynolds, I sent this work to him. In a letter dated October 14, 1978 he wrote: "Thank you very much for...your very-well-written...THE ECONOMIC PROCESS....I fear that I am Hamlet to your Fortinbras." Ever since then, in a hundred different ways he sustained my efforts to continue this work; yet, sadly, he passed away just when I resumed working on it and the proposal was accepted for publication.

Professor David C. Murphy has generously read part of the final manuscript and found a few slips of the cursor. Joshua Brackett has provided the proper name for a key mathematical relationship used in this work. Readers who have graciously extended editorial assistance are my wife, Joan M. Gorga, David S. Wise, George R. Feiwel, Mitchell S. Lurio, Norman G. Kurland, Dr. Robert L. French, Louis J. Ronsivalli, and David A. Nunes, who has been my toughest critic. I have not hesitated to incorporate their suggestions and to give them credit whenever possible. David Wise has been with me from beginning to end of this project. I owe him an additional note of gratitude: he has helped me strive for the right tone. The traditional disclaimer is most appropriate in this context: whatever outright error, whatever awkwardness of style, whatever obscurity of expression remains in this work is the sole responsibility of the writer.

Two student volunteers of the Center for American Studies at Concord, Richard F. Connolly and Ryan D. Banks, generously granted assistance for typing, proofreading, and basic book design. Ultimately a professional editor, Sandra F. Horwitz, and a professional book designer, Barry Rower, calmed my last fears of bringing this work to the judgment of the world.

Without my Moona's steering of our *oeconomia*, this work might have not been done. My wife is owed still another acknowledgment. Whatever degree of concreteness is to be found in this work is due to her long, subtle, and patient training of an absent-minded professor-without-tenure.

To all, *Gratias*.

Preface to Expanded Edition

*With the help of the reader,
this will eventually become,
as Benjamin Franklin said,
a new, and more elegant edition,
Revised and corrected
by*
THE (A)UTHOR

———

THE LITERATI, FOLLOWING CERVANTES, have been chasing the windmills for a few centuries now; the engineers, following Galileo, have been building better and better windmills; all the while, the oligarchs have been acquiring control of the windmills. Clearly, this is a situation that cannot go on indefinitely. How did it come about? What can be done about it? Answers to both questions must be based on a deeper knowledge of economics than is available today; available even to the best economists of today, as current events abundantly demonstrate. Evidently, there is much work to be done.

Hence, the primary function of this book is to set the process of economic enlightenment going, ideally with the help of as many people as possible. To this purpose, the book has been written in plain English and with a minimum amount of mathematics. Also, by changing all that needed to be changed, economics has been made again intelligible to people who need to know economics and to those who, by spending a fair amount of time on it, want to know economics.

Given these conditions, the reader might want to know why has the book not become a bestseller yet. There are at least three reasons. The hardcover was relatively expensive. The second reason is a bit more complicated. The book was subjected to a hurried review by Professor Paul Davidson, who, being a post-Keynesian economist, might have given reason to the editors of the *Journal of Economic Literature* to expect a favorable treatment. The book was published in May 2002; it was annotated in December 2002; the review appeared in December 2003. Professor Davidson, instead, got lost in the details of the transformation from mainstream economics to Concordian economics, which this book originates; inexplicably, he found in my book as well as in Keynes' General Theory—on which this book is built—statements that are not there: nowhere is in this book the statement I = H (investment equals hoarding) and nowhere is in the General Theory the statement I = S (investment equals saving). The first statement is contrary to every speck and fiber of my book; the second statement would be conceivable only if Keynes had solved the entire problem of economic growth. Quite reasonably Professor Davidson then dismissed my work, quoting Keynes' review of a book by Hayek: "The book as it stands seems to be one of the most frightful muddles I have ever read, with scarcely a sound proposition in it... It is an extraordinary example of how, starting with a mistake [here substitute unusual definitions for mistake], a remorseless logician can end up in Bedlam."

My sweet/sour consolation rested in the fact that I, an unknown writer, had been placed in the august company of Keynes and Hayek.

And I am still pleading guilty to being "a remorseless logician." I was sure then of the validity of my reasoning, not only because it was based, not on personal preferences, but on solid principles of logic followed "remorselessly"; I was sure especially because the work had been reviewed step by step for 27 years by Professor Franco Modigliani, a Nobel laureate in economics at MIT. My other faithful reader of 23 years was Professor Meyer L. Burstein, widely recognized as one of the sharpest minds in economics; and he never found anything wrong in my written or verbal expositions to him either. On the contrary, they both contributed significant building blocks to the progress of my work.

It is intellectually reassuring for me that all other reviews of the book have consistently been one more favorable than the other. For the entire set, please see http://www.carmine-gorga.us/id18.htm. My favorite review is that of Vincent Ferrini, our poet laureate in Gloucester, who prepared it for the local paper. In addition to many other flattering observations that I must omit here, he wrote: "In his book.... (Gorga) has the answers to universal poverty and the anxieties of the affluent.... A manual for a healthy mind, in a healthy body, in a healthy society." A few days after the appearance of this review, I happened to talk with Vincent. I mentioned that he had uncovered aspects of my work which were only latent in my consciousness, and I asked him how had he reached such an understanding. Deadpan, he said: "It is my task to go to the essence of things."

It is especially reassuring for me that neither I nor any of my readers have found the need to change much, beyond two issues of some substance, for the preparation of this expanded edition of

The Economic Process. The first change involves the specification that I meant the Doctors, rather than the Fathers, of the Church; the second, concerns the recommendation by Dr. Michael E. Brady to write equivalence relations using this notation: A ↔ B ↔ C, rather than A = B = C. Few formal changes, due to a most careful reading by Louis J. Ronsivalli, concern correction of spelling and layout mistakes as well as some missing words here and there in the interstices of the book.

In addition to price and an unfortunate review, a major reason why this book has not yet entered the consciousness of the economics profession resides in the complexities of paradigm shifts. The nature of this mental process was made clear by a mathematician and Fields Medalist at Princeton University, William Thurston. He put it in this striking fashion (*New York Times*, August 15, 2006, p. D1): "You don't see what you're seeing until you see it, but when you do see it, it lets you see many other things."

Two happy tasks are left for me. First, I will use the privilege of interpreting my own work to try to let the reader see in the next few paragraphs the paradigm shift operated in this work. *The Economic Process* presents a radical solution to the slavery of economic theory to the assumed equality of saving to investment: It does away with this widely acknowledged quagmire.

{FIRST HINT: In Thurston's terms, the reader has to see hoarding. [Rather than saving.]

(The reader will discover that the complexities are all in mainstream economics. And they are left behind. For instance, saving is a shifting idea that can assume 100,000 possible meanings! Pfew. *Pace* Professor Davidson, young economists and consumers of economics are entitled to draw a sigh of relief. Holding on to antiquated paradigms will not do forever. When placed side by side, as it is done in Appendix 1, "unusual definitions" will in time be preferred because they are consistently logical definitions.)}

{SECOND HINT: The reader has to see consumption as *any* expenditure. [Rather than expenditure on consumer goods.]

(Is not the purchase of goods hoarded or capital goods expenditure also?)}

To go a bit into one set of specifics, my decision to dispense with the assumed equality of saving to investment was not arbitrary. The rules of equivalence apply also to the relation of equality: the terms have to be reflexive, symmetric, and transitive. In mainstream economics, saving and investment do not respect these rules. Saving and investment are not reflexive. They do not consistently represent one thing and one thing only, because their usual definitions cover both items of wealth that are *productive* and items of wealth that are *non-productive* of further wealth. Hence the two terms cannot be symmetric. And they are not transitive either: there is no third term to which they are both equivalent.

Stated another way, it is impossible to resolve the contradictions of the quagmire of the equality of saving to investment, for a simple reason. Saving is indistinguishable from investment, because savings deposited in a bank are in fact an investment; it is the lowest form of investment. Hence the solution had to be radical. Saving had to be relegated to the field of finances and expunged from the field of economics.

There was a residue left from saving. What was that? Clearly, the residue is hoarding—like hoarding money under the mattress. I began to find my way out of the morass of mainstream economics once I introduced hoarding into the discourse. Hoarding represents all wealth that can indeed be "saved" because at the moment of the observation it is in a non-productive, hence static, and relatively safe state; and investment will then be clearly seen as all wealth that is in a productive state. The crucial step out of the morass was taken with the identification of investment as *income minus hoarding*.

That looked like a brand new statement. Upon much further and much later investigation, however, this apparently new statement in economic analysis turned out to be nothing but the mathematical formulation of the Parable of the Talents! The statement was not new at all. Looking at the issues retrospectively, the nightmarish nexus between saving and investment that Adam Smith established was broken; the fallacy that personal greed amounts to social good—a fallacy attributed to Adam Smith by many readers—was blinked away; and economic theory was reconnected with the millenarian tradition of warning against hoarding that reigned from Moses to Locke. Hoarding is clearly a selfish activity that might turn to social good only under extreme economic circumstances.

Looking at the issues prospectively, the pivotal statement that investment is income minus hoarding led to the conclusion that investment equals consumption (see page 25), namely the resulting *production* of all real wealth was separated from, and observed as being "equal" to, all monetary wealth. The two terms of the new equality, real wealth = monetary wealth, are reflexive and symmetric. Real wealth is always real wealth; and monetary wealth is always and everywhere only monetary wealth. Hence, one can look at the economic system from the point of view of real wealth and then from the point of view of monetary wealth and obtain a comprehensive view of the system. Were the terms transitive also?

The third term came from the world on institutional economics. Thus the equality of the two terms was transformed into a full-fledged equivalence, the equivalence of production to distribution and to consumption. This is the core of the book; this is the world that is depicted on the cover of this edition. Production means the production of real goods and services over any standard unit of time or, in technical jargon, aggregate supply. Consumption means expenditure of all monetary instruments over the same unit of time or aggregate demand. And distribution means distribution of ownership rights over the real wealth of aggregate supply and the monetary wealth of aggregate (effective) demand.

The reader is thus transported from the world of mainstream economics, a world in which the object of observation is The Market (exchange), to a world in which the object of observation is the economic process as a whole. A cycle of the process is ideally completed when the entire production of real goods and services is exchanged for the entire stock of monetary wealth; for this exchange to occur both producer and consumer must, respectively, be legitimate owners of real wealth and monetary wealth.

This is the origin of the world of Concordian economics.

My final task is to make three happy recommendations to the reader. First, if you trust the writer and are annoyed at the leaden pace of the mathematical and logical proofs in each step of the transition from mainstream economics to Concordian economics, please use a simple trick: skip the pages. I also have a second, bolder, recommendation to the reader: simply skip Part I and Part II. The third recommendation is this: please, keep in mind that this is a book on economic theory in transition from mainstream economics to Concordian economics observed at one instant in time.

Economists are at a disadvantage in relation to the lay reader, because, to use Keynes' phrase, they have to disabuse their minds of fallacies they were compelled to believe in in order to study economics.

The reader who at one paragraph or another should be lost in transition is encouraged to go to Appendix 1, which has been prepared at Louis Ronsivalli's strong recommendation and titled "Symbols, Meanings, and Definitions" in Concordian economics vs. mainstream economics; the reader who needs a broader view is encouraged to read Appendix 2, titled "Concordian Economics: Tools to Return Relevance to Economics"; the reader who needs an expanded view of the economic process is encouraged to read

Appendix 3, titled "Economics for Physicists and Ecologists." Observing the trajectories of the system over a business cycle we will define the "bubble," clarify much of the process of accumulation that leads to the bubble, and identify economic policies that bring us to a stable and just economic world. These two interrelated essays were published separately and are brought together here.

Even before the publication of *The Economic Process* I have had the opportunity to explore a number of social, legal, and political issues in which Concordian economic policies are immersed. Those essays are collected in *To My Polis, With Love: May Gloucester Show the World the Ways of Frugality* (The Somist Institute, 2008).

Much work is still in the cursor; and much work can now—ideally—be independently initiated by others. Hence the reader is heartily invited to contribute to the eventual creation of a truly "new and elegant edition, revised and corrected," of this work. Thus even Benjamin Franklin, whose connections to this work will gradually become apparent, can be expected to rest in peace.

CARMINE GORGA
July 16, 2009

Preface

The economic process was with us
at the appearance of the first human being.

Chances are it will be with us
as long as there will be people on earth.

Should we not therefore learn what the economic process is?

———

THE FACT THAT THE ECONOMIC PROCESS has arguably been with us ever since the dawn of men and women on earth has been justification enough for me to learn all that I could about it. To close one circle, let me immediately add a practical reason for this study. It can be gleaned from a deep observation by Paul Krugman at the end of his most recent book, *The Return of Depression Economics* (1999). The "peculiar thing" he noticed is that all of the critics of current economic policies "could, to some extent, be right."

It is a great privilege for me to invite the reader to join with me in the quest for an ever more precise knowledge of the economic process. Through the voyage, I venture to promise, the reader will eventually acquire a little more clarity about the extent to which each participant in the economic discussion is indeed right. Who knows? Some readers might, at a moment's notice, even be spurred to offer their own contributions to that discussion. As Bill Collier says, they will then become Concordians.

Now that I have blurted out the "point" of my work, allow me to enlarge it with some love and care into a small sphere.

This is the first in a series of studies that present the transformation of economic theory into Concordian economics. In this conversion, mainstream economics disappears as the linear, static, "dismal science" of textbooks and is replaced by an organic and dynamic structure capable of responding to the daily needs of concrete human beings. At the end of the journey, the reader's understanding of the economic system will change from a mechanical, Newtonian entity to a relational process.

Concordian economics is a three-level structure. At the first level, it enlarges the framework of mainstream theory by integrating the demand side with the supply side and giving equal standing to the institutional side of economics. Concordian economics reaches this goal by observing the economic life as a process that combines the production with the sale of goods and services and

relates both activities to human beings via the institution of ownership rights. Concordian economics distils this understanding into
a series of models on which a new national accounting system can
eventually be built. A referee of *The Journal of Economic Theory*
for my Manuscript # 91297, 12/31/91, has acknowledged that this
structure forms a "new analytic engine."

At the second level, Concordian economics encompasses the
field of economic policies. Drawing upon the spirit of the
Founding Fathers, the Transcendentalist authors, and many other
writers of the present and the past, and especially drawing upon
the spirit of Henry George, Louis D. Brandeis, and Louis O. Kelso,
Concordian economics opens up new possibilities for truly productive and just economic policies.

At the third level, Concordian economics reaches out toward the
field of practice through the transmission belt of economic rights
and responsibilities. These "tipping points" are not generic, but
specific rights and responsibilities. They form guiding principles of
daily action in the economic arena. In neo-Aristotelian fashion,
then Concordian economics leaves the determination of the specific content of these principles to the democratic dynamics of con-
tending wills and an innate sense of fairness in most people.

Only one aspect of the first level of the structure of Concordian
economics is covered in this book, the observation of the economic process at one instant in time.

                                            CARMINE GORGA
                                             July 16, 2001

Prolegomena
(Preliminaries)

THE STUDY OF ECONOMICS is the study of a mighty fortress whose inhabitants have the responsibility not to take change very lightly. To transform the nature of mainstream economics into a different entity, as Concordian economics promises to do, is a proposition that can be taken under serious consideration only by going beyond the façade of economic theory to observe how things are seen from the inside.

Once we acquire this worldview, we hear a surprising appeal: it is economists who, most of all, clamor to be freed from the strictures that mainstream economic theory imposes on them.

The appeal, we will gradually discover, is issued in many tones.

At this stage, to use Keynes' words, we can classify that appeal as a call to transform economics into a "simple" and "obvious" mental discipline.

The Need to Transform Economic Theory

Mathematics does help, but it cannot perform miracles.

———

A TRANSFORMATION OF ECONOMICS is long overdue. What makes this project urgent is the crisis that, as every economist knows, has by now wholly ensnared economic theory. The crisis is of such proportions that Amartya Sen, a Nobel laureate in economics, has proclaimed: "We must learn (economic theory), but not use it much."[1] Another Nobelist, Robert Solow, has concluded that economic theory is a case of "the overeducated in pursuit of the unknowable."[2] In epistemological terms, the crisis means that, as things now stand, it is impossible to reach agreement concerning the dynamics of the economic process.

There are many reasons for the crisis. The reader will discover that the theory is confronted with many anomalies, facts that do not fit into the theoretical structure of mainstream economics, and is riddled with many internal contradictions. These intellectual weaknesses are not tolerated in science. This is a crisis that has to be resolved.

The issue is not simply intellectual. The crisis has to be resolved because, through a long chain of causation, the weaknesses in economic theory are directly responsible for the most woeful conditions of modern life. Without understanding the economic process, can our efforts be truly productive? Without understanding the economic process, can we heal what deeply ails the civil society? Without understanding the economic process, can we solve the grave ecological problems of our age? Without understanding the economic process, can we close the gap that in a hundred insidious ways gnaws at our very soul, the separation of efficiency from morality? Putting it simply, can rich and poor alike enjoy the wonders of life if burdened with faulty economic theories and practices?

A Set of Structural Issues

The issues are complex. And because they are complex, if we approach them solely as economists, we fail. The crisis involves more than economics. The crisis is structural. Contemporary economic theory is locked into a paradigm, "a conceptual prison," in the felicitous phrase of former US Secretary of Labor Robert B. Reich, which permits only the observation of flows of monetary funds. Economists are thus prevented from directly observing stocks of goods, or the world of natural resources, for that matter. And they are prevented from observing how, in strict technical terms, the economy relates to concrete human beings. At the foundation of economics lies an abstraction, the rational human being.

Mainstream economists are aware that they operate in a closed world and want to get out of its strictures. Yet, in their struggle of escape, they have run into three strategic obstacles: they have issued a *premature* call for assistance to mathematics; they have neglected formal logic; and they have cut themselves off from their historical roots in the moral sciences. Reasoning more like natural than social scientists, and assuming that the economic system is ruled by impersonal forces, mainstream economists have trusted the belief that enlightenment will come from mathematics. Instead, they have removed themselves from the reality of concrete human beings and institutions and have become enmeshed into abstract mathematical models. Forgetting that Adam Smith was not a professor of economics but of moral philosophy, with logic at its core, many economists have separated themselves from their roots in the social sciences and have lost their sense of direction.

This is not an idiosyncratic indictment; it is rather common knowledge. In France, and gradually spreading throughout the world, this knowledge is being transformed into a student protest under the banner of post-autistic economics (PAE). In the fourth issue of its newsletter, pae_news@btinternet.com, Gilles Raveaud, one of the leaders of this movement has identified the key concern in these terms: "Our view is: courses can no longer focus on *tools* (maximizing under constraint, finding local and general extrema), but on *problems* (incomes, poverty, unemployment, monetary policy, international trade, European Union, developing countries, immigration, new economy, ecology, etc.). The tools would then be used only to the limit of their relevance for analysing such problems, and not for their own sake."

In *The New Yorker* of December 2, 1996, John Cassidy wrote comprehensively about this concern. But perhaps no one has made a stronger case than Alan Blinder, a professor of economics at Princeton University and former vice-president of the Federal Reserve Board. This is how he has put it: "...too much of what young scholars write these days is 'theoretical drivel, mathematically elegant but not about anything real.'" [3] If one listens carefully to mathematicians and natural scientists one hears worse things. One hears grumbling about the "funny math" used by economists.

There is nothing wrong with mathematics, of course. Mathematics does help. This is a refrain that is propounded most forcefully by Professor Paul A. Samuelson, the first American Nobel laureate in economics. Mathematics helps especially in the field of *applied* economics where, as Professor James K. Galbraith points out in the same issue of the PAE newsletter, "a series of particular models, drawn from a variety of intellectual and scientific traditions... help to structure thinking about empirical issues (which are) among the most hotly and openly contested questions in economics today."

Of course mathematics helps. The discourse in this book starts with a basic mathematical operation, goes through the presentation of an integrated set of simple mathematical models, and ends with a plea to apply the most up-to-date mathematical tools to economic reasoning. Without mathematics, in fact, it is unlikely I would have uncovered a series of weaknesses in economic theory. Without mathematics, it is unlikely I would have been able to carry the discourse forward from there.

Mathematics does help, but it cannot perform miracles. The issue is neither with mathematics per se nor with the application of mathematics to applied economics. The issue is with the relationship between mathematics and the current status of economic theory. The issue is with the attempt to use mathematics to fix whatever is wrong with economic theory as it now stands. Here mathematics is powerless. Mathematics cannot solve the basic cause of the crisis in economics, for the crisis stems from an insufficiency of precision in economic theory.

When the definition of saving, as calculated by Professor W. R. Goldsmith can assume one hundred thousand possible meanings, of what help can mathematics be? Definitions are like containers. Empirical data are accumulated into these containers and hypothetical relationships are established between the data; then, with theoretical exercises one manipulates the equations in order to extract all possible information from the data. But what validity does the information brought to light from any container possess, when the other 99,999 are necessarily left unexamined? The error is compounded by those who, through comprehensive investigations, attempt "to fit the curve" because, with the possibility of combining data extracted from different definitions of saving, they might be mixing apples with oranges. Worse still is the hope that mathematics can help economists choose which one is the best among those one hundred thousand possible definitions of saving. This is vain hope and proof positive that the economist has abdicated.

Economists have made a premature commitment to mathematics. Since the language of economics is imprecise and the language of mathematics is extremely precise, the two cannot quite mesh. Rather than accepting the limitations of this basic condition, economists have tried to force the issues. Blinded by the abstract beauty of their models, many economists have insisted on analyzing the superstructure of economic theory, and naturally they have found only few marginal faults. Fixing those faults, they have often thought to have made solid progress. Yet, not having gone to the source of the problem, they have eventually learned that they have only involved their reasoning in new hidden faults. For too long have economists been caught up in such a chase, driven by a saga of balancing contradictions. As a result, they have built a theoretical superstructure of laced intricacy, which, not unlike the leaning Tower of Pisa, does not rest on solid foundations.

Economists have neglected to seek assistance from principles of formal logic that have been painstakingly developed over thousands of years of intellectual effort. Recourse to the principle of identity, for instance, a principle which is much more ancient than Plato's study of linguistics, would have told economists that they have to arrive at definitions of economic categories that mean one thing, and one thing only. Only when this precondition is met can mathematics deploy its full power in relation to economics.

We will follow this directive in this book. And we will use mathematics, but not exclusively nor intensively. Avoiding the snare of excessive reliance on formal mathematical analysis, we will concentrate our attention on the foundations of economic theory in logic and, through common sense, on the substance of the economic discourse. This search leads to the discovery of anomalies in economic analysis. Thus, gathering the fruits of an Aristotelian injunction adapted by my father to modern needs, we will distinguish the form from the substance of things and always pursue the substance.

With the light of history as our guide, the focus of our attention will be on the development of the meaning of saving, investment, consumption, and income. Two major discoveries are in store for the reader. The reader will not only see that these entities, as well as their relationships to each other, are all inextricably tied to the meaning of saving; the reader will also see that, by altering the meaning of saving—whether consciously or not—economists automatically alter the meaning of all other terms in mainstream economic theory. And let us remember that the economist cannot legitimately choose among 100,000 possible definitions of saving.

Toward the Construction of a Practical Science

In other words, there is no *terra firma* in economic theory. Everything moves in accordance with the needs of the moment. While this condition can be challenging from an intellectual point of view, one must remember that the purpose of economics is not to provide an intellectual challenge; its purpose is to help solve vexing problems of daily existence. And in this regard, mainstream economic theory fails rather miserably. The condition of the cities, the condition of public transportation, the condition of the physical environment, the condition of the social environment all point to this conclusion. What is left is the roller-coaster excitement of the stock market. Clearly economic theory needs adjustment. And most economists agree with this judgment.

The central purpose of Concordian economics is not to make an analysis of mainstream economic theory for its own sake; it is not to revel in the discovery of anomalies and inner contradictions. Rather it is to make the reader realize that the flaws of that theory are so deep and so ingrained that they need healing. Hence, the purpose of this analysis is to make us bold enough to suggest that the existing structure needs so serious a reconfiguration that a new structure has to be designed in its place. As a note of reassurance, we are not alone in this journey. On the contrary, we will participate fully in the "struggle of escape" that was attempted by Keynes, as is especially evident from Volumes XIV and XXIX of his *Collected Writings,* and continues in many different ways to this very day.[4]

The escape suggested by Concordian economics is not a jump into some unknown territory; rather, it is a step-by-step progression that is guided by principles of formal logic. In the process, we will gather bits and pieces of the material from which a new structure unfolds logically and inexorably. The reader will recognize this structure as a faithful representation of the economic life in which we live.

Toward Concordian Economics

For a number of consilient reasons, I like to call the new structure Concordian economics. When fully developed, Concordian economics will be composed of an integration of three levels of reasoning: an enlargement of economic theory; a restructure of economic policy; and a method to transfer economic policies into practice through the organic implementation of economic rights and responsibilities. Only one aspect of the first level is observed in this work by taking a picture of the economic process as a non-mechanical system at one instant in time.

Even though observed only at such a fleeting moment, we will see that the new structure basks in a great degree of concord: anomalies and contradictions disappear from its inner structure; hence it is capable of offering a great degree of concord to the outside world. In the new structure we will find space for the demand side, the supply side, and the institutional side of economic analysis. These turn out to be three visions of the same reality, the economic process as a whole. We will also find that the dichotomy between micro- and macroeconomics, which vexes much analysis today, seems to vanish within the new structure: each model is capable of relating to the economy of the individual person, the family, the firm, the city, the region, the nation, or the world. The scale changes, but, in confirmation of Benoit Mandelbrot's discovery of fractal geometry and its applicability to so many fields, the structure of the economic process remains self-similar throughout. The new structure of Concordian economics also has the potential of closing the gap of understanding between ecologists and economists, because both can henceforth observe stocks of real wealth as well as stocks of financial resources, thus bringing to a close a discord that started in Concord between Thoreau and Emerson. As a small sample of the potential of closing the gap between the methods of analysis of economists and natural scientists, I offer this expression by Dr. Damon Cummings, a retired professor of hydrodynamics and control theory at MIT. Upon reading one of my papers in economic theory, he exclaimed: "This is how I build submarines."

Indeed, one of the unexpected benefits of applying rules of formal logic to economics is the opportunity to automatically close the gap that exists between economic logic and common logic—a gap that greatly hampers communication between economists and non-economists. To coin a maxim, economics is too important to be left to economists. People outside the economics profession are not neutral observers; they are deeply affected by decisions taken by economists and, as emphasized by rational expectations analysis, they in turn deeply affect policy decisions recommended by economists. They thwart economists' expectations. Sooner or later people outside the profession must take an active part in the economic discourse; sooner or later full accountability must be interwoven between concerned citizens and economists. Only then can the economic process give hospitality to morality.

To achieve this aim, as John Maynard Keynes well knew, economics must become a "simple" and "obvious" mental discipline.

... into "Simple" and "Obvious" Economics

The ideas which are here expressed so labori-
ously are extremely simple and should be
obvious.

JMK

———

IT HAS BECOME FASHIONABLE, for professional economists and laymen alike, to downgrade Keynes' system of thought. This work
does not follow that road. Even though it shall unavoidably provide ample and new ammunition to the traditional critics of
Keynes, this writer unabashedly admits that he remains in awe
before that construction. In fact, to make his position as clear as
possible, he will borrow from a rather famous passage by Alvin
Hansen. Professor Hansen, an early and foremost scholar of
Keynes, wrote: "Time and again when I thought I had discovered
this or that error in the Keynesian analysis, either on my own or at
the suggestion of a critic, I have been surprised to find how often,
upon examination, the point had already been anticipated and
covered in the *General Theory*."[5]

Neither shall this work follow the more traditional route of paying lip service to Keynes and then suggesting what he rather
"ought" to have said. No. The critical analysis of Keynes' thought,
which necessarily is no small part of this work, tries to interpret
what Keynes said in his own terms. And then it takes issue with
those terms—or, more specifically, with the form and not the substance of the *General Theory*.

This choice involves a reversal of the approach generally followed soon after the publication of that masterpiece. For a large
number of reasons, some of which will be touched upon at more
opportune moments, the majority of economists have found themselves compelled to take the form of Keynes' thought—namely, his
model of the economic system; and they have unwittingly abandoned the substance to its destiny. This writer, instead, has opted
for the preservation of the substance of the *General Theory* and for
entrusting its form to the history of economic analysis. (Treating
Keynes' model as the overall form of his thought is a most basic
assumption that will be *automatically* corroborated throughout
this work. In this context it can only be pointed out that, contrary
to what might currently be believed, Keynes did not attach undue

importance to his model: we shall soon observe what, from a substantive point of view, was his most important discovery.)

Direct and indirect evidence supporting this choice is overwhelming and in the following pages it will be distilled, drop-by-drop, to the extent that it is feasible.

A first sample of this evidence is provided here not so much to establish the legitimacy of the present work or even its continuity with Keynes' thought, but especially to stress that Keynes remained constantly aware of the limitations existing in his terms. Five short months after the publication of the *General Theory*, he wrote to R. G. Hawtrey: "Of course...the whole book needs re-writing and re-casting. But I am still not in a sufficiently changed state of mind as yet to be in a position to do that." In the same vein, nine months after this letter, he wrote to Professor Joan Robinson: "I am gradually getting myself into an outside position towards the book, and am feeling my way to new lines of exposition."[6] Indeed, as we shall see, in the "review of the reviews" of his book—the famous article of February 1937—Keynes had already developed "lines of exposition" which go beyond those of the *General Theory*. And the *General Theory* itself is replete with cautionary qualifications concerning the validity of his terms.

Yes, there is no doubt as to the legitimacy of the present work. (As to its validity, the reader shall be the judge.) The evidence is overwhelming. Keynes was fully aware of the limitations existing in his terms. And of course, as all great masters, he was fully able to work within those limitations. But, to the end, he was not able to discern what was the ultimate source of his troubles; what was the cause of the "laboriousness" in his exposition. In short, he was unable to discern what was the issue with his terms.

The Issue With Keynes' Terms

The "issue" with Keynes' "terms" lies in assuming, as he specified in the preface to the *General Theory*, that "...if orthodox economics is at fault, the error is to be found not in the superstructure, which has been erected with great care for logical consistency, but in a lack of clearness and of generality in the premises."

Keynes committed the fundamental error of not distinguishing between internal and external logical consistency. (Keynes' error lies in being too much an economist and too little a logician—even though his debut in the academic world occurred as a logician through the publication of his *Treatise on Probability*.) Centuries of accumulated thought and a scrutiny exercised by the most powerful minds in many countries leave no doubt that the superstructure of economic thought has indeed been built with great care for its internal logical consistency. But what of its external logical consistency?

Ah. This is another matter. This is the matter that is almost exclusively analyzed in these pages. The external logical consistency of economic theory is found riddled with glaring deficiencies; and such deficiencies are eliminated—hopefully to the satisfaction of the most exigent reader.

For instance, once it becomes apparent that both the definition of saving and that of investment contravene the principle of non-contradiction (because both definitions contain items that are physically productive and items that are physically nonproductive of further wealth), the principle of identity will require that the two types of wealth be separated from each other and that productive items, such as an orchard, are to be included in the definition of investment while nonproductive items, such as idle land, are to be included in the definition of saving. Ultimately, it will become clear that the word saving ought to be confined to the world of finance and that in the world of economics it should be substituted with the word hoarding. Following similar reasoning, lesser adjustments will be brought to the definition of consumption and the definition of income.

Most effort will be spent on the relation between saving and investment. Many reasons will be found to explain why the assumed relation of equality between them is not formally correct. Therefore, many tools will be used to separate from each other those two terms that forever seem to have been joined together, causing incalculable damage to the clarity and the usefulness of the economic discourse. Many economists call it the saving-investment quagmire.

Thus, through a number of simple mathematical transformations, buttressed by detailed economic reasoning, the structure that allows economists to observe only monetary flows is transformed into a structure in which, first, stocks are separated from flows; and then stocks and flows of real wealth are separated from stocks and flows of monetary wealth. Once these steps are taken, the two types of wealth are linked together through the legal institution of ownership rights. A relationship of equivalence is thus established among *production* of real goods and services, *distribution* of ownership rights, and *consumption* or spending of money for the purchase of financial instruments as well as consumer goods, capital goods, and goods to be hoarded.

The key concepts of economic theory are further refined and related to each other in a series of models that describe the economy from many points of view: e.g., the point of view of stocks and flows, real wealth and money, production, distribution, and consumption. These models are ultimately tied together into one organic and dynamic model of the economic system, graphically in this volume and mathematically in other volumes. The linear structure of mainstream economic analysis—a structure in which facts, and theories, are studied one by one as nearly independent entities—is transformed into an organically interdependent process. Thus each element of the economic system is synchronously related to all the other elements; and the static structure of mainstream economic theory is transformed into a dynamic structure in which a change in one element of the system is instantaneously related to changes in all the other elements.

This final result is an automatic byproduct. By closing the gap between the internal and external logical consistency of economic analysis, one develops economic analysis in full accordance with the rules of formal logic—namely, one makes that discourse fully intelligible to those who are ready to exert a minimum effort of attention and care over these matters. An interesting consequence then ensues. The gap between the substance and the form of the economic discourse is closed. Implicitly is thus brought to fruition one of the major, unrealized hopes of Keynes. In the preface to the *General Theory* he, in fact, stated: "The ideas which are here expressed so laboriously are extremely simple and should be obvious." In the following chapters we shall take the "laboriousness" out of the exposition. What remains are "extremely simple" and "obvious," but fundamental economic ideas.

Someone might legitimately ask, if these ideas are so simple and obvious, why are they not of common knowledge? The clearest answer to this complex question can be simply put. The most difficult thing to discover is the obvious.

The Road to the Discovery of the Obvious

With hindsight, the process of discovery of the obvious can be made quite simple. The only remaining difficulty arises from the number of issues involved. First things, first. The "sole end and purpose" of this work is the description of the economic process or, to put it in conventional terms, the analysis and the restructure of contemporary economic theory. To achieve this goal we will use the most basic tools of logic and, since there is, as always, a compenetration of the past into the present, we will intermittently resort to a historical analysis whenever we need the sustenance of thought elaborated over centuries of painstaking effort. Shining the light of history all through the structure of economic theory, we will find ourselves in a position similar to that of Howard Carter at the first sight of the interior of Tutankhamun's tomb in 1922. We will see "wonderful things."

In our archeological dig, we will peel a number of layers from the superstructure of economic theory in order to reveal its core structure. Through this exercise we will clearly see that—no matter the efforts to change it—the formal structure of economic theory has remained stubbornly constant ever since the first half of the twentieth century. Digging deeper, we will see that at center of this structure there is the void. Reassured by the observation of many economists who have compared this discipline to a black box, we will dig underneath the core structure and we will see that none of its single or compound elements respects the dictates of formal logic. Digging deeper still, we will see that the entire structure was laid on an older foundation; namely, Adam Smith's grand conception of saving. Not for nothing is Adam Smith called the father of economics. He took his position as tutor to the young Duke of Buccleuch quite seriously. Digging still deeper, we will see that such a conception is itself unbalanced because it lacks one essential plank, the meaning of saving as "not-saving," namely, consumption or future enjoyment, a plank that needs to be explicitly added to it in order to make common sense out of much technical economic reasoning.

Thus we shall observe the central core of contemporary economic theory, both as it stands today and as it has developed throughout its historical past. It is there, in fact, that the obvious lies buried: under layers and layers of tightly constructed thought. (This does not mean that "the truth" was known in the past, and has somehow been obscured by the forces of "civilization.")

Operating from inside, the first layer to pierce is that of contemporary economics. We shall gradually discover that this thought is wholly or partially locked into the terms—or as T. S. Kuhn would say, the paradigm—developed by Keynes: namely, his model of the economic system. Therefore we shall implicitly find ample justification for going directly back to Keynes.

With attentive listening to what he had to say we discover that Keynes, in turn, remained prisoner to an older set of terms; he remained prisoner especially to Adam Smith's conception of saving. It is on this conception, then, that we ultimately have to focus our attention. In addition, we shall also discover that Keynes remained equally prisoner to the linear tools of analysis developed especially by Alfred Marshall during the second half of the nineteenth century. Yet, much less emphasis will be placed on this matter because Keynes himself did not explicitly and exclusively use those representational tools and methods of analysis.

When liberated from all these incrustations, the obvious will appear—and will appear with a power of its own. It will free the economic discourse from its present strictures and will help us develop economic theory into an intellectual tool capable of facing the challenges of the day.

This writer would have studied Benedetto Croce in vain, if he were to leave the impression that henceforth the economic discourse will be completely "free." We shall, in fact, develop our own "incrustations." And we shall develop them, not only because that is the only way in which one can ever express thought, but also to leave something for future generations to do. It is up to them to tear down the structures we build; it is up to them to build their own abode in such a way as to fit their physical and intellectual measure.

Work Plan

The work is divided into five parts. Part I analyzes some overall weaknesses in Keynes' model. Part II analyzes a number of reasons for those weaknesses and suggests remedial solutions; ultimately, it presents a series of new models of the economic system. Part III analyzes the economic process as seen through the lenses of the new models.

Part IV deals very briefly with the issue of the foundations of economic analysis and how the new models have an inherent potential to destroy the dichotomy between micro and macroeconomics. A few concluding comments on the relationship between poverty and the economic process are offered in Part V.

As a summary of these introductory notes, our work plan can be compared to the "work plan" of a growing tree. The first (visible) thing to do is to crack some openings in the bark. The second is to shed the old bark away. The third is to grow new bark. The final result is the addition of a new ring all throughout the trunk and the major branches of the tree of economic knowledge.

PART I

Overall Analysis of Keynes' Model

THIS PART DISCLOSES THE EXISTENCE of major weaknesses in Keynes' model; hence, it establishes the need for the revision of that model.

Due to the extraordinary position occupied by this model, its weaknesses are also to be found—in whole or in part—in all prevailing economic analysis.

The focus is on the observation of the model itself, a tool of analysis that, once mastered, will first let us acquire a better understanding of the various types of wealth in themselves, and then will grant us a keener appreciation for various human activities revolving around economic wealth.

I

Keynes' Thought as the Apex
of Classical Economics

*Saving and Investment are the determinates
of the system, not the determinants.*
JMK

———•———

BEFORE WE SET OUT TO REVISE Keynes' model, it is only proper to try to understand what Keynes' thought really encompasses. He wrote a prodigious amount, but the core of his thought is contained in the *General Theory*, a book he published in 1936 in the very midst of the Great Depression. Keynes made one major discovery, and a long series of smaller ones. He discovered a different relationship between saving-investment and the rest of the economic system. As he succinctly but unmistakably put it, "Saving and Investment are the determinates of the system, not the determinants."[7]

This was *the* "revolution" in economic thought which Keynes accomplished and which he heralded in so many different and subtle tones. Classical economists, from Adam Smith through Marshall to Pigou, held the exact opposite view. For them, saving and investment determine all other quantities in the economic system.

Interestingly enough, most contemporary economists have gone back to the position of classical economists, thus annulling whatever revolutionary thrust was in Keynes' thought. For the Keynesians, saving and investment determine primarily and directly the level of income; and for the Monetarists they determine primarily and directly the rate of interest. Three other major schools of economics, namely, post-Keynesian economics, supply-side economics, and rational expectations analysis, have not changed the fundamental terms of discussion concerning the structure of the economic system and therefore remain outside the scope of this work. Post-Keynesians emphasize that some key components of

Keynes' thought, such as the short run, time, uncertainty, expectations, and money are not given appropriate consideration in Keynesian analysis. Supply-side economics is primarily concerned with economic policies. And rational expectations analysis is primarily concerned with the interstices between economic theory and economic policy.

We have to await the analysis of many more topics before we can pass a judgment on the validity of these opposing points of view. For the time being, let us observe only the general issue. The central point to realize is that, apart from the inversion in the *sense* of the relationship of saving and investment to the system as a whole, Keynes remained himself a classical economist. Indeed, he brought that train of thought to its apex.

This is an entirely new framework of analysis. The prevailing view is that Keynes' model is the most important and innovative aspect of his thought, and that *both* Keynes and the Keynesians abandoned the paths trodden by classical economists. Since the issues are riddled with intricate twists and turns, at this point we cannot do much more than adhere to the facts and proceed to give three proofs of the validity of the central statement that Keynes was a classical economist.

Keynes—A Classical Economist

Going back in time at least to the 1930's, a period of major transformations in economics, one will hardly find an economist who would deny that the study of economics is concerned with three major phases: production, distribution, and consumption of wealth. It was this overall understanding which created the classical school of economics. And yet, what was the practical application of this widely shared belief?

Keynes repeatedly emphasized that classical economists, particularly following Ricardo, had reduced the study of economics to the study of the theory of distribution— at the obvious expense of the theory of production and the theory of consumption. Keynes apparently saw that these *three* theories needed to be formally and rather indissolubly unified. This is what he proceeded to do—in his model of the economic system no less than in the *General Theory*.

And yet, due to the smelting and welding performed by his intuition, it is now nearly impossible to recognize the thought process he followed. This indeed is one of the major shortcomings of Keynes' model; and it is also one of the major reasons why contemporary economic analysis has followed so many different directions. Keynes himself provided very little assistance; and his insistence on his "revolution" threw economists even more off the path he had—intuitively more than analytically—trodden.

Keynes' reliance on intuition for the exposition of his theory might appear surprising; and yet, as we shall see, it is a recurrent feature. Skeptical readers will find in Moggridge's *John Maynard Keynes* (1976) an extensive treatment of this issue.

Three Sets of Evidence

When the issues are carefully analyzed, it becomes evident that Keynes was indeed a classical economist. At the end of the journey, in fact, we shall explicitly and analytically recognize the conceptual identity of the following elements which can be found respectively in classical economics and in Keynes' model: (1) *production* and the saving-investment system; (2) *distribution* and income; (3) *consumption* and consumption of consumer goods. These are, of course, "code" words that will be decoded as we proceed. The elaboration of their many nuances will provide the final proof that Keynes was a classical economist, but one point can be emphasized here. It was legitimate for Keynes to see the production of goods and services as the result, rather than the cause, of the economic process.

Do we need to await the end of the analysis to verify the validity of the position outlined here? To eliminate all doubt, yes. Some confirmation, however, can be found in Keynes' own words. The process of unification of the three separate strands of classical economic thought was made rather explicit in the body of the *General Theory*. The attentive reader of that work will discover that Keynes' definition of income—undoubtedly the central concept in his system of thought—is given in accordance with "two possible principles . . . one of them in connection with production, and the other in connection with consumption."[8] Does the definition, indeed the calculation—as he put it —of income from the point of view of distribution disappear from sight?

Not at all. The attentive reader will discover that, when the model is presented, the definitions of income so "laboriously" reached from the point of view of production and that of consumption are—apparently abruptly and inexplicably—no longer taken into consideration. In the model, the definition of income is presented—quite simply—as the sum of consumption and investment expenditure. This is none other than the definition of income from the point of view of distribution. It details how the yearly income is *distributed;* and how, for Keynes, it is distributed between consumption and investment expenditure.

An even stronger indication that Keynes meant to unify those three strands of classical economic thought, i.e., production, consumption, and distribution, is found in that passage of the *General Theory* in which he outlines his work plan: "Thus the analysis of the Propensity to Consume [i.e., the central element in the theory of consumption], the definition of the Marginal Efficiency of Capital and the theory of the Rate of Interest [i.e., the central elements in the theory of production] are the three main gaps in our existing knowledge which it will be necessary to fill."[9] Keynes then proceeded to fill these gaps. He did not proceed to abrogate the theory of distribution. In fact, he continued the paragraph just quoted by saying: "When this has been accomplished, we shall find that the Theory of Prices [i.e., the overall form of the theory of distribution] falls into its proper place as a matter which is subsidiary to our general theory."

As is well known, Keynes did not find the time to complete his thought. The structure of that thought, however, seems to be quite clear. It attempts to unify the three major theories analyzed by classical economists, no matter the extent to which they were analyzed: the theory of production, that of distribution, and that of consumption. As indicated, Keynes' thought represents the apex of classical economic thought.

In the following chapters we shall find not only more conclusive evidence for the validity of this statement, but also some of the reasons for its central importance.

A Narrow Gorge or One Ascending Peak?

To emphasize the central importance of the relationship between Keynes and classical economists, suffice it to say that every writer of economics from the 1940's onward has had to determine that relationship for himself or herself. Some have extensively dwelled upon it; others have been satisfied to dispose of it in a few lines. But no one could ignore the topic. To mention only a few names associated with it: Robinson and Harrod, Hicks and Samuelson, Modigliani and Friedman (four Nobel laureates), Hansen and Harris, Mises and Hutt, Clower and Leijonhufvud, Patinkin and Johnson, Lucas (a Nobel laureate) and Sargent, Milgate and Kates. The list could be much extended and refined; but then we would go far afield.

Keynes presented a synthesis. Indeed, to use a biological term, his theory represents a mutation. One can therefore find old as well as new elements in what he said. One can see either a cleavage—a narrow gorge—between Keynes and classical economists, and therefore two peaks (of varying size); or one can see an ascending peak as suggested here and indeed, through different justifications, in many other sources. Hence the unending controversy surrounding the overall topic.

In the following chapters we shall record some of the points of the controversy; but we will eschew the controversy itself. It is the framework of analysis established in this chapter that grants us such freedom. We have been concerned with the *core-structure* of the respective theoretical constructions. The emphasis on specific elements, the relationship among the various stated or implied elements of each construction, and the varying policy implications obtained by the discussants—all ineluctably issue from each theoretical core-structure.

A Clarification

The economist knows how true these statements are; but how can they be clarified for other readers? How can they be clarified in a few paragraphs? To simplify the issues, we shall first of all neglect the policy implications of different theoretical core-structures, not only because the linkages between theory and policy are rather complex, but especially because economic policy is not of direct concern in these pages.

It is clear that no matter which structure one deals with, greater emphasis can more easily be given to one element of that structure than to others. To simplify the issues, let us keep in mind that a "model" is a new/old tool of analysis: it is much used in computer studies today, but it derives from the ancient shipbuilding tradition of constructing miniature test models before undertaking full-scale production. Keynes' model performs essentially the same functions. Thus, using the image of test models of seafaring vessels, we recall that there are skippers for whom the shape, number, and arrangement of sails and masts—namely, the rig—are the most important elements. Others emphasize the role of the hull. Still others are primarily concerned with the living accommodations. They are all entitled to their opinions. And, depending upon the circumstances—the type of sea in which they are going to launch the vessel, the use they want to make of it, etc.—those opinions might be well founded. Even restricting to a minimum the number of basic elements, which ones should be stated explicitly? Which ones should be implied? Is the wind not an essential element of sailing? And what about the tides?

The same is true for the structure of economic theory. If divergent opinions can justifiably exist on the relative importance of the component elements of each core structure, it becomes apparent that opinions concerning the relationships among the various elements of each structure are bound to exist in even greater variety. Relationships, after all, are invisible entities. They are invisible to the naked eye, that is; but they do exist. And they do perform important functions. Too large a rig on too small a hull is going to cause problems. But, eliminating extreme cases, who can say what is the right proportion—the right relationship—between the two elements?

The economic system is, of course, composed of more than a few basic elements. That is bound to complicate the issues. Yet in this work we will not get involved with the selection of the basic elements composing the model of the economic system, nor with the rationale for this selection. Nor will we be concerned with the selection of the implicit elements of the model. We will simply trust Keynes' judgment on these points. As noted, we will remain satisfied with the bare analysis of the core-structure of that model.

And since the major concern is one of structure, let us focus on the central differences that exist between the structure of Keynes' model and the structure of the models we shall ultimately propose as its substitutes. These differences become sharper, perhaps, if incorporated in a brief description of the process that led to the new models.

II

Toward Concordian Economics

*The unleashed power of the atom
has changed everything save our
modes of thinking.*
Albert Einstein, 1946

———•——

THE ECONOMIC THEORY COMPONENT of Concordian economics takes its lead from the economics of Keynes. The economics of Keynes immediately blossomed into Keynesian economics. And Keynesian economics has become an incredibly complex and rich set of macroeconomic theories. Apart from boldly covering its own vast territory, Keynesian economics also stubbornly remains at the foundation of theories that have tried to challenge its major premises, theories such as Monetarism, post-Keynesianism, supply-side economics, rational expectations, and even input-output analysis. The reason for these linkages is that all mainstream economics, in its entirety or in part, in its wondrous variations, springs from the synthesis of classical economics operated by Keynes with his model of the economic system.

The word model does not exist in the *General Theory*. What we find in the middle of page 63, after detailed discussion of the meaning of each individual term, is, unheralded and unadorned, this construct in the form of three clearly hypothetical propositions:

(Given that) income = consumption + investment
(And given that) saving = income - consumption
Therefore saving = investment.

This is a syllogism.
The three propositions soon lost their hypothetical nature and were transformed into equations to represent the core-structure of

a model through which, as we will see, it is indeed possible to analyze the economic system as a whole. This set of equations represents the core-structure of mainstream economic theory, a core that has been expanded to include hundreds of equations. Yet these specifications have not affected the inner structure of the model.

———

I revised this model in 1965, after spending a summer in intense intellectual struggle with the *General Theory*. With John Maynard Keynes firmly leading me into his framework of analysis, I expectantly followed his reasoning. He was always clear, at times immediately, at times after some searching. In particular, I was seeking illumination on an issue that was dear to me: why, as firmly implanted in mainstream economics, saving is equal to investment.

Having lived in Southern Italy and graduated from the University of Naples, where the *Questione Meridionale* (the question of investment in that poor region of the country) is still a matter of vital concern, I had acquired a mixture of direct knowledge and some longstanding intuitions about the issue. For me, the problem could be reduced to a subset of the question: how does the economy emerge from a Great Depression, the great theme of the *General Theory*.

In 1960-61, those intuitions were reinforced in study and conversation at the Bologna Center of the Johns Hopkins University at the feet of a number of experts, including Professor Robert A. Mundell, the 1999 Nobel laureate in economics. I was then beginning to see how such an apparently simple statement as saving is equal to investment contains not only tremendous practical implications; it also stands at the very foundation of the entire structure of mainstream economics. Yet Keynes kept postponing the explanation. Finally, at page 328, this is what he said: A "view" which considers that saving is *not* equal to investment is "more usually supported by arguments which have no foundation at all apart from confusion of mind." This I took to be not an explanation, but abusive language.

Always the perfect scholar, however, Keynes, implicitly confirming the hypothetical nature of his system of thought, continued his sentence by stating: "It flows, in some cases, from the belief that in a boom investment tends to outrun saving.... This implies that saving and investment can be unequal, and has, therefore, no meaning until these terms have been defined in some special sense." This is the opening that set me on a voyage toward new horizons.

Rather than asking, what is saving, as economists have done ever since Turgot and Adam Smith, I turned the question around and asked, what is investment? Once I framed the second equation of Keynes' model in this fashion, the solution, as Bill Gates would say, came at the speed of thought: Investment = income minus saving.

Since this result was not immediately intelligible to some economists, I eventually changed it to: Investment = income minus hoarding.

Even though the result was dramatic, I do not wish for the recollection of this event to sound overly dramatic. I reached this conclusion, not through sheer intuition or great depth of knowledge, but through mathematical manipulation of the first two equations of Keynes' model. Since saving is equal to investment in that model, I experimented with what would happen if I changed their respective positions. Once I changed the second equation, the third resulted automatically.

I was presented with a new and decidedly different model of the economic system. This is a model that, in honor of the genius of John Maynard Keynes, I called (and, I still believe, ought to be called) the Revised Keynes' Model. Yet to increase clarity in communication, I have ultimately been convinced to call it the Flows model. I copyrighted this model in 1979.

Apart from its external appearance, everything is transformed in the new model: the internal structure is different from Keynes' model; the meaning of each term is wholly or partially changed; the relationships of the component parts to one another are altered; and the economic reality observable through the Flows model is much broader.

The differences are more easily observed by presenting both models in symbols:

Keynes' Model (KM)	Flows Model (FM)
$Y = C + I$	$Y = C + S$ (later, H)
$S = Y - C$	$I = Y - S$ (later, H)
$S = I$	I (later, P) = C (later, = D)

where

Y   stands for Income (to distinguish it from Investment)

C   for Consumption (in KM, expenditure *on consumer goods*)
     (in FM, *any* type of expenditure)
I   for Investment
S   for Saving
H   for Hoarding
P   for Production, and
D   for Distribution of ownership rights.

Nine tenths of the terminological difficulties presented by the
new model can be eliminated remembering that the meaning of
saving is *contracted* to mean hoarding (or production, ownership,
and sale of nonproductive wealth such as money under the mattress, idle gold, idle land, etc.). And the meaning of consumption
is *expanded* to include all expenditure of money or wealth in general: namely, expenditure for the purchase of consumer goods,
goods to be hoarded, and capital goods as well as expenditure for
the purchase of financial instruments.

———•———

Awed by the enormity of the discovery, in that distant 1965, I
wrote a few pages on a yellow pad and did not whisper a word to
a soul. Hopeful yet hesitant to explore the riches that I expected to
be there, I placed those pages in a desk drawer and went off to
fight first the War on Urban Decay (urban renewal) and then the
War on Poverty. By early 1973, having lost both wars, I went back
to those pages. Intuitively, I knew that the weaponry for successfully waging both wars lay in the new intellectual world in which
I found myself. At least, that was my hope.
    I was less deeply religious in those years. As a secular social sci-
entist I needed all things explained to me in clear and distinct
terms. The more I studied the relationship of equality between saving and investment, the more wanting it became. The more official
explanations I found, the more logical contradictions they
entailed. Although I do not remember the specifics, eventually I
exclaimed, "This is not science; it is dogma."
    Dogma. When the Catholic Church elevates a proposition to the
state of dogma, it is to put closure to a certain type of fundamental discussion. Arguments can go only so far; then the Church must
decide. If a train of thought leads nowhere but to confusion, its
sponsors ought to admit failure and start a new line of inquiry.
Dogma? Well, yes. But, in church affairs, the terms of the debate

are all there; they are all laid out in detail after painful detail; and they are available to anyone who might wish to reexamine the dogma. In economics, I found myself confronted by an unexamined dogma.

Where were the details of the dogma that saving is equal to investment? There is no record of a discussion to establish such a proposition or to analyze its inner structure. What made the situation more paradoxical is the fact that there is, indeed, in economics a long succession of attempts to escape from the strictures of that dogma. Yet all attempts have eventually led to failure. Kurt Godel's proof has the full explanation for this glaring deficiency in the structure of modern economic theory: the logical consistency of any closed mathematical system cannot be analyzed from within its own structure.

My hope to succeed where others had failed resided in the uniqueness of my problem. I had two mathematical models—two paradigms—in front of me, each serving as a tool of analysis to study the inner structure of the other. In addition, supported by the Flows model, I knew how to escape from the strictures of the equality between saving and investment. Potentially, this was a tremendous advantage.

In fact, I was faced with an apparently insurmountable difficulty. My problem was this: apart from my personal predilection, on what grounds was it possible to justify the escape?

Mathematics was out of the question. Many economists, from Professor Raymond G. Torto to Professor Otto Eckstein, recognized early that I was confronted with two equally consistent models of the economic system; hence the powerful tool of mathematics was entirely neutralized. Mathematics could not help me, or anyone else, determine what was wrong with Keynes' model or what presumably was right in the Flows model. Certainly the major weaknesses of Keynes' model were not in its mathematical structure, nor in the mathematical structure of the various theories that had been built on that model. The only certainty was that the economic *policies* built on the extant economic theory were not capable of solving problems of poverty and urban decay that demanded immediate attention.

When a practical field of investigation such as economic theory, whose sole purpose is to solve practical problems, is incapable of solving them, it must be seriously questioned and, if answers are not forthcoming, the search for a new theory becomes obligatory. Such a step is avowedly taken by any economist worth the traditional grain of salt. But surely a new theory would not be accepted on my recommendation. A framework of analysis that has sustained research for many centuries in many countries cannot be dismissed because it does not suit anyone's preference. I needed more serious grounds.

———

Between 1973 and 1976, I read economics texts with a renewed critical eye and found no such grounds. Worse, I discovered that there are no standards with which to examine the validity of any proposition in economics. With a gleam in their eye, many economists repeat Lewis Carroll's catchphrase about being masters of words and profess that economics is what they want it to be. Worse still, since economists show less than unanimity in their positions, nothing is firm. It was as if the economics universe were made up of a huge vortex: the more thoughts I threw in it the more they were absorbed, and disappeared into nothingness. I was alone in an intellectual black hole for days, for months, for years. Until I suddenly remembered that philosophic reasoning is supposed to be the final arbiter of intellectual questions. I went straight to Immanuel Kant. Anxiously I raced through his *Critique of Pure Reason,* until I found what I was looking for: the definition of the word concept, a fundamental tool of analysis in the theory of knowledge. I had reached solid ground. Finally, I was able to emerge from the black hole. How I came out of it is the story that is recounted in the following pages.

The full story will take additional volumes to relate, because a vast web of useful interconnections was displayed in front of my eyes as I gingerly passed from *philosophy* to *logic,* from *philosophy of science* to *epistemology,* from *quantum physics* to *chaos theory,* from *political science* to *theory of justice,* from *history of economic analysis* to *literary criticism,* from *theology* to *religion.* As soon as I found what I needed in each of these fields, most often with regrets, I had to pull a curtain on those vistas. I could not allow myself to be distracted from the task at hand. From the moment I discovered Kant's definition of concept, I started to put serious pencil to paper. As I went along, I gained more tools—standards, indeed—with which to examine the unexamined dogma that stands at the foundation of classical as well as mainstream economics.

Using those standards, I went on a journey to the logical foundations of economics. For it is there that its major flaws lie. There I discovered a few anomalies, facts that do not fit into the theory.

They served as an opening into the armature of economic theory. Once inside the structure, I gradually enlarged that opening and eventually put the entire Keynes' model on the operating table. Through the dissection of the model operated with the aid of a simple mathematical scalpel, I found cumulative grounds to convince, I trust, the most demanding reader of the need to revise Keynes' model of the economic system.

The Examined Dogma

Keynes' model requires revision because it is not a homogeneous entity. It is composed of two *concepts* and two *relations*. Income and consumption, although they stand in need of further important specification, are concepts: namely, they have an independent meaning of their own. Saving and investment, instead, have no meaning by themselves. To acquire any meaning, they have to be put in "relation" to income and consumption—or in relation to each other. Thus the model contravenes the standard of homogeneity, or internal coherence, a standard that is taken most seriously by philosophers.

Keynes' model requires revision because its first two equations contain exactly the same information. This shortcoming becomes immediately apparent once its first equation is rewritten as investment = income - consumption, and the second equation is kept as is, namely, saving = income - consumption. The model, in other words, contravenes standards of elegance and economy, standards that are taken most seriously by mathematicians.

Keynes' model requires revision, not so much because it contains redundant information, but especially because it does not contain essential information. The model is not a complete entity. As everyone knows, people hoard wealth. In the reality of the economic life, people do not spend all their annual income on consumer goods and capital goods, i.e., income is not the sum of "consumption" and "investment" expenditure, as indicated in the first equation of the model. This is an inadequate vision of the economic behavior of people; those who can afford to do so, generally, hoard wealth. They try to find ways to insulate part of their income from the vicissitudes of economic trends by hoarding it, setting it aside, hiding it away either directly or through expenditure on goods that can be hoarded. Yet, even though any item of wealth can be hoarded, Keynes' model does not allow for the possibility of formally including hoarding within its framework of analysis. Hoarding is not and cannot be included in any of the equations of that model.

Consequently, hoarding is neither defined nor taken into any consideration whatsoever by contemporary economic analysis. This is a serious anomaly that, as Thomas S. Kuhn pointed out, is not tolerable in science.

In other words, Keynes' model does not portray a realistic picture of the economic system. Students of philosophy of science take the standard of ever-increasing realism most seriously. This standard, as exemplified in Heisenberg's Indeterminacy Theorem—a theorem that can be paraphrased as "you can see clearly only one thing or one paradigm at a time"—will allow us to use the Flows model as a prism through which we will observe the strictures of mainstream economic theory and clearly see its inner flaws.

After looking at Keynes' model as a whole, we will also examine each one of its parts separately, and we will discover that not one definition of its component elements is constructed in a logically tenable fashion. None of its visible elements respects the principle of identity; and its major invisible element, namely, the relation of equality of saving to investment established in that model, is a forced mathematical equation that is not logically correct. It is not a true equivalence, as it must be according to the dictates of formal logic. The two terms are neither reflexive, symmetric, or transitive. Logicians take these standards most seriously.

Keynes' model requires revision because the proposition that saving equals investment, being a relationship between two relations, has no inherent content of its own. Rather, a varying content is forced upon it from the outside by different formulations of economic theory. Epistemologists take the standard of validity of individual propositions most seriously.

Keynes' model requires revision because the third equation hides a contradiction, not only between mathematical logic and formal logic, but more importantly between mathematical logic and economic reality. Thanks to the mathematical logic of the model, saving must be equal to investment. In economic reality, however, the two entities are not equal to each other. Serious economists take this contradiction most seriously. We will see that ever since the early nineteenth century much effort has been spent on the need to understand and possibly dissolve this contradiction. However, rather than looking at the logical make up of this contradiction that lies at the foundation of their theories, mainstream economists have turned their gaze upward, toward the superstructure, generally catapulting the theory into a more and more rarefied stratosphere of mathematical formalism.

Naturally, they have found only few marginal faults with it. The solutions, indeed, have always turned out to be temporary "patches" which, after raising great hopes and enthusiasm, were discovered to contain subtle contradictions of their own. A new patch had to be applied. This is the road that has transformed economic theory into a rational structure of carefully balanced contradictions.

The above deficiencies, many will agree, are too serious to be easily corrected. To paraphrase Keynes, they are carried over into every corner of our economic thought and economic policies. Indeed, there are many other minor shortcomings in the model that are not worth mentioning at this point. There is only one alternative to simply living with those flaws. One must revise Keynes' model; one must change the core structure of mainstream economics. It is this change that, I hope to show, gradually leads to Concordian economics.

Who is to blame for the condition in which we find economic theory today? It is possible to blame mathematicians for not forcefully pointing out to economists their misuse of mathematics and philosophers for the misuse of language or logicians for the lack of enforcement of rules of civilized discourse. But this is a regress ad infinitum. We know the story. Adam blames Eve; Eve blames the serpent; and I blame the cat, one Carmelite monk was overheard closing the circle.

There is no need to engage in the blame game. But there is need to realize that all the above deficiencies stem from the same source. They stem from innate shortcomings of rationalism.

It is indeed rationalism, the fundamental philosophical framework of the modern age, which has created the rationalizations and the tolerance for the set of contradictions that compose mainstream economics.

The Escape Vehicle

We will see that the consequences of the contravention of the many standards mentioned above are of fundamental importance to our discussion. We will be guided by those standards all along the way. Dissatisfied with the formal conclusion that saving and investment have no meaning and no inherent content of their own, much of the analysis will be focused on saving. Digging deeper, we will discover that ever since the publication of the *Wealth of Nations* in 1776 mainstream economic analysis has been caught in a web spun by Adam Smith's grand conception of saving. The in-depth analysis of this conception in the next chapters, buttressed by the analysis of the meaning of investment, consumption, and income, will give us not only the tools to take Keynes' model apart; it will also provide us with the material to build a new model of the economic system. We will see that, because of its many shortcomings, economic theory portrays an inadequate representation of three key phenomena of daily life, economic growth, inflation, and poverty. We will reach novel conclusions in all three fields.

The vehicle that allows us to escape from the deficiencies of Keynes' model is the Flows model.

While this model came to me in one intuitive instant, it has taken the better part of thirty-five years to try to understand its inner logic and to transform it into explicit expressions that can be communicated to other people—and the work is far from done. The following pages are but one attempt to deconstruct Keynes' model and to analytically construct the Flows model. This is the model given earlier in this chapter, a model that precipitates such innumerable changes in the entire structure of contemporary economic theory that, in effect, the old structure is torn down and the new structure of Concordian economics is built in its place. In the process, we will move toward the construction of an economic theory that is inherently organic and dynamic.

Toward an Organic and Dynamic Economic Theory

The change in structure from Keynes' model to the Flows model highlighted in this volume amounts to a transformation of mainstream economic theory from a linear and static to an organic and dynamic tool of analysis. This is a delicate operation that will be performed on the basis of economic, logical, and mathematical reasoning. Since the next chapters contain rather streamlined explanations of these transformations, their description cannot be summarized here. Mathematics is not of much help for this task: direct experience demonstrates that synthetic mathematical formulas, which express complex transformations in the logic of economics, inflict considerable pain on the careful reader and do not yield a great deal of enlightenment. These transformations, however, are rather easily perceived with the assistance of geometry. Hence, our immediate task can be reduced to this operation: we will transform a line into a sphere. This metamorphosis is outlined in the following paragraphs.

Step one. Take a line:

This starting point in our analysis is not arbitrary, because we want to transform linear economics into a dynamic and organic entity. More importantly, this starting point is not arbitrary because the entire analysis performed by mainstream economic theory can be made as complex as necessary by changing the shape of the line over time, by multiplying the number of lines, and rearranging them to intersect at different points. Yet, shorn of its myriad complexities, mainstream economic analysis can be crudely reduced to one line. The flow of funds, conceptually, is but one line. Indeed, in one of its original geometric representations, Dudley Dillard's 45° line diagram, the Keynesian analysis was performed with the assistance of only one line, overburdened though the graph eventually became with symbols. We are legitimately entitled to reduce the starting point of our analysis of mainstream economic theory to one line.

Step two. Since there is no definition of money in current economic theory, we will not ask—as contemporary Walrasian analysis asks—whether this line represents or does not represent money. We will not be interested in that discussion. But, through direct perception, we do know that the economic reality is composed of money *and* goods and services, therefore we will develop a series of mathematical models that will allow us to cut that line into two segments by separating real goods and services from money. Common sense knowledge tells us that the rules governing production, distribution, and consumption of the one (i.e., real goods and services) are totally different from the rules governing the other (i.e., money). Rather than one line, then, if we want to reproduce the economic reality faithfully we must be faced with two segments of a line. Thus:

---   ---

Step three. Rather than leaving the two segments along the same trajectory, as if there were no distinctions between real goods and money, we will make them face each other by placing them on two parallel lines. Real goods and money can not only be separated from each other; they can also be placed on two distinct conceptual planes, thus:

Step four. In order to see what happens *within* each segment, we will sequentially grab each one of them by its flanks and we will enlarge both of them to form two rectangles (when I became familiar with chaos theory I discovered such elegant expressions as "Smale transformations" for these sets of mental operations and these explanations by Benoit B. Mandelbrot: "The limit Peano curve establishes a continuous correspondence between the straight line and the plane."[10]) Thus:

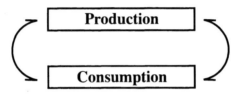

We have now made some room to see what happens within the segment of the economy that we call "real goods" and the segment that we call "money." In the attempt to observe the inner workings of the economic process as a whole, always at one instant in time, we peek inside the two rectangles, thus making them function as "Poincaré sections." Indeed, using the third equation of our Flows model as a guide, we will ultimately label one rectangle not investment, but "production" or aggregate supply *of real goods and services* and the other "consumption" or aggregate demand *of money.* In a fully dynamic context, we will eventually switch our point of view in order to observe the aggregate demand of goods and services as well as the aggregate supply of money.

Step five. We recall that real goods and services have their origin in the set of available natural resources, while money has its origin in the monetary authority. Tracing—ideally preserved from beginning of time to the present—the movements of real goods and services and money separately, and observing how they intersect each other, we will build a figure entitled "Flow of Values in the Economic Process." This figure is presented in chapter 14. (Once the monetary aggregate is broken down into its component flows, work that is not pursued in this volume, the figure, as I later learned through non-linear mathematics, becomes astonishingly similar to a "strange attractor.") If we were to "close" this figure, we would obtain a doughnut or the image of a cyclotron—a very crude but realistic interpretation of the economic reality in which goods and services are hurled at money by human beings in search of increasing welfare.

Step six. Once the rectangle of production is made to face the rectangle of consumption, the question arises, what or who links the one to the other? This is not an arbitrary question; rather, it is dictated by the formal requirements of the *principle of equivalence*. For any equivalence relation to be logically correct, there must be three elements.

The technical answer that we will give to our question of the link between production and consumption is "distribution" of ownership rights. It is clear that ownership rights are the invisible links that connect goods and money with people and institutions. Graphically, we will not enclose this term into a rectangle in order to simplify the reality and clearly signify the double function of the distribution of ownership rights, namely, rights over real goods and services as well as over money. Thus:

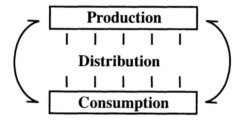

Step seven. From this moment on, the use of 3-D technology would really help. Barring its assistance, in a 2-D environment, the imagination of the reader has to be called upon to mentally place a point at the center of each rectangle, in order to determine its geometric center, and then to rotate each rectangle within this construction at ever-increasing speed about its center. (This operation was much clarified with the assistance of language offered by Louis J. Ronsivalli.) The reader who does this work will obtain the mental image of two, or three, overlapping circles, if distribution is enclosed into a rectangle of its own. The resulting figure forms a Venn diagram.

We cannot stop yet, but if we ask, what is a circle, we get toward the end of our labors. The answer is that a circle is a two-dimensional image of a sphere. To materially construct the sphere, we have to pick up any of the three circles by its two centers; one center is clearly visible, the other is in its back, its shadow image. If we pick up the circle by its two centers and we inflate the area between the center and the circumference, we obtain a sphere.

If we pause, we realize that we have thus transformed a line into a sphere.

Step eight. Let us repeat the last operation with the entire construction of the above figure and observe at once the three overlapping circles forming the Venn diagram. The three circles can be transformed into three intercompenetrating spheres: one into the other.

From a substantive or economic point of view, we will see that through these operations we transform linear activities such as production, distribution, and consumption into a set of complex processes, namely, the production process, the distribution process, and the consumption process.

Step nine. Let us simplify the issues and observe the three intercompenetrating spheres as only one sphere. The procedure is this: we need to change the perspective through which the three rectangles are observed. If they are placed on top of each other, we obtain three perfectly overlapping circles, hence only one sphere.

Substantively, we then reach an understanding of the economic process as a whole. And let us remember that the economic process is an inherently dynamic, complex process. It cannot be kept still. Observing it from the outside, with the help of two arrows connecting production to consumption, as in the following diagram entitled "The Economic Process: A 2-D Image of a Sphere," we can catch the moment of the exchange of (ideally, all) goods and services for (all) money existing at that one instant in time. The validity of this image is analytically confirmed by the other graph entitled "Flow of Values in the Economic Process" that has been mentioned above.

The Economic Process
A 2-D Image of a Sphere

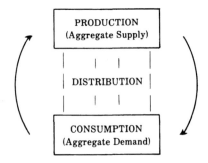

If we use 3-D technology or we mentally link each one of these figures in sequence, we obtain a geometric model of the economic process.

––•––

Through this geometric model, which in another volume will be presented in a mathematical form, we can pick up the discourse from where Keynes left it, namely, from the synthesis of the three separate strands of classical economic thought, i.e., production, distribution, and consumption. But we shall carry the discourse forward from an advantage point. Eliminated from the discourse are a number of inconsistencies that have proved to be traditional irritants to an immediate comprehension of the behavior of the economic process as a whole.

In broader terms, it can immediately be seen how much of the work done by economists ever since the publication of the *General Theory*, as well as in the more distant past, can be incorporated into this framework of analysis, and how the many links interconnecting that work can be identified and gathered together into a unified theory.

Not all this work will be done in this book, not only because of the magnitude of the task, but especially because we will remain satisfied with the analysis of the statics of the economic process. The study of its dynamics is reserved for other investigations. There we will observe the process not only as a flow of goods and services *from producers to consumers*, and a flow of money *from consumers to producers*, but also as a flow of distribution of ownership rights over *both* real and monetary wealth.

A Question of Perspective

In this book we will allow ourselves a contradiction in terms, namely, we will hold the economic process steady by analyzing it at only one instant in time. All the pieces will be placed in their appropriate box on the chessboard, as it were; but the pieces will not be allowed to move. In other words, we will obtain an instantaneous picture of the economic process. This picture yields, not a linear, but a spherical view; a view, not from the outside in, but the inside out. Recent literature on chaos theory is immeasurably helpful in explaining these differences. Thomas Petzinger Jr. has perhaps best described the applied methodological differences at some length in *The New Pioneers* (1999). He has shown how the method of nonlinear dynamics yields a non-Newtonian picture: a dynamic and organic or biological view, rather than a mechanical view.

Stocks and Flows

Intimately related to the above fundamental question of perspective is another issue. To obtain a dynamic and organic picture of the economic process, we need to be very clear about the distinction between stocks and flows. Once we hold the economic process steady, even for one instant, we no longer observe flows but stocks of wealth. Hence, we will use not only the Flows model to measure a *rate* of economic activity over time (although limited to one instant in time); we will also use the Stocks model to measure the *amount* of economic values accumulated up to the instant of observation. These values can be recorded with the help of any *numeraire*, be it dollar bills, labor-units, yards of silk, or beans.

The Stocks Model

The Stocks model is structurally and conceptually derived from the Flows model. Hence, it does not need much of an introduction. It reads as follows:

Wealth = (Consumer Goods + Capital Goods) + Goods Hoarded
Investment-assets = Wealth - Goods Hoarded
Investment-assets = Consumer Goods + Capital Goods.

This model will eventually help us close the gap between the language of the economist and the language of all other people; this model will help us close the differences in the field of vision between ecologists, who see mainly stocks of natural resources, and economists, who see mainly flows of funds. This model, when fully unfolded, will help us close the gap in methodology between economists and mathematicians.

The Stocks model is owed to suggestions and observations and so much prodding and probing by Professor Franco Modigliani that I doubt I would have ever developed it without his assistance. Ever faithful to the Socratic method, Professor Modigliani elicited this model, as well as those that we will examine later on, in a long series of conferences from 1976 to 1978. Nor did his assistance stop there; it has been carried out ever since through the exploration of the meaning of these models and their synthesis, work that will be presented in other books.

At this point the reader might ask, why so many models? At the limit, the economic process is not like a sphere as emphasized so far. The economic process is more like a prism that can be observed from many points of view. In order to avoid confusion, as we proceed we will specify each one of the angles of vision that we are adopting. When the structure of Concordian economics is fully developed, we will have at our disposal as many models as there are major viewpoints from which the economic system can and ought to be observed. And because of the existence of these many legitimate but partial visualizations, it becomes essential for economic theory not only to have a set of appropriate tools for each situation; it is also necessary to acquire a proper sense of the direction to be imparted to the system as a whole.

A Sense of Direction

In a somewhat distant past, everyone understood that the function of the economic system—and hence the function of economic analysis—was to free humanity from economic poverty; and, although not always explicitly stated, the economist wanted to free humanity from economic poverty, not for the sake of material riches, but to let people acquire time and energy to free themselves of spiritual poverty. This was, indeed, the noble goal that supported the work of eminent economists from Adam Smith to Marshall to Keynes, not to mention older economic thinkers from Aristotle to the Doctors of the Catholic Church. No longer. Apart from notable exceptions, economic theory has generally become the study of wealth, the study of how the stock market functions, and the study of how the rich become richer.

Indirectly, this type of analysis is of incalculable importance for human welfare. At its basis, however, there is the trickle-down assumption that once the rich get richer, all other people will benefit. This is a facile assumption that is not justified by the facts. At the peak of creation of incalculable amounts of wealth, the number of poor people remains in the billions, and the type of abject poverty to which they are subjected remains intolerable. The trickle-down assumption is too limiting of the human spirit, and thus it is not capable of bringing economic serenity to anyone. Clearly, economic theory has to regain its old sense of direction. If the elimination of absolute poverty is not the task of economic theory, which mental discipline can assume it? It must be axiomatic that the function of economic theory is indeed to solve the problem of economic poverty—directly, *mano a mano*, as it were. The analysis of this redirection is the task of the last two chapters in this book. There we will try to ascertain not only why, but how, this goal can be achieved.

There is much to be done before we reach that point. Let us start. The task at hand is the analysis of Keynes' model of the economic system.

III

Lack of Homogeneity in Keynes' Model

The hidden complexities of "a proposition."

———•———

KEYNES' MODEL OF THE ECONOMIC system is composed of two near perfect concepts (income and consumption) and two relations (saving and investment). Thus Keynes' model is not a homogeneous entity.

This lack of homogeneity is not simply a formal or esthetic shortcoming of the model. It is a substantive shortcoming. Once saving and investment are both defined as the difference between income and consumption, or defined in relation to each other as in the proposition that "saving is equal to investment," a number of logical consequences unavoidably follow. Through the observation of these consequences we shall gradually obtain an obstructed view of the economic reality.

Take away the concept of income or that of consumption, and the meaning of saving and investment almost completely vanishes. This consequence follows because saving and investment in contemporary economic theory are not concepts or independent entities. They are relations. They are mental linkages whose primary meaning is given by their relation to income and consumption. Take away the meaning of either or both entities, and you are left with very little because saving and investment, by themselves, do not exist—they do not exist as separate, independent entities.

The consequence that is of immediate interest is that by taking away the meaning of income and consumption, as in our hypothesis, both saving and investment lose all meaning. What is saving? What is investment? The argument is circular: saving and investment—it is said without batting an eyelash—are both equal to the difference between income and consumption. Circular reasoning has no standing in Western logic. And in most Eastern logic there is no circular reasoning either; but, rather, "complementary" reasoning.

Take away the meaning of income or consumption, and what remains is the *proposition* that "saving is equal to investment."

The Hidden Complexities of "A Proposition"

Let us focus our attention on the remainder, the proposition that "saving is equal to investment." A proposition—any proposition—does not have any meaning unless, as Keynes pointed out in his *Treatise on Probability,* it is related to a *corpus* of knowledge—i.e., a theory.[11] The classical example illustrative of this characteristic of propositions can be found in geometry: do two parallel lines meet? It is now evident that the proposition, by itself, has no meaning and therefore no answer can be given to the question, unless one puts it in the context of either Euclidean or imaginary geometry. In the first context, parallel lines do not meet; in the latter they do meet. The proposition that saving is equal to investment ought to be studied under the same stringent rules.

In this work, we shall adopt such stringent rules. They will be spelled out at more opportune moments. For the time being, let us confine our attention to the issue of the economic consequences of the lack of homogeneity in Keynes' model.

A More "Practical" Approach

So far we have observed that Keynes' model is composed of two concepts and two relations; and that if we take away the meaning of income or consumption, we remain with an empty proposition: the proposition that "saving is equal to investment."

However, if the hypothesis is too strong; if elimination of one or two of the entities to which saving and investment are related is too inconceivable a case, let us take a more realistic one. In contemporary economic theory, the meaning of saving and investment is subject to the vagaries in the meaning of income, consumption, and even saving or investment themselves. By altering the meaning of any one of these entities, the meaning of saving and investment is automatically altered—even when that happens inadvertently. This qualification is important enough to return to it at a later moment. For now, let us observe a general characteristic of economic theory. Economic theory is an apparatus like the inner workings of a clock. Any movement of one wheel is transmitted to all other wheels. And yet, the adjustment is not automatic. It has to be made to fit. Let us observe the major point.

Instead of insisting on the "abstract" question of the meaning of any one of those four entities—a meaning which has continuously changed over time and from author to author—let us talk of a "concrete" issue, the issue of the measurement of either saving and/or investment. It is evident that if one increases the level of national income, by adding to the calculations the income from stocks and bonds or, more radically, the value of housework—and one keeps the level of consumption constant—within the confines of existing theory, one automatically increases the level of saving and/or investment. There is a good chance of either change occurring in the future, and this change would carry with it important economic consequences. Would the resultant increased level of saving be considered as *real* saving? It clearly is a nominal increase. But, just the same, ought it not affect all projections regarding the future behavior of the economy? And by how much? Should one rather discount the influence of this nominal increase in the level of saving? Again, by how much? The psychological phenomenon of the "wealth effect" is rather well known, even though it is difficult to measure. A family whose assets are creating a nominal yearly income of, say, 2x instead of 1x is bound to feel wealthier and to spend more. It is this concrete action that is definitely going to affect the future, and this effect ought to be measured. The essential point is that a change in the concept of income brings about an automatic change in the concrete meaning, measurement, and effects of saving. (The reader who takes issue with the example selected here can make the identical case through a different hypothesis. And one can not only add values to the official accounts but also subtract them.)

The concept of consumption also is by no means quite fixed yet. What is the effect of a large influx of second-hand products on the market? In periods of prosperity, one expects large donations of second-hand products to charity organizations. In periods of depression, one expects those products to be sold to second-hand dealers. Yet such sales are not taken into account by present measurements and theory. The point is that consumption expenditure can be made to vary simply by changing the content of the word "consumption," and such changes are going to affect the measurement of saving and/or investment.

Even the meaning of investment is by no means fixed—except through conventions adopted by statisticians. A dwelling house, for instance, is counted as an investment. Since, when inhabited by the owner, it produces no income, should a house not be considered an article of consumption? Correspondingly, a car is considered a consumption item, even when it is used—at least in part—for business purposes. Should not this car be considered, at least in part, an investment? The point is that in contemporary economic theory the meaning and measurement of saving and investment are determined by the meaning and measurement of the entities to which they are related—be they income, consumption, or each other. Of course, there is no intention at this stage to argue the merits of these cases one way or the other.

Some Further Considerations

If it were necessary, examples could be multiplied. More important is to give some consideration to a major consequence of the lack of homogeneity in Keynes' model. Once one works with a model of the economic system that is composed of two concepts—however perfect in themselves—and two relations, one finds that the relationships that exist among those entities are determined a priori. Therefore, it is no longer necessary—indeed, it is no longer possible—to look at the economic reality as it is. The description of the reality is determined by those definitional conventions.

Specifically, it is thus predetermined that saving is equal to investment and that both are equal to the difference between income and consumption. Are these realistic assumptions? Do they reflect the economic reality? The point is, since saving and investment are defined as relations, and not as independent concepts, contemporary economic theory cannot even ask such fundamental questions.

These are only a few of the consequences, it must be emphasized, that follow from the lack of homogeneity in Keynes' model and specifically from the definition of saving and investment as relations. In the proceeding we shall discover more such consequences, which have a real impact on the clarity of the economic discourse, on the logical consistency of the structure erected by economic analysis, on empirical issues, on practical measurements, and on concrete economic effects.

So far, it must be stressed, the logical consistency of the structure of mainstream theory cannot be put into question. There is no rule that compels one to build a model composed of four concepts—a homogeneous model. Neither is there any rule that prohibits the imposition of a priori restraints on the formulation of economic theory. But clearly, on certain scales, the more formally coherent and the freer the theory, the higher a value is likely to be assigned to it. More important still, the content of such fundamental building blocks of economic theory as income, consumption, saving, and investment cannot be continuously made to vary at will. These changes affect the clarity of the economic discourse—and, through it, the vision of the economic reality.

IV

Simplicism—and Forced Doublespeak—of Keynes' Model

Each contradiction is subtly—and firmly—
balanced by the next contradiction.

ANY MODEL OF THE ECONOMIC SYSTEM, to be a manageable tool of analysis, must be simple. But it ought not to be simplistic. The interest of accuracy cannot be sacrificed to that of clarity. Everyone knows that people hoard wealth. Yet this phenomenon does not fit in Keynes' model and it disappears from any formal treatment of economic theory. Thus Keynes' model, eliminating the vision of the phenomenon of hoarding, reduces the understanding of the economic system to quite simplistic terms.

It should come as no surprise that the origin of this shortcoming resides in the conception of saving and investment as relations. Once saving and investment are defined either as income minus consumption or as equal to each other, there is no room left for anything else. The phenomenon of hoarding must disappear from sight. Those definitional relationships determine the description of the entire economic reality. Whatever is left from the difference between income and consumption must be either saving or investment; and whatever is saving must be investment, and vice versa.

For those who think that these are only formal or definitional issues, let us anticipate the very core of our findings: the phenomenon of hoarding has an overwhelming influence not only on economic growth, but even on inflation. And the incapacity of contemporary economic theory to observe the phenomenon of hoarding goes a long way to explain the theoretical as well as the real condition which obtains in those two fields. Let us then give our utmost attention to these matters of definition. Let us emphasize once more that, for contemporary economic theory, the phenomenon of hoarding does not exist.

What does an unbiased reading of the economic reality, instead, tell us? Out of the yearly income, one person hides numerous one-hundred-dollar bills in a safe deposit box; another stashes gold away; still another buys land and leaves it in an unused (as distinguished from "open") state, or a house and leaves it boarded-up; or he stockpiles raw materials, or ancient Mexican artifacts which need to be hidden away because they were smuggled into the country. These, and many others, are all documented facts. Their cumulative impact on the economic system can, at times, be quite considerable. How does economic theory take these facts into account?

Those items clearly are not consumer articles. Economic theory must, therefore, consider them either as saving or as investment. Indeed, it cannot decide and therefore considers them as saving-investment. Let us encourage economic theory to clarify its mind. Let us consider those items first as saving-investment, then as saving and, finally, as investment.

Are Those Items "Saving-Investment"?

The standard explanation is that saving-investment is a flow—whether of monetary funds or of goods and services, i.e., "real," wealth. There obviously are complications relating to timing, origin, and direction of that flow. They go beyond the present discussion and will be indirectly touched upon below when we break that flow into its component elements: saving and investment. Here we are only concerned with a static analysis of the issue. The question is: can there be an entity called "saving-investment"?

There clearly cannot be such a thing as saving-investment. One cannot have such an undefined and undefinable hybrid. One cannot have it both ways—especially when it is insisted that all factors in the economic system are sooner or later determined by the dynamics of saving *and* investment. The agglomeration of the two entities into one, called saving-investment, must necessarily be an inert factor. It takes at least two sticks to strike a spark. There is no dynamics there. Only when saving-investment comes into contact with something else, only then can it produce any effect. But economic theory has not discovered this "something else" yet. Therefore, those items cannot be considered as saving-investment—while leaving intact the remaining structure of economic theory. One cannot have it both ways in this sense either.

Since Keynes considered saving and investment as the determinates of the economic system, Keynes alone—and those who go beyond paying lip service in accepting his theories—could properly accept the existence of such an entity as saving-investment. Keynes in fact clearly stated that saving and investment are "merely different aspects of the same thing."[12] But even this conception does not eliminate other logical difficulties to be mentioned forthwith.

When one proceeds to define this agglomeration, this "same thing," one must still determine whether it has the characteristics of either saving or investment. (One could still consider those articles as having the *characteristics* of both saving and investment—as distinguished from *being* "saving-investment." This discussion, however, has to be postponed so that we can proceed in an orderly fashion.)

It might appear that the above does not address itself to the notion of saving-investment conceived as a flow. But it does. That notion can be explained only by maintaining that the flow is "first" saving and "then" investment. This explanation gives the whole case up. In fact, it is not even necessary to inquire when, how, or why this transition occurs. It is sufficient to recognize that this explanation has automatically split that agglomerate into two entities.

We can proceed.

Are Those Articles Saving?

Let us consider those articles as saving. Taking them one by one, one must conclude that those dollar bills, those raw materials, that type of land, etc., have the capability of being saved or preserved forever—or nearly so. Therefore, one can, indeed must, consider those articles as saving.

However, one can accept this inescapable solution only if one considers the issue in isolation and leaves both the conception of saving and that of investment isolated from each other. Those articles can be considered as expressions of saving, in fact—but what happens to the axiom of contemporary economic theory, the proposition that "saving is equal to investment"?

At this point a different mental mechanism is triggered. Those articles can be considered as saving, and the validity of the axiom that saving is equal to investment can still be safeguarded, only on one extremely important condition—provided, that is, that one breaks a tacit convention that has ruled economic theory ever since its inception. The convention—to which we shall have to return—is that investment ("capital" of old) is all productive wealth: productive of monetary income, or of real goods and services. This is economic investment. And it has nothing to do with financial investments. We shall return to the latter point as well.

Dollar bills in a safe deposit box, unused land, and stockpiles of raw materials left idle for a long time for any number of reasons can be considered saving only if one breaks the convention regarding the meaning of economic investment. In order to consider them as saving, even though those items are, in fact, so evidently unproductive of either income or goods and services, that convention is indeed broken. Since it is assumed that saving is equal to investment, those items are in effect automatically transformed into "productive" wealth. This is a clear-cut disregard of reality. The reality, as usual, takes (or should take) over.

And the reality takes over in its own unpredictable ways; first of all, through forcing strange twists in the language.

Are Those Articles Investment?

Some Unrecognized Consequences of Considering Those Articles As Investment

The items under consideration are dollar bills in a safe deposit box, unused land, stockpiles of raw materials that are not needed in the immediate future, and the like. Unless one confuses financial investment with economic investment, these items are so patently *not* investment that the issue does not deserve any consideration. We are therefore free to determine the consequences of the compulsory theoretical conclusion to the contrary.

As noted, by defining saving and investment as relations, a change in the meaning of one term automatically affects the meaning of the other—even when the change is unwittingly brought about. Let us look back at the situation in reverse order. Stating that those items are "investment" and equating investment to saving, economic theory has inadvertently affected the meaning of both saving and investment and, ultimately, the understanding of the economic function of those items from which we started. Specifically, saving has become no longer something which can be preserved more or less forever; rather it is something that produces wealth. Conversely, investment has become something which is nonproductive. Finally, those items have—by fiat—become productive of wealth. Mainstream economic theory compels us to assert that dollar bills in a safe deposit box, unused land, stockpiles of raw materials that are not needed in the immediate future, contrary to all reality, are items that produce wealth. To any unbiased observer, these are egregious anomalies.

These issues are so important that we have to return to them in order to close every possible escape hatch for the economist more than for any other reader. For the time being, let us observe some of the ultimate consequences of this central line of reasoning by asking a few pertinent questions.

Is it really necessary to pursue the economic discussion over this ever-shifting ground? Is it really necessary to be compelled to maintain that a packet of dollar bills kept under the mattress is productive, repeat, productive of wealth? Is it really necessary to break that convention concerning the meaning of investment that has been preserved for so long in economic analysis? Is it really necessary to alter in mid-sentence—as it fits the occasion—both the meaning of saving and that of investment? In short, is it really necessary to foster the Age of Doublespeak? A long chain of events can be thus summarized: economic theory dictates economic policy, and economic policy influences in a thousand subtle ways all other government actions and, thereby, exerts a direct and profound impact on all of our lives. If there is doublespeak at the beginning of the chain, there must be doublespeak at its end also.

Some day, someone will do a serious and thorough study of these relationships. This future scholar might also carry the inquiry into the analysis of the ways and means in which economic policies affect all the expressions of our existence—from modes of dressing to eating and sleeping habits. This is not economic determinism, however. A study must also be made of how politics determines economics. And so on. But let us return to our main point.

Within the confines of the mainstream economic theory, there is no escape. It cannot be overemphasized: in mainstream economic theory doublespeak is unavoidable. An escape from this stricture must be found.

Escapism vs. Escape

The current form of escapism adopted by mainstream economic theory is to assume that one must live with contradictions and with anomalies, namely, facts that cannot fit into the theory.

This book suggests that there is an escape. If the theory is changed, and if the economic discussion is firmly rooted in the soil of the Flows model, anomalies vanish, because all relevant facts are incorporated into a coherent framework of theory. Once that is done, we shall be able to study many phenomena, including the phenomenon of hoarding, and we will no longer be compelled to consider hoarding as investment—i.e., "productive" wealth. Conversely, investment will be considered as productive wealth, both explicitly and tacitly. The need for doublespeak disappears—and the simplicism that is inherent in Keynes' model is done away with.

For the time being, we must still remain within the confines of existing economic theory and ask a legitimate question: where is the internal logical consistency that Keynes claimed existed in that structure? A series of contradictions in terms, which we have found in that theory, is the exact opposite of logical consistency. Since this question will be raised again, let us try to settle it once and for all. The issue is one of standards. It has nothing to do with economic theory per se—directly, that is. These standards are not dictated by the internal logic of that theory. They are rather dictated exclusively by logic—whether "common" or "formal" logic. In other words, it is a rule of logic and not a rule of economics that conventions—whether they have ever been made explicit or they remain tacit—must be obeyed; and if disobeyed, they must be disobeyed explicitly.

Thus contemporary economic theory preserves its internal logical consistency, first, by operating on the basis of a tacit convention that investment is all productive wealth; then by overlooking the existence of this convention; and, finally, by altering in mid-sentence the meaning of both saving and investment. This is the cost at which that internal consistency is bought.

The internal logical consistency of that structure, it must be stressed, remains intact. Each contradiction is subtly—and firmly—balanced by the next contradiction. But how twisted can the economic discourse become? It is clear that something must "give." The ultimate concession appears at the level of the interpretation of the economic reality and therefore the formulation of economic policy—a subject that, the reader might sigh with relief, lies outside the realm of this work.

A general characteristic of contemporary economic theory might also be pointed out. The expressions of the Sibyl were of immediate comprehension; the ambiguities arose from a deeper analysis of the texts. Many economic expressions, instead, are indecipherable on the surface but become quite simple when unscrambled.

V

Lack of True Equivalence
in Keynes' Model

*The rules of equivalence "hold" even "for
equality (=) but are of far wider application."*

R. G. D. Allen

———•———

SO FAR THE DISCUSSION on the relation among income, consumption, and saving or investment has been held on the basis of general or common logic. In order to study the relation between saving and investment, which is contained in Keynes' model and in all manifestations of mainstream economics, let us use rules that have been established by centuries of elaboration in the field of formal logic—as well as in the field of mathematics. Both logicians and mathematicians speak cautiously of such vague terms as "equality." In its place, they prefer to talk either of identity or of equivalence. It is against the well-established standards governing both identity and equivalence, then, that one must judge the validity of the "equality" of saving to investment. Judged against those standards, that relationship proves to be technically incorrect.

The Relationship Between Saving
and Investment Is Not an Identity

The relationship between saving and investment cannot be an identity. Saving and investment are themselves relations in contemporary economic analysis. One would thus have a relationship (of identity) between two relations (saving and investment). In other words, if that relationship were to be considered an identity, we would be lifted into a rarefied atmosphere indeed: we would be enveloped by a pure mental construction without any substance, without any relation to the economic reality.

In any case, since Professor Patrick Suppes points out that "The relation of identity is an equivalence relation,"[13] we need not remain on this aspect of the total issue. (To clarify it somewhat, though, we might be helped if we consider "identity" as a relationship looking inward and "equivalence" as a relationship looking outward.)

We now consider the relationship between saving and investment as an equivalence.

The Relationship Between Saving and Investment Is Not an Equivalence

That relationship, we discover, is not one of equivalence either, because the terms are neither reflexive nor symmetric nor transitive—as the rules of both logic and mathematics command that they be.

The Terms Are Not Reflexive

Saving and investment are not reflexive because they are not exclusively identical to saving and investment respectively. By definition, they are both "equal" either to each other or to income minus consumption. (This point will become clearer still when we look deeper at the content of saving and investment; we shall then see that the concrete items generally covered under those umbrella-like definitions necessarily share economic characteristics with all entities to which they are related.)

The Terms Are Not Symmetric

Saving and investment are not symmetric either. This is the most delicate issue in contemporary economic analysis. Thanks to the influence of Frank Ramsey and D. H. Robertson, Keynes could not avoid giving a great deal of attention to it. In fact, he left behind traces of his thought that are invaluable for the understanding of the problem. Whenever he spoke of the "equality" of saving to investment (an equality which at times he also called "identity" and even "equivalence"[14]), Keynes grew very impatient and, uncharacteristically, even abusive with the reader who might have not agreed with him. He was clearly not satisfied with the condition in which he left the issue. This is the key quotation: "Thus the old-fashioned view that saving always involves investment, though incomplete and misleading, is formally sounder than the newfan-

gled view that there can be saving without investment or investment without 'genuine' saving."[15] How many qualifications. And
from the pen of John Maynard Keynes who certainly was not
prone to halftones. Let us observe these qualifications in reverse
order—those implicit as well as those explicit.

To state either that there can be saving without investment or
investment without "genuine" saving clearly is to misunderstand
the internal logic of contemporary economic theory. One cannot
alter that relationship without altering the entire structure of contemporary economic theory. This is the implicit assumption in
Keynes' position.

The explicit qualifications in Keynes' understanding of that relationship are as follows. The relationship for Keynes is "formally
sounder"—formally, as opposed to substantively; sounder, as
opposed to sound. And then that relationship is "misleading"—the
conception that saving is "equal" to investment in fact tends to
obliterate all that must be accomplished in order to transform saving into investment; thus that relationship tends to swallow the
entire theory of economic growth and leads to practices which cannot be analyzed here, but whose fruits, upon a moment's thought,
are fairly well known to all.

Finally, that relationship is "old-fashioned" and "incomplete."
That conception goes back at least to Adam Smith—thus one finds
a further confirmation that Keynes did remain in the mold of classical economic analysis. But, more importantly, that relationship is
"incomplete."

Why? How?

This characterization is so important that one would have
expected detailed explanations from Keynes. And yet, analysis
reveals that he could not totally satisfy either himself or his reader
on this point. He had to remain satisfied with the offerings of intuition rather than those of reason. This is indeed the essential dilemma in which contemporary economic theory is enveloped.

In fact, that is a characterization that becomes incontrovertible
only if one looks at the "substance" and not the "form" of the economic reality. Formally, to repeat with Keynes, there cannot be
saving without investment or investment without saving. But does
this position respect the economic reality? Not at all. As soon as
one looks at the substance of the economic process, i.e., as soon as
one looks at the economic reality without the assistance of prevailing economic theories, one realizes that, true, all investment
must correspond to some saving. This is a reality which can be better seen through the eyes of the law than those of economics: every

item of wealth, as soon as it is created, must be owned by someone; it must—economic analysis rushes to conclude— correspond
to someone's "saving." The right of property abhors a vacuum.
(As can be seen from this important connection, economics is not
entirely an autonomous discipline yet.)

But does every saving correspond to an investment? The answer
is positive if one is unable or unwilling to escape the straitjacket of
contemporary theories and is ready to twist the meaning of words.
The answer is positive if one breaks the tacit convention mentioned earlier that investment means "productive" wealth, wealth
that produces other wealth. The answer is positive if one does not
distinguish between financial and economic investment.

If one is not ready to make all these—and other—concessions,
one realizes that wealth which in act is inert, such as unused land
or dollar bills in a safe deposit box, cannot be considered economic
investment. Against those who did not concur, Keynes issued one
of his strongest possible warnings. He stated:

> The absurd, though almost universal, idea that an act of individual
> saving is just as good for effective demand as an act of individual con-
> sumption, has been fostered by the fallacy, much more specious than
> the conclusion derived from it, that an increased desire to hold
> wealth, being much the same thing as increased desire to hold invest-
> ments, must, by increasing the demand for investments, provide a
> stimulus to their production; so that current investment is promoted
> by individual saving to the same extent as present consumption is
> diminished.
>
> It is of this fallacy that it is most difficult to disabuse men's
> minds.[16]

Difficult, for certain; but perhaps not eternally impossible. (This
long quotation, incidentally, is a representative sample—not so
much of Keynes' style—as of what is here labeled "lack of clarity
in the economic discourse" due to use of prevailing "terms.") In
the substance of things, the naked truth is simple enough—as are
all truths: every saving does not correspond to an investment. The
two terms are not symmetric. One cannot exchange one term with
the other without falling into an "absurd, though almost universal" fallacy.

These conclusions must be obvious to the non-economist. And
yet, to make them incontrovertible to the economist, much more
remains to be done. Since it is impossible to formally and explicitly, namely, mathematically use the straightforward statement that

every saving does not correspond to an investment and include it within the framework of Keynes' model of the economic system, convincing evidence of the validity of this statement can be found only on another level of thought. It is discarding the distorting lenses of contemporary economic theory and transforming the theory from the bottom up that one clearly sees such a simple but fundamental truth: every saving does not correspond to an investment.

Then, and only then, one shall incontrovertibly realize that the terms of the presumed relationship of equality between saving and investment are not symmetric. One cannot exchange one term with the other and obtain the same meaning—let alone the same economic functions. A packet of dollar bills under the mattress does not perform the same economic functions; it does not cause the same results as dollar bills deposited in a bank, used by an entrepreneur in daily transactions, or even spent on the purchase of consumer items.

Substantively, the two terms are not symmetric.

The Terms Are Not Transitive

And the two terms are not transitive either. There is nothing in contemporary economic analysis to which saving and investment are equivalent. Keynes did not pursue this line of inquiry. We must be grateful to Professor Milton Friedman for offering this result in his Theory of Capital.[17] He found no other term to which saving and investment might possibly be equivalent. (It must be pointed out, however, that Professor Friedman was not looking for such a term.)

We shall find a third term implicit in the *General Theory*. But it is so hidden there that it has never been explicitly mentioned by anyone, Keynes included.

In summary, since the terms are neither reflexive nor symmetric (at least from a substantive point of view) nor (explicitly) transitive, the relationship of equivalence between saving and investment is not technically correct.

A Recurring Issue

The question remains: how does contemporary economic theory preserve its internal logical consistency? The answer is obvious: it ignores the rules of formal logic. Remaining within the confines of economic theory, one can neglect external standards. As soon as one opens the eyes to the larger reality of formal logic, however, it becomes no longer possible to use so vague a term as "equality." If one wants to provide his or her analysis with the sustenance of rules of correct reasoning elaborated by centuries of efforts in the field of logic, one must speak solely of either a relationship of identity or a relationship of equivalence.

And if one insists on using the term "equality"? There is no escape. One must remember with Professor R. G. D. Allen that the rules of equivalence "hold" even "for equality (=) but are of far wider application."[18]

Conclusively, tested against the rules of formal logic, the relation between saving and investment cannot be considered an identity nor an equivalence nor an equality. Therefore, the proposition "saving is equal to investment" is logically incorrect.

A Deeper Issue:
A Schism Within the Bowels of Mainstream Theory

Within the confines of contemporary economic theory, it cannot be overemphasized, one is forced to accept that logically incorrect proposition. Since what is left from income minus consumption is saving, and since saving is mathematically equal to investment in that model, one cannot formally demonstrate that saving and investment are asymmetric terms. There is no economic reality outside the framework of the model. One must simply accept the relationship of equality between saving and investment as a dogma.

But this compulsion does not make the proposition valid; it does not correct, nor does it obliterate, the internal weaknesses of mainstream economics. Indeed, those weaknesses are transmitted in a great variety of ways to the structure of whatever theory is built upon it.

We shall observe this conclusion at closer range in the next chapter. Here let us observe one central consequence: that dogma has created a schism in the bowels of mainstream economics. The asymmetry between saving and investment is not a passive entity. It affects the very core of mainstream economics. There it is reflected, and magnified, along the following fault lines. In theory, there are two asymmetric sets of conditions which are deemed to result in an increase in saving: an increase in investment and a decrease in consumption; while there are two symmetric sets of conditions which are deemed to result in an increase in investment: an increase in saving, and an increase in consumption. By themselves, both lines of reasoning are unobjectionable. Yet even though it literally represents a restatement of the first equation of Keynes' model, the second statement is not accepted as valid by all economists. And, unmistakably simplified, this conceptual asymmetry relating to saving and investment is carried into the realm of economic policy, whereby some are justified in believing that an increase in investment results from an increase in saving and others are justified in believing that it results from an increase in consumption, namely, a decrease in saving.

Such is the polarization that exists within the bowels of mainstream economics that the lack of symmetry between saving and investment is either not recognized at all or, taking refuge in its formally sound foundation, asymmetry is denied. Economists continue to trust in the presumed validity of the model. They go on building more and more intricate constructions on that basis.

If one were to ask, how can that happen, how can economists tolerate such contradictory statements at the very core of their discipline, the answer would be surprisingly simple. They find the ultimate justification for the presentation of their theories, neither in logic nor in the theory of knowledge, but in the prevailing philosophy of the age: rationalism. The point is so important that it deserves some undivided attention.

VI

Neither Classical nor Mainstream, but Rational Economics

Events of the last half dozen years have shown us how much economics remains an art rather than a science.

Paul A. Samuelson, 1973

———

THE TERM CLASSICAL ECONOMICS is a misnomer. Under the entry "classical," Webster reads: "Thought as soundly authoritative and standard . . . as *classical* economics." Were it for no other reason, after observing that the relationship of equality between saving and investment is technically incorrect, we can no longer accept classical economics as "soundly authoritative and standard." Classical economics is entirely based on the proposition that saving is "equal" to investment.

Indeed, we must realize that such a fundamental proposition has been shared—although in a variety of forms—not only by Keynes himself but also by Monetarists and Keynesians. Indeed, not even the other great trend of contemporary economic thought, the input-output analysis of Nobel laureate Professor Wassily Leontief escapes from assuming the validity of that proposition. Nor does any other expression of mainstream economics.

The fundamental importance of the relationship between saving and investment cannot be emphasized enough. It affects the entire structure of economic theory—in all of its wondrous manifestations. To mention—altering somewhat Professor Axel Leijonhufvud's analysis—only a few such ramifications, it must be recognized that such a relationship affects the theory of consumption no less than the theory of capital, the theory of the rate of interest no less than the theory of value or the theory of growth.[19]

More to the point, the importance of the proposition that saving is "equal" to investment is so fundamental that all schools of thought which share it should be classified alike. The mantle of classical economics, therefore, ought to be extended to cover all major contemporary schools of thought as well—and then the classification ought to be changed from classical to rational economics.

Rational Economics

The entire train of leading economic thought from Adam Smith to the present, with a few dissenters here and there, has been founded on a rather long series of rational explanations concerning the relationship between saving and investment. Since each explanation was well thought out, it could not be punctured from inside its own logic. But evidently it was still somewhat unsatisfactory, so each explanation in time was replaced with another one—equally rational, equally well thought out. And so on and on. Upon scrutiny, these rational explanations turned out to be mere rationalizations. Let us briefly review the historical evidence.

Adam Smith made the apparently innocuous observation: "Whatever a person saves from his revenue he adds to his capital. . ."[20] With the understanding that revenue today is called income and capital is called investment, nothing could be more obvious than Adam Smith's statement. We shall not, however, bring forward all the complexities involved in this or in any other of the positions listed below: we would go too far astray. We shall pick up some of the major issues as we proceed in the discussion.

With James Mill, what was implicit in Smith becomes explicit: "The augmentation of capital . . . is every where *exactly in proportion* to the degree of saving; in fact, the amount of that augmentation, annually, is *the same thing* with the amount of savings which are annually made."[21] With Mill, saving clearly is "equal" to investment.

These expressions were gradually transformed into the complex formulations of Say's Law.[22] One interpretation of this law can be simply put as follows: "parsimony" or some other psycho-sociological quality creates savings and, since "supply creates its own demand," there eventually results an "equality" of aggregate saving to aggregate investment. As is well known, Say's Law dominated economic thought all during the twentieth century—up to Keynes. (Apart from John Stuart Mill, who, trying to be clear and comprehensive, simply became prolix, Ricardo and Marshall were supreme technicians. Their powerful minds, no matter the ultimate intent, reduced the study of economics to an intellectual toy; exchanging the means—or tools—with the end, they reduced economics to the level of one single theoretical apparatus coming from nowhere and going nowhere: the theoretical apparatus of the laws of supply and demand. Keynes' tirades against Ricardo are well known;[23] less known perhaps is his characterization of Marshall's economics as "void of content."[24] This characterization is less known and, if known, its validity is generally discounted because Keynes himself did not fully escape from Marshallian "modes of thought and expression."[25] We shall evidently have to return at least to the major points so summarily treated here.)

Thus except for the "new-fangled view" of some neoclassical economists (including Keynes himself in1930[26]) that saving and investment are *not* equal to each other, Say's Law and its central proposition that saving is "equal" to investment remained uncontested for over a century. And it is against the many simplifying assumptions involved in any of the formulations of this law that Keynes opened his salvos in the *General Theory*. In the process of his reasoning, Keynes transformed the proposition that saving is "equal" to investment from a complex economic mechanism, which can be made to explain the entire economic process, to a definitional tautology. Only on this basis did he accept the conclusion that saving is "equal" to investment—but still accept it he did. More specifically, for Keynes, saving and investment are not only the product of an identical definition (both are defined as income minus consumption); they also are assumed to be the determinates, not the determinants, of the economic system. Thus the power of that proposition was completely spent. Say's Law was turned upon its head.

As stated in the first chapter, this was *the* revolution which Keynes accomplished and heralded in so many and different tones.

A Verification

The mathematician can quickly verify the validity of the previous assertions. The mathematician knows that, technically, Keynes' model can be written as follows:

Investment = Income - Consumption
Saving = Income - Consumption
Saving = Investment.

Written in this form, it appears immediately evident that both saving and investment share the same definition. And, if one takes the model at face value, it also appears immediately evident that saving and investment are indeed the determinates and not the determinants of the economic system. One simply needs to start the description of the economic process from the concept of income. (To proceed from there, the discussion becomes rather technical, "laborious," and even of limited range; but it can proceed. Keynes did just that. One therefore does not need to insist on the point.)

To follow the reasoning, the non-mathematician has to remember that for a term to be moved from one side of an equation to the other, its sign must be changed from plus to minus or vice versa. Economists and non-economists alike will agree that, had Keynes not had the stroke of genius to write that first equation as he actually did, either he might have not been taken seriously, or he might have been more readily understood. In either case, the history of economic analysis after the publication of the *General Theory* would have followed quite a different course. To say the least, one might have clearly seen that the economic discourse still revolved around the interpretation of the fundamental relationship between saving and investment, and that Keynes had simply added his own—revolutionary—meaning to an already long list of interpretations.

What Actually Happened?

A complex set of circumstances occurred after the publication of the *General Theory*. These events cannot be examined in detail without going too far astray. A few points will be covered in other chapters; at present we shall confine ourselves to the examination of this question: what happened to the proposition that "saving is equal to investment"?

Ever since the publication of the *General Theory*, there have been many other interpretations of that proposition. They cannot be listed here without unnecessarily burdening the discussion. Frankly, this shortcut is taken to avoid dealing with the distinctions introduced by Keynesians, led by the Swedish School of Economics, between "measured," "observable," or "actual" vs. "scheduled," "planned," or "desired" saving and investment. There are complexities in these distinctions that cannot be adequately treated in this work. And since they are built upon the proposition that *measured* saving, for instance, is "equal" to *measured* investment, there is no need for this detailed analysis either. The essential reason for this shortcut is to establish in a direct and immediate fashion a more important point. This goal is best achieved by picking up the discussion directly where Keynes left it: the state of powerlessness of the proposition that saving is "equal" to investment.

On the basis of the historical momentum it seems that it should have been easy to eliminate that proposition altogether from the realm of economic theory. Instead, the power of that proposition was left intact by the contemporary Monetarists who have never acknowledged the importance of Keynes' thought. Indeed, the power of that proposition was revived even by the Keynesians, who—as it has been more and more openly recognized—thus became inadvertently involved in a surreptitious counter-revolution:[27] a counter-revolution against Keynes. For instance, Professor Axel Leijonhufvud in 1968 categorically stated: "Keynes was not a 'Keynesian.'"[28]

This is how that proposition underwent a "counter-revolution" of its own. For the Keynesians, saving and investment came to determine primarily and directly the level of income; for the Monetarists, saving and investment continued to determine primarily and directly the rate of interest.

The dominance of Say's Law was reinstated in fact—even though its validity was often denied in words.

Thus the proposition that "saving is equal to investment" was transformed back into an operational entity. Indeed, it was explicitly put at the center of economic analysis: a position that it had only implicitly occupied before. This is certainly an improvement, because it invites direct examination; and yet that position carries hidden disadvantages as well. Since the proposition is logically incorrect, it was bound to affect the entire structure of economic analysis in many negative and subtle ways. Let us observe some of these effects.

Effects Upon the Structure of Economic Analysis

Leaving aside the many technical improvements brought forward especially by the full introduction of mathematics and statistics, the world of economic theory has reverted back not only to many positions but even to the fundamental composition of the past. This trend has been accelerated and accepted as normal through supply-side economics and rational expectations analysis.

Professor Joan Robinson, as *prima inter pares*, repeatedly and consistently insisted on the current reversion back to the positions held by economists in the past. Therefore, the point no longer needs to be proved. We are free to give a quick look at the issue of the formal composition of prevailing economic analysis.

We have already seen that the central importance of Keynes' thought consists of an attempt to unify the three major strands of classical economic analysis into a coherent, dynamic, and organic unit. Economists who came after Keynes annulled the value of this attempt. As we shall see, once again economic analysis offers a long series of theories that are only intricately related to each other.

Chain reactions are always composed of a large number of links. Let us interrupt the discussion at this stage then, so that we can firmly capture the major points in this review of the historical evidence. One essential point is that all theories, which are based on such a fundamental proposition as "saving is equal to investment," ought to be grouped together. And since they are all inevitably based upon a rational explanation of that fundamental proposition, these theories ought to be classified as rational economics. The other essential point is that all these theories, apart from sharing that bare proposition, have little else in common. To the extent that they give a different rational explanation to that basic proposition, the various theories are different from one another. Indeed, they are so different that one can easily fall under the impression that they are investigating completely different worlds, and not the same identical economic process.

If the reader objects that so far this work has provided not an analysis, but only a brief list of terribly shortened interpretations of the proposition that saving is equal to investment, the reader is absolutely correct. In Part II, we shall see why that proposition is not amenable to analysis. Lest we lose the overall importance of the point established here, let us now acquire a synoptic view of the total issue. Let us derive full value from the newly reached vantage point: the classification of mainstream economic analysis as rational economics.

An Overview: *Economics, still an Art—not a Science*

More than insisting upon any one of the crucial points that we have discussed so far, let us confine our attention to an overview of the issues. Ever since the publication of the *Wealth of Nations*, all leading economists have accepted, in one form or another, the validity of the proposition that saving is "equal" to investment.

The differences between each two such formulations are generally so significant as to give rise to completely different theories. And yet, if all these theories are seen as a group springing from a common root—and carrying with them at least some of the weaknesses implicit in that proposition—one must admit that those differences are marginal indeed. In any case, whatever the importance of such differences, since each one of these theories contains at least one strong element of truth, how can one rationally choose among them?

The only straightforward answer is that one cannot. There are no objective standards to help the professional economist—let alone any other reader—in choosing among all those different theories. The only means left are one's intuition and steadfastness. But intuition and steadfastness are more relevant to art than to science. One can thus see clearly displayed in front of one's eyes the wisdom contained in this passage by Professor Paul A. Samuelson, who in December 1973 could write: *"Events of the last half dozen years have shown us how much economics remains an art rather than a science."*[29]

That economics is indeed an art, rather than a science, is shown by a wealth of evidence—of which the unpredictability of the behavior of the economy and consequently the inaccuracy of forecasts are only symptoms. The long series of slightly divergent interpretations of basic economic phenomena is a much more important indication: it is from there that the long series of theories extant in economics branches out. And these are only the objective conditions of this field of study. Then there are the subjective conditions of its practitioners. These conditions are not less important to observe, if one wants to obtain a comprehensive view of our topic.

A Series of Super-Economists

The relatively long history of economic analysis is dotted with a series of super-economists—Superstars is the modern term. But who fills the spaces in between? There is a delightful analysis made by Professor Harry G. Johnson of the reasons why Keynes' thought was so quickly accepted by young economists. The passage that is relevant to this context reads: "It enabled the more enterprising middle- and lower-middle-aged like Alvin Hansen, Hicks and Joan Robinson to jump on and drive the bandwagon. And it permitted a whole generation of students (as Paul Samuelson has recorded) to escape from the slow and soul-destroying process of acquiring wisdom by osmosis from their elders and the literature into an intellectual realm in which youthful iconoclasm could quickly earn its just reward (in its own eyes at least) by the demolition of the intellectual pretensions of its academic seniors and predecessors."[30]

The central question is: would *this* "revolution" have occurred, had the history of economic analysis not been dotted with "Superstars"? As early as 1930, Keynes warned that economics "should be a matter for specialists—like dentistry. If economists could manage to get themselves thought of as humble, competent people, on a level with dentists, that would be splendid!"[31]

To become like dentistry, economic analysis has still to root its fundamental propositions into something more than purely rational explanations—i.e., mental constructions. Otherwise, more powerful minds or even bigger "Superstars" are bound to appear on the horizon and shall topple the previous construction. Like castles on the sand.

Provisional Conclusions

It would not only be premature, but impossible, and perhaps it will always remain impossible, to assess the damage done to the clarity—and the continuity—of the economic discourse by the presumed relation of equality between saving to investment. More than engaging in this impossible task, let us look at some of the fundamental reasons for the long existence of that incorrect proposition. Part II is devoted to this task, through which it begins the work of reconstruction.

PART II

Analysis of the Component Elements of Keynes' Model

THIS PART LITERALLY DISSECTS Keynes' model, and analyses each component element in an attempt to discover some of the reasons for the weaknesses observed above.

It is this analysis that dictates various solutions and ultimately the suggested revision of the model.

The focus is on the observation of the various categories of economic thought and economic wealth.

VII

The Dissection of Keynes' Model
and the Dissolution of the S-I Nexus

*I am more attached to the comparatively sim-
ple fundamental ideas which underlie my theory than to the particular forms in which I
have embodied them, and I have no desire
that the latter should be crystallized at the
present stage of the debate.*

JMK

EVER SINCE THE PUBLICATION OF THE *General Theory*, the analysis
of Keynes' model of the economic system has been conducted from
many different points of view, but the model itself—the overall
form of Keynes' thought—has never been literally dissected. There
is a good reason for this restraint. Not unlike a living organism,
that model, once dissected, cannot be put back together again. As
we shall see, through this operation one automatically steps out of
the internal logic of that model—and cannot logically re-enter it.

The analysis that has been conducted in the previous pages considerably eliminates this restraint. The model has so many deficiencies that its eventual loss will not be felt by economic theory.
We can proceed with our surgical operation, therefore, without
many mental reservations. We will separate each term from all others. There are overwhelming advantages in pursuing this course of
action. By separating the elements of Keynes' model from each
other, we will truly know, define, and understand them. Shocking
as it might sound to the uninitiated, we will learn that none of its
economic terms has been precisely defined yet.

The surgical operation we are about to perform is much simpler
than might be expected. There is only one important requirement.
Once the model is put on the operating table, one cannot let one's
vision be blurred by preconceived theories. He who dissects

Keynes' model is confronted, not with three, but with four entities: income, consumption, saving, and investment. These are the four explicit elements that will be separately analyzed in the following chapters. These are the subsidiary forms that, not unlike a Matreshka doll, contain the substance of Keynes' thought.

———•———

The requirement of proceeding without preconceived theories might appear obvious to the non-economist. The economist, however, is fully cognizant of the implicit relationships among all the terms of the model. The economist, therefore, will have difficulty in conceiving especially of saving as an entity separate from investment. This separation not only implies a dissolution of the internal logic of Keynes' model of the economic system; it even implies stepping out of the internal logic of the entire structure of mainstream economics. Hence the economist is left to wrestle with something that other readers might not see at first sight, namely, the relationship between saving and investment. The following pages are provided to alleviate these difficulties.

First, by isolating the nexus between saving and investment from the superstructure of economic theory, we will treat it as a system of thought of its own. Then, we will dissolve the nexus that exists at present between those two entities. Finally, we will gradually transform that relationship from one of equality to one of complementarity. Not all of this work can be finished in this chapter.

There are other implicit relationships in Keynes' model. They require no mention at this point. Otherwise they would be reduced to a sterile list, which becomes burdensome and worrisome. The challenge and intellectual enjoyment is in going through them slowly, one by one, at the appropriate time.

Stepping Outside the Logic of Keynes' Model

Let us quickly check the validity of the procedure for separating saving from investment. Taking Keynes' model at face value, and assuming that saving is indeed "equal" to investment, it is possible to substitute one term for the other in the first equation of that model—so as to read: income = consumption + saving. Leaving the second equation as is, otherwise one simply inverts the final result, the conclusion is reached that saving = saving. Through similar operations, namely, substituting investment for saving only in the second equation, one reaches the conclusion that investment = investment. The approach is legitimate. It is legitimate to separate saving from investment and to analyze them independently of each other. We then obtain the model of saving and the model of investment respectively, two models that have operational validity only at this juncture in the reasoning:

The Model of Saving

Income = Consumption + Saving
Income = Consumption + Investment
Saving = Income − Consumption

The Model of Investment

Investment = Income - Consumption
Saving = Saving
Investment = Investment.

It is doubtful whether the economist will be satisfied with this mechanical exercise. For the economist, much more is required because, even when separated from each other, the key question remains: what is the relationship between saving and investment?

Within the confines of mainstream economic theory, the relationship between saving and investment is and remains one of equality. It must be one of equality. Why have we done all this work, then, if we are still within the confines of that theory? The advantage of isolating the two terms from Keynes' model is that we are now free to observe the relationship by itself. We can ask whether saving is indeed equal to investment. In other words, we are no longer compelled to assume that saving is equal to investment. Rather, we are free to transform the nexus into a hypothesis and test its validity. The question indeed is: is saving equal to investment?

———•———

Before proceeding, we must realize the price we are paying for this freedom. It is worth asking whether we are still within the logic of Keynes' model. As pointed out above, once saving and investment are observed as two independent entities, Keynes' model cannot be put back together again. We have stepped out of its internal logic. Specifically, reflecting back, we realize that we have created two new models that, for identification purposes, we have called respectively the model of saving and the model of investment. To reconstruct Keynes' model from either one of these two models would involve us in a set of very arbitrary operations. We could never do it while respecting rules of logic. Since, as we have seen earlier, the terms are neither reflexive nor symmetric nor transitive, they cannot be logically linked to each other through either a relation of equality, a relation of equivalence, or a relation of identity. (Eventually we will discover they are linked by a relationship of complementarity.)

Working With the Hidden Complexities of "A Proposition"

We have stepped out of the logic of Keynes' model; saving and investment are now two independent entities. But we have not stepped out of the logic of mainstream economic theory. Until we find a new relationship between the two terms, we are faced with the theoretical compulsion that "saving is equal to investment." In a previous chapter we proved the negative; we proved that the relationship of equality between them is not formally valid. This discovery will forever remain an intellectual exercise unless we transform that relationship into a new and different nexus, without leaving the shadow of a doubt about the propriety of this procedure.

In Search of a New Relation Between Saving and Investment

Clearly, in our search we have to strictly adhere to the rules of formal logic. But this is not enough. At this juncture we are faced with the fundamental verity of epistemology: a proposition by itself has no meaning. How to proceed? How to proceed without being thrust back into the arms of mainstream economic theory? After many mental experiments, it became evident that the simplest solution to this conundrum was to transform the proposition itself into a "theory"—i.e., a mini system of its own. Thus a new a system of thought was born. This is a system that is composed of three elements: saving, investment, and the relationship between the two entities. We can legitimately call it the saving-investment system. We can now analyze that proposition on its own terms. We can look at it by itself and in its entirety. In this way we begin to bring forward some of the deeper reasons for the complexity and extraordinary resiliency of this apparently innocuous proposition. We will really know both saving and investment.

Three S-I Systems

In fact, once the proposition concerning the nexus between saving and investment is transformed into a system of thought of its own, we gradually discover that we are faced with, not one, but three systems: a *rational*, an *imaginary*, and a *real* saving-investment system. In the rational system, no matter its inner weaknesses, the relationship must be one of equality; in the imaginary system, we will ask whether the relationship is indeed one of equality; and in the real system we discover that the relationship is one of complementarity. We will study these three systems separately, the first two here and the third in a subsequent chapter.

The Rational Saving-Investment System

Neglecting the frequent resistance and the sporadic challenges, like that of Keynes himself in 1930, all prevailing economic thought ever since Adam Smith's analysis has been built on these shared beliefs: first, the belief in some commonly understood definition of saving; second, the belief in some commonly understood definition of investment ("capital" of old); and third, the belief that these two entities are linked by a relation of equality. In brief, all leading modern economists have consistently reached substantially similar conclusions concerning the structure of the saving-investment system. This structure, for reasons noted earlier, has to be classified as the rational saving-investment system.

We cannot right now be concerned with the tremendous difficulties that lie just underneath the appealing simplicity of these three basic beliefs. We can only ask whether a science can indeed be built on such vague beliefs as those listed above. The history of economic analysis, with its rapid succession of slightly different formulations of the same beliefs, has already given the answer.

Economic science cannot be built on those beliefs.

The root cause of this state of affairs can be found in one surprising factor. Rational explanations about the fundamental proposition of economic theory that "saving is equal to investment" have abounded. But there has been a dearth of analysis concerning its intrinsic nature. And no analysis could be made because, as we know, a proposition by itself has no meaning.

Thus all explanations, no matter how rational in themselves, were ultimately compelled to assume that the proposition was a valid one; and, consequently, it was assumed that it was only necessary to elaborate on the *modus operandi* of that proposition and on the effects it caused. It is here that art more than science became helpful. As far as the analysis of the nature of that proposition was concerned, one could take it either as a dogma: a proposition which must be accepted because it hides deep verities; or as a *pons asinorum:* a proposition which, leapt over, grants entrance into the magic kingdom of economic theory.

Either type of solution was manifestly unsatisfactory. Hence the rapid succession of slightly different formulations of those basic beliefs. Hence the different approach pursued here. Hence, the need to transform that proposition into a system of thought which can be analyzed in itself.

In the following chapters we shall be concerned with what is implied by the "commonly understood" definition of both saving and investment. Since we have already observed that the relation between the two entities cannot be one of "equality," we need go no further. We can abandon the Rational Saving-Investment System to its destiny; we can confine it to the history of economic analysis. But how to proceed from this point? Evidently, we must replace it with another system of thought. This is a system that, being truly free of any preconceived ideas, allows us to test the validity of any relationship we might want to assign as the nexus between saving and investment. This is a system that, for reasons to become evident in due course, is to be called the imaginary saving-investment system

The Imaginary Saving-Investment System

The logical derivation of the imaginary saving-investment system is also from Keynes' model. As in an ultra von Neumann's model, putting consumption at zero, it is possible to assume that all output is invested. In this fashion:

$$\text{Income} = 0 + \text{Investment}$$
$$\text{Saving } = \text{Income} - 0$$
$$\text{Saving } = \text{Investment}$$

or, in symbols:

$$Y = I$$
$$S = Y$$
$$S = I$$

where, as customary, Y stands for Income; I for Investment; and S for Saving.

From this system, respecting the rules of identity, we obtain:

$$Y = Y \text{ and } I = I$$
$$S = S \text{ and } Y = Y$$
$$S = I$$

(or, redundantly, S = S and I = I).

Discarding the identity of income, a concept that shall be dealt with later on, and inverting the position of the first two equations, we obtain:

$$S = S$$
$$I = I$$
$$S = I.$$

The last system of equations formally incorporates all three elements of the proposition that "saving is equal to investment." It takes mainstream economic theory at face value and, respecting such basic rules of logic as the requirements of the Principle of Identity and the Principle of Non-Contradiction, it assumes: (a) that saving is identical to saving; (b) that investment is identical to investment; and, (c) that saving is indeed "equal" to investment.

In an earlier chapter we have discovered that the *relation* between saving and investment is not an identity relation. At present, we will start the investigation as to whether—taken separately from each other—the content of saving and the content of investment remain true or identical to themselves throughout the discussion, namely, whether their definition does indeed respect the dictates of the principle of identity. This investigation will be continued throughout the next chapters.

Stepping Outside the Logic of Mainstream Economics

What is new in the imaginary saving-investment system? What is new is the freedom of its internal structure. The total independence of each proposition from each other allows us to transform the system into a set of hypotheses and thus test the validity of each proposition on its own terms. From "general beliefs" we transform the definitions of both saving and investment into propositions to be tested against the rules of the principle of identity and the principle of non-contradiction. From the compulsory proposition that "saving is equal to investment," we pass to the question: is saving equal to investment? By questioning it, we position ourselves—if it need be—

to step outside the logic of mainstream economics.

Thus we formulate the system in this fashion:

$$
\begin{aligned}
\text{Hypothesis \# 1:} \quad S &= S \\
\text{Hypothesis \# 2:} \quad I &= I \\
\text{Hypothesis \# 3:} \quad S &= I.
\end{aligned}
$$

We have already observed that the third hypothesis is not valid: in the reality of "simple" and "obvious" economics, saving is not "equal" to investment. We shall shortly observe that the first and the second hypotheses are not valid either. We will therefore be compelled to conclude that, except on paper, the system cannot logically exist. Consequently, its name is the *imaginary* saving-investment system. We must step out of the logic of mainstream economics. To do so, we have to acquire a deeper knowledge of the process in which we are involved.

The Function of the Imaginary Saving-Investment System

The function of the imaginary saving-investment system is to test the validity of some of the major strictures of mainstream economics. It allows us to make an independent analysis of both saving and investment by themselves and in relation to each other; and it helps us build yet another system of thought, a system which can logically exist. This is the *real* saving-investment system.

In brief, the imaginary saving-investment system functions as a space shuttle lifting us away from the realm of rational economics. From those heights (or depths), we shall examine the most recondite recesses of that system of thought. This is work that, as Heisenberg taught us, cannot be done while remaining within the realm of rational economics.

Once accomplished, that work will provide us with so much information that, upon reentry, we will have at our disposal all the material necessary to develop a new system of thought: the real saving-investment system; and upon it we shall build the outline of a new theory of economics, a theory that is here identified as dynamic and organic economics, a theory that in a forthcoming book will be more precisely specified as a *Theory of Economic Interdependence*.

Some Explanatory Notes

The operations discussed here can be deemed either very simple or very complex. Perhaps a comparison will clarify the issues. The function of the imaginary saving-investment system is identical to the function of the "blueprint" which might have been derived from a critical analysis of the horse and buggy. That blueprint would have made it possible to create an "ideal" or imaginary horse and buggy, an entity which, when actually built, showed us the transformation of the horse and buggy into the automobile. Similarly, the ultimate function of the imaginary saving-investment system is that of allowing the construction of the real saving-investment system.

The imagery of the horse and buggy is relied upon to make two points as clear as possible. First, the imaginary saving-investment system resembles a simplified Keynes' model or even an ultra von Neumann's model. And yet, except for an economic rationalization of its origin, it has nothing in common with either one of them. In Keynes' model, as in the rest of contemporary economic analysis, saving and investment cannot stand by themselves. They have no autonomous life of their own: they are relations, and not concepts. As such, they are not able to stand alone—not even to form an imaginary system. (In Keynes' model both saving and investment are supported by the structure of the model and by the entire theoretical structure of rational economics.)

In the imaginary saving-investment system, saving and investment are treated as if they could stand by themselves—at least formally or theoretically. And since they are found incapable of standing by themselves substantively as well, we shall have to build a new system: the real saving-investment system. This is a system in which both the content of the words "saving" and "investment" and their relationship to each other are fundamentally different from the ones to which we are accustomed. (The horse and buggy cannot travel at 55 mph without losing some of its own peculiar characteristics and thus being transformed into an automobile.)

The imagery of the horse and buggy is used to emphasize another important point. The internal conceptual coherence, functionality, and elegance of Keynes' model remain unaffected by the present analysis, just as the building of the automobile has not affected the conceptual coherence, functionality, and elegance of the horse and buggy. Stated differently, Keynes' model of the economic system is an independent world of its own: there is nothing that can either be added to or subtracted from it. (The impression to the contrary is due to a lack of appreciation of two factors: some additions and subtractions have actually built a different model; and others have simply made explicit what was implicit there.)

Looking at the same situation from still another point of view, it might be useful to restate what I have said in the introductory section. The present critical analysis of Keynes' model should not be confused with a lack of admiration on my part for Keynes' model and for most economic thought. Rather, the critical analysis conducted here ought to be viewed as a tribute to the laced intricacy of that thought. As implied in the preliminary material, the aim is to save, not to destroy, the Tower of Pisa.

But enough of these general considerations. The work that lies ahead consists of the following. We shall first observe saving and investment by themselves. We shall then discover the relationship that, in the economic reality, exists between them: thus we will construct the real saving-investment system. With that accomplished, we shall observe the concept of consumption and that of income. After applying a few refinishing touches to both concepts, we will have at our disposal all the ingredients necessary to construct the Flows model.

This model will grant us a clear and direct view of the economic process. To see the model exercise this function is work which lies too far ahead to be the subject of any discussion at this point. We have first to attend to the immediate task of analyzing saving and investment as independent entities.

VIII

The History of
the Word "Saving"

Everybody knows what is meant by saving.

Harlan M. Smith

———•———

WITH THE *IMAGINARY* SAVING-INVESTMENT SYSTEM as our theoretical support, we can proceed to make an independent analysis of each component element in Keynes' model. We shall start with "saving," and we shall start from a historical analysis of the development of this word. The purpose of the analysis is not only to discover some of the basic reasons for the weaknesses we have found in Keynes' model, but especially to forge the material out of which the Flows model can be built.

We shall soon see that the primary reason for the long, and troubled, existence of the proposition that "saving is equal to investment" resides in a surprising factor. Economic analysis has always proceeded without a precise definition of saving.

This statement, at first sight, appears so improbable that it deserves some careful examination. Let us review the evidence.

Synonyms Are Not Definitions

For all its acknowledged importance, saving has traditionally been given only scanty and indirect attention in economic analysis. All energies have traditionally been devoted to the examination of the functions which saving is supposed to perform in the economic system and the relationships it is supposed to have with other economic entities—let alone its relationships with such extraneous entities as sociology, ethics, and the law. This has been the tradition, starting with the early phase of monetary analysis (1600-1760) when saving—without ever being precisely defined—was immediately perceived, in the words of Professor Schumpeter, as an "obstruction to [the] flow of expenditure."[32] Adam Smith's *parsimony* was immediately perceived as the "cause of the accumulation of capital."[33] Senior's *abstinence* was immediately perceived as an essential component of the analysis of cost and the theory of capital,[34] and Marshall's[35] or Cassel's *waiting* [36] was perceived as the determinant of the rate of interest. As evidenced by this perusal, there is no definition of saving in the "early" economic literature. At best, there are many synonyms of the word saving; but synonyms are not definitions.

This fast-paced recitation of economic history brings us to the contemporary Monetarists, for whom saving—together with investment—directly and primarily determines (again) the rate of interest;[37] and the Keynesians, for whom those two entities directly and primarily determine the level of income.[38] Again, we find no definition of saving, but an examination of its functions.

If we explore less biased but authoritative literature, we find traces of the only conclusion which can be drawn from an examination of the word saving. For instance, in the *International Encyclopedia of the Social Sciences*, a work published in 1968, quite properly, there is no entry under the heading "Saving."

Faced with such consistent and convincing evidence that there is no acceptable definition of saving in the economic literature, we have only one alternative: we have to retrace our steps back to more solid ground.

In the *General Theory*, saving is one of the determinates and not a determinant of the economic system. In the *General Theory* there is also the conception that saving is "a mere residual"[39]—or, it could be said, a surplus from current income; a surplus worth saving presumably as a provision against lean years.

Thus we have come full circle. Stripped of all technicalities, Keynes' conception of saving seems to be akin to that which prevailed in Biblical times—and perhaps even earlier than that. This is a conception that was sharpened when men and women changed their status from nomads to farmers. In other words, this is a conception which, however expressed, seems to have remained amazingly constant since the dawn of history.

One general comment might perhaps be made at this juncture. Since words arise out of deeply felt needs, could the constancy of the conception of saving underlie a constancy of the economic problem experienced by men and women since the dawn of history? Let the historic case be as it may, what is the specific value to be derived from the history of the word "saving? This value, I would like to suggest, resides in the confirmation that there is still no precise definition for this conception, a conception which has been used so constantly in common parlance no less than in economic theory.

This lack of precise definition, in turn, explains why economic analysis could for so long hold such commonly shared beliefs concerning both saving and investment. This conception is so broad that it could embrace any shade of opinion. In order to reduce the danger of resting the case on a potentially biased and arbitrary conclusion, let us leave the stage to other discussants.

"Everybody Knows What Is Meant By Saving"

This, in brief, is the historical evidence. And it lends credence to a revealing statement by Professor Harlan M. Smith who, summarizing the results of an international symposium held at the University of Minnesota in 1952 on the topic of "Savings in the Modern Economy," did not find any better way of expressing the point made above than by stating—in quotes—"everybody knows what is meant by saving."[40] This is an indirect way of saying that nobody has really defined saving yet. Can, in fact, a science be based on such vague expressions as "obstruction to [the] flow of expenditure," or "parsimony," or "abstinence," or "waiting," or "a mere residual?" Clearly not.

As usual, this is not "simply" a theoretical issue. Professor Smith's full statement is as follows: "Although 'everybody knows what is meant by saving,' the measurement of it runs into definitional problems unsuspected by many."

This evaluation turned out to be an egregious understatement. Those "definitional problems" are conspicuous indeed. In a three-volume study of the topic Professor R. W. Goldsmith, examining the "specific (operational) definitions of saving," calculated that ". . . the number of theoretically possible variant definitions of saving as change in earned net worth is as high as $2^5\,5^5$ or 100,000."[41]

What is implicit in this last statement must be made explicit. All those possible one hundred thousand definitions of saving are all logically tenable. How can one scientifically choose among them? The answer is that no one can—except through an arbitrary decision. They who take this road have only their luck to trust; they have to trust that a large number of people will accept their arbitrary selection. But all theoreticians of the laws of probability make a point of telling us what is constant in luck: it soon runs out. One has only to wait for the next expert to try his or her luck. This much is clearly proved by the history of the word saving.

It seems evident: there is still a problem of the definition of saving. The sooner it is solved, the better it is. The proviso is that it must be solved, not in accordance with whim, but in accordance with standards created by centuries of thought—namely, by taking into full account, not only the standards of economics, but also those of logic and philosophy. This is the only route through which one can eventually obtain a precise definition of saving and on it build a science of economics.

IX

Beyond Adam Smith's
Conception of Saving

There can be no doubt as to the existence of ambivalence in the prevailing conception of saving.

———•———

GUSTAV CASSEL IN 1903 IMPARTED SUCH a crucial lesson to all aspiring critics that it must be recalled here: "Criticism cannot be very fruitful unless the critic really tries to come to a deeper understanding of the views of those whom he means to criticise, and unless he starts from the assumption that they have had *some* reason for their opinions."[42]

In order to obtain a precise definition of the word saving, then, we had better make an effort to understand (without even thinking of criticizing) what economists really have meant by that word. The key to the solution of the many problems presented by the persisting lack of definition of saving is that we stop considering the word as a simple entity whose meaning "everybody knows." The key to the solution of this problem lies in recognizing that we are faced with a complex conception.

To favor its immediate apperception, the full conception has been displayed in the attached graph entitled "The Spectrum of Opinion on Saving." With the help of this graph, and knowing the dates at which each opinion tended to prevail, it can be seen at a glance that the form or the "undecorated" shell of the word saving—not unlike a Fabergé egg—has remained the same over a long period of time; but its content and consequently its meaning have changed over the centuries. And the latest meaning quite often has simply been added to the previous ones. Individual economists might have picked and chosen one or more preferred meanings to which to cling; but the economic discipline as a whole has always been broad enough to accept all those meanings *at once*.

The Spectrum of Opinion
on
Saving

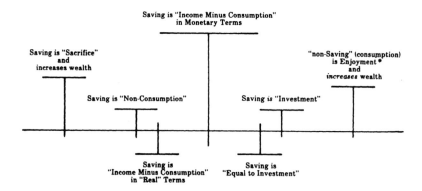

*Apart from other delicate issues of timing, every economist agrees that Saving serves purposes of *future* consumption and hence *is* "Future Enjoyment."

Notes:

— The spectrum seen dynamically is more like a pendulum.

— The polarization and splinterization of opinion on saving is just as likely to be found among different economists as within the soul of each economist.

— This spectrum has been drawn to reflect the corresponding spectrum of political opinion. Yet, there are such intricacies in the economic discourse and practice that they do not allow any preordained conclusion as to the effects which those views, if implemented as part of a coherent economic policy, are likely to cause.

A Complex Conception

Let us read the graph from left to right. The ever persisting but oldest meaning of saving is that of "sacrifice"—sacrifice, it is said, of present consumption needs in order to increase future income or future consumption.

(Clearly, we cannot analyze these "opinions." We shall simply confine ourselves to listing them.)

Very few technical economists would ever like to be caught, in a formal setting, saying that saving is "sacrifice." They prefer to convey the same idea by expressing it as "not-consumption." Thus saving, especially since the sixteenth and seventeenth centuries, becomes not-consumption. Both expressions, "sacrifice" and "not-consumption," convey the original meaning of saving—a meaning, to repeat, held from time immemorial and still widely persistent today. Suffice it to say that it was included in Keynes' model of the economic system. There one reads: saving = income - consumption; i.e., saving is "not-consumption" or, even better, saving is "income minus consumption." The latter is not only a monetary, but also a "real" expression of the definition of saving as not-consumption. In other words, one can see saving either as a sum of money or as a sum of goods.

The above set of expressions is singularly responsive to the exigencies of an agrarian society, a society in which they were developed—even though some of these expressions have only in recent years been formalized. Whatever foodstuff is not consumed, needs to be "saved," not only as seed for next year's production but especially as insurance against lean years. By extension, all other items of wealth—including money—that do not serve purposes of immediate consumption are also deemed to be saved.

Enter the Industrial Revolution, and the economic functions performed by agricultural products are largely replaced by new forms of wealth. Needless to say, the Industrial Revolution flourished in the eighteenth century; but it took, literally, millennia to develop. Hence the emphasis in economic theory changes. While the practical functions of saving remain identical, the content represented by that word becomes different. The content to which the word saving refers is no longer primarily agricultural foodstuff—but machinery, equipment, and supplies. With apparent justification, then, saving gradually comes to be defined either as "equal" to investment or even directly as investment. With investment obviously called "capital," this second major set of definitions of saving has been prevalent from the time of the industrial revolution to the present. It is at the foundation of contemporary monetary theory. It was also incorporated into Keynes' model. There one reads: saving = investment. Incidentally, since Keynes defined saving in monetary terms, he could alternatively use a large number of the above "definitions." But whatever he gained in flexibility, he lost in clarity. The *General Theory* has often been described as an "obscure" book.

These are the most common "definitions" of saving. And yet, were one to leave the issue at that, one would lose the thrust of that entire conception. One would not understand why the definition of saving remains the most complex and controversial issue in economic theory. What makes this definition such a peculiar item is an invisible element that nonetheless is included there. The clincher is the opposite of saving. It is an element that technically ought to be called "not-saving."

Let us pause and ask the crucial question: what is not-saving? It is evident that, in economics, not-saving means consumption. With this last invisible element that does exist in the conception of saving, we have come full circle. We started with the definition of saving as sacrifice and we have ended with the opposite of that definition—i.e., not-saving, consumption or "enjoyment."

Since this last component in the conception of saving is invisible to the naked eye, one can easily shut one's mind to its existence. But it remains there. And the resultant ambivalence in the conception of saving remains there with it.

Three Sets of Evidence

Is there any doubt as to the existence of ambivalence in the current conception of saving? We have observed that conception from many different points of view, and we have always reached the same conclusion. Crudely and directly, that conclusion has been reached with the analysis carried from within Keynes' model of the economic system, in which saving is defined as income minus consumption—namely, saving is a relation, and as such it must share characteristics with the entities to which it is related: income and consumption.

The construction of the imaginary saving-investment system has (formally) allowed us to separate saving from investment; and when the content of saving has at least briefly been analyzed by itself, it has become immediately apparent that it includes items which clearly are consumer items: a house inhabited by the owner, for instance.

Presently, we have observed the spectrum of opinion on saving; and, unless one wants to leave it as an unbalanced and incomplete set of opinions, one must include in it not-saving—i.e., consumption—as an integral part of it.

To repeat, one is entitled to shut one's mind to it; but there can be no doubt as to the existence of ambivalence in the prevailing conception of saving.

Some Effects of this Ambivalence

Shutting one's mind to the ambivalence residing at the core of economic theory is not without consequences. One misses the possibility of ever understanding the root cause of the dilemma in which all economic policies are enveloped today.

Since the present work is devoted to economic theory and not to economic policy, this issue cannot be adequately discussed here. But is it not true that there are two schools of thought dominating economic policy today: one which wants an increase in public and private saving and one which wants an increase in public and private consumption? The two views are irreconcilable. And they will remain irreconcilable as long as economic theory remains locked into the terms—the model, the paradigm, the understanding—which it uses today.

We have already seen that the cornerstone of this paradigm is the proposition that saving is "equal" to investment; and that its major weakness is the substantive asymmetry between the two terms. We have just seen how that "small" fissure, feeding on—and being fed by—the ambivalence inherent in the conception of saving, grows into an irreconcilable dichotomy. Let us follow that lead to observe how the scope of this dichotomy grows wider and wider.

The Scope of the Split in Economic Policy

The implications of the irreconcilable dichotomy at the core of economic theory are fully known to the experts in economic policy. They know full well how their field is split exactly down the middle—with the many advocating policies of higher consumption completely checked by the power of the few advocating policies of higher saving. Experts know how this split is carried over into every corner of the realm of economic policy: larger supply of money vs. smaller supply of money; lower interest rates vs. higher interest rates; lower taxes vs. higher taxes; higher wages vs. lower wages; larger public expenditure vs. smaller public expenditure. And on and on. Irreconcilably. The wisdom of Professor Galbraith's advocacy of "fine tuning" or the wisdom of Professor Friedman's advocacy of a "steady course" is lost—crushed as they are by the pressures of the two opposing points of view.

The concerned citizen can get a better glimpse of the implications of this dichotomy in economic theory by blowing up the picture and observing the relation between economic policy and political ideology. Thus one can best observe the twists and turns between intentions and effects that are caused by that dichotomy. *Pace* Fukuyama, on the university campus if not in international relations, the world ideology, however subdued, remains split between Communism and capitalism—with Communists in general pursuing a policy of higher saving and capitalists, as a whole when considered in relation to their ideological opponents, pursuing a policy of higher consumption. Who, in the end, has best served the interests of the "common" people? Who has best served the interests of the "privileged few"? Recall the ideology. It says that the Communists have the best interests of the common people at heart; and the capitalists have those of the privileged few at heart. Perhaps the treachery of these issues can be best recognized in its ultimate paradox: both "ultraconservative" capitalists and the majority of Communists apparently share the same preference—a preference for economic policies that foster high accumulation, high saving.

Not until we recognize the existence of this paradox of intentions, and we fully explore its myriad ramifications, shall we be able to clear the poisoned atmosphere of many national as well as international relations. The poison is not ideology. Human beings cannot live without some form of ideology: this is a mirror in which we look at ourselves—and discover that we are not alone, that there are many other people surrounding us. Ideology is a mirror that allows us to discover society. The bigger the ideology-mirror, the broader is man's conception of society. No. The poison is not ideology. The poison is a new/ancient one. The poison is self-adulation. It is self-idolatry. We are unsophisticated and direct these days. We do not need any Golden Calf; we put the image we have of ourselves on the pedestal.

And what is the image that ultraconservative capitalists have of themselves? The self-image is that of benefactors: whatever they advocate in the field of economic policy is for "the good of the people." Indeed, if one asks the same question of a Communist, one obtains exactly the same answer.

We must stop questioning intentions; we must stop attributing certain undesirable effects to "bad" intentions. This is too simplistic, unrealistic, and counterproductive an approach. If, instead, we start looking for the objective reasons of unwanted effects, we shall take the first decisive steps toward the solution of many international—no less than many national—problems that afflict our age.

The issues are that important. To insist on the point, only if we resolve the ambivalence in the conception of saving, the resolution of these issues can go beyond pure talk. With that ambivalence, there is much obfuscation in the discussion of these public matters.

Two Deeper Implications

Evidently, we cannot adequately explore every issue. We can only emphasize two key points. The entire conception of saving as it exists in contemporary economic theory—when all its component parts are not kept separate—fosters doublespeak. Indeed it fosters triplespeak: saving incorporates not only the meaning of saving, but also that of consumption and that of investment.

From Confucius to Orwell, let alone St. John the Apostle or St. Thomas Aquinas, all wise men have always guarded against the misuse of words. In fact, that conception fosters something worse than the use of poor language. It prevents the pinning down of responsibilities (that is always the ultimate intent of doublespeak). If the intentions are "good" and the effects are "bad"; or, vice versa, if the effects are good and the intentions are bad, how can we ever apportion responsibility for the specific economic condition in which we find ourselves?

One More Effect

At least another effect must be considered. The ambivalence in the conception of saving is insidiously but explicitly carried into Keynes' model of the economic system, and through this model into the body of economic theory. The second equation of that model, namely, saving = income - consumption, states that an increase in saving (which may be translated into an increase in investment, which in turn may be translated into an increase in output) within any given level of income necessarily has to take place at the expense of consumption. Or, alternatively, it states that the less saved the less available for investment.

This reading is not only clear and mathematically correct. It is also traditional. And yet, if this were the central message of the

General Theory, that work would have hardly elicited such strong criticism from so many economists. It would have hardly supported the claim advanced by many sources, including Keynes himself, that the *General Theory* is a "revolutionary" book.

The central message of that book is, instead, proclaimed in the first equation of the model. This equation, namely, income = consumption + investment, states that an increase in income can derive either from an increase in consumption or an increase in investment. A close analysis of the *General Theory* reveals that this was indeed Keynes' position. In fact, this position is explicitly stated: "Theoretically . . . there are *two* ways to expand output."[43] And Keynes immediately made it clear that the alternative is to "promote investment and, at the same time, to promote consumption." This is the logic of the *General Theory.* This is the justification for the claim, supported indeed by a long and tortuous line of reasoning, that the book is revolutionary.

In the end, such claims and counterclaims are not important. The central point is that, mathematically, both interpretations of the model are correct. It is only logically and dynamically that they exclude each other: the logic of the model—in part—is in contradiction with the logic of the *General Theory.* And no amount of practical compromise as to quantities and timing can ever fill the gap. Until we eliminate the ambivalence from the concept of saving, the gap is going to be filled with words.

A related consequence must also be mentioned. From this evident contradiction stemmed the basic need felt by the Keynesians to adopt the model—and discard the *General Theory.* Thus we come full circle back to the starting point of our discussion.

Whence Does That Complex Conception Come?

We must leave these overall economic, political, and moral implications aside. We cannot deal adequately with them. We must confine our observation to one final point. In order to get the full impact of the entire conception of saving, we must realize that it was all enclosed in Adam Smith's thought. And we must also recognize that economic theory has remained its prisoner ever since. Here are the relevant paragraphs from Adam Smith's *Wealth of Nations.* First: "Whatever a person saves from his revenue he adds to his capital . . ."

• What is saving here, if not "sacrifice"— or "not-consumption"?

- What is saving here, if not "income minus consumption"—both in "real" and in monetary terms?
- What is saving here, if not "equal" to investment— or, indeed, "investment" itself?

And the opposite of the notion of saving—or consumption—is also included in Adam Smith's thought, even though it is separated from the first notion by a few hundred pages. The other paragraph reads: "Consumption is the sole end and purpose of all production . . ."[44]

Readers who have not mentally joined these two paragraphs together have created all sorts of misinterpretations of Adam Smith's thought. Indeed, they have downgraded the stature of that thought. Adam Smith, although he placed great emphasis on the conception of saving as sacrifice, kept constantly in mind that such a conception is understood only if it is seen as a whole: only if it is seen as including not-saving or consumption as an integral part.

———

One more observation.

Such a complex conception as that of saving could be handled only by a mind as subtle and as comprehensive, and unhurried, as that of Adam Smith— and a few other economists who, for this reason alone, would deserve to be called classical economists. In the intervening years, however, the opposite mental qualities have tended to prevail: thus we have gradually eliminated, first, the two extreme notions of that conception; then we have played down the importance of the intermediate notions; finally, we have illegitimately reduced the entire conception to *one* number. It is this final outcome that makes that conception no longer tenable. The only alternative left to us is to transform that complex conception into an entity that can in fact be quantified.

To clarify these issues fully would take a great deal more than one brief chapter. It would take a critical review of the entire train of thought of mainstream economics. Let us simply conclude by saying, first, that the economic thought over a very long period of time has remained prisoner of Adam Smith's conception of saving: Keynes' *General Theory* no less than other systems of thought; and, second, that it is perhaps high time for us to go beyond that conception.

A Look Backward: an Unrecognized Schism

Before trying to go beyond Adam Smith's conception of saving, let us recognize one of the deeper consequences of that conception. The two statements quoted above foreshadowed the existence of a schism so deep in economic theory that it is rarely, if ever, openly mentioned: a schism that pits "orthodox" against "heterodox" economists. With no exaggeration, it can be said that mainstream economic thought has unfolded from, and alternatively placed greater emphasis on, each one of the implications inherent in the first statement by Adam Smith; and, similarly, unorthodox economic thought has wholly developed from the second statement.

Certainly this issue deserves much more careful attention than it can possibly receive in this work. Even though we shall fitfully return to it, we must recognize that if we do not acknowledge the existence of this schism, we certainly cannot heal it. Lack of official recognition is not the solution. The schism persists. In fact, it has always found a way to touch the major economic thinkers of every generation.

Nor does recognition of the schism cause automatic healing. There is much work to be done. The first step is to go beyond Adam Smith's conception of saving. And yet, the issues are so intertwined that we must immediately attend to a parallel task. We must recognize that there is a similar set of issues concerning the definition of investment.

X

Beyond Keynes'
"Definition" of Investment

Synonyms are not definitions

———•———

SINCE IT IS SO SURPRISING, let us start this chapter from its conclusion. As the reader might expect, there are basically the same
difficulties inherent in the definition of investment as in the definition of saving. Granted these conditions, the conclusion is
inescapable: there is yet no acceptable definition of investment in
economic theory. And since this result seems to be so improbable,
let us immediately call upon the assistance of authoritative literature. The second edition of *The McGraw-Hill Dictionary of
Modern Economics*, a work published in 1973, does not even
carry the entry "Investment."

———•———

Ours is not an age of definitions. In economics, we live on what we
have inherited from work done during the nineteenth and early
twentieth century. To speak of issues of definition is considered a
somewhat unscientific use of time. And yet, definitions perform a
crucial role. They either help or hinder communication. Today's
economic definitions leave so much latitude to the interlocutors
that they hinder communication.

Take the following passage from the *General Theory*. In it
Keynes speaks of a "radical cure" for contemporary economic ills.
Does this not sound like a warning bell to pay extra attention to
an important message? To be premised is that Keynes and his clos-
est collaborators in the 1920's and 1930's, leaving aside their
degree of success, are the last economists who, after Malthus, gave
serious attention to matters of definition. (Malthus wrote a
delightful, crystal-clear essay on these matters; but unfortunately

the work is unavoidably out of date.)

Keynes paid so much attention to definitions that, in substance, he went beyond Adam Smith's conception of saving. Yet he did not go so far as to establish either his own definition of saving or his own definition of investment. Indeed, if Keynes was a superb economist it is because he looked at the economic reality as it is. More often than not, he was unencumbered by his own or other people's definitions, theories, or models—or lack of definition, for that matter. This was his strength and, of course, his weakness.

One should not like to leave a wrong impression. Of course, let alone economists of the present, many economists of the past—even Keynes' own father, John Neville Keynes, who by all accounts is not considered a great economist—paid some attention to matters of definition. But, in general, they either belittled or rehashed them and, ultimately giving up in desperation, frustration, or compromise, they muddled the issues even further. And just because issues have been left so muddled, today most economists have come to shy away from matters of definition. They simply accept them as tradition has bequeathed them to us.

Specifically, Keynes alone—in substance—went beyond Adam Smith's conception of saving. But in what form did he leave these matters? The reader is invited to pass an independent judgment without undue influence from this writer. Here is the important passage mentioned earlier; there are many others: "The only radical cure for the crises of confidence which afflict the economic life of the modern world would be to allow the individual no choice between consuming his income and ordering the production of the specific capital-asset which, even though it be on precarious evidence, impresses him as the most promising investment available to him."[45]

Clearly, this is a case in which Keynes is addressing the fundamental issue of saving and investment; clearly the passage demonstrates that he had in mind something completely different from Adam Smith's conception of saving. But what was he actually saying? One interpretation of this passage might suggest that Keynes was the advocate of "consuming" all yearly income. First of all, this suggestion would be a practical impossibility: some machinery and equipment which is definitely part of the yearly production cannot be consumed or physically destroyed in one year, even if one wanted to. Second, this suggestion would represent a practical disaster: the level of income the following years would be severely reduced. Keynes was looking for "radical cures," not for disastrous cures. This is not what Keynes had in mind; he was not advocating consuming all yearly income.

A sub-distinction of this extreme interpretation might consider income only in monetary terms, and assume that the passage contains the recommendation to spend all yearly income on consumer items. This is an economic impossibility. The production process does not produce consumer goods in quantity and value equivalent to the total yearly income. The effect of this suggestion would simply be to drive the price of consumer goods up, and the sky would be the limit. Besides destroying the market for capital goods, this suggestion could not possibly be implemented on a national scale. Not all consumers are that foolish. They would resist implementing that recommendation. This is not what Keynes had in mind.

Another interpretation might reduce the entire statement either to a platitude or to a different impossibility: if investment is considered saving, one cannot see how "ordering the production of [a] specific capital-asset" would represent anything different from traditional economic suggestions about saving which clearly do not solve contemporary problems. The platitude assumes a magical transformation of saving into investment, an assumption that swallows up the entire theory of economic growth. And the impossibility concerns the insistence that an investment, namely, the production of a specific capital-asset, is indeed a saving: a specific capital-asset can be "saved" only as a metaphor or a theoretical abstraction; in the reality of the economic life, such an asset is in time physically destroyed—it is not saved. A platitude or an impossibility cannot produce a "radical cure" for the economic ills of the modern world. Clearly, this is not what Keynes had in mind either.

Why the Lack of Clarity?

Why is there such a lack of clarity on so important an issue as Keynes' recommendation of a "radical cure" for the ills of the modern economy? Reasons are always infinite. Let us remain on two of them. Clearly, one source of the difficulty must be related to the issue treated in the previous chapter: to reach an understanding of the above passage we need a clear definition of saving. Here let us add that we also need—and we still lack—a clear definition of investment.

The Issue of Legitimacy

Before taking the decisive steps to go beyond Adam Smith's definition of saving, it is necessary to ask important questions of legitimacy. What right do we have to take these steps? Is this an arbitrary and capricious activity? If we do take these steps, what right do we have to claim that we are "revising" Keynes' thought? Are we not going so far away from it that we sever all connections with it and, consequently, all connections with the history of economic analysis?

To cast away all these intellectual scruples, it is sufficient to recall the warning that Keynes issued only a few months after the publication of the *General Theory:* "I am more attached to the comparatively simple fundamental ideas which underlie my theory than to the particular forms in which I have embodied them, and I have no desire that the latter should be crystallized at the present stage of the debate."[47] This warning cannot be taken in isolation either. Were this book a reconstruction of Keynes' thought, one would need to develop the issue quite thoroughly. For our purposes, it is sufficient to highlight the crucial steps in that development. The most evident starting point is the intense discussion that occurred between 1926 and 1933 among Ramsey, Sraffa, Hawtrey, Robertson, and Keynes on the definition of saving. Included here must be Keynes' foray of 1930 attempting to build a definition of income whereby saving is not equal to investment. Only thereafter did Keynes return to the fold of rational economics—but with which frame of mind? All the reservations, which he had gradually accumulated and refined, expressed themselves in the careful qualifications of the *General Theory* over all definitional issues treated there. Yet, Keynes was still dissatisfied. And he insisted on this dissatisfaction not only privately to Hawtrey and Robinson, as pointed out at the beginning of our discussion; but also publicly as in the widely read article of February 1937 from which the above quotation is taken. There can be no doubt. Keynes was extremely serious about the warning that he was not "attached" to the particular forms in which he had embodied his ideas.

One more point. Against this background, it can be seen that Keynesian interpretations have not heeded that warning; on the contrary, they have heeded it in reverse. In the attempt to transform the model from static to a dynamic entity, those interpretations were compelled to add another rational explanation of the issues. They succeeded where Robertson, and the Swedish School of Economics, had failed. They succeeded in having the distinction between measured and scheduled saving and investment widely accepted. The form of Keynes' ideas remained intact; and, as far as the substance is concerned, there was a full—but unheralded— swing back to the substance of Say's Law. Saving and investment were again assumed to determine all other quantities in the economic system.

Keynes' "Definition" of Investment

Perhaps now is an appropriate time to heed Keynes' warning mentioned above. Anticipating the result of our findings, in the Flows model the "form" of the concept of investment is refurbished. It is presented as a clear-cut definition: investment is all productive wealth. What else did all economists ever intend whenever they spoke of either capital or investment? Indeed, what else did Keynes mean when he said: "Investment, thus defined [sic], includes, therefore, the increment of capital equipment, whether it consists of fixed capital, working capital or liquid capital."[48]

Actually, these are the breakdowns of the concept of capital—a concept that was never precisely defined, as is especially evident from the "exchange" between Marshall and Bohm-Bawerk. In fact, to fill this lacuna, Keynes adopted the word "investment." And he was convinced he had defined this term.

Actually, Keynes never defined investment. He expressed the idea through a variety of synonyms: "the purchase of an asset"; "the net addition to all kinds of capital equipment"; "the increment of capital equipment"; "the marginal efficiency [old 'productivity'] of capital"; or, more often, "net investment." These are all giveaways. But they are synonyms; they are not definitions of investment. Actually, some of these synonyms are so vague as to be confusing. But this is implicit in the point. Synonyms are not definitions. In any case, one cannot be misled. Keeping in mind what Keynes said in relation to the "equality" of saving to investment— namely, that this is an "old-fashioned" and only "formally sounder" view—one will not be misled. Whenever he spoke of investment from a substantive point of view, he always related it to such unmistakable entities as the entrepreneur, capital equipment, capital-assets, employment, marginal efficiency of capital, and the like. It is clear that for Keynes investment represents all wealth that, in act, is part of the productive process—all the wealth that in act produces other wealth.

To the Bottom of the Case

Once again, why so much lack of clarity about the definition of both saving and investment? Now perhaps is the time to go to the bottom of the case. We need to join the issues. We need to go beyond Adam Smith's conception of saving and beyond Keynes' "definition" of investment.

This feat can be achieved only if we neglect all prevailing definitions of saving and all prevailing synonyms for investment—and observe directly the economic reality that those definitions try to cover. All current definitions are based on shifting ground. Since they are generally used in rapid succession, each definition justifies the other. Together, they form an impenetrable entity.

In fact, it is only by pinning down all current economic "definitions" of saving and investment by inquiring about their specific content that one begins to break through the veil of words. Through this exercise, it becomes evident that all prevailing schools of thought agree that the content of the definition of saving is as follows: money, machinery, supplies, equipment, land, and all wealth in general that is not a consumer item. This, to be stressed, is also the content of the word investment. By looking at the economic functions performed by those items, first exclusively as saving and then exclusively as investment, we shall reach the root cause of all present difficulties.

The non-economist should be advised that contemporary economic theory does not take the value of past wealth into account, but only the value of the net addition to (or subtraction from) that wealth. The prevailing definition of saving and investment, it is recalled, is income minus consumption—namely, all wealth that remains from current or yearly production after immediate needs for consumer goods are satisfied. Indeed, one of the advantages of the Flows model in its static formulation, namely, through the Stocks model, is that it represents the value of all existing stocks. It freezes all flows at one instant in time, and allows us to observe not only the origin of the flows of goods and services, but especially the specific functions performed by those stocks.

We can now observe money, recently cleared land, machines, etc. from the point of view of saving. In subsequent paragraphs we will analyze those same items from the point of view of investment. Let us recall that, in accordance with mainstream economic theory, those items constitute the content of both saving and investment.

An Analysis of the Content of Saving

Money. It is evident. Some money in the form of currency can be "saved"—or preserved more or less forever—by hiding it in a safe deposit box or under the mattress. Indeed, only the money thus used can be properly considered as saving. Money used in any other way cannot be considered as economic (as distinguished from financial) saving: money which is kept on hand as "petty cash" performs the same function as a consumer item; and money which is either used—directly or indirectly, i.e., buying stocks and bonds—in the productive process or is deposited in a bank in any form of account is just like any other investment.

Money in a savings account (i.e., financial savings) clearly produces interest for the depositor; and money in a checking account clearly produces income for the financial institution in which it is deposited. To define the functions performed by these uses of money as saving is a contradiction in terms: such moneys are not saved. They are put to risk. The risk is evident if the money is used in the productive process; but it is equally evident when the funds are held by a bank. Banks suffer bankruptcies. The existence of the Federal Deposit Insurance Corporation (FDIC) and similar institutions reduces the risk, by spreading and/or shifting it on to other shoulders. The risk remains there, however. Funds thus used cannot be considered as economic saving. Risk is diametrically opposed to what is implied by the word "saving."

This argument relies on the assumption that one's powers of reasoning have not been unduly affected by such statements, of Vietnamese war vintage, as: "We had to destroy the town, in order to save it." In fact, were one to maintain that it is necessary to risk, to transform, and even to destroy wealth in order to "save" it, one would confuse increasing (or decreasing) wealth with saving or preserving it as it is.

Of course, if the money deposited in a bank—or somehow acquired by a corporation—is not lent out or otherwise used but is kept there for any extraordinary length of time, that money must be considered saving: saving by the institution. In other words, we must fix our eyes on the specific item of wealth and not on any of the economic operators—and then assume that they are engaged in an act of investment (or saving) simply because of the name or the label we affix onto those operators. (Needless to say, apart from considerations of current economic policy, a reading of the numbers in accordance with this definition is likely to shed some new light on the causes of the Great Depression. Much currency was kept idle in bank vaults.)

Conversely, if currency is used to purchase a stock certificate, this certificate can be "saved" forever—but the specific capital-asset it represents cannot be saved forever.

Machinery, supplies, and equipment. Unless they are kept idle for an extended period of time, machinery, supplies, and equipment cannot be considered as saving either. They are physically exhausted in the process of production. To consider them as saving is to do utmost violence to language. *Pace* Carroll, the fabric of the language, namely, the relationship of one word to the next, is torn to pieces when one makes each word assume any meaning desired.

Land. Not unlike money, land presents a complex case. Land that is put to use—any use, even public recreation—cannot be considered to perform the function of economic saving without doing violence to the language. But land that is kept unused can be properly considered as saving. (Use in this work is given the broadest possible interpretation: land which is kept open to be "used" by the eye for esthetic and recreational purposes cannot be considered "saving"; it is a "consumer good.")

In brief, no matter which specific item is examined, we find a series of major contradictions between the official definition of saving (and/or investment) and the content of those umbrella-like definitions. Not only do we find covered there items which cannot possibly be "saved," we even find clear-cut cases of consumer items: money in the hand of consumers, a home inhabited by the owner, land which is kept open to be enjoyed from an esthetic point of view. Are these not consumer items? And yet in contemporary economic analysis they are, and indeed they must be included in the definitions of both saving and investment.

The issues appear complex. They are not. How can one succinctly express the argument? The evidence gathered from this brief analysis of the content of the word saving, an analysis that will shortly be repeated in relation to investment, is very clear. The difficulty presented by that list of concrete items—a list that can be much extended—is that it includes too much. Put in the language of formal logic, the problem with the current definition is that saving is not identical to saving. The list of items included under that umbrella contains some elements that are clearly consumer items and others that are clearly investment items.

Conclusively, the current definition of saving contravenes the dictates of both epistemology and logic. As stated in an earlier chapter, saving in contemporary economic theory is not "reflexive." It is not identical to itself. Saving is not an entity that consistently refers to the same objective reality, a reality that performs the same economic function, throughout the discourse. Saving is not saving throughout. In symbols, in mainstream economics S S.

The first hypothesis of the imaginary saving-investment system is not verified. The "belief in some commonly understood definition of saving," which is such an integral part of the rational saving-investment system, does not have any foundation in logic. The language of mainstream economics is very imprecise. Indeed, we have here a further proof that saving in contemporary economic theory is not a concept. It is not an independent entity that can stand by itself. Rather, saving is a relation. And as such it must necessarily share characteristics or cover items that are proper to the elements to which it is related: consumption and investment.

An Analysis of the Content of Investment

These conclusions can be even more clearly seen by observing the same list of items examined above as representing investment now. Provided one does not confuse financial investment with economic investment, it takes too long a stretch of the imagination to consider money under the mattress, stockpiles of machinery and supplies held idle for any purpose, or unused land as an economic investment.

Economic investment must not be confused with financial investment. The world of economics and the world of finance ought to respect the same rules. But they do not. And here we are concerned only with the world of economics, not that of finance. The meaning of words pertaining to the two worlds ought not to be confused with each other.

That list of items, then, observed from the point of view of investment also includes too much. Indeed, it is no coincidence that the extraneous elements correspond in a complementary fashion. Quite apart from consumer items, *active* supplies, machinery, equipment, and money are extraneous to the concept of saving; just as money under the mattress or unused land are extraneous to the concept of investment. These are conclusions to be reached not only on the basis of "simple" and "obvious" economics, i.e., common logic, but also on the basis of formal logic. In contemporary economic theory the definition of investment does not yield an entity that is reflexive, an entity that is identical to itself. It does not refer to an entity that consistently points to the same objective reality, a reality that performs the same economic function throughout the discourse. Investment, in mainstream economics, is not identical to investment: it shares items with saving and even consumption. In symbols, in mainstream economics I I.

The second hypothesis of the imaginary saving-investment system is not verified. The "belief in some commonly understood definition of investment," which is such an integral part of the rational saving-investment system, does not have any foundation in logic. The language of mainstream economics is very imprecise.

The Issue of Reference

We have thus reached two important conclusions: in mainstream economics saving is not identical to saving (S S) and investment is not identical to investment (I I). The issue now is: to which field do these conclusions apply? Evidently, they directly apply to the imaginary saving-investment system, that system of thought which has formally allowed us to make an independent analysis of the component elements of the proposition that "saving is equal to investment." And since the imaginary saving-investment system logically derives from Keynes' model, one could abruptly say that our findings indirectly affect that model as well. This conclusion, however, would be unfair and ultimately untenable. In Keynes' model, saving and investment are defined as relations and therefore they must be equal to each other. Besides, that model is an entity that has nothing to do with the imaginary saving-investment system. Our conclusions are sufficient reason to revise Keynes' model; but they leave that model completely unaffected. One can only entrust that model to the history of economic analysis, to be appreciated for its boldness and elegance and especially as a steppingstone to further analysis. But one cannot in any way affect that model.

The Root of the Difficulties: Two Separate Concepts

The root of the difficulties presented by the prevailing definitions of saving and investment lies not in their "complexity." It lies not in the confusing reality that some items covered by those umbrella-like definitions are saved and can be saved almost forever, while others are put to risk or transformed and even physically destroyed while part of the productive process. The root of the difficulties lies in the lack of conceptual unity inherent in both definitions.

The root of all semantic difficulties analyzed above, in other words, stems from one simple source. That list of items includes two opposite concepts: the concept of productive wealth and the concept of nonproductive wealth. Hence the presumed "equality" of saving to investment, as stressed earlier, is not an identity. There are two concepts in each definition. There are two concepts, and not a single immediately identifiable entity, in each definition. And the two concepts perform diametrically opposite economic functions. Hence, the definition of saving, as well the definition of investment, that obtains in economic theory contravenes the dictates of the principle of non-contradiction.

We can now add the principle of non-contradiction to the principle of equivalence and the principle of identity as the list of principles of formal logic that are not respected by the most fundamental definitions in mainstream economic theory.

———

Words are not just words. They have consequences. And even before that, words do not stand by themselves. They are part of the fabric of culture. Were economic theory a closed world of its own, it might get away with the idiosyncrasy of using words as it pleases. But economics does not stand by itself. It has become increasingly dependent on the assistance that only mathematics can offer. And it is there that one finds the source of the mismatch between economics and mathematics. While mathematics respects the dictates of the principle of equivalence, the principle of identity, and the principle of non-contradiction scrupulously, economics does not. Hence the use of mathematics in economics is premature. Hence, by forcing the language and insisting on using mathematics prematurely, economics tears the daily reality of things, people, and institutions apart and attempts to find refuge in higher and higher abstraction. Economics becomes metaphor; the physical reality is given any meaning one desires; and economic reasoning, as Keynes put it, becomes a "haze where nothing is clear and everything is possible."

We must obtain a precise definition of saving and investment. We must make economics compatible with mathematics. This is a long-term goal.

The immediate goal is less ambitious. We want to make clear the passage of the *General Theory* in which Keynes speaks of a radical cure for the ills of a modern economy. In the next chapter we will see that to make Keynes' thought in that passage completely clear there is the need to list a third alternative: an alternative which allows us to see a full range of clear-cut choices and then to rank them; an alternative which was in the back of Keynes' mind, but which he did not, and could not, express. Contemporary economic theory does not leave room for this third choice. All that is not consumed is supposed to be saved; and that which is saved is supposed to be invested—and vice versa. The third and only logical alternative becomes evident when one goes beyond Adam

Smith's conception of saving in form as well as in substance and when one goes beyond Keynes' own "definition" of investment. Thus we will move toward a logically tenable definition of saving and investment. As a bonus we will discover the definition of hoarding.

XI

The Definition of Saving, Hoarding, and Investment

Three Suggestions
- *Let the word saving be reserved for financial savings.*
- *Let the concept of hoarding represent all nonproductive wealth.*
- *Let the concept of investment represent all productive wealth.*

IN THE PREVIOUS CHAPTER we have found that the prevailing understanding of saving contains two concepts and so does the prevailing understanding of investment. They are the concept of productive wealth and the concept of nonproductive wealth. Before we make any use of this discovery, we had better make sure that these concepts have indeed validity non only in epistemological reality but also in the economic reality.

The Reality of Economics

The theory of knowledge is just that, a set of tools to help us understand the reality of our daily lives. The verification of its validity does not lie in its own bosom, however; rather it lies in the very reality it tries to understand. The difference is between content and process: the content of the economic reality and the process as a set of rules of epistemology. (Needless to say, the reality is always filtered through theory. This is another layer of difficulty of our topic that must be eschewed here. This is pure methodology.) In other words, the grounds of the validity of the two concepts we have just found cannot be rooted in epistemology but in economics. If they fail this test, these concepts are not valid. It is in this process that economics does not become subservient to epistemology. It remains an autonomous discipline, and if it is wise it will fearlessly ask for help from its sister mental disciplines.

The concepts of productive and nonproductive wealth are clearly distinguishable from each other in economics. The starting point of the analysis resides in the basic assumptions on which this work is built: we are observing stocks of wealth at one instant in time. This starting point allows us to set aside for the moment all complications arising from increases in value due to movement in prices or population, be they shifts in relative or absolute price levels or even location, tastes, and preferences of the population. We observe a house or a plot of land, an industrial plant or a packet of currency. And then we ask the crucial question: is the item at this moment producing goods and services or even money income? (And not: is it capable of producing further wealth?) If the answer is positive, that specific item must be considered productive. If the answer is negative, the conclusion must be that the item is nonproductive.

If we want to complete the analysis, we must also determine the present market value of each specific item. (An even more complete analysis would require the determination of the reasons for which an individual owner would want to keep his wealth in an unproductive state. This examination will be performed only in part in this work. The quickest answer at this stage is that such reasons are infinite.) Six months or a year from now, we return to observe those "same" stocks of wealth. We then calculate the value of the goods and services or money income the productive items have produced: we measure their flow of productivity—i.e., their income value or earnings. This is the basis for the precise determination of the productive or nonproductive nature of each item. Item A, which was classified as nonproductive—and which has remained so during the entire time interval—obviously has produced zero income. Item B, which was classified as productive, has produced an income of a certain value. We thus find confirmation of the validity of our classification. (Changes in the economic function or nature of each item offer only practical, not conceptual difficulties. At the limit, all practical difficulties are eliminated through continuous monitoring.)

At this point we can do something more. We can also compare the market value of the two items: their respective capital appreciation. The simplest case is that in which there has been no increase in such value. In this case, the difference in the wealth of the individual owner—and the community at large—is due exclusively to the productive capacity of those specific items that have been classified as productive. And a similar difference can be established in the case of homogeneous increases in the market value of items A and B.

More interesting cases are those of non-homogeneous increases in the market value of those items. The reader can independently work out the various combinations. Let us look at the case of an increase in the market value of nonproductive items and the stability in the market value of productive items. The increase can even be such that the value of nonproductive items is now bigger than the original market value of productive items plus the value of the income that productive items have produced. The vital question then becomes: is everyone better off? Undoubtedly, the community as a whole is not; and the owner of nonproductive wealth is only nominally better off. If he has no outside income, he will be compelled to sell part of his capital. He cannot live on the nominal increase in the value of his wealth.

The "cases" can be intriguing. But the issue is incontrovertible. There is a substantial and identifiable difference between the concepts of productive and nonproductive wealth. At any one moment, non-consumer items are either productive or nonproductive specimens of economic wealth.

A last ditch effort is wholly warranted to specify the difference that exists between the two concepts. A piece of nonproductive wealth that gains in financial value, gains such value not by its own merit (or by what its owner does with it), but as a consequence of movements of population and market forces. To maintain that such an item of wealth is "therefore" productive does not only destroy the clarity of the economic discourse: at times those movements in population and market forces cause a decline in the financial value of the same item of wealth. That reasoning also denies the existence of a much larger reality: society as a concrete and independent entity. When the effects of society on wealth are clearly identified, there is no possibility of confusion between the concept of productive and the concept of nonproductive wealth.

To insist on the point, the distinction between productive and nonproductive wealth is so important that even if it did not exist in the economic reality—even if there were no distinction, in essence, between economic and financial value—we would need to force the language and invent it. The economic reality is so fickle that it is likely to transport our mind along with its movements. In fact, in deflationary periods money under the mattress increases in value; and in inflationary periods productive wealth is likely to lose value. Yes, even if the proposed distinction did not exist in reality, we would need to invent it.

Answers to an Important Question

Someone might ask how are such concrete, borderline cases to be classified: an oil well that has been capped? a silo of wheat that is not being emptied? In economic theory, as construed today, they are classified as investment and they are assumed to perform the function of equalizing present and future demand for those goods.

The answer to this important question is many-pronged. First of all, there is a practical issue to be solved that can be formulated as follows: "For how long?" This issue can be settled only by the economist who listens carefully to the technologist. There are functional time requirements in any industry that need to be respected. They are so obvious that they do not need to be elaborated upon. Within these limits, oil wells that are capped, for instance, must be classified as productive wealth.

The economic question arises as soon as practical and technological issues are settled for each specific case. Those goods that are kept unused beyond the technological time requirements for their non-use must be classified as nonproductive wealth. Economic theory must respect economic practices; but it has its own rigid demands that prevent it from adapting its logic to those practices.

But the question is not fully answered yet. One must also take into account the assumption mentioned above that those practices equalize present and future demand. This is an issue of economic dynamics for which scanty attention can be reserved in this context. Two aspects of it can be briefly mentioned. Those practices can be a consequence of oversupply. In this case one must admit that the entrepreneur has committed an error of judgment. Without entering too deeply into the issue of opportunity cost, one must conclude that both the entrepreneur and society as a whole would be better off if energies to produce the oil well, which now must be capped, had been devoted to producing solar energy; and those energies which were devoted to produce that wheat, which must now be kept in storage, had been devoted to producing corn or fresh fruit.

But what if that wheat or that oil are necessary right now; namely, what if those practices are a consequence of underconsumption? This question is immeasurably more complicated. It is composed of many sub-issues, only some of which will be treated later on. All too briefly, in an economy which is well run—by definition—there is neither oversupply nor underconsumption; and, most importantly, the requirements of the future are so calibrated that they are satisfactorily taken into account, a feat which is constantly accomplished by productive wealth and productive wealth alone. Thus the silo is of such capacity as to prudently satisfy not only the consumption needs of the entire year, but also foreseeable emergencies of future years. And it remains adequately full, not because it is not emptied, but because it is replenished in a timely fashion.

Evidently, we are faced with an intricate mixture of practice and theory. In a theoretical setting, we have to remain satisfied with settling theoretical questions. Upon careful consideration, the proposed distinction between productive and nonproductive wealth must be allowed to stand. Indeed, not until we separate the two concepts from each other shall we obtain incontrovertible, crystal-clear definitions of both saving and investment.

The Definition of Investment, Saving, and Hoarding

Implicit in the above analysis is all the material that is necessary for forging the economic definition of saving and investment. By making that material explicit, we can formulate the proper definition of the two terms. In the process, we shall also discover the economic definition of hoarding.

It is proposed that the tacit convention, which has forever permeated economic analysis, be totally respected by making it explicit. In other words, it is proposed that investment be defined as all wealth that—in act—is productive: productive of money, goods, or services. If we accept this definition, we automatically separate the concept of productive wealth from that of nonproductive wealth.

Conversely, it is proposed that saving be defined as all wealth that—in act—is nonproductive: all wealth that remains economically passive or inert for an extended period of time. Such a period of time will be determined, case by case, through conventions and practical constraints; perhaps it will be a year, perhaps much less.

Since the word "saving," however, is burdened with all sorts of emotive charges and since it has irremediably been taken over by the world of finance, it is further proposed that it be—quite simply—eliminated from the language of economics. It ought to be substituted with the word "hoarding." Hoarding clearly includes all forms of nonproductive wealth. And we must be careful never to use such expressions as "hoarding of capital-assets," but accumulation of capital-assets.)

———•———

How to make the issues a bit more concrete?

To complete the mental operation we have pursued so far, we definitely exclude all consumer items from the list of items representing wealth that is of interest to the economic process; then we mechanically put all the items that have traditionally been included in the definition of saving and investment in a long line. Soon we cut the line in two. And we include in the segment called saving—or, better, hoarding—all items which are nonproductive of further wealth; all items, instead, which are productive are included in the segment called investment.

The simplest way of thinking about the proposed definitions is to add the qualification "passive" to saving or hoarding, and "active" to investment.

Further Specifications

Economists will notice that the proposed definition of hoarding covers forms of wealth that can, indeed, be saved. Those included in our definition are forms of wealth that are largely indestructible, have low or non-existing carrying charges, and generally increase in value over time, automatically through the forces of the market and the movements of the population. And they generally increase in value over time whether there is a slight deflation or—with the exception of cash on hand—an inflation of monetary values. It is only severe depressions which affect the value of that wealth; but then the essential question to scrutinize is that of relative declines: the value of nonproductive wealth tends to fall less than the value of other forms of wealth. In fact, it is this distinctive characteristic that makes those items so attractive to buyers at certain times.

So far we have described the general case. To obtain a fuller understanding of the phenomenon of hoarding, however, we must realize one other essential characteristic: any item of wealth, given the proper conditions, can and will be hoarded. As a matter of record, once a few people started hoarding tissue paper and drinking water, those items disappeared from supermarket shelves in a matter of hours. And who can forget the long lines at the fuel pumps when in the 1970's people attempted to keep their car tanks always full? Or the long lines of supertankers waiting to be unloaded outside the harbor in Tokyo?

What to say of the quantity of goods hoarded? Clearly, this is a very important question. It is the quantity of goods hoarded, after all, which determines its relative effects on the rest of the economy. And yet, in this context, nothing more can be said on this issue than this: the quantity of goods hoarded varies over time, and not always in a predictable fashion.

The essential characteristic of items that can be hoarded concerns neither their physical nature nor their rate of accumulation over time, but their intrinsic economic nature. Those items have no economic (as distinguished from monetary or financial) value in themselves. Their economic value is realized only when they are transformed either into consumer items or into capital assets.

The crux of the matter hinges on a clarification offered by Professor Modigliani. Technically, it is not the existence of saving or hoarding of money that creates disturbances in the economic system. It is the uncertainty as to the quantity and the behavior of hoarding that creates disturbances. (If we pass on to the observation of "real" wealth, these specifications are of course of much more immediate understanding. We shall necessarily return to these points.)

The "Imprecision" of the Proposed Definitions

The proposed definitions might appear to be too imprecise to be satisfactory. Yet, whatever flexibility is preserved in them is kept, not to allow flexibility in the science of economics, but to reflect the condition of the reality that is the subject of economic study. Unlike a stone that—although changing—generally changes its nature rather slowly, one can have abrupt and entirely reversible changes in the economic reality. A gold ingot, which in accordance with the proposed definition may be classified as hoarding today, can become part of the industrial production tomorrow—hence, it ought to be classified as investment. And the day after it can be transformed into bracelets that are bought by a consumer and used as such—hence, the original ingot has been transformed into a consumer item. This is not all. At some time in the future, those bracelets can be melted down to form again a gold ingot. Often the economic reality changes, even though there is no change in its outward manifestations. Raw materials, which are bought to serve immediately in the productive process, can, for any number of reasons, be kept unused for an extended period of time. Should they not, accordingly, be classified differently, namely, as hoarding rather than investment?

Economic definitions are like nets. They alone can catch the ever-changing reality. But to perform this task they need to be fixed; they need to be sturdy. If not—if they are elastic and themselves mutable—they will let the moving reality slip by. And since, unlike fish or butterflies, the economic reality does not bear a name tag of its own, nor does it have an immutable color or form, elastic economic definitions will unavoidably let the economic reality slip by unrecognized.

If the basic function of theory is to bring order out of chaos, then definitions perform one more role that ought to be self-evident to those who have followed the arguments over the year 2000 United States presidential election. Agreed upon definitions reduce the number of disputes that are bound to arise in tense situations. Hence definitions are civilizing tools. Definition-nets also need to be so coordinated and complete as to cover the entire reality; but this is a different discourse: a discourse which pertains to the structure of any overall theory.

Statisticians need not be overly concerned with the "imprecision" of the language at this stage, even though all the qualifiers that have been used are worrisome. Statistical difficulties can be solved in advance of any counting, as they are usually solved, through the development of conventions; besides, the time frame in each case is crucial. Measurements—preferably of stocks as well as flows (through extended observations in time), and one hopes for eventual hard empirical data—can be taken every year. In particular stages of the economic cycle, they should be taken much more frequently. Whatever monetary funds are at those moments found to be used for the purchase of nonproductive wealth; whatever stocks of wealth are then found unused, i.e., neither used in the productive process nor as consumer goods, those funds and those stocks (after taking into account the technological requirements mentioned above) should be classified as hoarding. Stated differently, the statistical problems are considerable, but they can be solved. Indeed, they have to be solved if economics is ever going to become an exact science.

Some Advantages of the Proposed Definitions

The proposed definitions open up completely new avenues of research for economic analysis. Let us start with the observation of the most immediate effects of this new program of research. With the proposed surgery, we separate not only the concept of productive wealth from that of nonproductive wealth; we also automatically separate the two functions which, since ancient times, have been assumed to be performed by saving: "seed" for next year's production, and "insurance" against lean years. Investment will exclusively perform the function that "seeds" have always performed; and saving will exclusively perform the ancient function of "insurance" against lean years. The effects upon the clarity of the language will be especially appreciated during the discussion on economic growth and inflation.

For the time being, let us return to some crucial issues that have already been extensively covered. Saving and investment have now clearly and irrefutably become asymmetric terms—formally as well as substantively. Does this alteration not cut the ground underneath past controversies? Were not the extraneous elements, which we have found included in the prevailing definitions of both saving and investment, intractable irritants? Without any firm theoretical guidance, productive items were included in the definition of saving, and nonproductive items in that of investment. Separating one category from the other, we can clearly see that every saving does not—indeed, cannot—correspond to an investment. Items which are hoarded automatically become nonproductive and thus fall into one category, that of saving or hoarding; productive items fall into the other category, that of investment. The possibility of confusion between the two is drastically undermined.

Furthermore, if the suggestion to abolish the word saving from the language of economics is faithfully respected (even though, to capture its linkages with the past, such suggestion cannot be respected in this work), the definition of financial savings as term deposits of money in financial institutions is left completely undisturbed. This definition can be left undisturbed because, observed from an economic point of view, the practice of financial savings contains the homely and eternally valid recommendation not to spend more than one's income—an issue of microeconomics which, provided it does not involve hoarding, does not have macroeconomic effects. One's financial savings can indeed be put to good use by someone else's economic investment of those funds.

The word hoarding unequivocally conveys the idea of wealth which—in act—is nonproductive from an economic point of view. Such substitution makes not only the language of economics in general much more clear and understandable; it also eliminates a large number of obscurities from the *General Theory.* The passage quoted earlier, and much more economic literature, becomes quite clear. What Keynes had in mind as the "radical cure" for the Depression is the elimination of every aspect of hoarding.

We now have a full range of choices. The addition of hoarding as a distinct category of economic thought clarifies the choices expressed by Keynes; and makes it clear that he was indeed suggesting a national policy which would include a combination of the choices he had listed, but would exclude all forms of hoarding.

This is no conjecture. Clearly, he had in mind the existence of a third alternative to either spending all one's income on consumer items or ordering the production of specific capital assets. Let us read the rest of the paragraph. Keynes said: "It might be that, at times when he was more than usually assailed by doubts concerning the future, he would turn his perplexity towards more consumption and less investment. But"—and here comes the clincher—"that would avoid the disastrous, cumulative and far-reaching repercussions of its being open to him, when thus assailed by doubts, to spend his income neither on the one nor on the other." The third alternative that Keynes had in mind was hoarding.

This again is no conjecture. Keynes closed that passage by stating: "Those who have emphasized the social dangers of the hoarding of money have, of course, had something similar to the above in mind. But they have overlooked the possibility that the phenomenon can occur without any change, or at least any commensurate change, in the hoarding of money." The subset of the third alternative that was *not*, and could not be, made clear by Keynes is for a person to spend part of his income on items that can be hoarded. No money is hoarded, but the effects of hoarding are all there. To clearly see this subset, one has to distinguish real wealth from monetary wealth and stocks from flows, as we are doing in these pages.

The proposed definition of hoarding makes it, indeed, clear that the level of "hoarding of money" can remain the same or even be reduced. But money can still be spent on items that can be hoarded: unused land or gold, art "objects" which are not to be enjoyed by the owner or the public in general, jewels to be hidden in a safe deposit box, even machinery and supplies which are stockpiled for psychological, speculative, or strategic purposes. These are all items that, in the traditional terminology, can be "saved"—and can be largely saved forever, for reasons to be further clarified later on. Needless to say, many more topics need to be examined before we can decide whether we can accept or reject Keynes' "radical cure" for the many economic ills of the modern world: a national economic policy to avoid hoarding.

Finally, the effect of the proposed definitions upon the psychic resources of economists, let alone laymen, should not be overlooked. Today one is torn by the push and pull of two sirens: saving and investment. And their push and pull is stronger than that exercised by Scylla and Charybdis upon Ulysses. Unnoticed by the traveler, they often switch places. With the proposed surgical operation, we compel both saving and investment to remain in their place. The subjective leanings of the traveler can now be forcefully expressed and openly followed. At the destination, one will at least find what was expected. (The presence of subjective leanings is undeniable. Perhaps one anecdote will suffice. When a technician, whose name shall remain unmentioned, was shown a paper on the Flows model, he suggested to eliminate the definition of investment in order to preserve intact the current definition of saving.)

A Summary

This chapter can be summarized in the following three sentences. It proposes: (a) that the word saving be replaced by the word hoarding; (b) that the concept of hoarding represent—with the exclusion of consumer items—all nonproductive wealth; and (c) that the concept of investment represent all productive wealth.

The Question of Standards

This is not the place to add to the above. Rather, it is important to realize how contemporary economic theory preserves its internal logical consistency in the face of all its evident contradictions. The answer is twofold. Internally, when one contradiction is detected, a patch is found. And when it becomes evident that the patch contains a new contradiction, the cycle starts anew. Thus the internal logical consistency of economics has become a set of balancing contradictions.

As far as external logic is concerned, the answer is quite simple. Economic theory has not been subjected to any outside standards of logic, epistemology, or philosophy.

And, not unlike many other mental disciplines ever since the Renaissance, deep in its innards it believes that its autonomy requires absolute internal freedom.

Standards of Logic

For instance, without distinguishing between economic and financial investment, economic theory feels free to borrow from the language of finance and say—without fear of getting enveloped in a tangle of serious contradictions—"People invest in a boarded-up house, or in gold, or ancient artifacts."

And yet, what is proper to the world of finance is not proper to the world of economics. Economics is—or ought to be—a science. Finance is a practice. Thus the world of finance can legitimately borrow a technical term—investment, in our case—from the world of economics and use it loosely. The same opportunity is not available to the world of economics, if it chooses to be a science. In economic theory, investment, just as much as hoarding, must mean one thing—and one thing only. (Indeed, to be an autonomous discipline economics has to be separated not only from the language of the law but also from the language of finance.)

Through respect for such simple standards of formal logic as the principle of identity and the principle of non-contradiction, one eliminates the need for double- and triplespeak, thus facilitating communication among people; one also obeys standards elaborated by centuries of thought in the fields of economics, logic, and philosophy. We shall have occasion to return to the first two sets of standards. Let us look at the third set, the application of a basic tool of the theory of knowledge, namely, the use of the definition of concept.

Standards of Philosophy

Rather than following the more stringent standards for the definition of a concept that were elaborated by Benedetto Croce (since we would need the knowledge of many other topics before we could verify their application), let us check what Immanuel Kant had to say on this account. Kant, the father of the "modern" concept, stated in a key passage:

> *In every cognition of an object there is* unity *of concept, which may be called* qualitative unity, *so far as we think by it only the unity in the comprehension of the manifold material of our knowledge . . . Secondly, there is* truth, *in respect to the deductions from it. The more true deductions can be made from a given concept, the* more *criteria are there of its objective reality. . . Thirdly, there is* completeness, *which consists in this, that the plurality together leads back to the*

unity of the concept, according completely with this and with no other concept.[46]

If one applies these standards to the traditional definitions of saving (or hoarding) and investment, one discovers that they do not obey these standards. By the same token, the newly developed definitions indeed

- Offer a unity in the comprehension of the manifold material of our knowledge;
- Can be, and shall be, subjected to many criteria to check their objective reality;
- From the plurality of items they need to cover, they lead the mind back to the unity of one concept—with the exclusion of all other concepts.

Through our work, both saving and investment have been transformed from vague conceptions to precise concepts. And once they have become concepts, the function that they perform in economic theory has also been automatically transformed from that of a relation to that of an independent entity. The reader will recall that, in mainstream economics, both saving and investment are related to income, consumption, and to each other. In Concordian economics, they stand by themselves as independent entities.

We have eliminated all extraneous elements from the definition of both saving and investment. With help of the hypotheses established within the context of the imaginary saving-investment system, entities which, within the context of the rational saving-investment system, were not identical to themselves, have been transformed into entities which are now identical to themselves: from $S \neq S$ and $I \neq I$, we have passed to $S = S$ (or $H = H$) and $I = I$.

In essence, we have stepped out of the internal logic of contemporary economic theory. More specifically, we have stepped out of the internal logic of both the rational and the imaginary saving-investment system. We have entered the world of the real saving-investment system.

A Sub-Distinction

We will return to these topics in order to complete the construction of the real saving-investment system.

For the time being, whatever haziness is left in the mind of the reader in relation to the concept of hoarding might be further dispelled by one distinction introduced at the suggestion of Daniel Bubly, an environmental engineer. The distinction is between "liquidatable" and "non-liquidatable" hoarding-expenditure. The former relate to all those expenditures on nonproductive wealth, e.g., unused land, which can eventually be transformed back into liquid capital at the discretion of the owner. The latter relate to those expenditures whose economic value can never be recovered again. Among the latter expenditures, one ought to include all forms of economic waste: not only those that result from willful activities; but also those that result from involuntary unemployment, strikes, and the like. These may be classified as forms of forced waste.

Having finally discovered the economic definition of both saving (or hoarding) and investment, let us pass on to the observation of the relationship which in the economic reality exists between the two entities. Thus we shall complete the construction of the real saving-investment system.

XII

The Real Saving-Investment System

*The most difficult thing to discover is the
obvious.*

⸺⸺

ALL ECONOMISTS HAVE BEEN FACED with a difficulty at a level that
appears obvious—and it is not. This, indeed, is the difficulty of
dealing with the obvious: the obvious is devious. Unless it is
checked and re-checked in all possible manners, any one statement
can be utterly misleading.

The obvious is what every economist worth his or her traditional grain of salt knows instinctively: there must be a relationship
between saving (or hoarding) and investment. It is obvious, the
relationship must be there. But what is the relationship that links
the two? Once the relationship of "equality" between the two elements is dissolved, without leaving a shadow of doubt, what is one
left with?

With arbitrary "definitions" of both saving and investment done
away with, and with the definition of hoarding firmly in place, we
can go beyond the veil of words. The ancient definitions of both
terms, in fact, compelled us to accept the relation of "equality"
between the two terms as an unavoidable consequence. With those
constraints now gone, and with a model of the economic system
composed of four homogeneous and independent elements, or
(nearly) full-fledged concepts, we can look at the reality—and let
the economic reality determine the type of relationship that exists
between saving and investment.

The solution lies in observing the problem not as a single proposition, but in its entirety. "Saving-investment" has in fact often
been called a system—i.e., a unit; but it has never been treated as
such. If we want to treat it as a system, we discover that there are
three component elements in it: saving (or better, hoarding), investment, and the relation linking the two. This ground, and more, has

been covered before.

We have already determined that, in Concordian economics, saving—or better, hoarding—can be defined as a concept, namely, as all nonproductive wealth and thus can be presented as an identity ($S \equiv S$ or $H \equiv H$). We have reached the same conclusions regarding investment. By defining investment as all productive wealth we have been able to identify investment as an identity ($I \equiv I$). What is the relationship between the newly defined saving and investment? This search shall now engage our attention.

A Relation of Complementarity

The key to the solution of the problem lies, as it often does since words express the shared wisdom of too many people, in the very word "system." This word implies a unit that is complete by itself. Nothing can be added or subtracted from it without destroying the organic unity of the system. In other words, if saving and investment do form a system, they are all that the system requires. In mathematics, such a unit is symbolized with the number 1. It can be expressed with the number 1 or 10 or 100 or any other such finite number. If the sum (and it has to be a sum—otherwise there is no "simple" unit here) of saving and investment does indeed form a system, that sum must be equivalent to 1. We can thus write: Saving + Investment = 1.

The essential characteristic of saving (or hoarding), it will be recalled, is that items so classified have the potential of being transformed into investment. Indeed, some of them can also be transformed into consumer goods; but, as it will become clearer when we discuss the concept of consumption, the distinction between consumer goods and capital assets is a spurious economic distinction. For a quick disposition of this matter, if a consumer item is exchanged for money, its economic nature cannot be distinguished from any other investment-asset: the consumer item has become productive of money income. And if the item that was hoarded is used by its owner as a consumer product, since the change has no direct effect on the economy, the action remains outside the province of the economic process and, as such, outside the professional interest of the economist.

In other words, it might be useful to stress, the sum of saving and investment is equal to all existing stocks of wealth that are of interest to the economic process. Thus we can directly and constantly write: $S + I = W = 1$. This formulation is not only an equivalence; it is also the first logical link in the chain of thought which gradu-

ally allows us to build the Stocks model, a model we have enunciated earlier for clarity of exposition but we have not yet built. If
we were to start the analysis indirectly from the Stocks model
itself, our equation would read: S/W + I/W = 1; or, starting from
the Flows model, S/Y + I/Y = 1. These expressions and what follows from them lead to the same results. However, they are more
complex formulations. And especially the second expression tends
to make us lose sight of one fact of fundamental importance. This
year's income is not the result of only last year's net investment,
but also of the investment which occurred many years prior to
that. That formulation, in brief, makes us lose sight of the existence of past wealth.

There is a major advantage in the use of the basic and simple formulation of the saving-investment system given above; namely,
Saving + Investment = 1. It brings to the surface the relationship
between saving and investment with unequivocal and immediate
evidence. At any one moment, if there is more saving (or hoarding)
in the economy, there must be less investment—and vice versa. Any
increase (or decrease) either in saving or investment increases (or
decreases) the total wealth available to the economic process, let us
say from 100 to 110 (or 90). Now we simply put 110 (or 90) as
equivalent to 1. The size of that quantity—or of that system—does
not matter. At the limit, it can be zero or infinity: at this "special"
or logical moment, both zero and infinity are systems; they are
whole entities; they are a unit. They are equivalent to unity, which
is symbolized as 1. Thus, if we have saving at a value of 75, investment must be at a value of 25—or respectively 0.75 and 0.25; otherwise, what we are observing is not a system.

What is the relationship, then, which in reality exists between
saving and investment? Such relationship is one of complementarity: when one value increases, the other must decrease by the same
amount.

Formally, this relationship can be written as follows:

$$\text{Saving} + \text{Investment} = 1 = \frac{\text{Saving}}{1 - \text{Investment}}.$$

Perhaps the last term of this expression ought to be clarified for
the non-mathematically-minded reader. Let us assume that Saving
= 0.25; then, investment, as stated above, must be equal to 0.75.
Thus, substituting the numbers for the words, one reads:

$$\frac{0.25}{1-0.75} = \frac{0.25}{0.25} = 1.$$

Mathematicians might prefer to see this relationship expressed as follows:

$$\frac{S \text{ (or } H)}{1-I} = \frac{0.25}{1-S \text{ (or } H)} = 1.$$

In plain English, this expression symbolizes a relationship of complementarity. The value of one term increases by the same amount as the value of the other term decreases. We have thus found the relationship that in the economic reality exists between saving and investment. We can now build the real saving-investment system.

The Real Saving-Investment System

With the definitions of saving (or hoarding) as all nonproductive wealth, and investment as all productive wealth that have been reached earlier, we have all three elements in the saving-investment system clearly determined. We can now formalize the system by writing:

$$S = S = npW \qquad\qquad H = H = npW$$
$$I = I = pW \qquad\qquad\qquad I = I = pW$$

or preferably

$$S + I = 1 = \frac{S}{1-I} \qquad\qquad H + I = 1 = \frac{H}{1-I}$$

which, in plain English, reads:

Saving (or Hoarding) = Unused land, etc. =
        Nonproductive Wealth
Investment = Machinery, Supplies, etc. =
        Productive Wealth
If the sum of saving (or hoarding) and investment is
        equivalent to unity, only then is saving (or hoarding)
        in a relation of complementarity with investment.

Needless to say, each one of the three expressions is an identity. All terms in each expression are reflexive, symmetric, and transitive. Saving (or hoarding) is reflexive because it is identical to itself—and nothing else: all wealth that is nonproductive is all and only saving. Saving is symmetric because the term can be exchanged with either the term nonproductive wealth or its own specific list of items, and one always reaches one and only one concept. Saving is also transitive because saving and that list of items is always and only equivalent to the same concept: nonproductive wealth. This check can be extended by applying it to each and every term in all three expressions—never reaching contradictory results.

To clarify the above, let us recall that an identity is an equivalence relation. Briefly, through the identity relation one looks inward, increasingly deeper into one entity; and through the equivalence relation one looks outward, at increasingly broader aspects of the same entity. The former relation puts an entity more in contact with itself, and the latter puts the same entity always more in contact with the outside world. We shall have occasion to observe these distinctions at closer range.

Thus the saving-investment system offers a high degree of internal as well as external logical consistency. It "makes sense" internally—on each one of its own terms. It makes sense externally—all terms in that system respect age-old standards of formal logic. Let us neglect the meaning of the word "concept," which has been known and scrutinized and at each step of the way increasingly formalized by many thinkers from Socrates to Benedetto Croce. Let us recall that the rules of equivalence, already known to Aristotle, were codified by Boethius in the VI Century A.D., and from him they passed through the Scholastic Doctors and have reached us with a number of refinements which are not crucial to our context.

The above saving-investment system, then, appears to satisfy not only the rules of internal and external logic. It also appears to make economic sense—even though the demonstration of the existence of this "sense" has to wait a while. At this stage, let us simply point out that the system ought to be called the real saving-investment system—as opposed to the imaginary saving-investment system, and as distinct from the rational saving-investment system.

The latter system, as we have seen, is common to all extant economic thought from at least Adam Smith, whether through Keynes or not, to the Keynesians, the Monetarists, and the Neo-neo-classicists. This is a system which, as suggested in a variety of ways, ought to be discarded, because it is founded on a rational explanation—always so clearly unsatisfactory that it has been repeatedly replaced by a different and completely new explanation, an explanation which has never had any foundation either in the economic reality or in logic. As distinct from it, the real saving-investment system ought to be accepted because it is indeed—in brief—"real."

With this conclusion, it is not denied that within the realm of rational economics saving must be equal to investment—just as the proposition that "parallel lines do not meet" remains a necessity within the realm of Euclidean geometry. Conversely, as the proposition that "parallel lines meet" belongs to non-Euclidean or imaginary geometry, so the proposition that saving is not equal but complementary to investment belongs to the realm of Concordian economics.

The Historical Significance of the Real Saving-Investment System

Even though elaboration upon it shall come later, let us not lose sight of the historical significance of the newly found real saving-investment system. With the recognition of lack of validity in the proposition that saving is "equal" to investment, and with the statement that saving (or hoarding) is complementary to investment, we have hopefully brought to a halt a long train of thought intensely pursued by mainstream economics. Completely new avenues of research open up to view.

In the beautiful simplicity of mathematical symbols, we can now write:

$$S \neq I \; ; \; \frac{S \text{ (or H)}}{1 - I} = \frac{I}{1 - S \text{ (or H)}}$$

namely, in Concordian economics, saving is not equal to investment; saving (or hoarding) is complementary to investment.

In the thorough expressiveness of plain language, what we are saying is this: out of any yearly income, the more spent on actively engaged capital-assets, the less remaining to be spent on inert items which can be hoarded. In a well-run economy, the amount we spend on consumer items does not affect that choice; it is the production process—or the choice exercised last "year" between hoarding and investment—which determines what is available as consumer items this year. What we might wish now on this score is immaterial; we cannot "consume" more consumer items than have been produced. Assuming that the economy is well run, we cannot even "consume" less: all the production available is necessary to satisfy our needs. (In practice, the economy is not well run; but this is a different type of discourse which belongs to the field of economic policy and not that of economic theory.)

When all "nuisance" values are taken out of the context, the real saving-investment system advances only one proposition: the more we spend on investment, the less we have for hoarding—and vice versa. The proposition is of immediate understanding, evident and, at least to this writer, incontrovertible.

Will the real saving-investment system prove to be so strong a dike to hold the pressures of centuries of thought? Will it be able to arrest the momentum of that thought and divert its energies toward other directions, other pursuits? Only time will tell; the future is in the lap of the Gods—and the lap of men and women.

XIII

A Sartorial Movement
Turning Keynes' Model Inside Out
or
Turning Mainstream Economics
into Concordian Economics

Quick Comparisons

	Concordian Economics	Mainstream Economics
Saving	Financial savings	100,000 possible definitions
Hoarding	Nonproductive wealth	Does not exist
Investment	Productive wealth	Identified only through synonyms

RATHER THAN BREAKING MUCH new ground, this chapter is designed to achieve only minor objectives. This moment is taken not so much to recapitulate each and every argument developed so far, as to shed additional light on terrain already explored in order to become fully aware of where we have been and where we are going. The basic purpose of the chapter is to let us acquire complete control of the process of conversion of mainstream economics into Concordian economics.

Physicists can use beautiful representations and succinct expressions to render this transformation absolutely evident and incontrovertible. Not being a physicist and not speaking exclusively to physicists or even to some contemporary sculptors, I shall use—perhaps to just as much profit—a more earthly imagery. The process in which we are involved is like turning Keynes' model of the economic system inside out. This is a movement that is well understood by any tailor. When he has nearly finished a hat or jacket, he does exactly what we are doing with Keynes' model. He lines it and then turns it inside out. (The technical expression, I am told, is "right side out.")

And that is what Keynes, perhaps only for lack of time, did not do. He did not give us a finished product. The model needed to be refurbished and then turned inside out. As it is now, the original model shows all the rough edges of a hat or jacket that has not yet been lined and turned inside out. Since all the rough spots are on the outside, they are not even noticed by many economists who have rushed to wear that model. From the inside, from the point of view of the professional economist, that model feels comfortable—undoubtedly more comfortable, at the moment, than the model we are presenting here. Remember, the rough edges of Keynes' model are all on the outside; it is only laymen who brush against professional economists wearing that model who feel those rough edges.

Of course, neither the internal logic of Keynes' model nor the description of the economic reality obtained through this intellectual tool is easy to understand. This difficulty, encountered by laymen no less than by some economists, provides one additional reason why the model needs to be revised or turned inside out. Yet, the very last reason for revising the model is perhaps the most important. The model is incapable of yielding a description of the economic process as a process. The model is static—and all attempts to make it dynamic have failed and are destined to fail. Keynes' analysis is "period analysis": it stops and goes, and then it stops again. And, in its Keynesian interpretations, that description breaks down at the level of the asymmetry between saving and investment. (The existence of this asymmetry is, in turn, the reason why Keynes chose his peculiar type of analysis.)

———

Once the need for revising Keynes' model is no longer argued, the focus of the discussion shifts onto the method to bring this effect about. So far we have exercised many mathematical operations on the original model, and we have obtained parts of the Flows model. We will now offer three methods to turn Keynes' model as a whole inside out.

A Tri-dimensional Method

The first method for turning Keynes' model inside out, the simplest method, consists of visualizing a hat that lies on the tailor's table before the hat is lined and turned inside out. Lying on its brim, with its rough edges on the outside the hat does not permit us to give a look inside it; by the same token, Keynes' model does not allow us to look inside the economic system; the system has often been compared to a black box.

Grab the hat by the brim; turn it inside out; look into it. You can see everything that occurs inside it.

The most important understanding to bring home from this topological excursion is that we have to conceive of both models, not as linear but as tri-dimensional containers of information.

A Two-dimensional Method

A second method for turning Keynes' model inside out relies on a two-dimensional method. It uses the model in its symbolic form and gradually rotates all elements of the model starting with any one of its symbols, but that for income. The first shift is optional; all other are a mechanical consequence of the first.

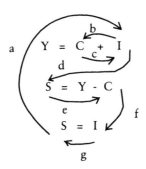

In detail, following the economic and mathematical reasoning outlined in earlier chapters, these physical operations can be described as follows:

a) Move S from the third equation to the position of I in the first equation

b) Move I of the first equation to the place of C in the first equation

c) Move C to the original position of I in first equation, and obtain Y = S + C

   d)   Move I from the first equation to the position of S in the
         second equation
   e)   Move S from the second equation to the position of C in
         the second equation, and obtain I = Y − S
   f)   Move C to the original position of I in the third equation
   g)   Move I to the original position of S, and obtain I = C.

The three equations that have been isolated from the context of
this rotation of all elements of Keynes' model themselves form the
three equations of the Flows model: Y = S + C; I = Y − S; and, I =
C. In other words, through a mechanical method, we have
obtained exactly the same results as we have obtained through all
other operations in this study of the transformation of mainstream
economics into Concordian economics. In brief, the elements of
the original Keynes' model remain the same in the Flows model,
but by changing position in relation to each other they acquire a
new meaning and change the internal structure of the model.

A Flattened One-dimensional Method

A third method relies on conceiving of Keynes' model literally as a
jacket, so that we can more closely look at the movements that
each of its component elements has to go through in order to pass
from mainstream economics to Concordian economics. This literal method has the advantage of letting us observe one movement
at a time. So far we have devoted considerable attention to the
transformation of saving to hoarding; we have, in other words,
reduced that vague but very large conception to one single concept:
all non-productive wealth. Let us now grant some additional attention to another element of Keynes' model, investment.

The Concept of Investment as the Pivot

All methods for turning Keynes' model inside out become clearer
if, with our mind's eye, we actually see that the concept of investment performs the function of a pivot. All movements from mainstream to Concordian economics revolve around this concept. This
concept, after a few refinements, as we have seen in the previous
chapter, remains exactly the same in both models. The refinishing
touches relate exclusively to its form.

    We have thus heeded Keynes' warning not to remain too
attached to the forms in which he cast his thought.

    The definition of investment as all productive wealth, which is included in the Flows model and the Stocks model, is exactly the same as that which, in substance and not in words, is included in Keynes' original model.

A New Definition of Saving

It is the definition of saving which had to be formulated anew. We have spent already much time on this topic to remain on it here. In both the Flows model and the Stocks model, saving—or better, hoarding—is all nonproductive wealth. The ancient, grandiose conception of saving had to be deflated to the status of a single concept. (The jacket had to be pressed and lined.)

And then, with the definition of saving and that of investment finally obtained, it has become relatively easy to change the relationship between those two entities from one of equality to one of complementarity. Through this operation, we have turned Keynes' model almost entirely inside out.

What remains to be done is to put a few refinishing touches on both the concept of consumption and that of income. This will be done in the next two chapters. There we shall elongate, stretch out both concepts: figuratively, both sleeves in our jacket. Here let us remain a little longer on the twist which has been imparted to the relationship between saving—or hoarding—and investment.

A Relationship of Complementarity

Once saving is defined as all nonproductive wealth and investment as all productive wealth, it is evident that the two entities can no longer be "equal" to each other. Were one to preserve that type of relationship, one would say that a boarded-up house is "equal" to, i.e., performing the same economic functions as, a factory alive with activities; one would see no distinction between gold bullion which lies in some heavily guarded fortress, and gold bullion which sits in a building ready to be used in industrial processes or transformed into jewels. One would say that money under the mattress is just as good for the economy as money deposited in a bank. Examples can be multiplied. They ought not to be necessary.

The central point is that once saving is defined as nonproductive wealth and investment as productive wealth, it no longer makes any sense to say that saving is "equal" to investment. Indeed, this clearly appears to be not only an incorrect statement, but also an empty one—empty from a logical as well as an economic point of view.

It now becomes more evident that in order to fill that empty statement, to give substance to it, one rational explanation had to be followed by another rational explanation. A statement by itself does not have any meaning. To give to any statement a definite meaning, one needs to support it with a full-fledged theory. And this is exactly what happened to the long train of thought that has been labeled rational economics. One theory—unconsciously—succeeded another simply to explain the validity of that statement from a slightly different point of view. But this is like trying to erect a building from the top down. Any light breeze will topple it.

Perhaps this matter ought to be put in stronger terms. Once one rationalization—or the entire theory justifying that relationship—was found wanting, it was far easier to build yet another rationalization and another theory than to examine all the issues involved there. In fact, the reader who is sensitive to matters of structure underlying any written work is aware that nearly every previous chapter has dealt with some of the issues arising from only one proposition, the proposition that saving is equal to investment.

No matter which approach is chosen, the point remains the same. A proposition by itself has no meaning. To acquire a specific meaning, it has to be part of a context—and the fullest possible context is a full-fledged theory. There is no getting away from these requirements.

The same requirements have, consciously, been met in the construction of the Flows model, an operation that still needs to be completed—with one difference: no longer by superimposing a theoretical structure upon a basic proposition, but by developing (less ambitiously and hurriedly) such a proposition itself into a system of thought. Faced with the massive historical evidence concerning the rise and fall of so many theories, we have isolated the basic proposition on which all those theories rest, namely, the proposition that "saving is equal to investment;" we have broken it down into its component parts and found three elements: (a) saving; (b) investment; and (c) the relationship between these two entities. All three elements have been put together again into a system—the imaginary saving-investment system; imaginary because it cannot logically exist. In other words, we have taken economic theory at face value and assumed that

$$Saving = Saving$$
$$Investment = Investment$$
$$Saving = Investment.$$

The independent analysis conducted on each of these component parts has revealed that all three assumptions are invalid. We have found that in contemporary economic theory, saving is not "equal" to saving—and saving alone; investment is not "equal" to investment—and investment alone; and, finally, that saving is not "equal" to investment.

At that point, it has become evident that the saving-investment system itself—whether in its unconscious ("rational") form or in its conscious ("imaginary") one—had to be turned inside out, in order for it to make logical as well as economic sense. The concept of investment has remained the same (in substance, though not in form) in both the rational and the imaginary saving-investment system: the tacit convention through which it had been expressed for so long has been made explicit. Saving, instead, has been changed to hoarding: a complex conception through which saving was—unconsciously—expressed for so long has been reduced to a clear-cut definition. And the relationship existing between these two entities has been twisted and transformed into one of complementarity. Ultimately, it is this relationship that has essentially been turned inside out. The result is the real saving-investment system.

Advantages of New Definitions and Relationships

At this point, the professional economist has a decided advantage over other readers. He or she can now clearly see the change or "movement" concerning the relationship between saving and investment through the use of conventional, synthetic expressions. What used to be the marginal propensity to save (MPS) is transformed into the marginal propensity to hoard (MPH); the marginal propensity to consume (MPC) is made equivalent to and replaced by the marginal propensity to invest (MPI); and the relationship between MPS and MPC (which in contemporary theory is one of complementarity and is written: MPS + MPC = 1) can no longer be kept in front of our eyes. It has to be turned inside out, and replaced by: MPH + MPI = 1. The resulting change consists in this, the marginal propensity to consume is no longer complementary to the marginal propensity to save—and therefore to the marginal propensity to invest. The marginal propensity to consume is now equivalent to the marginal propensity to invest. (We will return to this operation in due course.)

The understanding of the multiplier also changes accordingly. With MPC equivalent to MPI—and implicitly equivalent to MPD (a new entity: the marginal propensity to distribute)—the analysis of the multiplier (a) is stripped of any form of automatism that has entered into it; (b) is fully integrated into Keynes' principle of effective demand; and, (c) is integrated into Leontief's input-output analysis. General equilibrium analysis thus becomes the analysis of the effective and/or optimal mix of inputs—namely, the analysis (*à la* Piero Sraffa) of the cost of factors of production (plus desired profits = Keynes' aggregate supply function)—to obtain the desired level of output. The desired level and composition of output is, in turn, determined by the expected propensity to consume (= Keynes' aggregate demand function).

Finally, the propensity to consume—respecting (*à la* Kaldor) the internal dictates of MPD—is divided into three elements: a propensity to buy consumer goods; a propensity to buy capital goods; and a propensity to buy goods which can be hoarded. Once the propensity to buy capital goods is isolated, observed from the point of view of production, is broken down into its component elements, and these elements are tied to their own technological coefficients (multipliers), only then can we start making predictions about the future level of output. (Leontief's analysis cannot be allowed to remain in a no man's land, nor can it be fitfully grafted onto Keynes' system of thought.)

Obviously, these are relationships whose elaboration belongs to a dynamic analysis of the economic process—a topic that goes much beyond the task that can be performed at present. Suffice it to say that there is no such thing as "the multiplier." Rather, there are as many multipliers as there are mixes of the factors of production—including money. (And, incidentally, it is these mixes that determine the level of employment—and not the level of investment per se. In fact, two identical levels of investment measured in monetary terms can determine two entirely different levels of employment.)

Also, with practice we should eventually gain a detailed and comprehensive understanding of the combined effect of all experienced multipliers. It is then that we can begin to develop a clear understanding of something that might be called the organic growth path of the economy as a whole. This is the ultimate result of the changes suggested in this work.

The economist will realize that the changes from mainstream economics to Concordian economics, although subtle, are of fundamental importance. They will be appreciated especially by other readers. The concerned citizen who has understood the real saving-investment system can no longer be lost in the language of economics. With the real saving-investment system one simply says that at any given moment the total amount of hoarding plus the total amount of investment is equivalent to unity. Equally, the

A FEW VERBAL CONTRADICTIONS
in the Current
Economic Discourse

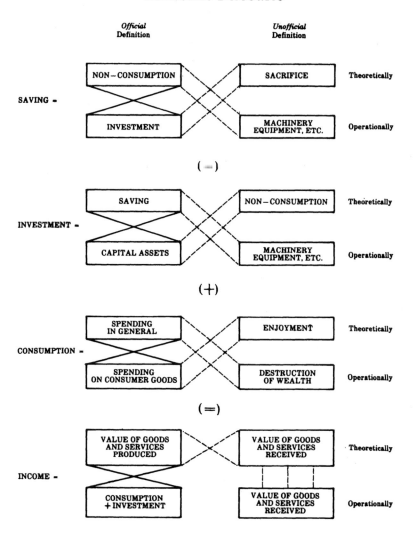

"extra" or marginal income (which is now being earned) is divided between a "propensity" or a decision to hoard and a decision to invest. The reader who wants to be more specific can say that one's extra income (just as one's total income) is divisible between hoarding and buying of consumer or capital goods. The reader who prefers a purely monetary terminology can say that one's extra income can be directly hoarded or it can be divided among expenditure on items that can be hoarded, expenditure on consumer goods, and expenditure on capital goods—as well as expenditure to purchase financial instruments.

A Few Consequences

There are innumerable consequences that follow from the above "sartorial" movements. Some of them will be explored in the next chapters. At the moment one consequence cannot be passed by silently. A large part of the economic discourse is taken out of the realm of dogma and art and is thrust into the light of science: the mind is now presented with a set of propositions which it can freely and immediately grasp, because they are free of contradictions. By stating that the more wealth kept in unproductive uses, that much less is kept in a productive state, namely, as capital-assets; by recognizing this twisted reality of the relationship between saving (or hoarding) and investment, there is no longer any need to interject verbal contradictions into every step of the economic discourse. A few such verbal contradictions in the current economic discourse have been recapitulated in the attached diagram bearing this title. (No attempt, however, is made to discuss again the content of the diagram.) Those contradictions were all necessary and they all balanced each other out; thus they formed a structure with internal logical consistency.

That consistency was acquired at such heavy cost because one wanted to start the discourse from a "straight" proposition—namely, a direct relation between saving and investment. The relation is indirect. The relation is one of complementarity. Once this reality is recognized, not unlike Franklin's rod, it will attract all lightening which happens to occur in the atmosphere of economics. We can now proceed with the building of a new structure—a structure which is safe; a structure which is well protected; and a structure which rests on the solid foundations elaborated by centuries of logic no less than economic thought; a structure, finally, which is immediately intelligible.

To verify the validity of the last statement, compare the complexity of the language that prevails in economic theory with the simplicity of the statements of Concordian economics. As a representative sample of the language of mainstream economics, the following might suffice: "In the pure theory of individual behavior, saving is represented essentially as the consumption of future commodities. Any funds allocable to current consumption that are not so allocated become available for future consumption. Specific future commodities may be associated with savings, but a certain residue to be passed on to heirs or simply accumulated in the form of paper claims is also part of savings." Etc., etc.

No source is cited for this quotation, because it is impossible to be fair to its author. To be fair, one ought to analyze the quotation, putting it in its proper context and comparing it with similar expressions. Besides, the purpose here is to highlight the clarity of the following propositions of Concordian economics:

- Saving is always and everywhere a financial phenomenon
- Hoarding is all nonproductive wealth
- Investment is all productive wealth
- Consumption is spending
- Income is the value of goods and services that are either produced or distributed or exchanged during the course of the year.

We will analyze the last two propositions in the next two chapters.

XIV

The Concept of Consumption

Quick Comparisons

	Concordian Economics	Mainstream Economics
Saving	Financial savings	100,000 possible definitions
Hoarding	Nonproductive wealth	Does not exist
Investment	Productive wealth	Identified only through synonyms
Consumption	Spending	Spending on consumer goods

———

OVER THE CENTURIES, the meaning of consumption has undergone numerous changes, but these changes have, at times, been so subtle as to pass almost completely unnoticed. The Reverend Malthus, when he wrote his crystal-clear essay on *Definitions in Political Economy* (1827), still held a conception of consumption that must have been expressed as soon as the first economic thought was formulated. "Consumption," he said, "is the destruction wholly or in part of any portion of wealth."[49] This definition appears to be so obvious that it is still frequently used.

However, this is a rudimentary definition that is wholly irrelevant to economic theory. Destruction of wealth is a concept which might be valid in the physical world—and even there its validity is questionable because, as a famous law of thermodynamics maintains, in nature nothing is created and nothing is destroyed; everything is simply subjected to transformation. In any case, even if the concept of destruction of wealth were fully valid in the physical world, it would still be irrelevant to the world of economics. Just as it is important to develop a science of economics that is independent of the rules of financing and the law, so it is important to develop it independent of the rules of all physical sciences. Economists, in brief, must be economists first. After, they can be lawyers, financiers or, physicists.

Let us leave the issue of the autonomy of economic science aside. What happens to the concept of consumption after Malthus? Enter Alfred Marshall. With his keen mind, taking a leaf from Senior, Say, and J. S. Mill,[50] he affirms that there are subtleties in the economic concept of consumption which an economist can disregard only at his own risk and peril. He stated: "*Consumption* may be regarded as negative production. Just as man can produce only utilities, so he can consume nothing more. He can produce services and other immaterial products, and he can consume them. But as his production of material products is nothing more than a rearrangement of matter that gives it new utilities; so his consumption of them is nothing more than a disarrangement of matter, which diminishes or destroys its utilities. Often indeed when he is said to consume things, he does nothing more than to hold them for his use, while, as Senior says, they 'are destroyed by those numerous gradual agents which we call *time*.'"[51]

Clearly, with Marshall, the concept of consumption tries to free itself of the strictures of the physical world. It has taken off into a world of pure economics, but we are left in mid-air. We see the physical world below, and it is solid and reassuring. We look up and do not know where we are going.

It is one of Keynes' major accomplishments to have taken the concept of consumption from that precarious position and landed it on safe ground—a theoretical ground to be sure, but safe nonetheless. Keynes clearly developed the concept of consumption in terms of sales: "total sales made during the period," he said.[52] We have landed. To make the concept totally clear, we need to generalize it a little further as follows. Consumption is expenditure of money. Consumption is spending. This is a clear-cut economic concept. We need go no further.

Beyond Lies a Slippery Road

Had Keynes also stopped here, he *might* have clarified his own and our minds on this issue—and if he had looked farther back in his and other people's thought, he might have clarified his own and our minds on many other issues. But Keynes could not exercise this degree of restraint. He was *"in a hurry,"* as he acknowledged (even) in 1931 in his *Essays in Persuasion*.[53] He went an additional step; and he muddled his own ideas and ours as well. Where did Keynes actually land? He landed on a slippery ground. When he got up, he found himself in possession of only half the concept of consumption: consumption had become expenditure on consumer goods. In his original definition, the attentive reader will recall, there was no such qualification. Consumption was expenditure, period. Gone from the concept is expenditure on capital goods— let alone expenditure on items which can be hoarded.

This outcome raises some intricate questions of scholarship that cannot be fully untangled here. It is arguable in fact whether Keynes obtained his definition of consumption as a conscious or an intuitive act; indeed, it is even arguable whether this writer is not "stretching the point" by implying that Keynes actually reached a definition of consumption by itself. On the assumption that the truth lies somewhere between these positions, let us confine our attention to substantive issues.

What is important to realize is that, no sooner had Keynes healed one split in the conception of consumption, he got it involved in another one.

The Existence of a Further Split

It is interesting to notice that the split that has traditionally plagued the concept of consumption has with Keynes shifted locus. The split inherent in the etymological origin of the word consumption between, as Webster says, "to buy" and "to take wholly or to destroy," has been shifted to involve a distinction between expenditure on consumer goods and expenditure on capital goods. It is this latter split which now needs to be healed, if we want to build a whole concept.

To achieve this aim, we have to ask: why this halving of the concept of consumption—a halving which has been fully accepted by all Keynesian and non-Keynesian writers? Finding an answer to this question implies retracing the mental steps taken by Keynes. The knowledge thus acquired will not only indicate the weak spots in his analysis; it will also indicate some of the lacunae we have to fill in order to be fully convinced of the validity of the "whole" concept of consumption which has been suggested above.

The key answer to the reason why the concept of consumption has been halved resides in the internal dynamics of Keynes' model. Once those terms are accepted as he presented them, there is no escape. Consumption must be defined as expenditure on consumer goods—otherwise it cannot be distinguished from the concept of investment; and the concept of investment, we shall remember, is there "equal" to saving.

Of the need to distinguish between investment and consumption once that model is adopted, there is no question. Keynes was fully aware of it. He stated: "Expenditure on consumption during any period must mean the value of goods sold to consumers during that period..."[54] But he was also aware of the complications arising from this obligatory decision—a decision, he continued, "which throws us back to the question of what is meant by a consumer-purchaser." The foundation of this "question," as it can be seen, is circular. Yet, even more "specious" than the establishment of this unnecessary vicious circle, is its suggested escape route. How did Keynes resolve the question?

He suggested that any arbitrary decision would do—but of course he substituted the qualification "arbitrary" with a less harsh word. Here is his solution, which he advanced so quickly that no opportunity to think is given to the reader. The sentences that are here separated from each other were written as a continuum. "Any reasonable definition of the line between consumer-purchaser and investor-purchaser," he said, "will serve us equally well, provided that it is consistently applied." The matter is left wholly to the discretionary judgment—of statisticians. The economist has abdicated.

An indirect, but quite strong, confirmation of the inadequate current state of affairs concerning the definition of consumption is obtained through a perusal of the *International Encyclopedia of the Social Sciences* (1968). The work does not even carry the heading "Consumption." These are some of the costs to be paid in order to preserve contemporary economic doctrine intact and still preserve a degree of internal logical consistency.

———•——

We have obtained a familiar set of conclusions. The economic discourse is mired in arbitrariness and contradictions as a consequence of lack of respect for the canons of formal logic. We have found another major building block of contemporary economic theory that does not respect the principle of identity. The difficulty presented by the current definition of consumption is that it includes too little. As evidence of internal cohesion, the reader might keep in mind that the definitions of both saving and investment that prevail in mainstream economics contain too much.

One spends money when one buys capital goods or goods to be hoarded; yet, these expenditures are not classified as consumption. Put in the language of formal logic, the problem with this definition is that consumption does not consistently mean spending. As stated earlier in relation to similar cases concerning the current definition of saving and investment, consumption in contemporary economic theory is not "reflexive." It is not identical to itself. Consumption is not an entity that consistently refers to the same objective reality throughout the discourse, namely, spending of money. Its meaning is arbitrarily cut off at spending of money on consumer goods. (In barter, the spending is done through the exchange of real wealth.) Consumption is not consumption throughout. In symbols, in mainstream economic theory $C \neq C$.

With the Flows model, there is no need for the interjection of anyone's "reasonable" decisions; there is no need for economists to shy away from their tasks. They cannot leave questions of economics so open. They have to resolve them—in a clear, non-arbitrary, non-contradictory fashion.

To achieve this aim, we need to introduce some further requirements in the discourse; and these requirements become clearer if we acquire a closer understanding of the primary functions of the purchase of both capital goods and consumer goods, and then we distinguish the latter from items that can be hoarded.

The Primary Function
of the Purchase of Capital Goods and Consumer Goods

With only a quantitative difference, the purchase of consumer goods causes the same primary economic effects as the purchase of capital goods. They both transfer financial resources (or, in a barter economy, other wealth) from the consumer to the producer. Indeed, since the production process involves a gradual growth in value, the purchase of either type of products also requires a compensation for this growth—i.e., an "extra," which generally is called profit.

Obviously, the growth in value is due to many factors: first of all, the transformation of natural resources into economic wealth; then, the passage of time—which, as seen immediately in agricultural processes, implies automatic growth; finally, all the other factors, such as the "conveniences" involved in any transformation operated by the production process whether it be in form, size, or simply location.

Now that we have observed the similarities in the purchase of a capital good and a consumer good, we can better understand the quantitative difference mentioned above. The purchase of a consumer product causes an outflow from the economic system of a value that is equivalent to the value of the items purchased. This loss is not immediately recognizable because it is fully replaced by an equivalent monetary value. (Monetary values are here considered as funds validated by the production process and temporarily held in store as a legal claim on real wealth.)

The purchase of a capital-asset, instead, does not only replace the value of the asset with monetary values—as the purchase of a consumer product does. It also increases the total value of the system, first, by a value that is equivalent to the monetary value of the asset itself and then by a value which is equivalent to the asset's own internal growth.

In brief, it can be said that while the purchase of a consumer product increases the value of the economic system only to the extent of the profit, the purchase of a capital-asset—in addition to the profit—causes an increase in the value of the system which is fully equivalent to its own (growing) value.

Perhaps these relationships are better observed through the attached diagram entitled "Flow of Values in the Economic Process." Since this work is confined to the statics of the economic process, these flows cannot be followed step by step. They can be seen only as an image frozen at one instant in time when the picture resembles that of a "strange attractor." If one wants to go a step further, one has to close the two halves of the doughnut and conceive of a shape not unlike that of a nuclear super-reactor, a cyclotron. In the reality of the economic life, in fact, it is hard to keep flows of monetary wealth as neatly separated from flows of real wealth as we are attempting to do in this study.

A Reminder of the Existence of Secondary Functions

Consumer goods can re-enter the economic system if they are sold as second-hand goods; some of them can even be pledged as security for the issuance of loans. The secondary economic functions performed by consumer goods end there. Beyond that point lies the area of personal enjoyment which those goods provide for their possessor. Thus we leave economics and enter the realms of psychology, sociology, politics, esthetics or morality.

The secondary functions of capital goods are exactly the same as those of consumer goods—and many more in addition. They offer both to their individual owner and to society as a whole the possibility of the renewal of present income levels and the growth of future income. These functions are extraordinarily important; but they cannot be explored in this volume. Here it is sufficient to emphasize that most capital goods enter the economic system via the same route as all other economic items: via exchange. They are

FLOW OF VALUES
IN
THE ECONOMIC PROCESS

Monetary Authority

Natural Resources

Exchange

Money	
Consumer Goods	
Productive Wealth (Capital — or Investment Assets)	
Nonproductive Wealth (items which can be hoarded)	

produced and they are sold. They are bought, in other words, by those who—either directly or indirectly, through hired managers—make use of them. And, who, in today's world, has no use for capital goods?

Rather than insisting on the secondary functions performed by the flow of consumer and capital goods, let us instead realize why it is essential to keep items that can be hoarded as a separate category of economic thought. This distinction is essential because, by themselves, items that can be hoarded are in limbo: they can either become consumer or capital goods.

An Important Distinction: The Role of Items That Can Be Hoarded

First, when items that can be hoarded are owned by their own producer, they might call not even for one exchange. The simplest case is that of the independent miner who hoards whatever he has "produced." Wealth is thus immediately subtracted from the economic system—and nothing replaces it. Nor does this wealth satisfy immediate needs.

Much more important, however, are the following characteristics. Items that can be hoarded are by definition nearly indestructible. Hence they are clearly differentiated from both consumer and capital goods. Knowing the average life expectancy of the latter products, the producer can plan on their reproduction. Thus they form a rather steady (and large) market. Items that can be hoarded, instead, create only a small and highly erratic market. One tends to buy such products only at particular stages of the business cycle.

Finally, items that can be hoarded are by definition scarce; their cost is high; and their resale frequency is totally unpredictable. Indeed, it is this last characteristic which makes them so potentially dangerous: they lie there—like felines in wait—ready to spring on the market at a moment's notice. It is these products that bring a high degree of irrationality to the behavior of the market. There is no link between the existence of goods hoarded and economic necessity, except perhaps via psychological thoroughfares.

Perhaps the economic role performed by the purchase of nonproductive wealth is put in sharper focus if contrasted with the purchase of consumer or capital goods. The differences consist mainly of this: (a) consumer and capital goods cannot easily be resold; (b) when resold, they are often sold at a loss—while items which can be hoarded are generally resold at considerable gain;

furthermore, (c) when consumer goods are resold, they are made available in a different market: the market in which money is by nature scarce and goods are plentiful, whereby their sale tends to function as a further depressant on prices. (Of course, conditions change in periods of severe deflation; the relative relationships, however, will not change considerably.)

We shall return to these points during the discussion on economic growth and inflation. At the moment, let us remain satisfied with the above general characteristics. Now that we have acquired a closer understanding of the primary effects which flow from the purchase of major categories of real wealth, it is more urgent to introduce some further requirements which enable the economist—more than other readers—to obtain a clear understanding of the suggested definition of consumption.

Some Further Requirements

The solution proposed here—in addition to defining consumption as, simply and wholly, spending—is that the question of the distinction between consumer and capital goods does not need to be raised at all. The concept of consumer-purchaser, or that of consumer goods, is extraneous to pure economic theory. It is a spurious concept. Indeed, since the attention of the economist today is not devoted to "the causes of the wealth of nations" but to the economic process itself, all three concepts—the concept of wealth, that of destruction of wealth, and that of consumer items—have to be considered spurious economic concepts.

The production of consumer goods is only one of the results of the economic process. There are many others. Once consumer goods have been sold, they no longer belong to the economic process. And as such they are of no interest to the economist—except as a secondary check upon one's reasoning and calculations. They serve a limited purpose if one wants to distinguish among various kinds of purchases—i.e., capital goods from goods of immediate consumption, and both from goods that can be hoarded. (Only the last distinction is necessary and meaningful; and the concept of consumer goods is especially useful if one wants to consider the total value of existing "wealth," whether or not it is of immediate interest to the economic process. Also to be kept in mind is the fact that consumer goods can reenter the market as second-hand goods). As far as "consumption" is concerned, purchases of consumer goods represent an expenditure just like all other expenditures: be they for capital goods—goods which produce other goods—or goods which can be hoarded. Once consumer goods are sold, and provided they are not resold as second-hand products, they are outside the professional purview of the economist.

For confirmation, let us look at the issue from another point of view, that of producers. They do not see any difference between consumer and capital goods—or between "consumer-purchasers" and "investor-purchasers." They look at other producers as potential consumers of their products. They scan the market and produce, not in accordance with the prevailing theoretical distinction, but in accordance with the availability of purchasing power that is ready to be spent. Producers sell to other producers as well—these become, in turn, the "final" consumers.

No. There is no logical validity in the prevailing distinction between consumer and capital goods. And there is no historical validity either. The first act of production of capital goods was not performed as an end in itself—as it might be today. The first "production" of the stick or stone, our first tools, was accomplished to obtain more consumer goods and, possibly, to obtain them with less effort. One was—and is—the logical and historical extension of the other.

But, someone might still object, are not consumer goods destroyed in the physical sense? Yes. Just like capital goods; the latter, too, are destroyed in the physical sense. It might only take longer. (There are in fact preserved in museums and in old homes "consumer goods" which were created centuries ago.) To repeat, there is no logical distinction there.

What interests the economist is the flow of funds generated by any purchase. Consumer goods generate (in quantity as well as quality) such a flow, toward the producer—as do capital goods or goods hoarded. It is this flow of funds that is of interest to the economist. Incidentally, one can clearly see why the concept of the physical destruction of wealth lies outside the interest of the economist. A sale, any sale, is an exchange of either money for goods or goods for money. In this process, there is no destruction of wealth. Both transactors get something in return. Indeed, they both get something extra in the exchange—i.e., a profit: otherwise there would have been no exchange. This is a result upon which Professor Friedman has consistently insisted. But it is not a new discovery, as it was known to Aristotle.

The miser might say: I have given away money and received goods that are destined to be destroyed in the physical sense—while money is not. The economist can only console such a person by reminding him or her that, as Keynes rephrased the old dictum pronounced by Adam Smith, "Consumption—to repeat the obvious—is the sole end and purpose of all economic activity."[55]

The extension advocated here of the concept of consumption to cover expenditure on consumer and capital goods—in addition to expenditure on items which can be hoarded—is, by contrast, logically as well as historically valid. Indeed, it even echoes the classical distinction between "productive" and "unproductive" consumption. Thus, together with much of what is contained in the Flows model, this extension recaptures a large part of the spirit that is contained in an old stream of economic thought. Those efforts cannot be thrown away—as is often done today—with impunity.

Finally, the extension of the concept of consumption to cover all expenditures is not only logically and historically correct; it is also modern. The consumer obtains a status equivalent to that of the producer: they are both "prime movers" of the economic system. Producers can manufacture as much as they want; it is the consumer who brings (or ought to be free to bring) the economic process to a close. Only then the cycle starts anew. Without the final act of the consumer, the production effort is sooner or later brought to a screeching halt.

A Look Backward

If it were necessary to search for the central distinguishing feature between mainstream economics and Concordian economics, we would find that for mainstream economics the prime movers of the economic system are savers and investors; while for Concordian economics the prime movers are producers and consumers.

A Warning

Cutting the nexus between saving and investment, Alan Reynolds points out, Concordian economics necessarily blurs the theoretical distinction between consumer goods and capital goods. Therefore, it is necessary to stress that the practical value of this distinction should never be taken for granted. No matter the theory, however, one can be sure that the forces of the market will never take it for granted.

A Look at the Work Ahead

At this point there might still be a gray area concerning the relationships between consumption and investment, and maybe even the relationships between expenditure on items that can be hoarded and expenditure on capital or consumer goods. These matters will be investigated in the more appropriate context of the discussions on economic growth, inflation, and poverty. To advance smoothly, these discussions will come after some undivided attention is given to the production process, the distribution process, and the consumption process.

A final word. By extending the concept of consumption to its full length, we have gone a step farther in our "sartorial movement." We are closer to the full turn from Keynes' model to the Flows model. What remains to be refurbished to make this model completely intelligible is the concept of income.

XV

The Concept of Income and
The Flows Model as a Whole

Quick Comparisons

	Concordian Economics	Mainstream Economics
Saving	Financial savings	100,000 possible definitions
Hoarding	Nonproductive wealth	Does not exist
Investment	Productive wealth	Identified through synonyms
Consumption	Spending	Spending on consumer goods
Income	Goods and services produced, distributed and sold	Goods and services produced and sold

INCOME IS THE VALUE OF GOODS and services produced over one year. This is true, but it is a partial view of the concept of income. This is a more complex concept than is revealed at first sight. The above definition, in simplified terms, is obtained through the observation of income from the viewpoint of production. As such it can be symbolized by the letter "P." There are other views, however.

Income can also be seen from the vantage point of consumption. It represents the yearly expenditure of money to purchase the goods and services produced over the same period of time. The two views ought not to be confused with each other. This view of income can be represented with the letter "E" or "C."

And then there is the observation of income from the point of view of distribution. This view yields knowledge on the distribution of yearly income among the major types of expenditure, namely, purchase of consumer goods as well as purchase of capital goods and services that are available for sale. This view of income can—and eventually will—be represented with the letter "D." Yet, to simplify the discussion and to emphasize that it is indeed income that we are observing, it is here symbolized with the letter "Y." (We shall see that the investigation of the concept of income observed from the perspective of distribution also leads to an understanding of how income is distributed among people.)

The three views amount to the same thing. These are not three separate items, but three views of the same entity. In symbols, they can be written in this fashion:

$$P = C = Y \text{ or } P = E = Y.$$

Finally, there is the relationship between income and wealth that also needs to be taken into consideration. By convention, income is the flow of wealth produced—or distributed or bought—over one year. But income can also be seen as the amount or the stock of wealth produced, distributed, or bought over the same length of time as carried over ever since time immemorial. (The same applies to the concepts of investment, hoarding, and consumption.) To emphasize this distinction, we have been examining two models of the economic system and not one: the Stocks model and the Flows model. However, since the economic reality is in constant movement, the notion of stocks serves more analytical than operational purposes. We can therefore set the notion of stocks aside. Confining our observation to the concept of income, we concentrate attention on the formulations given above: $P = C = Y$ or $P = E = Y$, formulations which are conceived in terms of flows over time or simply as activities.

This is a complete description of income. It is a fully blossomed concept. And, incidentally, it is a true equivalence. Each term is reflexive, symmetric, and transitive. So far we have expressed these characteristics in terms of logic; but this intellectual approach is well known to Christians and other religious persons. An equivalence relation allows one to observe the same entity from three points of view. The object is identical. And yet, each view is different. Each view gives us a better understanding of the subject we want to observe. All views are essential, but full knowledge is obtained only through a view of the totality of the issue.

The instrument for obtaining a view of the totality of the issue—in our case, the totality of the economic process—is the Flows model. However, it must be realized that we have not yet formally constructed this model. We have presented it in chapter 2 solely for clarity of exposition. In addition, we have already built its inner invisible structure: the real saving-investment system. Now that we have all the ingredients for its construction, we can finally attend to the task. (It would be repetitious to build the Stocks model; the two models are functionally different, but structurally identical.)

Model Building

Ever since Keynes presented his model of the economic system, many other models have been created for a variety of reasons. Some of them include hundreds of equations—or statements. Without even thinking of analyzing those models, let us simply add another specimen to the list. This is a basic model that will be elaborated upon in the following chapters through the English language, and minimally through the language of mathematics. This is a basic model that, as far as its appearance is concerned, is quite similar to Keynes' model. Apart from its form, however, the substance, the structure, the meaning, and the implications inherent in this model are totally different from those of Keynes' model.

Without further ado, let us proceed with the construction of this model. In a more appropriate context, we shall see that Keynes' model does not include a definite sense of perspective. Let us avoid this important pitfall. Let us build our model from the point of view of the consumer. If this is done, it will be seen that all other viewpoints are not excluded; they are, at once, made very definite.

Our starting point is the vision of the decisions to be taken by the consumer regarding the disposition of yearly income. At this stage, to achieve a greater degree of generality we will leave it indeterminate whether we are considering money income or real income. We will be specific later on. The first decision, obviously, is whether to spend or not to spend one's income. Were the economic system running smoothly, this decision would be made by everyone continuously and on a significant scale. As the system works today, this is still a decision taken by everyone; but for most people, in most cases, it is an empty decision. No matter the practical limits, if the proposition "to spend or not to spend now" is universally true, then the first equation of our model can be written as follows: Income = Hoarding + Spending—or, to use a more preferable terminology:

$$\text{Income} = \text{Hoarding} + \text{Consumption.} \qquad (1)$$

Hoarding, of course, can be a direct activity: one can directly hoard one's income whether it is in the form of money income or real wealth. But hoarding can also be an indirect or secondary activity: one can spend one's "real" or money income to purchase items which can be hoarded. The latter kind of expenditure certainly is a type of spending. Also, it is possible to conceive of the income not spent as a consumer item. Thus one could reduce the first equation to this form: Income = Spending. Yet, such a reduction would diminish, not enrich our understanding of the economic reality. It is better to leave the first equation as written above; besides, it expresses all possible forms of hoarding.

Once the decision is reached to spend part of one's income, the next fundamental decision is whether to spend it on consumer or on capital goods. This is a refinement that is not formally and explicitly included in our basic model, not only to keep it as simple as possible, but also because—as noted—this is not a necessary distinction. Were we to write it explicitly, we would extend the first equation to read: Income = Hoarding + Consumption of Consumer Goods + Consumption of Capital Goods. (Interestingly enough, this is as far as Keynes went in February 1937, when, still in search of "new lines of exposition," he wrote that income is divided "in some proportion or another between spending and saving." This is the first equation of our model. His, it is recalled, was Income = Consumption + Investment. But there is more. In the same article, he also said: "Incomes are created partly by entrepreneurs producing for investment and partly by their producing for consumption." Is this not our split of the concept of consumption into purchase of capital goods and consumer goods? This is no longer the Keynes of the *General Theory.)*

In a well-run economy, the decision to spend on consumer or capital goods also ought to be taken by everyone. Leaving practical limits aside, for those who do have the latter choice, what is an expenditure on capital goods? It clearly is an investment. This statement fully respects traditional terminology.

To see how traditional terminology coincides with the logic of the terminology developed here, it is to be remembered that consumer goods are not explicitly taken into consideration in the present model: once they are immediately consumed by the producer or they have been bought by the consumer, they are automatically and instantly excluded from the economic process. However, what replaces them is their equivalent in monetary values that pass from the buyer to the producer. Hence, this equivalent value clearly has to be classified as investment. It is in the hands of producers now.

(Less rigorously, traditional terminology could be made to coincide with the terminology adopted here through an enlargement of the definition of investment. The reasoning is as follows. Money not hoarded is actually spent. This activity is at present exclusively defined as "consumption." By changing the mental framework to which we are accustomed, we could also validly say that all money that is spent is actually "invested"—namely, it is entrusted to some other form of wealth; it is transformed into something else. This posture would then lead us to state: even an expenditure on consumer goods can be considered as an "investment" in the future, an "investment" in the well-being of the economy. This economic necessity becomes especially evident in times of stress, when people tend to reduce their expenses even for consumer goods—and, those who can, send their capital abroad.)

In any case, since consumer goods are out of the economic process and therefore are no longer taken into consideration, how can we formally express the concept of investment? Within the context of our basic model, investment can be nothing else but the difference between income and hoarding. Thus the second equation is:

$$\text{Investment} = \text{Income} - \text{Hoarding.} \qquad (2)$$

The reader can experiment with the possible relationships that might exist among the four basic concepts comprising our model. This formal check will confirm the validity of the proposition as written in (2) above. No more can be said on it in the present context.

Once the first and second equations are determined, the third emerges inescapably:

$$\text{Investment} = \text{Consumption.} \qquad (3)$$

Investment and consumption share a common formal definition. They are both defined as income minus hoarding. We shall see, however, that the relationship between these two entities is more than one of equality. It is a true equivalence.

To anticipate the gist of the future discussion, it might be well to stress that the validity of the distinction between investment and consumption is purely one of perspective through which the economic system is observed and, as such, it is extremely important. One is the point of view of the producer and the other is the point of view of the consumer. We shall certainly return to it. And to avoid possible confusion between the concept of investment as elaborated so far and the tradition developed after Keynes, in the balance of this work we will be using the term production more than investment—and we will never use the expression investment process. Rather, we shall use the expression production process. This word substitution will more directly connect us with discussions held since the dawn of economic analysis. For the time being, let us simply pay attention to the logical and historical subtleties involved in the distinction between investment and consumption.

Here is that gist. The very first act of production—i.e., reaching for the apple (?) on the tree—was nearly indistinguishable from an act of consumption. Today, in a money economy, this relationship should be even more evident: an act of production makes consumption possible; and consumption, in turn, creates anew the need for production. Indeed, in a money economy, with an act of consumption one does not only convey the message of a need for more production; one even transfers the financial resources that allow others to continue their productive activities and prosper. As pointed out above, the prime movers of the ecosystem are producers and consumers.

We have thus finished the construction of our basic model, the Flows model. Of course, the level of generality kept here does not help to clarify the issues; we need to observe each issue at close range in order to dispel doubts and possible gray areas.

The Flows Model: an Overall View

Before we proceed with the observation of the economic process that is obtained with the aid of the Flows model, let us observe the model itself as a whole. In this form we can now study it with our accumulated knowledge (if we do not, we "hoard" that knowledge):

$$Income = Hoarding + Consumption$$
$$Investment = Income - Hoarding$$
$$Investment = Consumption.$$

This model can be examined from many points of view. For the time being, let us acquire an overall view of the model with the help of the newly developed concept of income. In this model, income is described from the viewpoint of distribution. That is the meaning of the first equation: it wholly describes the distribution process, whose ultimate economic result is the distribution of income among capital goods, consumer goods, and goods which can be hoarded. But does the description of income from the point of view of production and from the point of view of consumption disappear from sight—as in Keynes' model?

Not at all. Income from the viewpoint of production is described in the second equation; and income from the point of view of consumption is described in the third equation. This, however, is only a descriptive or logical analysis of that model. We have to wait for its economic description, a more detailed description, before we can fully ascertain whether the second equation describes the entirety of the production process (whose ultimate result is the production of income). Equally, we have to wait for that description to realize that the third equation completely describes the consumption process—whose ultimate result is the exchange of goods and services between producers and consumers.

Some General Characteristics of the Model

Surely, the Flows model has great internal consistency, and it also has the following major characteristics. It is not simplistic. It is homogeneous. It is technically impeccable (if one may say so). It has full external consistency as well.

The model is not simplistic. It describes every aspect of the economic process; it describes the totality of the economic reality. Nothing is left out. Starting from the terms of the Flows model, we can begin to analyze the entire economic reality, and we shall never have to shut our eyes to any of its aspects or to observe them through the distorting lenses of dogmas and verbal contradictions. The entire analysis is of direct and immediate comprehension.

The model is homogeneous. It is composed of four concepts. Each entity has its own unmistakable identity—a meaning, that is, which is neither derived from nor can be confused with that of any other entity. Hoarding is all nonproductive wealth. Investment is all productive wealth. Consumption is all spending. Income is the sum of goods and services that during a year are either produced or distributed or consumed.

More accurately, our four concepts describe activities that revolve around the production, distribution, and consumption of productive as well as nonproductive wealth. From a static model, we have passed to a dynamic one. And yet, for analytical purposes, we will continue to hold steady the moving reality and pretend that it can indeed be frozen at one instant in time.

The model is technically impeccable. It makes not only economic and mathematical sense; it also makes logical sense. Thus it has full external consistency.

A Shortcoming of the Model

We shall not rest on these laurels. At a more opportune time, we shall be able to apply quite stringent tests in order to fully verify the existence of this external logical consistency—which at this moment is more claimed than demonstrated.

The model, however, has one major shortcoming. Whether in its static formulation (the Stocks model) or in its dynamic formulation (the Flows model), it still does not describe the economic process as a mixture of real goods, money, and ownership rights as it is in reality. This shortcoming will be overcome in chapter 23. There we shall formally interject money into the model, and we shall see how this operation leads to three closely interlocked formulations of the same model. It is these three formulations that, together, will describe the economic process in movement.

Since this work is devoted to the study of the statics and not the dynamics of the economic process, we cannot provide any further analysis of the model at this time. As it stands, the Flows model is a satisfactory tool. It will help us understand the economic process to the extent that is feasible in a single work. Indeed, using the model in this fashion, we shall also learn to better understand the model itself.

Let us proceed with this assignment then: the description of the statics of the economic process. This is the ultimate task of the present work. And since—formally—this is a new and separate task, let us proceed under the aegis of a new and separate heading.

PART III

Analysis of the Economic Process

THE THEORETICAL UNDERPINNINGS of this work have all been shaped and fastened. Hence, more than expounding a new theory of economics, this part presents an organized description of economic facts. It clarifies the structure that has already been built, and it fills a few interstices left open so far.

The intellectual tool that will help us achieve this goal is the Flows model.

The focus is the observation of the various types of economic activities.

XVI

The Economic Process as a Whole

Only when the entire production is sold
to the consumer is the economic process
completed; and the cycle can start anew.

———

KEYNES' MODEL OF THE ECONOMIC system looks at the economic process as if it were looking at a coin from the side of the rim (or, technically, the point of view of the balance sheet). In other words, normally, that model permits but one view of the economic process: vertically, from outside in or from the top down. This is not to say that with extremely piercing eyes, or with the help of modern scanning machines, one cannot see everything in it—the whole coin. The majority of observers, however, lack this extraordinary capacity. As a result, the model gives free rein to the imagination to determine the size and the shape of both the face of the coin (production) and its reverse (consumption), and to determine the relationship that must exist between those two sides (distribution). To wit, that model permits but one view of the economic process: from outside in or from the top down.

Worse. The observer who ventures to look at any one of those three aspects composing the economic system is under no compulsion to examine the remaining aspects. Thus is specialization born in economics: some economists learn—in total isolation—all about the production function; and others learn all about the demand function. Few economists today study the distribution (function)—indeed, the term does not even exist. As a consequence, experts no longer agree with one another on fundamentals.

Furthermore, the vision of the economic system over time can only be obtained through a succession of still snapshots: the national product at one time is in a certain relationship with the national product at another time; but the opinion as to how the system moved from one stage to another can be as varied as the understanding of each economist—at each moment in his or her personal growth. (If in doubt on the validity of these statements, ask, for instance, two economists: what is the effect of a tax cut?)

The Flows model eliminates all these technical shortcomings. It illustrates the economic process in its entirety. The model makes clear that if one observes just one of its component elements, one has not yet observed the economic process. By the same token, it leads to the observation of those elements one at a time: the production process; the distribution process; the consumption process.

The vision of the economic system from the viewpoint of the national product (i.e., "the rim") is still allowed. But it becomes clear that this is a static view of the economic reality. Indeed, the Flows model makes clear that the national product is but one of the results of the dynamics of these three component processes. Put in different terms, Keynes' model *is* static; the Flows model, instead, is inherently dynamic. And we are holding the reins of our observation at only one instant in time. Thus we are forcing the Flows model to function as a static tool of analysis.

More. The Flows model compels one to observe the relationships that must exist among the production, distribution, and consumption processes. In brief, they must be equivalent to each other—or, as previously written, P = C = Y; they must be "in equilibrium" in order for the entire economic process to function in a smooth fashion. Production must be in equilibrium with distribution, and distribution with consumption. The attached diagram entitled "The Economic Process" might help the reader to understand these relationships at a glance.

There are many issues. Some of them will be treated as we proceed; others will have to be reserved for later studies. Let us touch upon two of them at this point. First, in the context of dynamic and organic economics, the notion of equilibrium implies a moving, dynamic and, indeed, organic entity. Second, the diagram is—as it ought to be—capable of being immediately and intuitively understood. However, some technical notes have been appended to clarify that it is not an arbitrary entity. Its origin does lie in economics, logic, and geometry. In any case, the graph is an entirely new form of representation of the economic reality. Even though we shall become more and more familiar with it as we proceed, it ought to be sufficient to point out that it can be read as follows.

Only when the entire production is sold to the consumer—be the consumer, in turn, a consumer of capital goods or of finished products—only then is the economic process completed; and the cycle can start anew. (In reality, as Mitchell S. Lurio points out, the process is continuous.) For the process to be partially or, concep-

The Economic Process

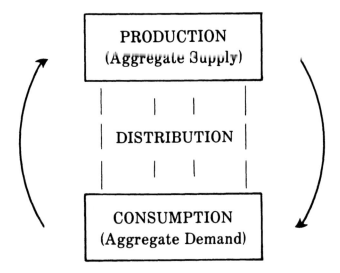

Notes:

- Rotating the two rectangles, at ever increasing speed, about the geometric center of the diagram one obtains a circle. And what is a circle, if not the visual image of a sphere?

- This graph is a development of Keynes' formulation of the Principle of Effective Demand: namely, all what happens at the *point* of intersection between the aggregate supply and demand functions. The link is briefly put in these terms. What is a point, if not the smallest sphere? (Or, conversely, what is a sphere if not a big point?) Also, mathematical functions are represented by a *line* – and what is a rectangle, if not an enlarged line?

tually, totally completed, the consumer must somehow possess the means—in money, or wealth in general—to acquire that production. The distribution of wealth, in other words, must somehow have occurred before the transaction can take place. (In rare cases today—just as in primitive economies—the three phenomena occur simultaneously: the economic operator produces wealth, has ownership rights to it, and sells it to himself. After that, he can do as he wishes. He or she can destroy it physically, preserve it in a museum or derive personal and direct enjoyment from it. The destiny of that wealth is of no interest to the economist, as an economist.)

These, then, are the three major components of the economic process: production, distribution, and consumption. They are in themselves complex elements. As a first approximation, to make them more concrete it might be helpful to see them in this simplified light: production as goods and services; consumption (spending) as money; and distribution as a person's bundle of ownership rights over wealth. It is these three diverse elements that ultimately make up the economic process. They will have to be observed one by one.

All this is obvious. And yet, strange as it may seem to the non-economist, today this is a novel vision of the economic process. Before proceeding further, then, let us try to allay possible fears in the economist. First, this is a simplified vision of the issues. Second, consumption is taken to mean "monetized wealth"—wealth that, in a modern understanding of Say's thought, facilitates the transfer (or purchase) of wealth. Third, with the expression "distribution has to be seen as a person's bundle of ownership rights over wealth," the ultimate economic effect of the distribution process is not denied here: largely through prices, "distribution" is the agent for the allocation of resources in the production and consumption process. There are issues, however, which precede economics. These are issues of justice. They must be taken into account by the economist. They cannot be glossed over. In Concordian economics they are explicitly taken into account via the transmission belt of economic rights and responsibilities, the determinants of property rights.

Finally, let us emphasize that this is not a novel vision of the issues at all. It is largely Adam Smith's vision. It is therefore necessary to recall that Adam Smith closed the last edition of his *Theory of Moral Sentiments* (1790) regretting that he would not be able to carry forward the program of research he had outlined for himself at the end of the first edition of that work (1759). And what was that program of research? To use our terms, he proposed to study the legal and institutional aspects of the economic process. The fact that Adam Smith did not translate his vision into print is no indication that the task cannot or should not be performed. Above all, that is no excuse for remaining under the spell of Ricardo's magic; that is no excuse for not trying. That is work which still remains to be done. Indeed, the situation is at once more simple and more complex than it appears at first sight. Much of this work has already been carried out by a peculiarly American school of economic thought: Institutionalism, a school represented by many outstanding thinkers from Veblen to Gruchy to Galbraith and, through Ronald Coase (a singular Nobel laureate in economics), from R. C. O. Matthews to Oliver E. Williamson. What remains to be done is to integrate the findings of this school of thought with those of mainstream economics.

In this book we shall prepare the groundwork for this integration. For the moment, let us try to preserve a unified vision of the economic process in its entirety a little longer. How does one, technically, reach this understanding?

A Technical—and Historical—View of the Economic Process

The starting point is a brief discussion of what Keynes called the principle of effective demand. The principle of effective (or effectual) demand is the product of a long and noble tradition in economic analysis. It was well known to Sir James Steuart, a contemporary of Adam Smith.[56] Steuart evidently was not able to put that concept across; it was quashed by Adam Smith,[57] even though Smith himself was compelled to acknowledge that "Consumption is the sole end and purpose of all production . . ." (Consumption, as we shall see, is a major element of the principle of effective demand.)

Other efforts to revive that principle were subsequently made, notably by Malthus and Keynes himself,[58] but to no avail. The principle of effective demand, when mentioned at all, is still symptomatically translated as the theory of effective demand. The two notions, as we shall shortly see, have very little in common with each other.

The tradition surrounding the principle of effective demand is not only long and noble; it even covers some of the most controversial issues in the history of economic analysis. Indeed, the issues are so controversial that they are consistently hidden from sight: they are swept under the classical rug. If we list the major protagonists of the discussion over time, and add all relevant names, we are able to find the root cause of the official reticence even to acknowledge the existence of the controversy.

In code, as it were, the tradition can be summarized in this fashion: Smith vs. Steuart; Ricardo vs. Malthus; Pigou *(et al.)* vs. Keynes.

So far so good. But how to explain the long gap in time between Malthus and Keynes? The fact is that the gap was filled. But it was filled with such an assault on the foundations of capitalism that it has created a schism and a political tradition of its own. The person who filled that gap—as Keynes openly admitted—is Karl Marx, of course. And all major economists of the second half of the last century, from J. S. Mill to Marshall or Walras, secretly labored very hard to undo what Marx did—with little success, it must be added. These are issues that are either confronted directly or they do fester below the surface.

In truth, the various issues can be more comfortably and openly treated now because a brilliant lawyer-economist, Louis 0. Kelso, has finally "exorcised the demon." He has brought Marx back into the fold of the central economic tradition through a major work he published with Mortimer Adler, *The Capitalist Manifesto* (1958), and a short article entitled "Karl Marx: The Almost Capitalist." [59] These titles are so descriptive that they require only brief elaboration. Kelso's thesis is that Marx's analysis led him to propose an appealing but wrong solution for the ills of the modern world: the abolition of private property in the means of production, namely, abolition of private property over capital-assets. For Kelso, instead, the cure for the ills of capitalism is widespread capital ownership: Universal Capitalism, as he calls it. Is it necessary to recall the parallel diagnosis that the proper solution for the ills of democracy is more democracy?

With Marx brought back into the fold of humanistic economics—a fold in which the young Marx would have felt quite comfortable—we can not only bring the controversy up to date by mentioning the names of the major protagonists involved in the last dialogue or, better, lack of it: Samuelson *(et al.)* vs. Kelso. We can also rationally approach some of the basic theoretical issues that exist in the principle of effective demand.

The Theoretical Content of the Principle of Effective Demand

Let us start the analysis from ground zero. The principle of effective demand is not yet part of the common economic knowledge.

Why? To answer this question we have to see how Keynes treated that concept. The issue deserves some careful attention, because Keynes categorically stated that the principle "is the substance of the General Theory."[60]

We have it on the authority of Professor Samuelson that the chapter on the principle of effective demand is "difficult";[61] and this difficulty has so affected the understanding of the *General Theory* that the work as a whole has nearly unanimously been classified as "obscure." There are in fact a number of good reasons for this classification. Let us point out the major one here. The chapter on the principle of effective demand has been read in the light of Keynes' model of the economy—and it has been overlooked that the model barely occupies half a page in that entire book. Indeed, it cannot be emphasized enough that the *General Theory* was not written in the light of that model. The two, in fact, are completely different entities. They do not match. They are irreconcilable. (This is the central reason why, since one must choose between the two, it has been suggested in this work that the model be discarded.)

Keynes specifically stated that " . . . the point of the aggregate demand function, where it is intersected by the aggregate supply function, will be called *the effective demand.*" [62] The issue, barring all technical complications, can be reduced to this blunt question: aggregate demand—and aggregate supply—of what? If one studies that chapter using the interpretive lenses of the original model, the answer is inescapable: aggregate supply of *saving* and aggregate demand for *investment*. In that model the conclusion is, in fact, reached that S = I. And, since a relationship of equality must respect the rules of equivalence—unconsciously, but unavoidably—one ends up writing the principle of effective demand in this form: S = I = PED, where PED stands for principle of effective demand. (The effective demand, in fact, for Keynes is neither the undefined aggregate demand, nor the undefined aggregate supply; but a third element: the point where the two meet.)

Incidentally, on this basis alone, it should be evident why the theory of effective demand, namely, the theory which is concerned with the aggregate demand function, ought not to be confused with the principle of effective demand: aggregate demand is only one of the three elements composing that principle. Furthermore, in this principle we have found the third term, PED, which implicitly transforms the relation of equality between saving and investment into an equivalence relation. Making this hidden assumption explicit, however, does not cure the deficiencies of that proposi-

tion. On the contrary, it simply reveals the deepest problem existing within its deepest underpinnings. If one proceeds on this
assumption, in fact, one goes nowhere. At the end of this line of
inquiry there is nothing new. There is no additional knowledge to
be gathered on that principle. One then returns to that chapter of
the *General Theory* in which the principle of effective demand is
barely enunciated, and the conclusion is reached that the chapter
is not only difficult, but even obscure.

Yet the chapter's intent is to make us understand in a few bold
strokes "the substance of the General Theory." The conclusion
becomes inescapable: The *General Theory* itself is obscure. This
verdict has been passed so many times, both officially and unoffi-
cially, that documentation is unnecessary. The *General Theory* has
become a "classic"—one of those texts that is frequently referred
to, but rarely studied from cover to cover. After all, it is assumed
to have been fully understood and its value fully extracted. Why
"waste time" on it any longer? Leaving these issues of scholarship
aside, what must be insisted upon is the direct relationship
between the "obscurity" of the principle of effective demand and
the "obscurity" of the *General Theory*. The linkage was established by Keynes himself: one is the substance of the other.

In this work we are no longer bound by the old model. We have
discarded it. And we have developed a new model in which a completely different conclusion is reached—i.e., Investment =
Consumption (I = C). Let us use this model to understand what
Keynes was attempting to say. The question "aggregate demand
and aggregate supply of what" can now be answered in this fashion: aggregate supply of all goods and services produced; aggregate
demand (in a money economy) for all money available—money
that must have already been somehow distributed. The entire issue
is clear. When the available supply of money—whether in the
aggregate or in individual units—is ready to be exchanged, and it
is indeed exchanged for the available supply of goods and services, only then have we an effective demand: a demand which is concrete; a demand which is totally realized. (The laws of supply and
demand are, after all, an integral part of economic analysis.) Thus
the principle of effective demand can now be written:

$$I = C = PED \text{ or better, } I \leftrightarrow C \leftrightarrow PED.$$

To be more precise, we ought to say that the demand for "I"
must be in equilibrium with the supply of "I" (read, goods and
services); and the demand for "C" must be in equilibrium with the

supply of "C" (read, money). When these four functions are in
equilibrium with each other, only then do we have a smooth-run-
ning economic system. This is a technical clarification that can be
safely neglected in the present context and is to be taken up again
in a subsequent chapter. Let us now return to our central line of
reasoning. We have left it at the conclusion that I = C = PED.

The language is still cumbersome. The expression "principle of
effective demand" can be confusing. It is better to replace it with
the expression "economic process." Therefore, we can simply say
that when the entire production is exchanged or sold—i.e., consumed—only then is the economic process completed and the cycle
can start anew.

In symbols, then, we ought to write:

$$I = C = EP,$$

where EP stands for economic process. Even better, however, is to
write

$$I = C = D \text{ or better, } I \leftrightarrow C \leftrightarrow D,$$

where D stands for distribution. Thus we have a concrete equivalence; and, what is more important, we make explicit what is
implicit in that process: the phenomenon of distribution of income.
[Incidentally, remembering that we have written "income" as P =
C = Y, we realize that we have now come full circle: investment (I)
and production (P) are identities, just as distribution (D) and
income that is distributed (Y) are identities. The Flows model represents the total economic reality, logically and conclusively.]

Perhaps we gain in clarity if we rewrite the first and the third
equations of our model in the form in which they have finally been
developed. Thus we can write:

$$(P = C = Y) = (I = C = D).$$

And since an equality must be an equivalence, we can also write:

$$(P = C = Y) = (I = C = D) = EP.$$

The entire economic process can now be simply expressed thus-
ly: production is equivalent to consumption and both are equivalent to distribution. Since each one of these three elements is a
complex entity in itself, they are better called respectively: produc-

tion process, distribution process, and consumption process. As they are here listed, they represent a logical and temporal progression. For ease of exposition, however, we shall observe them in a different sequence: the production process first, the consumption process second, and the distribution process third.

Before we go on to analyze these three processes, which are by themselves three aspects of the same economic process, we need to go back in history for a while. Let us, in the next chapter, compare and countercheck our reasoning with how economic analysis has traditionally described this process. This task is, after all, the entire task of economic analysis. Indeed, even before that, it is better to tackle a number of general questions that will help us fuse together the analysis of the particulars. In other terms, we will bring one step forward the theoretical analysis performed by Professor Nicholas Georgescu-Roegen in his *The Entropy Law and the Economic Process* (1971).

The Definition, Representation, and Study of a Process

The word "process" in this work is not meant to describe a linear series of actions heading to a certain end—with the "line" perhaps as wide as necessary to accommodate the "flow" of goods and services. Rather, the word is taken to express a feedback mechanism that is the result of (at least) two forces acting on each other and producing a material or immaterial entity. The forces, which can vary from a minimum of two to infinity, meet in a variety of ways thus creating either a harmonious interplay or a clashing explosion: as we have seen, the economic process is the result of at least the forces of production, distribution, and consumption. The size, the shape, and the movement of the "entity" is determined by the way in which those forces combine to form the process.

In geometry this entity can be represented, not by a line, but by a sphere or any other solid: this, incidentally, as analyzed in chapter 2, is the proper way to visualize the given diagram entitled "The Economic Process." One simply needs to rotate the diagram at ever-increasing speed about its geometric center. (The line is the *trace*, or the appearance, left by the movement of the solid.) In mathematics a process is described, not through a single equation, but through a system—or systems—of equations. The best computer models generally describe processes.

A process is not simply change. A process is the change of an entity. A process is this entity in movement. The entity can be as "simple" as a stone or as "complex" as a planet or even the entire universe. To comprehend the stone, sooner or later, we follow three approaches: we establish an equivalence relation. First, we study, i.e., we contemplate the stone by itself by breaking down its various qualities: shape, size, color, etc. Then we go inside the stone and analyze its physico-chemical properties. Finally, we look outside the stone to discover its geological formation, its relationship with other elements, with the total composition of the earth, etc. Through these mental operations we discover the continuity that exists from one entity to the other, and this continuity leads us to comprehend the Whole. (At the suggestion of Louis J. Ronsivalli, it is good to specify that the order of observation can vary from the one given here.)

In essence, we establish "natural" boundaries—an operation that allows us to concentrate our attention on a limited area of the reality, i.e., one process at a time. This concentration allows us to look inside, within those boundaries, undisturbed by all that goes on outside those boundaries. Thus we discover that there are processes going on within each process: that each process is the result of at least two forces, namely, an infinite regress or an infinite progress.

Specifically, having briefly observed the economic process as a whole, or better, by itself, we can shortly proceed to look inside it. But we shall not follow the infinite regress; our analysis will have to be rather shallow. Nor will we observe the outside of the process: that exercise would gradually lead us to the study of the legal, political, esthetic, and moral aspects of society as a whole. It is only then that we would really bring the economic process within our sphere of comprehension. We shall have to be much less ambitious than that.

The Question of Measurement and Prediction in Economics

Unlike solids of physics, the "solids" of economics have two properties: (a) they can *abruptly* grow or shrink in size; (b) their movement in space-time can abruptly accelerate or decelerate. These two properties explain the impossibility of precise measurements and prediction in economics. Stated differently, there are forces in economics that cannot be measured in advance of their occurrence: ultimately, those forces spring from the free will of concrete human beings.

After the magisterial work done by Professor Georgescu-Roegen, there is very little to add on this point. Following his lead, what needs to be specified is that the impossibility of precise measurements does not make economics any less of a science. And not only because measurements are simply an aid to any science, but also because we can measure ex post the effect of those imponderable actions. As stated earlier, a solid leaves a trace. This trace can be measured in economics—and, unlike physics, the trace is "solid" enough. It is the economic system as it has evolved up to this moment.

Learning as much as we can about the past, we can then begin to make predictions about the future. But these predictions are exactly that: they are predictions; they are educated guesses. They have no certainty. Any degree of probability attached to them can be one hundred percent wrong. Forecasts that state otherwise are sheer salesmanship. The history of too many crucial forecasts has proved this much.

What then is the usefulness of forecasts? In the impossibility of obtaining any certainty about the future, under normal circumstances they are useful as a broad guide to action. Even more than that, they are useful in narrowing down the number of alternative courses of action. But one has to be prepared to take into account that the path chosen with the assistance of forecasts can be one hundred percent wrong.

XVII

Simplistic Descriptions of the Economic Process

*What Adam Smith described is the actual
practice followed in the world of finance.*

———·———

A SUPERFICIAL READING of the history of economic analysis leaves
the mistaken impression that there are nearly as many descriptions of the economic process as there are writers of economics.
This impression could not be further removed from the truth.
Stripped of all technicalities and shifts in emphasis, which make
them appear more numerous than they actually are, in the relatively long history of economic analysis there has been only one
coherent description of the economic process—and, stretching
the point, it is possible to obtain two major descriptions of this
phenomenon. One is the interpretation given by Adam Smith
and the other is the interpretation given by John Maynard
Keynes.

A Nagging Question: What About Marx?

Many are ready to state that Marx was perhaps the only economist who ever described the economic process as a process and in
its entirety. From their point of view, they are right. However, what
is also true is that Marx has had no direct influence on the development of rational economics. (His indirect influence is a completely different story.) The system of logic he used, dialectic logic,
made his intellectual world nearly impenetrable to economists who
used rational logic as their supporting system of thought. What
crossed such barriers was only a flurry of words, which relate to
issues of logic and political economy more than to issues of economic theory.

Adam Smith's Interpretation of the Economic Process

Adam Smith's interpretation is nothing more than a magnification of his conception of saving. This is the penultimate reason why that conception is so complex and has been so resilient. (As we proceed, we shall discover the ultimate reason for its resiliency.) Let us observe that conception now from this overall point of view. Adam Smith stated: "Whatever a person saves from his revenue he adds to his capital, and either employs it himself in maintaining an additional number of productive hands, or enables some other person to do so, by lending it to him for an interest, that is, for a share of the profits."[63] And, without letting his reader (or even himself) think of all the complexities which exist in between, he continued: "As the capital of an individual can be increased only by what he saves from his annual revenue or his annual gains, so the capital of a society, which is the same with that of all the individuals who compose it, can be increased only in the same manner."

Just as Adam Smith's conception of saving could not be considered complete without including in it his view of consumption, so it is with his understanding of the total economic process. Let us read his view of consumption, then, in a somewhat extended fashion: "Consumption is the sole end and purpose of all production; and the interest of the producer ought to be attended to, only so far as it may be necessary for promoting that of the consumer. The maxim is so perfectly self-evident, that it would be absurd to attempt to prove it. But in the mercantile system, the interest of the consumer is almost constantly sacrificed to that of the producer; and it seems to consider production, and not consumption, as the ultimate end and object of all industry and commerce."[64]

The temptation to issue facile comments shall have to be suppressed. The reader, however, is invited—to say the least—to link this quotation with the history of the principle of effective demand and with the relationship between Adam Smith and Sir James Steuart. Just like "rational" mules, we have to wear our blinders and move on.

The above quotations give, in a nutshell, a description of the entire economic process as understood by Smith. Through "parsimony" or some other psycho-sociological characteristic, a person does not spend all of his income to satisfy immediate needs of consumption. He rather saves part of it. And what he saves is immediately added to his capital—whether directly or indirectly by lending it to others for a share of the profit. There is no need here to emphasize how much Adam Smith simplified the issues—even in the field of production on which he focused his attention, let alone the fields of consumption and distribution to which he simply paid lip service. To prove the validity of this assertion, a brief analysis of a few key steps in Smith's reasoning should suffice.

The Simplicism of Adam Smith's Interpretation

For instance, not every one is able to save. More importantly, not all savings lend themselves as immediate additions to one's capital. If income is seen in "real" terms, it becomes apparent that certain types of income (or production) are so perishable that they cannot ever be "saved." But even if income is seen in monetary terms, not all savings can be "added" to one's capital. After Keynes' analysis, it ought to be apparent that in certain situations the more one saves the less one adds to one's capital: during inflationary periods, monetary funds—no matter how held—tend to lose value. The value of money depreciates so fast that one finds himself less rich the more one tries to save. And, because of the upheavals created by inflation in the world of production, no one else wants to employ those funds either. (The same happens in periods of deflation, in which the loss might derive from lack of income.)

This set of simplifications in Adam Smith's thought is directly due to another momentous set of simplifications that result from his overlooking all the pitfalls to be overcome before one can pass from the description of the economy of the individual to that of the nation. Indeed, the central reason for the near-universal acclaim which is—and must be—bestowed upon Keynes is that he filled, as he said, a sizable number of "gaps" in our knowledge in this area.[65] It is Keynes' filling of these gaps that gives us today a better understanding of the complexities involved in the transition from the individual to the national economy. It is this understanding that marks the difference and dates Adam Smith's thought.

To simply touch the surface of the issues, it can be said with Keynes: "Though an individual whose transactions are small in relation to the market can safely neglect the fact that demand is not a one-sided transaction, it makes nonsense to neglect it when we come to aggregate demand. This is the *vital difference* between the theory of the economic behavior of the aggregate and the theory of the economic behavior of the individual unit, in which we assume that changes in the individual's own demand do not affect his income."[66]

As seen above, the more one saves in an inflationary or severe deflationary period; the more one exercises his right to a "negative" demand, the more one reduces the total size of the economic system. The reverse happens in cases of "positive" demand, i.e., consumption. One's own demand, however small, is bound to have a positive effect on the economy as a whole. Then everybody prospers. (No attempt, of course, is made here to analyze the details of each combination and permutation involved in these oversimplified "cases.")

These are some of the "vital" complexities that Adam Smith, and so many other economists after him, overlooked—and some still insist on overlooking. But this is not the central point. The central point is that, if the economy were always to run smoothly, one could add one's savings to one's capital. And for what reason? Evidently, to increase one's future consumption level. Remember, for Smith, "Consumption is the sole end and purpose of all production."

This is the central point, then: Adam Smith's conception of saving represents a first approximate description of the economic process as a process. In fact, the person who—after saving part of his income—has a larger capital now, will increase his future income. But he or she will not spend all that income. Some of it will be saved. And it will be added to capital—which will further increase future income. And on, and on. The process is organically, although approximately and simplistically, described in its entirety—or nearly in its entirety.

Reasons for the Resiliency of Adam Smith's Description

Now that Adam Smith's description of the economic process is displayed as fully as possible, we can easily discover the ultimate reason for its extraordinary resiliency. Indeed, now we can discover why no school of thought in economics has ever been able to stay for long out of the shadow of Adam Smith's thought. What Smith described is the actual practice followed in the world of finance. A person must already have some capital—he or she must have "saved" some income—before becoming eligible to borrow money that, with wisdom, will be invested; and through expertise, cunning, and luck, it can increase one's future income.

Some Broad Considerations

In this theoretical as well as practical system, someone might ask: what happens to the person who earns so little income that he can never satisfy his consumption needs—let alone save some of that income? The century of Spencer developed a clear-cut answer to this question: the Devil take the hindmost. The phrase has disappeared from our daily vocabulary; but the practice followed by financiers that gave rise to that statement still persists.

Let us remove our blinders for a while and try to observe the situation in *tutto tondo*. It would be easy to blame financiers for this situation; but the criticism would neglect the reality. Financiers are not paid to think. They are not paid to manifest their "social conscience." In the reality of the world, the only reality that must here be respected, financiers are paid to reduce the risk for their investors and to increase their income. The practice of requiring an "equity position" before a commercial loan is extended or the "down-payment" before a mortgage for the purchase of a home is issued—i.e., some of the tangible proofs of the existence of previous savings—actually reduces the risk in lending money. The loan is "secured" and, if worse comes to worst, at least a part of it can be recovered. Financiers are paid to perform tasks whose procedures have been developed through centuries of experience, and they—on the whole—perform those tasks admirably. To say the least, they perform their tasks not less well than lawyers and doctors—or even priests, rabbis, and ministers.

It is the economist who instead, perhaps first and foremost, is paid by society to think. It is the economist whom society is begging to develop a "social conscience" for everyone—a social conscience that makes economic and financial, no less than political, sense. When the economist fails to think and to design practices which—taking into full account the financial needs of society—reconcile the social, the ethical, and indeed the economic needs of society, that economist fails miserably in the performance of the tasks of his freely chosen profession.

Not that such economists have never existed or indeed do not exist today. Now and then one finds such an "ideal" economist. Adam Smith was one of them. Alfred Marshall was another. Keynes, to remain at a safe distance from the contemporary and therefore necessarily biased scene, was still another. And that is the only reason why they—and so many others—have earned the admiration of nearly every other economist first, and the admiration of so many laymen thereafter.

And yet, were one to leave these broad considerations at that, one would leave them on a cerebral and complacent note. The reality of the world is considerably different from the reality of the intellect. Economic practices are still dismal; there is still a dismal lack of understanding of basic economic principles abroad. And the result is unavoidable. Economics still wears the stamp of Carlyle's indictment: economics is still largely considered the "dismal science."

Even though one might give the impression of dancing the minuet, one step forward and two steps back, it has to be stressed that this characterization of economics is only partially accurate. What is discredited today, it must be realized, is not economic theory per se—which in many quarters is being studied harder today than ever before, and whose magnificent structure is being appreciated now perhaps more than ever in history. It is our prevailing economic policies that are almost fully discredited. But then it must be remembered that, even though they have largely been based on his theories, Keynes himself had very little to do with the development of such policies. As he said in the opening paragraph of his preface to the *General Theory,* "This book is chiefly addressed to my fellow economists. I hope that it will be intelligible to others. But its main purpose is to deal with difficult questions of theory, and only in the second place with the application of this theory to practice."

And what were these "difficult questions of theory"? If we want to catch their essence, we have to realize that they were all partial attempts to outline Keynes' own description of the economic process. Let us observe this issue at closer range. Let us put our blinders back on again.

Keynes' Partial Descriptions of the Economic Process

Let us recall those difficult questions of theory. Such questions are numerous. A number of them have been examined, however briefly, in these chapters. Others will be observed momentarily. But—to remain exclusively within the area of fundamentals—they can all be reduced to a series of attempts made by Keynes to break away from "old" ideas that, he concluded in that same preface, "ramify. . . into every corner of our minds." As preeminent among such attempts one must mention his attacks against Say's Law (which is an elegant and tightly construed reformulation of Adam Smith's understanding of the economic process), his formulation of the principle of effective demand, and the presentation of his brand-new model of the economic system.

All these, and many other similar attempts, judged individually, were not entirely successful. Many of his ideas were disregarded from the very beginning; others, for good reasons that cannot be analyzed here, were subjected to a surreptitious "counter-revolution"; and still others were so adapted to other needs that nothing of Keynes is left in them. And yet, it is not individually that Keynes' attempts have to be judged. They must be judged collectively. The net effect of those cumulative attempts was to accomplish exactly what he promised. Each one of those attempts shot such gaping holes in the structure of classical economics that the structure collapsed—irremediably and irretrievably.

Ultimately, the net cumulative effect of those repeated attempts was to break away from Adam Smith's description of the mechanics of the economic process. The net effect literally was, as Professor Samuelson once put it, to "swallow the classical system as a special case."[67] But that system—no matter how battered—was still there. And Keynes did not find the time, first, to sweep the debris away, and then to develop his own unified, coherent description of that very process: his own castle. What he left were many partial descriptions of the economic process.

A major proof of the validity of this interpretation is his use, even though necessarily haltingly, of period analysis. Keynes builds the description of the economic process around the concept of income—and no longer around the idea of saving. Hence saving becomes a "mere residual"; hence saving becomes one of the two "determinates," and not a "determinant," of income. Then the analysis stops abruptly; and, through the device of the multiplier, starts again with the concept of income.

It is at this juncture that economic theory tried to dart off into economic dynamics and general equilibrium analysis in which, since everything is related to everything else, as Professor Samuelson stressed in his *Foundations of Economic Analysis* (1947), it is no longer significant to distinguish what is the cause and what is the effect of any event. Yet, it is precisely at this juncture that economic theory becomes enmeshed in abstractions of such vastness that the tree of economic knowledge vanishes into the clouds of pure thinking in which, as Keynes put it, "nothing is clear and everything is possible."

This effect, which perhaps is more dominant now than at Keynes' time, is the most evident symptom of the current crisis in economics. The roots of the crisis, as we know, lie in the saving-investment quagmire, an immovable obstacle that Keynes tried to circumvent with the use of period analysis, and the Keynesians tried to ignore with their general equilibrium analysis.

But not everything is possible in economics. There are logical obstacles that cannot be ignored. The debilitating question for economic analysis remains: how does one pass from saving to investment? Hence the high hopes of building a truly dynamic theory are continuously dashed away. Hence the effort to create a truly general equilibrium analysis is still premature.

Not everything is possible in economics. In addition to the logical obstacles, there are factual obstacles that cannot be ignored. The key debilitating question remains: which one of the 100,000 possible definitions of saving is to be thrown for processing into the cauldron of general equilibrium?

Without the knowledge of how to pass from saving and investment, without the knowledge of which one is the appropriate definition of saving, one can build a magnificent economic theory; but this theory cannot be of any assistance in the field of economic policy. That is the test for economics. Economic does not have a theoretical end in itself. Economics is a practical science.

A Practical Coda

Leaving issues of high theory aside, the practical implications of the different theoretical approaches might now become clearer to the reader. Keynes' use of period analysis was his most piercing attempt to deflate Adam Smith's conception of saving. It was his most poignant attempt to steer the discussion away from efforts to design policies which foster "higher saving," or often self-defeating austerity and sacrifices; and get on with the task of designing policies which foster "higher consumption," as a deserved reward for one's efforts.

This is only one specific case of Keynes' attempts to describe the economic process as a process; there were many others. And all justified the general claim, as well as his own in a letter to G. B. Shaw, that he had written a book that should have "revolutionized" people's economic thinking.

To elaborate upon these attempts within the present context would tend to do great injustice to Keynes and the Keynesians. It is better to close this chapter by observing that the net cumulative effect of Keynes' efforts was to prepare the ground for a major revision of economic theory. Indeed, it is safe to believe that, had Keynes had enough time and patience, he would have accomplished this feat himself. But this was not to be.

The Simplicism in Keynes' Work

Someone might ask at this point: what is "simplistic" in Keynes' description of the economic process? What is simplistic is not the description itself, but two assumptions on which that description rests. The first assumption is that one can use a clever analysis to get around an intellectual obstacle of such magnitude as the saving-investment nexus in economics; the second assumption is that ideas, which admittedly were expressed so "laboriously," would ultimately be sweeping readers off their feet for long, sustained action. In addition, it must be stressed that those ideas were expressed piecemeal, and could not all be logically fitted together.

To clarify this issue somewhat, the *General Theory* has to be compared to one of the great paintings of the cubist school. The painting provides many partial descriptions of the subject studied. It is the viewer who, knowing many things, puts the pieces together. The viewer who does this work comes away from the painting with a total—and analytical—understanding of the subject.

We shall now try to become such a viewer. The ongoing description of the economic process as presented in these pages attempts to do just that. Its value, however, lies not so much in the overall view it offers as in the analytical paths—almost new paths—which it opens up. Let us proceed along these paths, then.

The analysis will first lead us to understand the bare structure of the production process, the consumption process, and the distribution process as entities in themselves. And then, combining those entities together, the analysis will grant us a better understanding of such concrete phenomena as economic growth and inflation. Riding on the crest of these waves, we shall also attempt to understand what economic poverty is.

XVIII

The Production Process

Wealth has its source in applications of the
mind to nature.

Ralph Waldo Emerson

———•———

KEYNES MADE CONSISTENT EFFORTS to escape, as he said, from old
"modes of thought and expression."

What were they? The modes of thought and expression on which
he had been brought up were all enclosed in the Marshallian
instruments of analysis—a formidable apparatus which explored
every possible corner of the laws of supply and demand: the blades
of a scissors, as Marshall called them. Graphically, the two blades
are two lines on a graph—itself a series of lines.

For the reader who detects a seeming contradiction between the
above and the ideas expressed in the previous chapter, it might be
pointed out that, substantively, Marshall did not change the content of Adam Smith's thought. In any case, at issue here is the form
of Marshall's thought. Indeed, the issue is with the limits of all linear diagrams.

The Limits of Linear Diagrams

A great many people are familiar with this type of graph, with the
conditions such graphs represent, and the logical as well as economic premises on which this type of analysis is based. These
issues are not of concern here. Of direct concern is Keynes' reaction to or, more specifically, his attempt to escape from those strictures. It must be realized in fact that, from many points of view, his
was not much more than an attempt. In fact, notwithstanding all
efforts, Keynes remained prisoner of those modes of thought and
expression. His analysis is a classical Marshallian analysis. Indeed,
at the insistence of his pupil and later Professor Roy F. Harrod,
Keynes even included one Marshallian diagram—the only dia-

gram—in the *General Theory*.

It is no wonder, then, that economic theory has rather fully reverted again to that type of analysis. Economic literature is replete with "functions," the mathematical expression of a line; and with linear graphs and diagrams: lines that generally intersect at one or more points. It is as if economists had never heard of Marshall McLuhan. The reader who is familiar with McLuhan' s analysis will not only be able to link linear graphs and diagrams with rational economics; he will also realize the essential pitfalls of all linear and rational analysis. Compelled to eliminate from its purview all that surrounds the "line," this analysis tends to rationalize and greatly simplify the issues. It also tends to have no sense of direction, i.e., it comes from nowhere, except the mind of its maker; and it goes nowhere in particular, except toward the preferential biases of that same person.

This is a matter that must be put in stronger terms. It is as if physicists were to neglect Newton, let alone Einstein, and were still to use exclusively Euclidean geometry and physics. Professor Robert Clower showed himself acutely aware of this issue. In 1960 he stated: "The fruits of the Keynesian Revolution have been, and are being, gathered primarily by a new generation of economists, a generation that has finally accustomed itself to thinking in terms of points and planes instead of curves and crosses."[68]

The next generation of economists will have to accustom itself to thinking in terms of solids moving in space. Only in this way will the seeds sown by Keynes fully blossom. Crosses, lines, functions will still be of help; yet, more than lip service will then be paid to Keynes' model. The model, a non-marginalist tool, will actually be used to examine—to say the least—the simultaneous effects of any economic operation on the production process, the distribution process, and the consumption process: our "solids" in economic space.

Will we deepen our understanding of the interrelatedness of the issues if we realize that the shortcomings of rational economics must be laid at the feet of rationalism? If we do that, we will also realize that the shortcomings of rationalism can be encapsulated in one sentence: rationalism abuses the usefulness of the shortcut of extending the point into a line, and avoids transforming it into a sphere; therefore, each point in the analysis is stretched along linear patterns, rather than being enlarged into an organic and dynamic entity. To put it positively, the underpinnings of this work present a first attempt to expand rationalism into relationalism.

The Production Process (PP)

$$\underline{\text{D} + \text{A} \rightarrow \text{PP}}, \text{ where: } \text{D} = \text{Division of Labor; } \text{A} = \text{Added Activity; and, PP} = \text{Production Process.}$$

Notes:

— In Hegelian terms, D can be seen as thesis and A as antithesis. Then, PP becomes the synthesis.

— The graph can also be seen as a representation of the continuing movement of thought, which from a synthesis leads to an analysis and from there to a new synthesis. (Not all past analyses lead to a new synthesis; at least, not all at the same time.)

— As such, the graph can also be read as representing the path of evolution of economic science — or any other science.

Credits:

The graph has been reproduced and adapted from *The Economy of Cities* by Jane Jacobs (New York: Vintage Books, 1970), p. 58.

The Discovery of the Production Process

Be the case as it may, since Keynes was not fully able to escape from the old modes of thought, it is no wonder that his successors are still thinking in terms of production function, or line—and not in terms of production process. For the overwhelming majority of economists, production is still a linear activity and not a process.

Indeed, it is no wonder that it is a non-economist who first discovered the production process—without giving it a distinctive name, but simply calling it "a process." Indeed, since every modern economy has evolved in the city, it is no wonder that it was an eminent urbanologist who first discovered that process: Jane Jacobs. And it is finally no wonder that economists so far have not taken cognizance of this important discovery: specializations are so divisive today that they function as barriers against the free movement of thought.

Ms. Jacobs' discovery is best illustrated with the use of her own diagram, a diagram that is attached under the heading "The Production Process." Ms. Jacobs starts her analysis by taking issue with Adam Smith's principle of division of labor (anathema to economists, of course) as only a partial explanation for the production process. She then develops another principle, the principle of added activity, and creates the following formula:

$$DL + A \longrightarrow nDL,$$

where DL stands for division of labor, A for added activity, and nDL for new division of labor.

Subsequently, she adjusts that formula to read:

$$DL + nTE + A \longrightarrow nDL,$$

where nTE stands for new trial and error. In summary, we encounter a description of the production process as it was, as it is, and as it will be forever—unless one changes the nature of the world.

Men and women work: they measure their energy and creativity against natural resources. Thus they create wealth. It is noted that wealth, economic wealth, is created only as a result of human activity. Wealth is not to be found in the "natural" state.

This is the essence of the production process. Men and women go on with this simple yet exhilarating activity rather indefinitely; always searching for better and new ways to perform that same function. It is here that the principle of division of labor enters into play. Each task is broken into its component parts, and each person specializes in the performance of one task. The majority of people continue in their repetition. A few look for even better ways. Some break those tasks into even more finite components; but others do something completely different. They invent a new gadget, a new tool, a new consumer product, a new service.

Pace Adam Smith, all these new items do not "divide" existing work. As Jane Jacobs correctly points out, they create new work. They add to the sum total of work that can be done at any given time. It is the principle of added activity that is triggered here. This principle includes the notion of technological advancements, but it is broader in scope. The principle of added activity comes into play even when—strictly speaking—no development in technology has occurred. The purest case in which the difference between the two manifests itself is in those new products and services that are determined solely by cultural or esthetic requirements. A new fashion, or a new fad, can be introduced utilizing exclusively existing technology. The two notions coincide if one conceives of technology in the broadest possible sense, as the art of producing goods and services.

It is the combination of the two principles, however defined, that creates the dynamics of the production process. Behind both principles stands that spark of creativity that arranges matters in such a way as to produce wealth—just as it arranges matters in such a way as to produce a masterpiece in literature, music or art. Indeed, it is that spark of creativity which—to make the production of consumer goods of easier accomplishment—also creates the machines.

At this point, we are no longer confronted with two "factors" in the production process. We now have three of them: labor, natural resources, and capital, i.e., machinery, tools, supplies, equipment, etc. This is a position that, although firmly established by classical economists, has been nearly lost of late. To try to avoid a repetition of this fate, let us simplify the issues. Once what stands behind it is made explicit, this simplification should no longer be dangerous. Let us rewrite the formula for the production process using almost entirely traditional terminology. The formula thus reads:

$$\text{Man} + \text{Capital} \longrightarrow \text{Production.}$$

It is worth stressing that it is preferable to speak of "man" rather than "labor"; and that "capital" in this case always includes land and natural resources.

What is new in the discussion held here, then? What is new is not only the way in which the traditional position is reached, but especially the form it assumes. No matter which one of the two formulas is used, they clearly indicate that we are speaking, not of a linear activity, but of a process.

And the "process" never stops. The principle of division of labor is activated over again. Some person will soon begin to look for a better way of producing the newly invented gadget, tool, consumer product, or service. This person divides the task into its component parts—until someone else comes up with a *newer* gadget, tool, consumer product, or service. And on and on and on.

People who scoff at this type of activity are requested to think in these terms: to think of doing away with all—not, simplistically, some of—the existing gadgets, tools, consumer products, and services. And one is not justifying expensive, useless, unimaginative, ugly, wasteful, distracting, annoying, noisy, injurious, harmful, cruel, inhuman products and services—whether in their being or in their making. No. One is speaking of a simplistic mental attitude.

Facile tirades aside, what Jane Jacobs describes is indeed a process: that which was missing in Adam Smith has been found. The principle of division of labor by itself could not create a process; and, therefore, it could not ultimately even be understood. To repeat, it takes at least two sticks to create a spark. Indeed, what Jane Jacobs so convincingly describes and analyzes in a wealth of historical examples taken from many continents, is more than a simple process. As the word implies, it is an organic process:

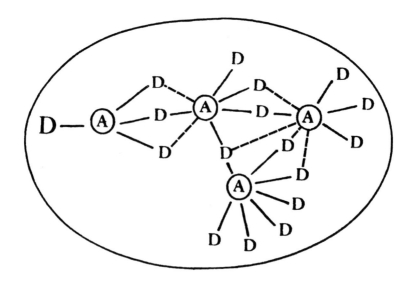

that is the way in which all living things operate, grow, and die.

In order to capture this understanding of the production process at a glance, it is sufficient to draw a line around the figure given above. One then obtains the diagram on the preceding page, a diagram which might be called "The Production Process: A Reformulation."

The viewer simply needs to transform the static image into a dynamic one. And the viewer will be assisted in making this transformation if the concept of the production process is replaced, at least for a moment, by the vision of any organic matter, from a simple cell to the entire universe.

Economic Requirements of the Production Process

Apart from sheer delight in reading the details of the process, and apart from useful repetition, there is little more included in Jane Jacobs' work that is of essential interest to our discussion. Since that "little" more is quite precious still, we shall try to capture it while speaking of economic growth. The present discussion can be closed. However, brief reference has to be made of the purely economic aspects of the process—aspects that are so well known that they do not require much attention. These are the requirements that have to be met in the economic world for the production process to stay on course. The first requirement is that the marginal efficiency of capital be equal to the market rate of interest. This is a requirement that was especially emphasized by Keynes.

If one is not the actual producer, it is easy to say that as soon as someone has the idea for a new gadget, tool, consumer product, or service, the idea ought to be immediately implemented. If one is the actual producer, one must take—whether consciously or instinctively—a tremendous number of factors into account. What is the likely effect of the new idea—if translated into being—upon the present level of activity? Is it somehow going to disrupt it? What are the innumerable factors that are necessary to translate that idea into reality—are they all available? What is the cost of each one of them? Would one get a better return from a different type of investment? These are some of the factors that must be taken into consideration. Expressed in technical language, they all contribute to the creation of what is called the marginal efficiency of capital or, simply, how much return do I expect from the extra effort? This return is then judged, not in the abstract, but against a concrete yardstick: the current rate of interest.

I shall make the effort involved in the investment only if the expected return is greater than the rate of interest—and up to the point at which they are equal. If the rate of interest is greater than the expected rate of return, if I can, I will even transform my "capital" into liquid capital and deposit the proceeds in a bank. I shall then get a greater income than if I had invested my capital in machinery, equipment, etc. As Adam Smith well knew, and yet this simple truth is so disrespected today, "It is better . . . to play for nothing, than to work for nothing."[69]

To use Professor Bain's expressions, the above does not say anything concerning the right of entry into economic markets nor the right of access to financial markets. To repeat, the discussion on the economic requirements of the production process can be—and, were this a dynamic analysis, it should be—much enlarged to include a close examination of such issues as the theory of the firm, the law of diminishing (and increasing) returns, the role of technological innovations, of (Schumpeterian) entrepreneurship, of (Robinsonian) imperfect competition, and the like. But the above, in simple terms, is the first economic requirement that exists in the economic process.

The second is that I do indeed realize the expected rate of return. If I do not, I shall not be able to stay in business for long. And what does this mean? It means that I must be able to sell—at a profit—whatever product or service I have decided to produce, otherwise I shall not be of economic use for long. This requirement was emphasized by Adam Smith in his analysis of "the market."

This second requirement is implicit in the first. However, since the time sequence for its verification is different, it is better to mention the latter requirement explicitly. We will look at this requirement separately in the next chapter—and from a novel point of view: the point of view of the consumption process. Indeed, let us emphasize that this second point of view through which "the market" can be observed is eminently proper. To consider the market only as part of the production process leads to a contradiction in terms and to confusion of mind; and, in any case, this writer has nothing to add to the wealth of information existing on the latter well-known point of view.

Before we embark upon this discussion, however, let us address ourselves to a few general issues. Let us start with the issue of measurement of the production process.

What Is to Be Measured?

Economists tend to reduce all the complexities of the production process to a single set of numbers, and hence a single line: the line representing the flow of value of goods and services produced over a determinate period of time. So be it. Practices ingrained over many generations are not going to change overnight. But let us not join them in their surprise whenever their forecasts turn out to be far wide of the mark.

The practice of measuring only the value of goods and services obliterates the vision of the human element that constitutes such an integral part of that process. Apart from lip service paid to the principle of division of labor, the substance of the economic discourse generally proceeds on the basis of the fiction that the process goes on by itself. And this fiction, together with the lack of recognition of the principle of added activity, is not even the major shortcoming in the current measurement of the process. After all, it could be said that those principles are taken into account ex post. More important still is another phenomenon.

No attention is ever paid to all other results of the production process. And yet the list of such results is truly endless. To mention but a few of them, lives lost: lives enhanced; ears pierced by shrieking sounds: ears delighted by the sounds of music; idle hands: industrious hands. And this is not all. One needs also to take into consideration such other factors as trees felled: fields of wheat; rivers polluted: killer-rivers brought under control; oceans streaked with oil spills: oceans ploughed by cargo and sailboats; noxious fumes in the air: spaceships.

To highlight other effects to which we will return from another angle, the production process, as a human institution surrounded by other human institutions, also directly creates rich and poor people—with all that these expressions imply.

These are effects that objectively exist; and therefore must be taken into account by the economist. And many of them are indeed taken into account by an economist as refined as, for instance, Nicholas Georgescu-Roegen—an economist who does not bow to the almighty arithmomorphic concept, as he calls it, even though the expression might be simply translated as God Number.

Incidentally, many of these effects are taken into account by the entrepreneur. It is only the statistician, then, who is put under severe strain by the existence of those effects. But we all live under certain limitations. The sooner statisticians acknowledge the limitations they are under, the better off we all are. Indeed, at that point we might seriously begin to push those limitations back a few inches.

The Assistance Provided by the Laws of Supply and Demand

It might appear from the above that a bulwark of traditional eco-

nomic analysis, namely, the influence exerted by the laws of supply and demand over the production process, is totally neglected.
This is not so. Once the notion is dismissed that those laws are
impersonal "market" forces, it is immediately realized that they
are implicitly taken into account through the principle of division
of labor as well as the principle of added activity. And this is not
enough yet. It is also necessary to dismiss the notion that economic operators react only to the pull of money and wealth; this is the
assumption of the rational economic man on which those laws
rest. In reality, there are many other forces at play: fears, power,
status, envy, hate, altruism, etc.; and such forces are not necessarily irrational either. Furthermore, they operate not only in the production, but also in the distribution and consumption of wealth.

These statements barely scratch the surface of the issues. There
are many more simplistic assumptions in the field of microeconomics—assumptions that, too often, from there are bodily trans-
planted into the field of macroeconomics. We cannot go any deeper into these issues, nor can we stress them every time we touch
upon the microeconomic underpinnings of our analysis. The reader who is interested in these issues will find a wealth of information and much enlightenment in the rigorous analysis made by
Professor Harvey Leibenstein in his *Beyond Economic Man: A
New Foundation for Microeconomics* (1976) or by Herbert A.
Simon (a Nobelist in economics) in his *Models of Bounded
Rationality* (1997). These analyses have gradually grown into a
field of its own, behaviorism, and they have become so prominent
that the 2001 John Bates Clark medal was awarded to one its most
creative practitioners: Matthew Rabin.

Of direct concern is one simple point. Once simplistic conceptions of the laws of supply and demand are done away with, and
without of course determining a priori to what extent they are
indeed applied in today's economic world, those laws reappear in
all their splendor and potential effectiveness. In fact, then it
becomes evident that there is no such thing as a single "aggregate
supply" and a single "aggregate demand." Even without reverting
to microeconomics, one can discern many such schedules at work
in the economic system.

To state it clearly, the producer—meaning the productive process
as a whole—has at least to be seen as an entity which requests as
well as supplies goods and services; and as an entity which requests
as well as supplies money.

But these are issues that are better treated through a dynamic
analysis of the subject. Let us break off the discussion at this point

and stress that these general considerations, *mutatis mutandis*, ought to be repeated while observing the economic process from other points of view. Yet, not to tax the patience of the reader unnecessarily, they will no longer be mentioned.

Some Broad Considerations

There are so many broad ramifications of the above issues that they can neither be analyzed nor listed in this book. Let us, nonetheless, proffer a word of caution to those who pursue traditional modes of thought and expression. The principle of division of labor does not involve mechanical repetition; it expresses continuous creativity—a creativity that appears especially evident when the principle of added activity is cast into the mix. The most important result of studying the two principles in conjunction with each other, however, is that production can no longer be conceived as a linear activity. It must be conceived as a process. And the essential characteristic of a process is that there is no beginning and no end to it; there is only continuous transformation.

This phenomenon has some far-reaching intellectual implications of its own which will have to be analyzed under the rubric of *Organic Logic* and *Complementary Knowledge*. But one consequence can properly be mentioned at this point. Once production is no longer conceived as a linear activity, but as a process, the power of persuasiveness is taken away from rational economics. It becomes necessary then to continue the transformation of economics into dynamic and organic or Concordian economics. But, specifically, why?

The practical reason is simple. A line is so fragile that it can hardly be considered as an entity that has no beginning and no end. We tend to think of it as a finite entity. This conception tends to confirm our belief that a line can abruptly snap. Or at least we fear that it can snap. And in fact, when production is conceived as a linear activity, it does snap; thus quite often causing recessions and depressions. The historical repetition of these occurrences reinforces our fears—which we individually try to allay by accumulating and hoarding as much wealth as possible. As we shall see, this cure is worse than the disease: it ultimately is the cause of the disease.

Production considered as a process—or as a sphere—might help to assuage those deep-rooted fears. A sphere does not abruptly snap. A sphere conveys the idea of lasting strength. If this is true, and inherently that important, let us spend a moment realizing how the production process can be pictured as a sphere. The previous graph, entitled "The Production Process: A Reformulation," can already be seen as a sphere. The viewer simply needs to transform the image from a two-dimensional to a tridimensional one. To facilitate this operation, and at the same time unify our visual method of representation, the production process can be illustrated in another way, as in the diagram entitled "The Production Process: Another Representation." This diagram does not need any word of explanation, except to note that rotating the two blocks at ever increasing speed about the geometric center of the diagram, one eventually obtains the mental image of a sphere.

The Production Process
Another Representation

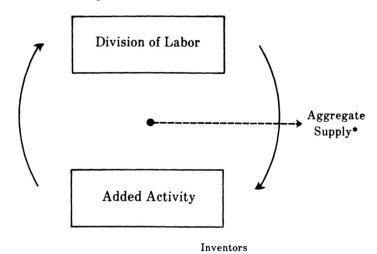

*"Aggregate Supply" is a convenient, synthetic expression. Unless it is related to the *innumerable* concrete results of the Production Process in the physical, social, legal, economic, aesthetic and moral world, the expression becomes a mere abstraction.

XIX

The Consumption Process

*The consumption process is the interaction of
the availability of goods and services on the
market and the readiness to spend money.*

———•———

CONSUMPTION, IN CONTEMPORARY ECONOMICS, means spending; it
does not mean destruction of wealth. This much we have realized
in the previous pages. But how do we pass from the observation of
a category of thought to the observation of the activity involved in
spending? The transition is made possible by a familiar tool of
analysis, the notion of process. The consumption process, then,
describes all that is involved in the act of spending—not only from
the point of view of the individual person, but also from the point
of view of the economic system as a whole.

Lest we lose sight of our central concern, however, let us be
aware that, with the aid of the Flows model, we are observing the
same entity—i.e., the economic system—from three different
points of view: production, distribution, and consumption. Of
direct interest at the moment is the observation of the economic
system from the point of view of consumption. Since this is a novel
vantage point, let us delineate some of its general characteristics.

Just as we have observed the production process and not the
production function (or line), so we shall observe the consumption
process and not the consumption function. This is the first characteristic. The second characteristic is that the consumption process
is the result of many forces, some of which are generated within
the production and others within the distribution process. In fact,
observed dynamically, the consumption process represents but one
instant in time: the instant in which a transaction actually occurs—
ideally, the transaction involves the total output of the system. We
shall, however, insist on a static observation because, only through
the expedient of halting the moving economic reality, the consumption process acquires a configuration of its own. Only in this
way can we understand the mechanism that stands behind the

scene and is required for the exchange to take place.

To put its configuration in sharper focus, let us realize that the consumption process is a hybrid composed of goods and money which, if not observed as an entity of its own, can easily lead to misinterpretation—especially by the economist and the business-man or the businesswoman. Each of them tends to observe only one of the two elements that compose the hybrid, the element of course with which they are directly familiar. And they tend to neg-lect the entity as a whole. Entrepreneurs think of consumption as an extension of the production process and economists think of it as an extension of the distribution process.

What we should essentially realize is that consumption is itself a process. Thus it must be composed of at least two elements. They are: availability of goods or services and readiness to spend money. We can even express this process with a formula:

$$AoG + RtS \longrightarrow EX,$$

where AoG stands for availability of goods, RtS for readiness to spend, and EX for exchange. An exchange, in other words, occurs only when those two central elements are present. An exchange is a consumption process that has been completed.

Visually, the consumption process can be represented through the familiar, attached diagram bearing this title. Essentially, the process involves an exchange of wealth. In a monetary—as opposed to barter—economy, it involves an exchange of money for goods and services. Or, conversely, it involves an exchange of goods and services for money.

This is the essence of the consumption process. However impor-tant it is, this "essence" of course does not tell us much. Nor is recourse to the economic literature of much assistance. Indeed, this point must be expressed more directly. For a variety of reasons, we do not have a detailed knowledge of this process yet. To mention only one such reason, ever since Adam Smith implicitly attacked James Steuart for the latter's approach of observing the economy from the point of view of consumption, economists have been very reticent to tackle the issue. And those who have dared have not been spared by the leading economists of every age. Traditions acquire an aura of respect. Combined with the laziness of mind that they tend to foster, they become easier to accept than to break up. The tradition with which we are concerned, entangled as it is with the history of the principle of effective demand, is quite involved indeed.

The Consumption Process

Producers

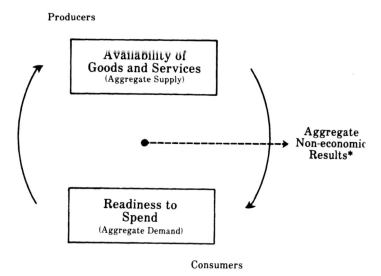

Consumers

---

*From the exchange of goods and services for money, and vice versa, there follow innumerable social, legal and political results—but, with the exception of the physical transferral of wealth, there are no *direct* economic results. In a free exchange, both parties give up and receive something of an equivalent value. Indirectly, however, the Consumption Process is the spring of the entire economic process.

Reasons always come in a bundle, and a twisted bundle at that. Rather than pursuing the discussion on this general level, let us first make explicit some of the practical consequences that flow from the general lack of knowledge of the consumption process; and then let us be more specific about the limits of the existing knowledge on this topic. After that, we shall offer a few suggestions that might somewhat reduce those limits.

Some Practical Consequences

As stated, the consumption process is composed of the interaction of at least two elements: the availability of goods and services on the market and the readiness to spend one's money to purchase those goods and services. The entrepreneur who considers only the availability of goods to the consumer neglects the second equally important element in that process: the readiness of the consumer to spend money.

Business people engage in a well-known series of activities such as marketing, merchandising, advertising. They consider these efforts so much part of the production process that they include them in their ledgers as categories of the cost of production. Thus entrepreneurs are correct in considering consumption (the sale or exchange of products for money) as an extension of the production process—but they are right only in part.

First of all, they would indeed be wrong if they were to neglect the fact that the availability of goods on the market must be considered from the point of view of the consumer. Entrepreneurs need to produce what the consumer wants. In other words, even before starting production, entrepreneurs (as well as economists who are concerned with the totality of the economic process) need to take a host of sociological, esthetic, and cultural factors into account. Entrepreneurs who assume this proper perspective enhance their chances for success. This is not all. There is something else that no one ought to neglect: consumption is also an extension of the distribution process.

This gap is not filled with advertising; rather, it is filled with serious misconceptions regarding advertising. The proper function of advertising is not to induce desire to spend, but to inform consumers of the existence of goods and services available for sale. Manipulative advertising cannot affect the readiness to spend. If money is not there, the induced desire does not suffice. Apart from destruction of lives, induced desire has a primary effect on the production of income. Thus manipulative advertising, at best, has only a potential and delayed influence on the consumption of future income.

Indeed, the lack of understanding of the entire consumption process on the part of the entrepreneur has another even more grievous consequence. It is the fundamental reason for the entrepreneur's lack of concern about the ways and means through which consumers acquire their spendable income. This is such an important and widespread deficiency that it creates innumerable consequences of its own. These consequences ramify into so many areas and into so many facets that we had better abandon the terrain of this practice and take refuge into the realm of theory.

The availability of income is the essential prerequisite for the readiness to spend—a prerequisite that completes the hybrid and establishes the link with the distribution process, a topic which will be dealt with in the next chapter. Here, let us simply point out that the entrepreneur generally does not receive much assistance from the economist in learning about the totality of the consumption process. In fact, at this point it might be useful to investigate what does the economist know about the consumption process.

The Limits of Our Knowledge on the Consumption Process

The most important discovery to be made from a perusal of the economic literature is that the economist generally tends to become interested only in the second half of the consumption process. Is it necessary to editorialize that, if the entrepreneur is somewhat justified in not seeing the consumption process as a whole, the economist has much less of a justification? Yet, even Keynes neglected to see it as a process. He observed only the second element mentioned above, the readiness to spend. And he observed it on such a high level of abstraction that failed to adequately emphasize its relationship with such concrete issues as those involved in the phenomenon of income distribution.

Keynes observed only the readiness to spend. He found it dependent on the size of income, and propounded a psychological law in accordance with which the large majority of consumers tend to spend always a little less than their income. He called such entity the (marginal) propensity to consume. Many consequences were observed by Keynes as being dependent upon this psychological law. They are not of interest right now. The important point to realize is a different one.

With the exception of Professor Modigliani's effort to establish the validity of the "life-cycle hypothesis of consumption"; with the exception of Professor Friedman's effort to analyze the possible consequences of the hypothesis that consumers receive a "permanent income" (a hypothesis which will become even more fruitful if it is no longer based on admittedly "inappropriate concepts of income and consumption"[70]); and with the exception of the effort made by many writers of monetary theory to reintroduce in the economic discourse the hypothesis of the existence of a "silent auctioneer" in the market, to the knowledge of this writer there is not much new in the field of consumption theory. Certainly, not much can be expected from those who, like Professor Kaldor, maintain that "Capitalists earn what they spend, and workers spend what they earn."[71] Finally, in addition to many detailed, highly specialized and technical studies, mention must be made of Professor Sraffa's efforts to study the consumption (and production) of commodities by means of commodities. This approach, however, has greater value as a "Prelude to a Critique of Economic Theory" than—if one really could so neatly separate the issues—as a breakthrough in the field of consumption or even distribution theory.[72]

Older or classical writers were, of course, hampered in their vision of the consumption process by the conception of consumption as destruction of wealth. And other writers, like Professor Katona, are held back by their lack of distinction between the consumption and the distribution process—whereby they introduce at this point the "ability to buy." The latter element, as we shall see, is an integral part of the distribution process. All contemporary writers are, of course, hampered by their conception of consumption as expenditure on consumer goods.

These are the limits of our knowledge on the consumption process. As can be seen, they are rather striking and constricting. It is, therefore, hoped that the Flows model and the terms of the present discourse will open new avenues of theoretical and applied research in this field. What this writer has to say in this area is hypothetical and tentative at best.

Quite apart from the indicated necessity to study the process as composed of two major elements—availability of goods and readiness to spend—it seems that, first of all, research has to be intensified in the direction of the distribution of income. But we shall have something to say on this issue in the upcoming chapter. Second, it seems that economic research has also to be intensified in the direction of a deeper knowledge of the readiness to spend or propensity to consume. And it is here that a few specific suggestions are offered.

A Few Suggestions

First of all, let us be concerned with the issue of terminology. Both expressions, "readiness to spend" and "propensity to consume," are too abstract. They are useful just because they are so general and all-encompassing; but they do not lead to concrete, specific, indeed economic knowledge. For this purpose one must recur to a specific economic term. This term is "the market."

Before entering into the merits of the following observations, one more caveat must be expressed again. The market, in this context, must be observed from the point of view of the consumer. Otherwise, one reverts back to the observation of the Production Process.

It is on the issue of the market observed from the point of view of the consumer that this writer would like to add two specific suggestions. First, that there are three market configurations to be dealt with, and not one; second, that, to study the "mass consumption" market, the law of increasing prices and decreasing performance might be of great assistance.

Three Market Configurations

Economic—as distinguished from psychological—analysis, it is suggested, might with profit be directed toward the examination of an ancient hypothesis. This hypothesis, advanced in slightly different terms by Johann Becher in 1668, is that there are three (not one) market configurations: a luxury market, a mass market, and a second-hand market.

This hypothesis was not examined by Adam Smith. And it has never been taken into consideration by later economists. Only market analysts know full well that it is impossible to speak and deal intelligently with such an aggregate conception as "the market"—as Adam Smith preferred to do.

To insist on one point, Adam Smith's conception of the market is also not appropriate because it looks at that entity from the point of view of the producer, and not from the point of view of the consumer. Thus the central question is: how does the consumer view the market? The suggestion is that the consumer places himself (or herself) either within the luxury market, the mass consumption market, or the second-hand market. And the consumer neglects the other two markets. This appears to be the reality. But of course the economist can hardly limit the range of observation to that extent. The economist must look at the characteristics of all three markets. Let us do just that.

A brief analysis leads one to believe that there is considerable value in Becher's hypothesis. Certainly, the luxury market seems to behave in nearly the same fashion as the second-hand market. Here the laws of supply and demand seem to behave in practice as they are supposed to behave in theory. The only, minor, difference consists of this: while constraints in the luxury market exist on the side of supply, in the second-hand market constraints exist on the side of demand. More explicitly, in the luxury market the price of an article is no deterrent to a sale. The market is limited only by the extent of supply. Here prices behave exactly as the theory of supply and demand says they ought to behave: in simplified fashion, scarce supply + high demand = high prices. And prices are not set arbitrarily either; they are in direct relationship to costs. Otherwise, if prices could be raised arbitrarily, the profit margin would increase tremendously. And a large profit margin—unless one were operating in a monopolistic market configuration—sooner or later would attract competition which, for many reasons, would bid costs up and therefore reduce the margin of profit. (Notice that the latter mechanism is not generally mentioned in discussions concerning "free competition," especially because there are many other countervailing forces at work in the field.)

The reverse takes place in the second-hand market. Here the supply is virtually limitless. Constraints, however, exist on the side of demand: people who buy second-hand products have a limited quantity of money at their disposal. And, again, the laws of supply and demand rule nearly supreme in this market as well. Prices tend to be low since the supply is large and the effective demand is limited. The profit margin remains within "normal" limits, mainly because with any increase in prices the demand is further restricted.

But what happens in the mass consumption market? This market, after all, occupies not only the central but a dominant position in the modern economy. As is becoming increasingly more evident, the laws of supply and demand do not apply to this market. And prices bear only a vague relationship to costs. What controls prices, and the supply of goods or services, no less than the demand for those goods and services, is an intricate web of corporate and governmental rules, regulations, and practices. Many an economist, not to mention the concerned citizen, has been lost in this web. Perhaps the reality is that such rules, regulations, and practices are so numerous, so confusing, and so contradictory that they cannot possibly be understood by anyone—especially with the aid of generalized tools of analysis. The computer, of course, might be of assistance here.

Needless to say, it is important that we make an effort to understand those rules. The limit of tolerance for the existence of hidden rules has proved to be traditionally short. Besides, with the benefit of hindsight, it has generally appeared that hidden rules—whether they were made by the few or a majority of the people—were detrimental to everybody. Certainly, one is hard put to find any group of people who thoroughly benefit from whatever rules exist in the present chaotic condition of the world market economy. It is important, then, that we try to understand at least some of those rules. Only in this way might we be able to take charge of our own destiny in "the market."

The Law of Increasing Prices and Decreasing Performance

What can an unbiased consumer observe? Through relatively long observation, it appears that the mass market is also ruled by a major economic law. This is not the law of supply and demand; but a law that this writer would like to call "The law of increasing prices and decreasing performance." Close attention to the behavior of the mass consumption market suggests that there is considerable validity in this law.

That there is a long trend of increasing prices in the mass consumption market is not a new observation. That there is a corresponding long trend of decreasing performance is not frequently observed—and, if observed, it is not recognized as tenable, for a variety of reasons. First, our memories are generally short: it is only "old people" who tend to remember how extended the life of houses, appliances, clothes, machinery, etc. used to be. Second, we are too often bombarded with the dictum that such and such is a new "improved" product: there is nothing like repetition to distort the truth. Third, the phenomenon of obsolescence is not only accepted as a "law of nature"; it is even deified today: it is called planned obsolescence. Consequently, the idea is rationalized as being good for the economy because it creates jobs—as if work were meant to be inherently destructive. Fourth, the long trend of decreasing performance—in services, no less than in products—is not easily recognizable because it is not a continuous trend. The awesome apparatus of the physical sciences is, indeed, called upon to alter that trend. Considering the size of the effort, the marvel is that the trend is not *reversed*.

A fifth reason why the long trend toward decreasing performance is not generally recognized also ought to be mentioned. Changes in quality are most difficult to measure. And whatever is not easily quantifiable is often simplistically denied the right to existence.

In any case, the law of increasing prices and decreasing performance is not officially recognized—even though it is sporadically talked about—because the economic mechanisms through which it operates are not easily recognizable. As a spur to in-depth research, here is one such "scenario." When prices increase (and in the chapter on inflation we shall see some of the reasons why they do) many effects take place. Consumers buy not a product; but, as an old school of economics used to say, they buy "utilities." And consumers are not engineers—nor do many of them have enough money to exercise a free choice. They rarely distinguish between short and long term utilities. If the immediate "utility" appears to be good enough, consumers tend to shift allegiance from a sounder to a cheaper product—"cheap" both in the old traditional meaning and the meaning that the price is lower. Producers of a sound product at first lose customers; then they restrict their margin of profit. At this point they are left with three basic choices: they either leave the market; or raise the price, losing more customers; or lower the quality of their product. Often, no matter how painful it is to the conscientious provider of the product or service, the third choice is the first one. Thus the long trend of decreasing performance is set in motion. And it is only sporadically interrupted by the repeated efforts of technicians, engineers, and scientists in every profession.

Prima facie evidence for the validity of this law is to be found in its converse, as exemplified in the computer market at the turn of the millennium: when prices decreased, quality and performance tended to increase—often spectacularly.

One certainly needs much more supporting evidence than is possible to provide in this sketch before passing a final judgment on the existence—let alone the limits of validity—of this law of increasing prices and decreasing performance. This law seems to dominate the economics of the mass consumption market. It seems to deserve attentive scrutiny.

Besides, this law is not new. It is a restatement of the most ancient "law" in economic analysis, Gresham' s Law. This is a law that has been independently discovered not once or twice, but three times: by Oresme (a French monk) in the fourteenth century, by Copernicus (the astronomer) in the sixteenth century, and by MacLeod (a Scottish economist) in the nineteenth century. It is MacLeod who mistakenly attributed this law to Gresham, the founder of the London Royal Exchange in the sixteenth century.

The law of increasing prices and decreasing performance is a restatement of Gresham' s Law. Poor money, the law says, drives good money out of circulation. (If a bad and a good currency are in circulation at the same time and both are "legal tender," i.e., have the same legal value, everyone will use the bad currency first and will tend to save, hoard, or monopolize the good one.) Poor services and poor products appear to perform the same function: they drive good services and good products away.

One would like to close this chapter with the following words of the renowned Professor Frank H. Knight: "I disclaim originality—anything very original in economics would be wrong anyway. . . ."[73]

It is only necessary to add that the observation of such phenomena as described above should be repeated over time—and certainly extended to include capital goods and items that can be hoarded.

XX

The Distribution Process

*The distribution process is the interaction of
availability of a money supply
and ability to obtain part of that supply...*

*Evidently, nearly every consumer is willing to
receive the total supply of money available.
How does society control the flow of funds?*

———·———

ONCE MASTERED, THE DISTRIBUTION PROCESS—in spite of its many
twists and turns—can be observed exactly as if it were a gravity
flow: just like water which, temporarily held in a reservoir, eventually flows downstream. The difficulties, which do exist, are not
really in such a flow. The difficulties lie mainly in a host of related
issues that prevent a clear vision of that relatively simple and continuous event which, in large part, occurs daily under our very
eyes. Let us briefly analyze these issues one by one. Let us start
with the so-called theory of distribution.

The Theory of Distribution

If one asks what is the theory of distribution, the economist
answers that—technically—it is wholly contained in the theory of
prices. One thus goes to consult the theory of prices, and one discovers that it is not much more than the laws of supply and
demand fully displayed in front of our eyes. The "extra," it is
maintained, is contained in the monetary theory. From this stage
on, the line of reasoning becomes increasingly "complex."

We must let Keynes speak directly to the point. After all, as
Professor Leijonhufvud has incontrovertibly demonstrated, Keynes
was not a "Keynesian." He was a monetarist. (A monetarist, with
the small "m.") Keynes said, and since the passage is still so largely valid it deserves extensive quotation:

So long as economists are concerned with what is called the Theory of Value [and *therefore* Distribution; we shall come back to this point], they have been accustomed to teach that prices are governed by the conditions of supply and demand . . . But when they pass in volume II or more often in a separate treatise, to the Theory of Money and Prices, we hear no more of these homely but intelligible concepts and move into a world where prices are governed by the quantity of money, by its income-velocity, by the velocity of circulation relatively to the volume of transactions, by hoarding, by forced saving, by inflation and deflation *et hoc genus omne;* and little or no attempt is made to relate these vaguer phrases to our former notions of the elasticities of supply and demand. If we reflect on what we are being taught and try to rationalise it, in the simpler discussions it seems that the elasticity of supply must have become zero and demand proportional to the quantity of money; whilst in the more sophisticated we are lost in a haze where nothing is clear and everything is possible.[74] (Perhaps it is due to passages like these that the *General Theory* is kept as much as possible out of the classroom.)

Thus, taking contemporary economic analysis at face value, we have to conclude that the theory of distribution is indistinguishable from the theory of money and prices. And yet, the deeper one goes into these issues, the less one learns. At the end of the search "we are lost in a haze where nothing is clear and everything is possible." If we are dissatisfied with this state of affairs, we must retrace our steps.

We must go back at least to the *terra firma* of the laws of supply and demand. We must cut through the confusing and circular thinking represented by the attempted use of the theory of money and prices as "the" theory of distribution. In other words, we have to discard the "theory": we must proceed unassisted by the theory of distribution. Since there is no such theory, no loss is incurred in abandoning it—or the host of surrounding "soft" theories.

Yet, if we did so directly and immediately, we would automatically be leaving the theory of money and prices completely cut through and dangling. Indeed, we would be leaving even the laws of supply and demand suspended in a no-man's land. A few observations need to be made on these issues.

The Theory of Prices—*a Synonym for the Laws of Supply and Demand*

The theory of prices, to the extent that it has been developed, is wholly contained in the laws of supply and demand. Period. (We shall see that even the phenomenon of inflation can be largely explained through the mechanisms detailed by those laws.)

The laws of supply and demand are seldom and sparingly applied in today's reality. Period. (The conditions for the application of those laws are nearly nonexistent today. They range from perfect competition to full access to all necessary information.)

With these two points firmly established, the discussion can continue—and perhaps even become intelligible. Let us proceed on this basis. It is not the fault of the theoretical economist if, in general, prices do not behave in accordance with the laws of supply and demand. Rather, it is the fault of policies often designed by practical economists and generally followed by business and governmental leaders. As mentioned in the previous chapter, in the mass consumption market—the market that counts—prices are governed by an inextricable and incomprehensible web of corporate and governmental rules, regulations, and practices. All too often, those prices are not classified as market prices but as "administered" prices.

Theory must respect the reality, but it cannot "adapt" to it. Theory cannot be formulated to please daily practices. Stated in other terms, if people contravene the laws of supply and demand, it is their privilege to do so. In so doing, however, they have to be made to understand that they have lost their right to expect the consequences foreseen by those laws. As stated in the previous chapter, it seems that an entirely different economic law rules the field: the law of increasing prices and decreasing performance.

Indeed, on the whole, the fault of the economist lies elsewhere. It lies in somehow making people believe that those unapplied laws could magically cause the expected consequences. God is good, but not that good. Civil authorities are good, but not that good. When we disobey laws, every mental discipline warns us that there are consequences to be paid. Economics is the only exception. (And then, faithful to its propensity for doublespeak, in a separate context it states: "There is no such thing as a free lunch.")

A theory of prices, which confines itself to restating the laws of supply and demand, and which extends itself to teaching about the conditions which must prevail for those laws to be triggered and the consequences to be expected from the working of those laws, is perfect as it is. This is what especially Alfred Marshall did—and, although his effort was deftly branded by Keynes as "void of content," this is all that can actually be done in the field of economic theory. It is up to economic policy to bring "content" into that structure, so to give it daily life. Marshall was too much of a "pure" scientist to become a policy-maker.

In any case, there is certainly room for improvement in any theory; in fact, the validity of this homily is brought home by many an exciting development in the field of contemporary microeconomic analysis, represented as it is by such outstanding names as Arrow, Kantorovitch, Koopmans, and Debreu (all Nobel laureates). But the major point remains that one must first learn the lessons Marshall—and Ricardo, of course—taught. After that, one must try to translate those lessons into daily reality—not the other way around. Theory cannot be formulated to accommodate contorted daily practices.

This is all that can and, indeed, must be said on the theory of prices—the theory, to repeat, and not the practice of prices, i.e., the various pricing policies as they are actually implemented. In short, the theory of prices is an elegant synonym that stands for a more awkward expression: the laws of supply and demand.

Still largely left to be unexplored in the theory of prices is the analysis of that area which lies between microeconomics and macroeconomics. Specifically, what are the conditions for the application of the laws of supply and demand to the macroeconomic world? Due to the persisting schism that exists between micro- and macro-economics, this is an area which has not really been explored yet. In this area one must still conclude with Keynes that one ought not to "attach much value" to manipulations expressing in extended equations the relationship between prices and the quantity of money; and that the best purpose of such manipulations is simply "to exhibit the extreme complexity" of those relationships.[75] (Perhaps someday computers will really be of help in this field.)

From the theory of prices rooted in this rich soil spring enormous practical consequences. They cannot be dealt with here; but one of them cannot be passed silently by. This is a practical consequence with theoretical implications—implications that this writer hopes to explore in another study.

Toward the Healing of a Schism

The theory of prices placed in the above context—combined with the revision of Keynes' model as presented in this work—has the potential of healing the breach that exists today between macro- and micro-economics.

In particular, the Flows model seems to describe as much the economy of the individual and the firm as the national or, for that matter, the world economy.

This is not to say that the differences that do exist among various economies are going to vanish. Rather, it is to say that the differences in the mental attitude with which we currently approach the study of those economies can be gradually made to disappear.

The Theory of Money

The theory of prices is bigger than monetary theory; one only needs to realize that it affects real as well as monetary wealth. The theory of prices is like the sap that is to be found in every part of a living tree. Monetary theory, instead, is an entirely different entity. It is one aspect of the tree itself. Monetary theory is one aspect of economic theory, one aspect of the economic process. The other two aspects concern the real economy and the institutional side of economic affairs.

These statements can be somewhat clarified through the use of the following diagram:

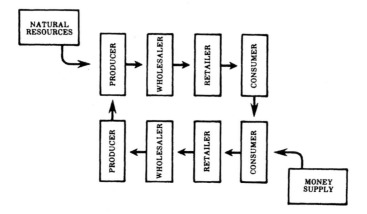

This diagram describes the economic process in greater detail than has been possible so far. The upper part describes the flow of goods and services that pass from the producer to the consumer and represents the real economy; the lower part describes the flow of money from the consumer to the producer and represents the monetary economy. In this volume we are not paying any attention to that part of the economic process that is represented by the flow of money from the consumer to the producer. And we are further assuming that the economist can indeed measure the flow of goods and services without the assistance of money, however money is identified and its value determined.

This is a strong assumption.

The economist, in fact, does not observe flows of "goods and services." He (or she) leaves this task to the engineer, the technician, and the student of nature. The economist looks only at flows of economic values. But this is an entirely crude approach, a great simplification of reality. It represents a structural weakness in our mental attitude and overall knowledge of economics that cannot be easily overcome. In fact, no attempt has been made to overcome it in this work. To emphasize in the strongest possible way the need to distinguish values relating to the real economy from values relating to the monetary economy, it is only in chapter 23 that the revision of Keynes' model is presented in a strict monetary formulation. (One of the advantages in keeping the two formulations so separate is to avoid the rather common pitfall of switching, in mid-observation, the lenses through which the economic reality is and can be studied; namely, from the monetary to the "real" lenses, and then—likely—back again. Back and forth.)

A Reformulation

Since the issues so briefly treated thus far are numerous, interrelated, and contorted, let us reformulate them using more direct expressions. Let us stop pretending that the theory of money and prices can serve as the theory of distribution. The theory of money or monetary theory represents one aspect of economic theory; as such it is somehow related to the phenomenon of distribution of wealth and income, but it cannot itself be the theory of distribution.

Equally, the theory of prices is not the theory of distribution. Structure to the theory of prices is given by the laws of supply and demand. Were those laws fully applied, they would explain how prices are determined in the real no less than the monetary or financial sector of the economy. Since those laws are not applied today, one must find other explanations for the determination of prices. As seen earlier, the only realistic, truthful, and unbiased explanation one can find is that, especially in the mass consumption market, prices concerning the real economy are determined not by the market but by an intricate web of administrative rules and regulations. The "administrative" unit is either the government or the corporation or both.

In any case, prices—however determined—do in turn determine the allocation or distribution of resources in the field of production. Producers select their production "mix" or their production "function" on the basis of existing prices. Guided by technology and science, they tend to use more of one resource and less of the other, so as to provide an acceptable level of goods and services and ultimately to maximize profits. Leaving aside the important issue of how they are determined, prices also allocate resources among consumers. Consumer-purchases, just as much as producer-purchases, are vastly affected by existing prices. This much is certain. But do prices determine the allocation or distribution of money among consumers as well as producers?

They clearly cannot. Money must have already been distributed, before prices can be determined. Is not this a self evident proposition?

In a modern economy, consumers need to have money at their disposal in order to trigger the mechanisms detailed by the laws of supply and demand and thus influence prices—to the extent that they can—in the micro- no less than in the macro-economic world. Producers, it must also be remembered, are themselves consumers when they shop for the things that they need. It is only in a barter economy that the important step of the distribution of money can be properly neglected in theory as well as in practice.

The theory of prices interpreted as the theory of distribution, in other words, begs this important question: how is money distributed? This is the question that will be investigated as soon as we fully extricate ourselves from the maze built by the many existing, but unrelated, theories. This question, above all, leads to the observation of how economic matters are related to real people and how wealth is distributed among people.

Now that we have found the "proper place" into which, as Keynes envisaged, the theory of prices must "fall";[76] now that we have observed what is meant by monetary theory, we can pick up—again—the discourse on the issue of distribution from where we left it: at ground zero. But now, with a few obstacles removed, we can start afresh. And on our way we shall find some more root causes for the difficulties which economic theory encounters in this field.

Let us start with the fundamentals.

The Theory of Value

The first and foremost difficulty lies in the theory of value, as

Keynes mentioned *en passant* in the lengthy quotation given above. The theory of value is like the "spirit" of economic theory: it overshadows all discussions; it remains silent; indeed, nowadays it is rarely even mentioned; but it is there. Indeed, the theory of value is like a window left open in the structure of economics; the window from which the vast horizons of sociology and psychology, politics, morality, and even esthetics are glimpsed by the economist. In the final analysis, it is in these fields that one finds the springs of the "value" of things. These are vast and pleasing horizons. But one can really enjoy them only when the structure of economic analysis and the internal management of that structure are in good order. Otherwise, one has to attend to other less pleasing tasks.

The way to avoid dangerous drafts while attending to the latter type of tasks is to close the window tight—and to be concerned solely with economic value. In turn one can, rather brusquely, say that economic value is all that two people operating in the market determine it to be. No more, no less. It is only through the market exchange that the economic value of anything becomes "effective," i.e., fully realized.

Those who might harbor doubts as to the validity of this "theory" are invited to spell out those doubts to the "inventor" of the Pet Rock! He knows what economic value is; and he implicitly also knows that it is indeed the "theory of value" which determines the actual practice of distribution of wealth. People try to acquire possession of all that they believe has value.

There are some theoretical questions that must of course be resolved in order to dispel doubts on the validity of this direct approach. As Keynes implied in the above quotation, observed at the instant in which an exchange occurs, there is no difference between economic value and prices; and, unless one wants to get entangled in flimsy theoretical constructions, there is no better alternative. Besides, observed at any other moment, the difference between economic value and prices is not obliterated at all. One is primarily the result of social, psychological, esthetic, and even moral forces; the other is primarily the result of economic, legal, and institutional forces. Consequently, in the price as a manifestation of economic value, we have one result that is determined by the clashing of these two complex and largely intermixed sets of forces. As stated, economists—as economists—have nothing to say about those forces. They can even indulge in their contemplation and eventually, as any other lay person, try to shape them after they have put the economic house in order.

Using more technical jargon, once the interest of the economist is shifted from fascination with the notion of wealth to the analysis of the economic process, an old dichotomy disappears. The economist then completely loses sight of the "value in use" (whether or not hidden, as in Menger, in the utility theory of value) and concentrates the attention on "value in exchange." The unmanageable theory of value—an intensely philosophical and cultural affair that cannot be resolved by the economist alone—is thus reduced to the practical market theory of value.

This theory of value not only places the theory of distribution in its proper context; it also helps to pinpoint a notion that must have troubled the inquisitive reader. This is the notion of wealth, or, more precisely, the notion of economic wealth. Economic wealth is everything ready to be exchanged on the market, and everything involved in the preparation for such an exchange. Excluded from it (in addition to money, as we shall shortly see) are especially consumer goods that, once bought, are not offered again for sale; excluded from it are also skills and other intellectual qualities. What labor exchanges are the services of its skills and intellectual qualities—not skills or intellectual qualities themselves.

Undoubtedly, these are "complex" and controversial issues. One can hardly hope to have settled them once and for all. But in this context nothing more can be added to them. Thus we can, finally, attend to our appointed task. Directly, that is.

The Distribution Process

The phenomenon of distribution of income and wealth is not a theory; it is a practice—a process, to be exact. And a process can only be described and then understood as it is, or not be understood at all. Theory has very little to do with such a description. Let us look at the process of distribution in this light, then. Incidentally, the phenomenon of distribution of wealth ought to be distinguished from the distribution of income. Mostly, the latter slowly determines the former. Thus it is with the latter that we shall primarily be concerned.

Technically, the process of distribution is that process through which the legal ownership of wealth changes hands from one person to another. In a different context, in which undivided attention could be given to it, it would be possible to observe the many ramifications and the many theoretical implications of this concept. Here let us limit our concern to some pedestrian, but concrete, and strictly economic aspects. (Let us note that if producers consume what they produce, there is no such thing as distribution of wealth. From which it also follows that the consumption process is a powerful agent in the phenomenon of distribution: strictly speaking, through the consumption process the economic—or physical—ownership of wealth changes hands from one person to another.)

First of all, let us understand what is being distributed. If commodities bought commodities, as economists of the caliber of John Stuart Mill or Piero Sraffa maintain, then one would need to see how the yearly gross national product (GNP) is distributed among people. The GNP is in fact exclusively composed of goods and services—not of money.

One can, of course, follow this route; and in a more complete treatment than is possible here, one should. Closer to today's reality, however, is the route suggested by Professor Clower, who categorically states: *"Money buys goods and goods buy money; but goods do not buy goods."*[77] Let us observe the process of distribution of money, then—with the warning that money is treated here as any other physical commodity: a global commodity representing, for short, goods and services. (Money is many things, not excluding a tangible representation of the right of property or a claim on wealth.)

The process of distribution of money can thus be seen as a flow of funds *into* the hands of consumers. (Picking up the flow from there, we can also mentally link the three processes mentioned in this work as constituting the economic process. From the hands of consumers, money is exchanged for goods—i.e., consumed—and passed on to the producers. Thus operates the economic process. Thus people create the economic process.)

The distribution process can synthetically be described as follows:

Availability of a Money Supply + Ability to Obtain Part of that Supply ➤ Distribution of Money.

There are two parts to the process, then. Let us observe them separately—visually first, through the attached graph. In a more complete treatment of the issues, one would need to look at the distribution of ownership over real wealth in addition to ownership over monetary wealth. Since the roots of the distribution of ownership over real wealth are more legal than economic, even though it has clear-cut economic implications for economic policy the description of this phenomenon will be skipped here. But it has to be kept in the back of our minds.

Availability of a Supply of Money

For many technical as well as political reasons, ever since the dawn of civilization, to "supply" money—in a large variety of forms—has been a function of the government, often, through a monetary authority. In the United States today, this authority resides with the Federal Reserve Board. Of essential interest to us is not a description of the mechanics of that operation, but an understanding of the basic assumption that rules the "creation" of money. The assumption is that the monetary authority estimates the value of the total sum of goods and services to be produced in the year, and puts at the disposal of consumers (!) a quantity of money which—taking into account the supply of money already existing in circulation—corresponds to the total value of those goods and services to be actually distributed. In the terms developed in this work, the monetary authority has to make sure that the total supply of money is equivalent to the value of the gross national product (P); in symbols, $M = P$; or, following Keynes' terminology, $Y = P$ where both M and Y represent the total money supply. If these two values are equivalent to each other, they will also be equivalent to the total value of "consumption" (C): i.e., equivalent to the total amount of money which consumers are ready to spend. Thus we have reconstituted our basic equivalence of income: $P = C = Y$; or $P = C = D$, where D stands for distribution.

As Professor Modigliani carefully specifies, this equivalence does not need to be established through a one-to-one relationship; it is sufficient to adopt a criterion of proportionality.

We shall assume that the monetary authority is indeed capable of avoiding all the pitfalls involved in the calculations and that it does indeed reconstitute that equivalence. As a further simplifying assumption, let us consider the total supply of money, literally, as a whole that stands, in a kitty ready to be distributed to the people. (We have thus found the water reservoir mentioned earlier.) Let us, in other words, not differentiate among the many kinds of money that do exist or between money which is with the monetary authority and money which "at the beginning of the year" is already in the hands of consumers. Let us also neglect, as we have neglected so many other technicalities, the effects of the velocity of money. It is clear that money can be used more than once during the year; hence, doubling the velocity of circulation is (nearly) the same as doubling the total supply. This is an extremely important factor that, since it can only barely be controlled, is tantamount to

The Distribution Process

Monetary Authority

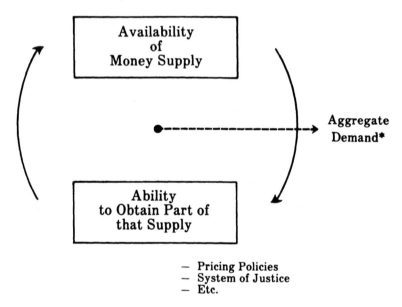

*"Aggregate Demand" stands for all forms of payment, including in-kind, which in any society are necessary to obtain wealth produced by others.

reducing the awesome power of the monetary authority. In addition, this is an extremely important factor because it indicates that the laws of supply and demand—however repressed—are still there to lend all the assistance they are allowed to lend.

Incidentally, there are many other ways in which the power of the monetary authority is cut down to size and the laws of supply and demand reassert their intrinsic power. As Jean-Baptiste Say was fond of emphasizing, people, too, "create" money through sheer word of mouth and paper notes. All these issues, however, belong to a more detailed treatment of the topic.

Finally, we have to neglect the most treacherous aspect of the entire operation: the supply of money created by the monetary authority is not "neutral." It has a great influence on prices, hence on its own value and the market value of the yearly output. This discussion, however, belongs to the description of the dynamics of the economic process. In this context, we can only assume that the monetary authority is indeed capable of establishing the M = P equivalence.

With all these simplifying assumptions, we have thus been able to exhaust the description of the first part of the distribution process. Now a supply of money is available. How is the second part carried out? How does money actually filter down to the consumers?

Before we observe this flow, let us pause to consider a few implications of what has been observed so far. They are important, surprising, and interesting.

Say's Revenge

With the observation that the monetary authority must re-establish the M = P or Y = P equivalence, we have implicitly recognized the need for the application of Say's Law. No matter how far back one tries to push that law, it leaps to the forefront once again begging for revenge. Let us realize why. (Of course any automatism that might have been implied in that law, i.e., "supply creates its own demand,"—has been excluded here. It is the monetary authority that consciously establishes or should establish the equivalence between total output and total supply of money. Total output constitutes "aggregate supply"; and total supply of money when it finally reaches the hands of consumers constitutes "aggregate demand.")

Say's Law is nothing but a belated application to economics of sound bookkeeping practices and principles whose discovery is usually credited to Venetian merchants of the fifteenth century, and are actually much older than that. In order to provide a double check (as opposed to contemporary doublespeak) on their business operations, merchants invented the double-entry bookkeeping system. The system does more than double-check the validity of one's additions and subtractions; it implicitly informs us whether, where, and even when, any business operation goes off balance. It functions as a warning bell. The business *system* can sustain only that much strain, on one side or the other of the balance: debits or credits; inputs or outputs; assets or liabilities; supply or demand.

At the beginning of the nineteenth century Jean-Baptiste Say finally suggested that such bookkeeping principles and practices ought to be applied to the national economy as well. And so Say's Law was born. (It is one of the latest misconceptions to believe that only contemporary economists have dealt with national or aggregate economics.)

Say's Law and controversy go together in economics. Since every time it is mentioned, no matter how, that law creates a stir, let us pause to think. What does a bookkeeping balance really say? It says that the books must be balanced; it does not say how they are to be balanced. This is what Say's Law really tells us: nothing more, nothing less. In fact, it is only an in-depth observation of specific economic operations that can reveal how the books are actually balanced. Very briefly: if the national accounts are balanced both formally and substantively, we are going to have "normal" economic growth. On the contrary, if they are balanced only from a formal point of view, we are going to have either inflation or less growth than we could potentially have. Say's Law provides a starting point for these investigations.

A more detailed analysis, which cannot possibly be conducted here, would reveal a further and perhaps deeper facet of that law. Say's Law is the formulation, in Say's own terms, of the principle of effective demand. It is this hidden characteristic which ultimately explains the extraordinary resiliency of that law.

Need for Triple-check

Indeed, since Say's Law can be such an anchor of strength in our reasoning, calculations, and daily operations, let us think a little more and a little harder. What is the double-entry bookkeeping system, if not a partial recognition (and a belated application) of a much older principle of logic? The double-entry system is an equivalence cut short; it is an equivalence that has not yet fully realized its potential.

In fact, it gives us only a superficial indication of the conditions for the short-term (usually one-year) "equilibrium" of the firm—no less than the conditions for the short-term equilibrium of the national economy. With ecology, and many other developments, coming of late to the forefront of our consciousness, we have begun to realize that the short-term equilibrium is not a completely satisfactory entity. We need to balance our "books" over the long-run as well. This is one form of a triple-entry system of bookkeeping that sooner or later will have to be invented.

Business accounts must be made "to balance" at least over the average life expectancy of capital equipment: about seven years. Indeed, national "accounts" must be made to balance over the average life expectancy of various business cycles: not only five to seven years, but even forty to fifty years. In order to evaluate the efficiency of our economic system, recessions and depressions (to say the least) must be taken into full account—literally, scientifically, statistically. We need a triple-check on our operations and our reasoning. Logic is that demanding. Man's mind is that demanding.

Quite apart from other possible uses, a triple-entry bookkeeping system would provide the material for a fuller, more comprehensible and realistic economic discourse. In that light, one could clearly see the importance of Professor Modigliani' s "life-cycle hypothesis of consumption" or Professor Friedman's "permanent income" hypothesis; on that basis, one could truly build a solid economic policy. Clearly, these are issues that cannot be explored at any greater depth in this context. We must break off the discussion at this stage, but not before emphasizing perhaps the most important characteristic of this work. The seed of the triple-entry system of bookkeeping is contained in the equivalence $P = D = C$.

As we have acquired a more comprehensive understanding of the conditions that surround the first part of the distribution process, i.e., the availability of a supply of money, we can now proceed with the observation of the second part.

Ability to Obtain Part of the Money Supply

Evidently, nearly every consumer is willing to receive the total supply of money available. How does society, no matter the reigning political ideology, control the flow of funds? The answer cannot be found exclusively in economics—even though economists would like to believe that they, as economists, can provide the full answer.

When economists maintain that the flow is controlled exclusively or even primarily by economic laws, they show themselves believing in an imaginary construction: a theoretical assumption in accordance with which the flow is supposed to be controlled by the laws of supply and demand. Presumably, the laws of supply and demand determine the price of commodities; and whoever has earned enough money to pay that price shall apportion to himself a corresponding amount of existing wealth. In this way the distribution of wealth is supposed to occur. It is all supposed to be so automatic, so impersonal—and even so fair. Adam Smith went as far as to say that each person is in the process led by an Invisible Hand. (This expression, it must be pointed out, is just as much misrepresented here as it is in many other places; but this is another story.)

Economists who have a minimum of respect for scientific accuracy, however, qualify the answer—to say the least—to maintain that the flow is controlled by the laws of supply and demand only to the extent that they are applied. And since our economists also know that those laws are only partially applied, they go in search for the rest of the answer somewhere else.

Through this search, one shall find that the rest of the answer lies in the concrete system of practical justice as it prevails at a certain time and a certain place. To dispel any doubt on this extremely important point, let us first observe what the nature of money is. Money is not wealth. It represents wealth; it is the image of wealth. As often repeated, burn all existing money and you have destroyed almost no wealth at all. Money is not another economic commodity. Money is a legal commodity. Actually, money is a contract between the holder of the note and society as a whole. Money then is a legal institution—a claim on wealth—that, like many other similar institutions, creates economic consequences of its own. These consequences are not the subject of this discussion.

For confirmation, through a series of instantaneous snapshots, let us now observe the flow of the distribution of money as it exists in the capitalist world. (In non-capitalist countries, the practices are different; but the principles are essentially the same.) Since the issue is rather long and convoluted, let us call for the assistance of "visual aids."

If the flow were to be observed downstream, it would appear like the delta of a river. It would be composed of seven branches— outflows or channels, as in this graph that can be entitled "Personal Income":

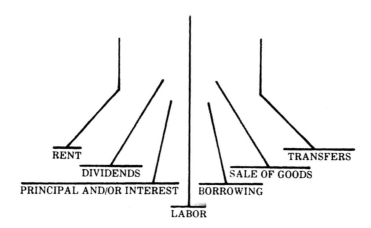

Close examination reveals that so far mankind has not invented any other way for a consumer to receive income, i.e., money. All seven channels are self-explanatory. (A historical analysis of this breakdown would reveal not only how, where, and when were those channels "opened," but also how, where, and when they are used today. In particular, it would be found that non-capitalist countries deprive themselves entirely of the use of a number of these channels.)

A convenient synthesis of the seven channels into three, however, requires some explanation. Rent from land and/or structures, dividends from ownership of stocks, retrieval of principal and/or receipt of interest from loans to other individuals and corporations (bonds) or deposits in a financial institution, sale of goods and borrowing—are all terms that can be subsumed under the category of capital. Thus ownership of capital, performance of labor, and receipt of transfer payments are the three major channels through which money is distributed.

The reduction of the seven channels to three is an important step in our analysis of the flow of income distribution. It allows us to shift our point of observation from the delta to the origin of the flow. (It is in fact one of the characteristics of organic processes that the end is always a beginning—and vice versa.) As is well known, neither people who receive transfer payments nor those who receive labor-income have direct access to the national kitty of the money supply. Such access is reserved to the central government and to financial institutions. This is an intermediary step in our process. As it can be seen, it has nearly nothing to do with the laws of supply and demand; it is almost entirely determined by legal and institutional arrangements. Whatever is left to observe, is only a vague hint of the existence of the laws of supply and demand.

The central government is encouraged to borrow money from the monetary authority (and other private sources), following a counter-cyclical pattern—i.e., to borrow more when the demand in the economy is slack. To emphasize its distance from the laws of supply and demand, this is called "autonomous demand." Indeed, the central government in such cases is encouraged to run huge deficits. (Remember the implicit warning contained in Say's Law.) As far as financial institutions are concerned, they are governed by a web of rules and regulations and follow practices that are necessarily destined to alter the theoretical mechanisms of the laws of supply and demand.

In any case, we are now one step removed from the source of the flow. In order to observe what happens between this step and the delta, we have to analyze the flow at closer range. After the money has reached financial institutions and the federal government, how does it filter down?

Here again we see only a vague hint of the existence of the laws of supply and demand at work. Certainly, transfer payments proper—whether operated by the government or by financial institutions (to and from foundations, for instance)—have nothing to do with the laws of supply and demand. And what about the loans, and/or government contracts, which are issued as political and personal favors—or simply to pursue a mirage as misguiding and unreachable as every mirage is: the policy of "full" employment? What about interest rates or cost overruns, which are allowed under those same contracts? What about straight government loans, loan guarantees, and outright grants to profit and nonprofit organizations? What about the loans which are denied in order "to kill" a competitor? What about the myriad of other practices which exist in the real world of business and finance, let alone the underworld of plunder and murder which exists whether or not the state is one of declared belligerency? These are all concrete factors in the distribution of income. Do they have anything to do with the laws of supply and demand?

More important than all those activities, it might be hard to believe, is the practice of financial institutions lending money only to people who already (!) have money. This practice is the linchpin in the construction of the economic system as it exists today, and as it has existed for centuries; the practices mentioned before are simply the spokes of that great wheel. Contrary to the usual justification for this practice, it must be remembered that as far as "sound" financial practices are concerned too many rich people entrust their wealth to managers who have little or no wealth of their own. Indeed, the great merit of ongoing efforts in the field of micro loans is precisely the demonstration that money can safely be lent to people who do not have money. In any case, the central point in our discussion is another one: how much does this practice have anything to do with the laws of supply and demand?

All this is not to deny that the laws of supply and demand or, more generally, the consumption process—namely, the exchange of goods for money—remain, literally as well as figuratively, the hub in the distribution of money and wealth. If there were no exchange, wealth would stay always in the same hands: apart from forcible extortion, there would be no distribution of wealth. But since in a voluntary exchange both parties receive something in return, and something of an equivalent value, the consumption process functions as a revolving door. No more, no less.

These are only a few of the links in the long chain that leads to one result: the concentration of the ownership of the wealth of nations in a few hands. (In Communist countries, ownership belongs to the state; but control remains as concentrated in a few hands as in capitalist countries. Undoubtedly, even more so.) The correlation between people and wealth is this: the largest portion of existing wealth is owned by a small number of people; and the reverse is also true: a small portion of existing wealth is owned by a large number of people. In order to see clearly this first major twist, which stands in the background as an essential ingredient of the flow of income distribution, let us explicitly draw these two blocks of our total diagram or flow-chart; and let us link them together:

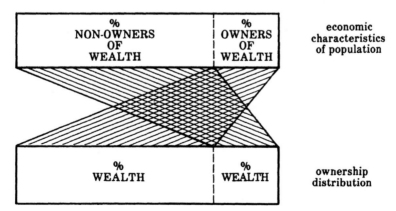

No actual percentages are given, besides stating that the sum of the parts is equal to one hundred, not only because they are subject to small variations from point of view to point of view, from time to time, and place to place; but because precise percentages tend to trigger a famous Parkinson's Law: while one quibbles over the precise accuracy of the smallest possible figure (in our case, a few—necessarily few—percentage points), one loses sight of the total picture. And the total picture is not only important, but incontrovertible: a large portion of existing wealth is owned by a small number of people—and vice versa.

If we pause an instant, we immediately realize why this pattern of distribution of wealth is such an essential ingredient in the distribution of current income. Remember, financial institutions generally lend money only to those who—somehow—have already acquired wealth. (Of course, it is not, nor can it be—and indeed it should not be—their concern to inquire how people acquired their wealth. Would anyone like to create such a super-censor? If so, whose standards of morality ought to apply?)

Past wealth is used to borrow money from financial institutions. Hence money filters down from those institutions toward the final consumers. Indeed, much borrowed money is soon reinvested; and, if the investment is sound, one will receive an even bigger income in the future. Thus wealth tends to beget wealth. But we are not interested in the future wealth right now—except to emphasize that the second block in the process of distribution of money, which has been observed above, looks like the end of the flow; and it is not. It is a mere beginning in its own right. There is in fact considerably more. Indeed, the next two major blocks in the distribution process are composed of elements that are relatively little known. Both require rather extensive explanatory notes.

In our discussion of the production process we have, in essence, observed that Man + Investment-Assets Production. Investment-assets are those actively engaged in the production process: tools, machinery, land, supplies (in part, natural resources), etc. Evidently, these assets are less than the total value of wealth observed in our previous block. We have to discount the value of all consumer products such as homes, their furnishings, clothes, and all nonproductive goods such as gold under the mattress, land which is held for speculation, conservation or recreation purposes, etc. This point can perhaps best be illustrated with the use of the following two diagrams:

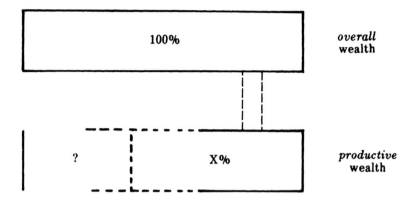

Productive wealth clearly is less than the totality of wealth in general. Two questions arise: first, what contributes to the totality of the productive effort—or what makes our "open" diagram equal to one hundred percent? The answer is simple: the "value" of labor. The next question concerns the determination of the apportionment of that total (one hundred percent) between the two items, which for short shall be called capital and labor.

Surprising as it may seem to the uninitiated, there are no precise accounts of either the value of that total or the value of the component parts of that total. This condition is the direct result of the interest of contemporary economic theory, which is concentrated upon the value of "flows" and not the value of "stocks" of goods and money. The measure of the flow of the river does not, and cannot, give the measure of the depth and the capacity of the lake.

Hence, at best, one finds estimates of the value of stocks. Existing estimates concerning the value of productive wealth can be derived especially from the work of Professor R. W. Goldsmith. To the knowledge of this writer, no one has yet even attempted to measure the value of labor. What exists in this area is owed to the work of Professor Simon Kuznets, Professor Robert M. Solow (two Nobel laureates), Professor (and Senator) Paul H. Douglas, and the work done at the National Bureau of Economic Research under the directorship of Dr. Arthur F. Burns, a former chairman of the board of the Federal Reserve System. Through their methodologies, however refined and extended to gather information all over the planet as evidenced especially by the Penn World Tables, economists have calculated the value of income received by labor over long periods of time. These computations then have to be taken as the only available indirect estimates of the value of labor. The reasoning is as follows.

The value of labor apparently is that which exists on the market today; or what employers pay employees—thus functioning as direct distributors of income. With the aid of existing computations, it can be said that this value tends to hover around seventy-five percent of the combined productive effort (or total income). Hence the market value of capital "must" be put at approximately twenty-five percent of that total. We have apparently solved our two problems. The totality can be called *"market* value of contributive shares to production." Hence our "open" diagram now reads:

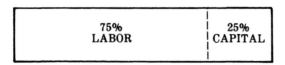

| 75% LABOR | 25% CAPITAL | market value of contributive shares to production |

Once again, this would appear to be the end of the story. But it is not. The compulsion which we have been under, i.e., the need to assign a figure of twenty-five percent of the total productive effort to capital, is a strong indication that there is something wrong either with our reasoning or our calculations—or, as proves to be the case, with the perceived reality. That compulsory twenty-five percent appears to be an extremely low figure—especially if one considers the value of the accumulation of past capital stock. (Conversely, the seventy-five percent contributive share attributed to labor appears to be an extremely high figure—especially if it is agreed that labor does not sell skills and intellectual qualities, but only the services of those skills and qualities.)

Let us now look at the reality unassisted by prevailing statistical computations, which, however well-founded, had to be taken into account as mere facts. In other words, we no longer look at the "market" value of those two factors of production. Instead, we look at their "actual" value. Our task is to determine the *"Actual* Value of Contributive Shares to Production." This computation evidently is an estimate. The calculation is treacherous and, in the absence of figures developed and counterchecked by many minds, it is uncertain. Louis O. Kelso, the noted lawyer, financier, and policy-maker, risked such an assessment, and he incurred the wrath of many an economist. But his reasoning seems to be unexceptionable.

This appraisal of Kelso's position, in the face of strong official criticism, might appear to be either naive or preposterous. Instead, there is a solid reason why much weight should not be given to the wrath of mainstream economists on this point. The attentive reader will notice that such wrath arises out of a not-so-subtle misinterpretation of their relative positions: Kelso talks of the value of income produced, and mainstream economists talk of the value of income received by labor. There is a manifest gap between the two entities; but the gap is more likely to be observed by a lawyer—such as Kelso—than by an economist. No matter what the root cause of the misunderstanding on this point is, one must conclude that the official criticism is misdirected. We can proceed with our discussion.

When one discounts from the current market value of labor the effects of featherbedding and boondoggling, of make-work and make-believe work, inflated wages, and the cost of all labor which could be eliminated—with today's state of the art—through a fuller application of automation techniques, the impression of the soundness of Kelso's reasoning seems confirmed. A large part of the total value of production is actually contributed by "the machines" and a little is contributed by labor. Simply think of a man with a bulldozer and a man with a shovel—and the shovel already is "capital." No doubt with some exaggeration, especially since he did not seem to make full allowance for an intangible element—human organization—which is "pure" labor or labor-unassisted-by-capital, Kelso put those shares respectively at ten percent as the contribution of labor and ninety percent as the contribution of capital. Capital here includes land. Without excessive concern for accurate figures, then, let us link together the two blocks in the flow or distribution of income that we have now discussed:

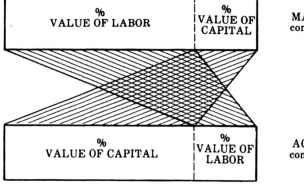

Again, a major twist in the flow of distribution of income. The market value of labor is higher than the value of existing capital-assets, but its actual contribution to the value of the new total production seems to be relatively lower than that contributed by capital. Again, this seems to be a fact. There are many reasons and many explanations for this fact; they are of concern to economic policy. Of direct concern is a third group of two blocks in our description of the flow of income distribution.

The two blocks respectively are: the one observed above concerning the value of the actual contributive share to the total production and the final distribution of income as it actually occurs today. The two blocks linked together read as follows:

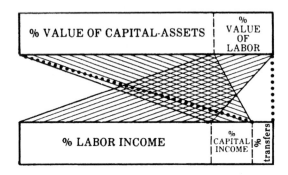

Still another twist. Labor is generally receiving a larger share of income than it actually produces; and the owners of capital a smaller share than they—through their ownership of land, machinery, and equipment—actually produce. What does it all mean? All too briefly, it means that, whereas the large majority of people lost ownership and control over the means of production long ago, capitalists have lately lost ownership and control over the fruits of capital.

Again, we run into overpowering issues of economic policy that cannot be adequately treated here. Our concern must be limited to the description of the facts. Hence, we notice that both capital and labor transfer shares of their income to people who, for a variety of reasons, cannot directly participate in the productive effort. It is to be noted however that, although the recipients of transfer payments do not directly contribute to the production process, they are an integral part of the distribution and the consumption process. They receive money, and they spend it. Thus they are an integral part of the overall economic process.

There are some strictly interconnected implications of the last observations that deserve to be highlighted. If people who receive transfer payments are such an integral part of the economic process, it will be seen how problems of distribution of income and wealth, which start as problems of justice, automatically become problems of economics. The hoarding of wealth, for instance, is self-defeating: it is a totally passive action that wilts away. Wealth which is invested and whose fruits are equitably distributed, instead, comes back to its original owners in the form of profits— after having sustained people's lives. Hence justice loses its frequently given connotation of being a vaguely sentimental, impractical, and idealistic affair, whose moral tinges need to be suppressed in the "cruel reality" of the world. Justice, indeed, becomes the very hidden motor of the economic system; justice makes supreme practical and economic sense.

Unfortunately we have to abandon these important but still incidental observations in favor of the resumption of our central line of reasoning. We have yet to see the end of the flow. There is still another characteristic to be mentioned. (Is not the word "flow" an egregious misnomer? Would an engineer ever dare to call it so? Would engineers ever tolerate such a pattern in any of their constructions?) The final characteristic is this: of the seven channels which we have observed at the beginning of the description of the flow of distribution of income, one (labor-income) carries approximately seventy-five percent of the load—and the remaining six carry the balance. Engineers take note.

This final segment of the flow can be illustrated as follows:

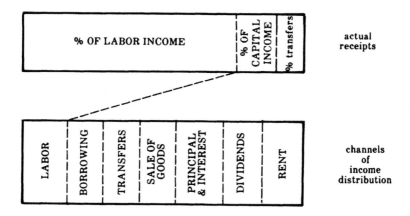

Thus we have come full circle. We are exactly at the point from which we started. In the impossibility of repeating what has been said so far, perhaps a whole diagram which joins together the key steps observed above might function as a summary of this discussion on the second component part of the distribution process. The attached diagram is entitled "A *Simplified* Flow of Distribution of Income" because it eliminates a large number of intermediary steps. The aim of the diagram is to provide a synthetic, not an analytical, view of the flow as a whole—at one instant in time.

There is, undoubtedly, a host of issues here. They cannot be analyzed in this context. Suffice it, perhaps, to say that not until those many knots are unsnarled, will the flow of distribution of income be a smooth one. Indeed, not until then shall we have a smooth-functioning economic process. (Perhaps it should be emphasized that the question of a smooth process must not be confused with the issue of the "redistribution of income." Income is already being distributed and then re-distributed. Could one risk here a not altogether facetious observation? In the final analysis, people seem to get exactly what they deserve.)

In closing, we need to remark that, were we able to study the dynamics of the distribution process, we could clearly see how the money thus distributed eventually results in a certain mix of capital goods, consumer goods, and goods that can be hoarded. We would, in other words, see how the distribution of money is ultimately transformed into the distribution of real wealth. But this task has to be reserved for other investigations.

For the time being, it might be useful to tie more closely together the three aspects of the entire economic process observed so far. As highlighted in their respective illustrations, the major function of the production process is to create a specific aggregate supply (of goods and services); the major function of the distribution process is to create a specific aggregate demand (essentially represented by a *supply* of money or wealth in general at the disposal of consumers); and the major function of the consumption process is to establish a moving, organic equilibrium between that aggregate supply and that aggregate demand. Clearly, these issues are so completely interwoven that they should always be considered dynamically and as a unit.

To get a glimpse of the totality of the issues, let us observe two phenomena in the next two chapters: economic growth and inflation. We shall conclude our work with some observations about economic poverty. The knowledge acquired so far about the eco-

A Simplified Flow
of
Income Distribution

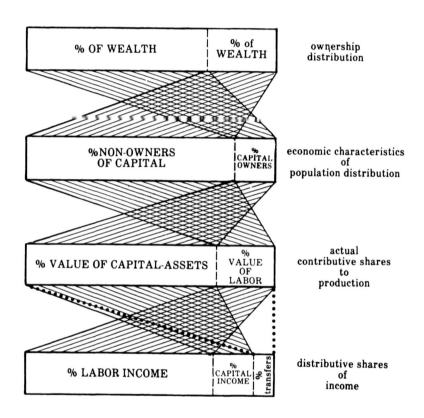

Notes:

— This is a *simplified* flow. Other clarifying steps are included in the text.

— Actual percentage figures are withdrawn to avoid the pitfalls outlined by one of the major Parkinson's Laws.

nomic process as a whole will allow us to make a first approximate analysis of those key phenomena in our economic—and indeed social, political, and moral—life.

XXI

Economic Growth:
The Normal Outcome of the
Unfolding of the Economic Process

The work of economic development
occurs when the "miracle of growth"
is not followed by pauses, recessions,
and depressions.

———•———

BECAUSE GREAT FAME AND RECOGNITION have quite properly been
bestowed upon Adam Smith, he must also bear the burden of great
responsibilities. And nowhere are the unavoidable weaknesses in
his thought more evident than in what has lately been called the
theory of economic growth. Here, the fundamental error in his
thought lies in not distinguishing the ends and means of man from
the ends and means of the economic process. Because of this failing—which of course was a distinctive characteristic of his age—
Adam Smith ended up attributing both sets of means and ends to
an Invisible Hand.

The two must be separated from each other and, while the ends
and means of Man can largely be attributed to an Invisible Hand,
the ends and means of the economic process are to be attributed
directly to the visible hands of many men and women.

If we do not make this distinction, the economic process becomes
enshrouded in absolute mystery and dotted with miracles. The cita-
tion of the Italian—or the German, or the Japanese—economic miracle is the direct descendant of that failing in Smith's thought. And
the misuse and inappropriateness of the word "miracle" in this
context is not without practical consequences. Notwithstanding
the warning of such eminent specialists as Albert O. Hirshman,
it has made us confuse the phenomenon of reconstruction with

the phenomenon of growth.

The Works of Reconstruction

More or less consciously, we look at the reconstruction of the European and Japanese economy after World War II as "the model" to follow in order to obtain economic development in the Third World. In addition, that model is often looked upon as containing policy recommendations that need to be followed in order to obtain community growth in so many decaying cities or larger geographic areas, i.e., the so-called "pockets of poverty" within the "developed" economies of the world.

All efforts plus billions of dollars—and other currencies—expended in the fitful attempt to implement the policy initiatives inherent in that model have dismally failed. The failure itself, whose existence needs to be neither proved nor qualified, has been unable to deter a repetitive call for a Marshall Plan for the cities or a Marshall Plan for "developing" countries. Perhaps an analysis of the structural weaknesses of that model might convince its proponents that even if such a plan were comprehensively implemented the result would still not be satisfactory.

Undoubtedly, there are many causes for this result. For each effect, there is always an infinite number of causes. Learning about the largest possible number of those causes is essential to avoid the repetition of the most common mistakes; but to mention all those causes indiscriminately carries with it a double jeopardy. It carries the danger of confusing both the reader and the writer. To let the reader obtain a clear view of the problem, on which basis further inquiries can be advanced, let us turn immediately to the root causes of that failure.

Causes lie in a deficient analysis, and consequently in a treatment based on the wrong diagnosis. The analysis, which has been neither detailed nor general enough, overlooks the profound differences which exist between the European or Japanese economy after World War II and the "underdeveloped" or the "ghetto" economy. In addition, this analysis fails to appreciate the profound differences that exist between the works of reconstruction and those of development.

In the vast literature on economic growth there is a vivid illustration of the difference between reconstruction and development. True—it has been pointed out either by Professor Rosenstein-Rodan, Professor Manlio Rossi Doria, or some other authority in the field—bombs did contribute to the collapse of the European and Japanese economy; but bombs simply destroyed key centers of production and key lines of transportation and communication. To undertake the work of reconstruction, therefore, it was sufficient to restore those key points to their former function.

Not that the "patching" work of reconstruction was easy. But it was not that difficult either. The areas surrounding the "holes" caused by the bombs were still very much intact.

Consider now the economy of the ghetto. It is often said that these areas are "bombed out." The description is accurate; the devastation is near total. What exists there is a delicate web of tenuous economic relationships. The threads are so thin and stretched out that they are ready to snap at a minute's notice. Within that network, one can often find "pockets of wealth." And is the economy of the developing world much different? Indeed, one is hard put to characterize either of them as an economic system. In the "underdeveloped" and the "ghetto" economies, it is not a question of patchwork. Rather, one needs to create centers of production, communication, and transportation *ex novo*.

Quite apart from the solidity of the underlying structure of "miracled" economies, the collapse of previous activities proved to be an—economic—blessing in disguise. One did not need to consider the impact upon existing plant and equipment of the adoption of new scientific and technological advancements, whose creation had been accelerated by the war effort conducted in the United States no less than in those countries themselves. More often than not, the replacement cost of previous plant and equipment with the use of old technology had, for various self-evident reasons, become prohibitive. And the cost of the new equipment was lower than the expected revenue. In addition, especially thanks to the Marshall Plan, financial capital was rather plentiful. Therefore, rates of interest were generally lower than the "marginal efficiency" of proposed capital-assets. Finally, the needs were evident—a factor that ought not to be underestimated; and the public's demand to have those needs met was exceptionally strong. (Where is such a demand in relation to the "underdeveloped" and the "ghetto" economy?)

With the necessary financial and business requirements in relatively good order, and secure that likely errors would not only be absorbed by the profits obtainable during the period of expansion but even morally justified, one business executive and one corporate board after another gave the green light to the proposed investment. The "boom" was well underway; and the miracle could not fail to appear on the horizon.

This was the work of reconstruction—fully completed. But was this a work of economic development? No. That work would have proved to be one of economic growth only if the miracle had not been followed by pauses, recessions, and near-depressions.

Not until we learn how to avoid such economic—let alone social—calamities as pauses, recessions, and depressions can we say that we have mastered the field of economic development. By themselves, voluminous treatises will not do. They cannot be substitutes for that final proof.

Economic Growth

And what is economic growth? Economic growth is the normal outcome of the unfolding of the economic process.

The phrase might sound cryptic. Let us expand upon it. But let us start from ground zero. Let us first observe some of the characteristics of organic processes, not in the abstract but by relating them to the economic discourse. Then we shall become better equipped to deal with such a complex phenomenon as economic growth.

To put it more categorically at the outset, there is no difference between the process of economic growth and the economic process itself. What one actually observes is the process of economic growth or decay. It is in fact impossible to study the one without the other; and when that is done, it is realized that the center of observation is simply the economic process in its concrete manifestations. (This phenomenon was well understood by classical economists. They had no separate theory of growth.)

Some General Characteristics of Organic Processes

If the economic process is indeed an organic process, as these chapters portray it to be, it is necessary to get acquainted with some of its general characteristics. In organic processes, there is neither a beginning nor an end to it; they are coterminous with life. This is the first, predominant characteristic.

Let us immediately relate this characteristic to two issues connected with economic analysis. In the nature of organic processes we can find not only convincing evidence of how fruitless is one of the major controversies revolving around Say's Law—the controversy, that is, as to whether it is production or consumption which is "more important" or comes "first." We can also see how fruitless it would be to pass any judgment on the question left open in the first chapter. This is the question as to whether the sense of the relationship of saving-investment to the rest of the economic system, which Keynes discovered, is more "accurate" than the sense accepted by the majority of economists. The issue, we shall recall, is whether saving and investment are the determinates or the determinants of the economic system. In the briefest possible terms, it all depends on the place and time of observation. Within the context of its own theory, in fact, each sense is accurate and performs its own distinct set of functions. But that is not the question.

The question is that, because of those two different approaches, one is presented with two completely different sets of theories: to use Professor Leijonhufvud's terminology, The Economics of Keynes vs. Keynesian Economics. (Of course, from this point of view, Keynesian economics is quite close not only to classical economics, but even to Monetarist theories.) If those two (or more) sets of theories appear to be "close enough" to each other, it is due to a simple fact. Neither set has ever been completely spelled out. The missing parts in each have, for the most part, not been provided by later explanations. On the contrary, these have often broken away from their respective base lines just enough to become derivative theories in their own right. As noted, we are not presented with two theories; but with two (and more) sets of theories.

Rather than getting involved with those differences, it is preferable to emphasize that all those theories—considered as one group—are completely different from the economic "theory" which is outlined in this work. Those are rational theories; this is a dynamic and organic theory—or more precisely, a dynamic and organic, though unavoidably incomplete, presentation of existing facts. Facts are always infinite and always changing; and in this work the dynamics are kept in check because the economic process is observed at only one instant in time.

This distinction leads us to the very essence of organic processes: they cannot be rationalized. There is no theory of trees; no theory of kidneys. And, properly speaking, there can be no theory of economics either. Either one faithfully and accurately describes the economic process as it is, or one builds abstract rationalizations: castles in the sand that collapse at the touch of reason or the touch of reality.

This is not a call for irrationality and chaos. Far from it. Reason—and the full expansion of reason represented by theories—is indispensable especially for the diagnosis of illnesses. And so there are, and there must be, theories to investigate the causes of the illnesses of trees and kidneys—as well as the illnesses of the economic process. But such an investigation can be proficiently carried out only when the normal condition of those phenomena is truly understood. Therefore, rather than building a theory of economics, we must be concerned with studying the infinite details of the actual phenomenon of the economic process. Indeed, economics itself must be defined as the study of the economic process. And economic theories can be built only to study the causes of the illnesses or deviations from the "normal" process.

As far as the study of the process itself is concerned, one cannot build a theory. It can simply be presented as an organized description of economic facts—a task that cannot be finished, if it can ever be finished, in these pages. The basic difference with mainstream economics would become incontrovertibly evident if one were allowed to introduce the language of biology into the economic discourse. Thus economists would stop talking of consumption, investment, etc. as rather abstract entities; they would, instead, present them as organs: organs that are an integral part of moving and living organisms. But the relative ease with which ideas could then be expressed, would carry with it the danger of losing all contact with the past evolution of economic analysis—as well as the danger for economics of losing its autonomy to biology or other natural sciences.

This loss of autonomy would be a serious drawback. Economics is not a natural science, and it cannot be made such for a very simple reason. It does not respect the law of impenetrability of bodies. As we have seen, for instance, hoarding has the capability of transforming itself into investment—and then at times back again to hoarding. Similarly, what has so neatly been divided here exists as a unity in reality: the production process is an instrument of consumption, no less than an instrument of distribution of income. And there are many more relationships of this type. Besides, the loss of autonomy for economics, which would rather automatically ensue from the adoption of the language of other organic sciences, is not really necessary. (What is necessary is a change only in our mental attitude towards economics; and this will necessarily come slowly and gradually.) That loss in fact is not necessary because the language of economics, as it has evolved, already carries with it the ability to represent organic phenomena. A "system" for instance, if it indeed a system, is an organic entity observed from a static point of view. And a "process" is an organic entity observed from a dynamic point of view.

Incidentally, should this work not have been entitled "The Economic System"? Technically, yes. But the expression economic system is generally understood to mean a system of political economy. This work does not cover such an aspect of economics. Also, the word system tends to convey the notion of a static and inflexible entity. The economic system is not static and inflexible. Far from it. It is organic, non-mechanical, non-Newtonian. To express these points more forcefully, while at the same time attempting to dispel a rather common misconception, Keynes did not analyze the capitalist system. *Mutatis mutandis* (what needs to be changed relates exclusively to the political and juridical institutions surrounding it as well as all issues of political economy), the theoretical economic system analyzed by Keynes is neither capitalist nor Communist—and it can be either.

If someone asks how the economic system becomes the economic process—the process of growth or decay—the answer is simple: the system has never stopped being a process. It is our mind that, for ease of analysis, has made that entity a system; it is our mind that has observed it as if it was, and could be, static. The entity itself has never ceased being a process—as the titles of the previous chapters tried to convey. Indeed, the entity itself has never ceased being a process composed of many strictly interrelated processes. The economic process as a whole—in short—is the result of the production process, the distribution process, and the consumption process. One can mistakenly see them as boxes within boxes; or one can more properly see them as living organs within a living organism.

In an organic system or an organic process, then, there is nothing that is "more important": all parts have an identical importance. Take away even the smallest possible part, and the process—or the system—will break down. (The cost of the eventual repair of that part is a totally different matter from the question of its intrinsic importance; in any case, in the repair cost of the smallest part one has to include the cost of idleness of the total system.) Also there is nothing in an organic process that comes "first": either all the elements are there at once, or the system does not work at all. (The question of the timing involved in the preparation necessary for each smallest or largest piece to be created, to join other pieces, and to form the system, is a totally different matter as well.)

Now perhaps we begin to have a fuller appreciation of the expression, economic growth is the normal outcome of the unfolding of the economic process. And yet, for further assistance, let us think about the growth of a human being. Once the baby is created—an amazing process in itself—no one makes the baby grow.

One can deny food or overfeed a baby; but no one makes the baby grow. The baby naturally grows; another wondrous and, no matter what one reads in the natural sciences, mysterious process in itself.

These, then, are some of the characteristics of organic processes: (a) there is no beginning and no end to them; (b) they cannot be rationalized; (c) the smallest component part has exactly the same importance as the biggest one; (d) all parts have to be present at once in order for the system to function; (e) it is a mystery how they are set in motion; (f) it is a mystery how they actually grow—except to say that they grow or decay through internal, organic processes. (The work of science is to reduce the area of mystery.)

Let us now briefly use these characteristics to obtain a closer understanding of the process of economic growth.

Economic Growth as a Dynamic and Organic Process

Just as no single person makes the economic system grow from the outside, so nothing external makes it grow. The system grows and organically transforms everything with which it comes in contact to serve its purposes—purposes that, unless they are guided by men and women toward a specific goal, are simply purposes of growth or decay.

No single person or group of persons determines the process of growth or decay, because everyone contributes to that result: from the hermit to the hustler; from the old man who sweeps the floor to the corporate executive; from artists or scientists who introduce a new vision of the world to government planners who try to steer the economic system toward their own vision of the world.

We are now able to see with clarity the extent to which Adam Smith was correct. The process of growth, as all other processes, is an invisible—indeed, a mysterious—one. His conception of the Invisible Hand is vindicated. But there is also a visible part to the process. This is the economic system; and that is what we have largely observed in the previous chapters. We have even broken it down, pretending that it was a static affair. Also the importance of the difference between reconstruction and growth is more easily identified now. Indeed, to put that difference in sharper focus, let us think in these terms. Let us elaborate upon the differences between a war hospital and a nursery—be it a baby or a tree nursery. The practices are sharply different; and the results are also different.

But all this describes the process of economic growth in a figu-

rative way, contrasting it to a set of negative images. Is there no
other way? Basically, there is no shortcut. The alternative is to
repeat each and every step mentioned earlier in the discussion on
the production process, the distribution process, and the consumption process—and then to go forward by tying all those steps
together and observing all the interrelationships among those
steps. And there are gaping holes in this discussion that cry out to
be filled. Those gaping holes have been left as they are confidently
relying upon two essentially exploitative assumptions: first, the
knowledge of the reader; and then the existence of a neat distinction between economic theory and economic policy whereby we
have excluded from our range of observation all matters which
pertain to economic policy. Of course, this distinction does not
exist in reality. In reality, economic policy shapes economic theory
and economic theory shapes economic policy. Furthermore, some
readers might not have the knowledge to fill those gaps. But these
are the unavoidable risks taken when entrusting so delicate and
complex a process as the process of communication between
human beings to so crude an instrument as the written word.

There is left, however, one possibility of filling some of those
gaps—and this possibility shall be exploited here. This possibility
consists of simplifying and adapting to our purposes a series of diagrams developed by Jane Jacobs in her appendix to *The Economy
of Cities*. Let us unabashedly proceed with this exploitative work.

A Visual Representation of the Economic Growth Process

In the discussion of the production process we have observed that
Man + Capital Production. In the discussion of the distribution
process we have essentially transformed that formula into the following diagram, which can now be given the name of
"Production—Stage I" with an index number of one hundred:

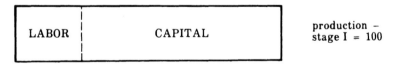

Through the work of the principle of added activity and the
principle of division of labor, we can also graphically see how the
production process grows:

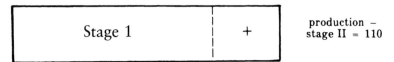

We could continue indefinitely along this road. This attempt, however, would be a mere mental exercise. To observe what happens in the field of economics, we have at least to combine the production with the distribution and consumption processes. Thus we can graphically represent the path of growth (or decline) of the economic process as a whole through the following diagram:

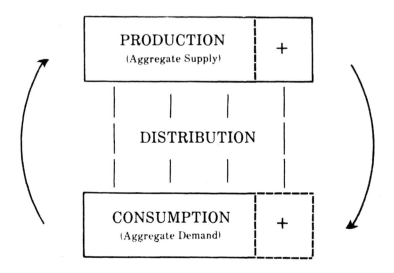

Since this section is intended to be a mere visual representation of the process of economic growth, no analysis is provided to explain the last diagram. But three points need emphasis. First, from this diagram it is immediately recognized that the notion of equilibrium in economics does not imply statics; it does not imply stability or tranquility. Economic "equilibrium" is a constantly moving, dynamic, organic phenomenon. Second, from this diagram and this notion of equilibrium it follows that the laws of supply and demand—as Keynes rather forcefully tried to demonstrate—apply to the world of macroeconomics more clearly and fittingly than to that of microeconomics. Third, it cannot be stressed enough that just as there is an infinite set of conditions which make the economic system grow, so there is an infinite set of obstacles which can make it decline. Since it is impossible to provide a complete list of the former, no adequate list can be provided of the latter.

In the next chapter we shall focus on the major concrete obstacle that the economic process faces in a modern economy: inflation. As a synthesis of the discussion carried out so far about the process of growth, let us briefly observe a generally temporary, and easily corrigible obstacle. Following the implicit hypothesis of an increase in production, if the monetary authority does not increase (as Professor Friedman would heartily favor) the supply of money from index base one hundred to, say, one hundred ten, and if this increased supply of money does not reach the hands of consumers who are ready and willing to spend that money, the increased production cannot be sold—or, greatly simplifying things, that production would have to be sold at a loss. Then the process of growth would not proceed on its path. Indeed, in the long-run the economic process would—as at times it does—decrease instead of increase. To be made explicit, the above statements rely on the assumption of a constant value of the money supply. It can now be immediately seen that economic growth is indeed the "normal" outcome of the unfolding of the economic process. If each process within the overall economic process does not encounter undue obstacles, the normal outcome cannot be other than growth. This is how the economic process operates.

With the preliminaries taken care of, we are free to approach the core of the issues. A few essential characteristics of the process of economic growth can be firmly grasped if, instead of looking backward at what has previously been said, we move the discourse forward. We need to observe some of the imaginary and some of the real requirements for this process to get started.

Three Imaginary Requirements

Those who are even remotely familiar with the field of economic development will notice that (at least) three commonly mentioned requirements for economic growth have disappeared from the discussion: the need for savings; the need for plenty—plenty of labor, plenty of financial capital, plenty of natural resources; and the need for full employment. These are three imaginary requirements. Let us briefly see why.

The Presumed Need for Savings

With saving (or hoarding) defined as all nonproductive wealth, it is clear that savings are not a requirement for economic growth. Quite to the contrary, they impede economic growth—because they withdraw from the economic process resources which otherwise might be transformed into investment.

Once the relationship of "equality" between saving and investment is definitely dissolved, as it has hopefully been done in this work, there is no longer the danger of running into what we shall soon see as a series of verbal and conceptual pitfalls. One can no longer say that in the final analysis savings are technically investment, or use any variation of this expression. The clarity of the discourse gains immeasurably. Certainly, were it not for the existence of a long series of misconceptions engendered by the prevailing verbal quagmire, we could even leave the issue with the above general statements. However, to dispel the last vestiges of doubt, we had better proceed gingerly.

The ownership of savings, whether "real" or financial, of course, still remains one of the requirements for the acquisition of financial capital; but this is an entirely different function from that which savings are supposed to perform. As Louis 0. Kelso vividly points out, this function of past accumulated wealth is one of "insurance" against possible future losses. (But then he fails to add that this function can be—and is—performed by capital goods or even consumer goods, just as well as by nonproductive wealth.) In fact, because he sees savings performing exactly this insurance function, Kelso has been able to design economic policies that take care of that financial requirement. Such policies lie beyond our present field of observation.

And what is the economic function that savings are generally supposed to perform? They are supposed to "pay" for investments. This is a gross misconception. It can never be emphasized strongly enough. Savings do not pay for investment. As Kelso insists, investments pay for themselves. Indeed they must pay for themselves and even leave a surplus—otherwise they are not, and ought not to be, undertaken. This is a simple but fundamental truth which becomes evident when the production process is seen as a dynamic and organic process and when the terms of the economic discourse are made to mean exactly what they say. This is a simple but fundamental truth that has always been recognized by every true economist. Kelso recognizes it, even though his theoretical structure is so skimpy that one even hesitates to call him an economist. Of course Keynes recognized it. He stated that one ought "to speak of capital as having a yield over the course of its life in excess of its original cost."[78] Adam Smith also recognized this simple but fundamental truth. He stated: "Though the manufacturer has his wages advanced to him by his master, he, in reality, costs him no expense, the value of those wages being generally restored, together with a profit, in the improved value of the subject upon which his labour is bestowed."[79]

How else to make the point? Perhaps the point cannot be made with words. Perhaps one ought to become an entrepreneur and directly experience that simple but fundamental truth. Perhaps, to clearly see the point one ought to start implementing many of the economic policies designed by Kelso, i.e., one ought to remove the obstacles which exist in the field of financing, not by subverting those practices, but by finding wholly "modern" ways to meet those requirements.

Barring the advantage of a comprehensive vision of the issues that only super-economists seem to be able to acquire and barring the benefit of direct experience, how can we—the majority of the people—be made to understand clearly the fundamental truth that savings do not pay for investment? Maybe the best way to exorcise the common misconception to the contrary is to return to its historical origin.

It was Quesnay (1758) who, if he did not invent that conception, certainly made it appear incontrovertible. He made the observation that capitalists, by definition, are those who "advance" their capital to keep the production process in movement. This factual observation of "financing" growth or "advancing" capital was soon confused with the hypothesis that savings pay for investment, and the latter proposition became part of a tightly constructed system of thought. It then became a matter of dogma to maintain that the role of the capitalists is to pay—through their savings—for economic growth.

Capitalists benefit from—they do not "pay" for—economic growth. This contradiction in terms was insufficient to let many economists stop and think that workers also advance something in that process. They advance their labor: i.e., their capital. They are never paid before their work is completed—whether the time involved is a day or a week. As far as timing is concerned, then, there is no difference between workers and capitalists.

But what about risk? Whenever a product is not sold, or it is not adequately paid for, workers are also penalized. Thus they too incur a risk. Furthermore, whenever capitalists advance their capital, through careful selection they risk little and on the average they risk nothing. It is only in periods of great economic distress that capitalists suffer losses; but then everybody suffers. The issue is one of relative sufferance, relative risk—and not one of absolutes.

In brief, whether by saying that savings pay for investment is meant to advance capital or to wait for returns or to risk a loss, the expression hides a long series of gross misconceptions. In time, investments pay for themselves. Period. And time is not money. Time is life.

At this point the argument becomes either philosophical or circular. Obviously, we cannot insist on the philosophical aspects of the issue; but we do need to close the circularity of the economic argument. When it is said that "in time" investments pay for themselves, the economist might grasp at the straw and maintain that past savings are still necessary to sustain the life of both the worker and the capitalist—if not the life of the investment itself. The circularity of argument can be eliminated by realizing a simple fact. It is current consumer and capital goods that allow one to go through the waiting period. Current consumer and capital goods are neither savings nor are they the result of past savings. They are the result of past investments that have paid for themselves and have left a surplus to boot.

Semantic issues always carry a message. They signal either clear thinking or muddled thinking. But final immunization against muddled thinking is not acquired through mere words. As stated, it is through a comprehensive view of all the issues or through the impact of direct experience that the truth affirms itself. Certainly, in words, one can only monotonously repeat: for the process of economic growth, savings are not necessary. Indeed, they have never been necessary for such a purpose either historically or logically or, in fact as well as in theory, economically. Let us observe these different points separately.

Savings in Fact and the Meaning of Cost in Economic Theory

The observation of crude facts is cryptic but unobjectionable. There is nothing that creates an investment, except the act of investment itself. Admittedly, this is rather cryptic. But the search for the conditions of an investment outside the act of investment reintroduces, through the back door, the role of savings in the production process; and this leads to unpredictable consequences. At the unconscious level, it confuses savings with natural resources. At the conscious level, it neglects the important train of economic thought represented by the meaning of cost.

To believe that savings create, or pay for, investment is to confuse savings with natural resources. It is to confuse them from an economic point of view. It is to believe that natural resources—which are indeed necessary to carry on the act of production—are man's "savings." There is no foundation for this belief. Savings and natural resources have nothing in common.

Natural resources do not even constitute economic wealth. It is only as a result of the production process, i.e., when man applies his energies to those resources, that they become economic wealth. Not before. And then economic wealth is still undifferentiated. One must still distinguish among consumer goods, capital goods, and goods that can be hoarded. And when this distinction is made, it becomes clearly evident that neither consumer goods nor goods that can be hoarded have anything to do with the next stage of the production process. It is capital goods or investment-assets—those assets that, by being productive, pay for themselves—that are essential to this stage. While consumer goods are at least an essential part of the consumption process, goods that can be hoarded are essential to neither. They become a part of the distribution process and from there, at times without one exchange, they get out of the economic process as a whole. They are hoarded. (They can of course re-enter it, either as consumer or as capital goods. But then they automatically lose their economic nature as hoarding.)

Perhaps the best way to eliminate confusion in this area is to examine the facts of primordial existence. When the first men and women, with their bare hands, picked nuts and berries or caught fish and fowl, they used natural resources directly as consumer items. When they began to collect stones and metals for fear of their disappearance tomorrow, or to deprive someone else of their use today, they used natural resources as items that can be hoarded. (But if they used those resources for their own beauty as articles to adorn their neck, they used them again as consumer items.) And then, when they used sticks and stones as tools to aid them in the production of more wealth, they used natural resources as capital or capital-assets. These are the connections that existed—and still exist—between natural resources and wealth. Do any of these connections have anything to do with the conception of natural resources as "savings" which "pay" for investment? Sticks and stones, our primitive instruments of production, did not have to pass through the stage of "saving." They immediately became capital, thanks to the very decision to use those resources as invest-

ment-assets. To repeat, there is nothing that creates an investment—except the act of investment itself.

Quite apart from the facts, believing that savings pay for investments is not in keeping with a long train of thought that has been
explored in the field of microeconomics. This effort is concerned
with the economic meaning of "cost," and it has rather firmly
established that cost must mean "opportunity cost." The cost of
anything is not what we "pay" for it—but what we cannot obtain
once we have made our choice. As Vivian Charles Walsh philo-
sophically puts it, "The cost of Marina is Karen."[80] Patience.
That's life. More traditional economists than Walsh have
expressed the idea differently, but the soundness of the idea is
unquestionable. Frank H. Knight accepted it; Lord Keynes accept
ed it—even though it seems that in vain he tried to "sell" it, by
insisting that "the rate of interest cannot be a return to saving or
waiting as such . . . . in fact it is the reward of not-hoarding."[81]

The host of theoretical and practical implications which exist in
these positions have to be set aside to continue with our central
line of reasoning. The vantage point of opportunity cost, in fact, is
important not only in itself but especially because it allows us to
understand what financiers mean by financial savings. We thus
approach the very root cause of all confusion concerning the economic meaning of saving.

Financial Savings

A venture, any business venture, makes financial sense—and thus
becomes eminently "bankable"—if it reduces the financial costs of
performing any business operation. If a new machine, for instance,
reduces fuel consumption by twenty- to thirty percent and produces the same results as an existing machine, it automatically
reduces the current costs of energy by the same amount. The
machine is then said to generate "financial savings." This is the
ultimate basis on which it is incongruously argued that savings pay
for the investment.

It is sufficient to consider that those "savings" are not accumulated before but during the life of the investment, and indeed are
generated by the investment itself, to realize how much confusion
is engendered by the meaning of financial savings. (Money deposited in a bank is called "financial savings." But this practice has
nothing to do with the issues discussed here. As pointed out earlier, money deposited in a bank is economic investment. In any case,
were growth truly hampered by lack of financial paper, this need

would soon be filled.)

One can never hope to change the practical expressions that prevail in the world of finance. One can only insist on the need to keep the two worlds separate. Only then can one also insist that the proper expression to be accepted in the world of economics is: "investments pay for themselves"—and leave a surplus to boot, which is represented by the life of machinery or the service which continues to exist after its initial financial cost has been paid out.

Properly interpreted, of course, the notion of financial savings performs important functions. It not only permits us to enter Buckminster Fuller's world of "ephemeralization," the process of achieving more, or at least the same, with less; it also permits us to obtain a fleeting glimpse of the source of all economic progress. We do more today than ever before; and we could potentially do infinitely more. But the spring of economic progress does not lie in financial manipulations. It lies in improved technology; it lies in the infinite inventiveness of people. This inventiveness permits us to do more with less; and, with the energies we spare, we can do even more.

A quick look at savings in history and in logic confirms the validity of the above observations.

Savings in History and Logic

History tells us that the first persons on earth did not have savings at their disposal. And yet, they set the economic process in motion. So can we.

If an idea does not make sense historically, it cannot make sense logically. To understand this relationship fully, one needs to know that Giambattista Vico equated the *verum* to the *factum*. What has already been done, i.e., the "factum" or history, is the only source of certain knowledge. In the absence of such a pillar of contemporary thought, let us use a different tool of analysis.

To be certain that the concept of saving (or hoarding) has no logical validity for economic theory as a whole, let us apply to it one of the ultimate tests of logic which, in another chapter, will be applied to all other concepts as well. So far, we have observed saving (or hoarding) as an identity, i.e., Hoarding = Dollar Bills in a Deposit Box, Unused Land, etc. = Nonproductive Wealth. Can the concept also be construed as an equivalence relation?

It cannot. The only possible equivalence would be the following one: Hoarding = Dollar Bills in a Deposit Box, Unused Land, etc. = "Hoardability." This construct does not withstand the test of logic. As soon as we extend the list of concrete items that can be hoarded, we realize that many—and not all—consumer or capital goods can also be hoarded. "Hoardability" is not a distinctive characteristic of exclusively one set of articles of wealth. Hoarding is a spurious economic concept.

This characteristic of hoarding has been withheld so far, in order to make the discourse as plain and as gradual as possible. However, whatever gray area might have existed in the reader's mind regarding the difference between saving—or hoarding—and investment should now be completely dispelled. Nonetheless, since the point is novel and complex, a few more words might be useful. Not only any item of wealth, but even machinery or equipment that—in act—remains idle for an extended period of time, clearly is not productive of further wealth. Therefore, it is not investment. It is hoarding—whether voluntary or forced hoarding.

We should free ourselves of the habit of looking at the moving, changing, fickle physical reality and expect that it can tell us anything about economics. We should start looking at the economic reality through the lenses of fixed, firm, immutable categories of thought. That is the only way not to be confused by the changing facts.

But enough about savings. Enough about savings as one of the imaginary requirements for economic growth. What about plenty?

The Presumed Need for Plenty

Neither historical nor logical evidence supports the view that in order to have economic development one needs plenty of labor, plenty of financial capital, or plenty of natural resources. It is the characteristic of organic processes not to have plenty—but just enough of all the necessary ingredients. On the contrary, both scarcity and plenty spoil such processes. If the argument is too abstract, a look at the historical evidence might help.

The historical record is abundant, quite open, and clear for all unbiased persons to observe. Many countries with plenty of natural resources have not experienced any appreciable degree of economic growth. The list of these countries is long and too well known to be repeated here. Instead of providing specific examples, we will look at the converse situation: the case of states with no appreciable natural resources. Take the case of Massachusetts: sparsely populated and yet the richest state in the United States of America for a long time—and then richest where it was most populated, around Boston. As Louis D. Brandeis noted, Massachusetts has one of the rockiest soils on God's earth. And no minerals. No diamonds. No oil. No coal. But the boulders that needed to be removed, were removed. They were removed by men and women who, by emigrating from their countries of origin, had finally acquired the legal right to flex their muscles and remove them; and if the boulders proved to be too stubborn, they were bypassed by people who had finally acquired the legal right to use their brain to get around those boulders and start new endeavors.

Once again, how to express this simple but fundamental truth that the world of economics is neither a world of scarcity nor one of plenty? Thanks to the work of conservationists and ecologists, the fetish of plenty, the fetish of "affluence" is out of style these days. Let us insist on the presumed scarcity, then, here is where the pendulum is "resting" now. Is there any historical evidence of scarcity? The good Reverend Malthus—elaborating on a population growth trend that had been discovered by Benjamin Franklin, and by Botero earlier still—did not show much faith in nature after all. But today, we do not need to have faith. It ought to be sufficient to look at the historical record. Malthus' dire—indeed, dismal—predictions did not come true after all. With billions more people, we have more than ever before. (And we would have more, and better quality, if we only understood and respected a few basic economic principles.)

This is not an age in which the study of history is cultivated. This is the age of science. But, even using this perspective, to blindly repeat that we live in a world of scarcity is not an affront to Buckminster Fuller—let alone Einstein?

Yet here, too, doubts exist. That the entire stock of natural resources of the earth is not worth more than a few days of sunlight, is taken by some as a justification for despair—and indirectly, feeding on the natural insecurity of human beings, as the ultimate justification for hoarding. On the contrary, this fact actually ought to be taken as an index of our inefficiency—an index of waste. With the same few passing days, we are wasting energy from the sun that is equivalent to all the energy producible by our natural resources from now until the end of the earth.

No. It is not the infinite amount of natural or any other resources that creates economic wealth. (Certainly, financial capital is a worldwide commodity—as abundant as writing and speech.) It is economic freedom that creates wealth. Wealth is the product of economic freedom. Wealth is the product of economic freedom that is "fully" employed.

So we come directly to the third major—imaginary—prerequisite for economic growth: full employment.

The Presumed Need for Full Employment

The policy of full employment, instead of being accepted as an organic result of the theory of growth, has become its major tool or goal. This twist has caused innumerable theoretical consequences in a variety of fields, the most important of which is a break in the functionality of the act of employment: the central function of work has been transformed from the production of goods and services to the production of money.

Employment solves three theoretical economic problems at once: (a) it satisfies the supply side of the economic equation—or better equivalence; namely, it satisfies the requirements of the production process; (b) it satisfies the requirements of the demand side—or the requirements the consumption process; and, (c) it also satisfies the requirements of the distribution process, namely, it is an essential ingredient in the distribution of income.

In an inherently organic world, as the world of economics is, each action produces an infinite number of consequences. (Sidney Harris, the noted newspaper columnist, was fond of pointing out that the liver performs more than five hundred functions.) Contrary to a prevailing economic doctrine, therefore, the policy of full employment can attempt to solve all three economic problems at once—but it needs to solve them organically. And this is what the policy of full employment has generally failed to do. Starting with the second half of the twentieth century, a technical understanding of the theory of economic growth has led to a misguided use of the function of employment. Too many jobs have been pressed upon the production process, not because the process required them directly, but because they were a means to distribute income.

The list of such jobs is too long and too well known to be repeated here: the unions and the government have pressed for the acceptance of practices that range from featherbedding to boondoggling. The ultimate result has been the near-complete transformation of the function of employment from work-to-produce-goods to work-to-earn-money. In the process, the ancient dream of automation has come within our reach; but it has been compelled to bear only few fruits.

There are many non-economic consequences in this transformation. Our concern has to remain with the economic consequences—whose list is confined to the following ones: the production process has produced less, not more; not being naturally called for the performance of the appointed tasks, the function of the "extras" has been to create obstacles and to become a hindrance to the smooth functioning of the economic system; more money has been distributed than has been earned; there has been a lack of exploration of the potential inherent in other channels for the distribution of income outside the labor channel. The most important consequence has been to lock economic theory into the straightjacket of the discredited Phillips curve or the belief that there is a trade-off between unemployment and inflation. This belief, like the Sphinx, is hard to die. It was resurrected under the name of NAIRU (Non-Accelerating Inflation Rate of Unemployment). It did not come true in a climate of inflation, and it has not come true in a climate of deflation: in the 1970s we experienced both rising unemployment and rising prices; in the 1990s we experienced both rising employment and stable prices. The belief is like a straitjacket that does not allow economic theory the freedom to think of real problems and work on real solutions. Nothing can be done about it from outside the framework of economic theory. Economic theory alone can free itself of this straightjacket.

It is fervently to be hoped that the framework of analysis developed in these pages can be of assistance in the performance of this task. The theory of the trade-off between unemployment and inflation maintains that full employment can be reached only at the cost of inflation. Due to contrary evidence, faith in the theory has been shaken; but it still persists. To try to dispel it completely, let us now look at the limitations existing in the prevailing conception of full employment, we shall devote the following chapter to the examination of the second factor of the trade-off theory, the issue of inflation.

The policy of full employment sets up a false goal. This is the ultimate reason why, notwithstanding the concerted effort of politicians and economists starting with the second half of the twentieth century, that goal has so sporadically been reached. Nor will it ever be reached and maintained for long—if pursued directly. Full employment is a condition that either exists here and now, or it does not. To set it up as a goal does not facilitate its achievement. To set it up as a goal is to transform it into a mirage. To put it differently, full employment is the result of a long string of conditions that in this text are synthetically listed under the expression of "normal unfolding of the economic process."

This is the goal, then: one must look at all the conditions that cause a smooth functioning of the system. If the economic system functions properly, it will generate full employment of all economic resources—not the other way around. Pressing for the achievement of full employment hinders the proper functioning of the system, and thus makes full employment impossible to achieve. To repeat, full employment is a result. It is not a prerequisite. It is not a goal. The goal ought to be the exploration and then the establishment of the conditions that make the economic system run smoothly.

Unburdened of the task of making this inquiry, since it belongs to the field of economic policy, we can more profitably devote some attention to secondary theoretical issues which exist in the policy of full employment as formulated at present. Although the numbers change with the prevailing economic and political winds of the moment, following Lord Beveridge we shall define as full employment that national policy which aims to obtain employment for ninety-seven percent of the labor force—or three percent unemployment rate. This is the definition at its best. And we shall not even mention that the ideal three percent unemployment rate is a national average which hides fifteen percent unemployment rates in the rural pockets of poverty; twenty-five percent unemployment rates in the urban ghettos; fifty percent unemployment rates for disadvantaged youths; and seventy-five percent unemployment rates on Indian reservations.

The hour is late and the discussion must be cut short. First set of questions: does the "ideal" and almost never realized nor—within prevailing legal and institutional arrangements—for long realizable three percent unemployment rate constitute "full" employment? In many countries, this policy condemns millions of people—on a revolving basis, to be sure—to unemployment. Is that full employment? Does this policy ever look into the eyes of those millions of people; or into the eyes of the dependents of each one of those millions of people?

Second set of questions: full employment, of what? Here, faithful to its propensity to doublespeak, the prevailing economic discourse finally—but inappropriately—becomes literal. That policy is primarily in search of full employment for labor. Full employment of capital-assets is often included only as an afterthought. And, what about full employment of all other resources—especially those resources that are generally hoarded? The prevailing economic discourse cannot even ask such a question. Those resources are mostly considered investment. A sub-question should clarify the issues somewhat. Is this a full employment policy or is it a wage policy?

Third set of questions: full employment, for what? The usual answer is: for consumers to receive income, so that they can spend it and keep the economic system "going." Having only a dim awareness of the existence of seven channels for the distribution of income, the prevailing economic discourse does not even recognize the simple engineering problem of overloading one channel with up to seventy-five percent of the total flow—and leaving the other six channels "underemployed." And, as that discourse has not faced up to this engineering problem, it cannot even ask more fundamental questions, such as: at the cost of how many trees unnecessarily felled, shops filled with "junk," rivers polluted and ocean bottoms raised with "surplus" material—at what ecological cost is that ideal rate of three percent unemployment acquired? (Incidentally, does all that waste conjure up images of scarcity?)

Needless to say, once engineering and ecological problems are swept under the rug, to ask the final—the human—set of questions is considered "idealistic" and "philosophical." The questions are: was man born to "earn" a living? When did men and women lose their right to live? When did they lose their right to be the proud owners, not so much of the wealth that God created, as of the wealth that they themselves contribute to create? Rather than insisting on this line of questioning, it is better to pass on to the observation of a few real requirements for economic growth.

A Few Real Requirements

To list all the requirements for economic growth to occur, it would be necessary to repeat, to expand upon, and even to add to all the steps mentioned in the previous chapters. This clearly is an impossibility. Time therefore is better spent cementing the discussion held so far by bringing forward three requirements that are implicit in the preceding paragraphs. The first is the issue of the right dosage of natural resources, stocks of capital, and human resources; the second is the need to find a substitute for saving; the third is the overall prerequisite of economic growth: economic freedom.

The Right Dosage

In order to have normal economic growth, the notion of the right dosage has to be substituted for the notion of plenty as well as the notion of scarcity. What the right dosage is cannot be determined abstractly; it varies in relation to time and place. Indeed, the whole "secret" of economic growth lies in determining this question of the right dosage in a concrete and practical setting.

Having disposed of the abstract question of the measurement of the right dosage, we are free to address some core issues concerning the content of this notion. It goes without saying that economic growth does not occur without natural resources, human resources, and—once the process of growth has somehow started—previous stocks of capital represented by machinery, equipment, etc. These are such obvious requirements that, were it not for a series of misconceptions regarding them, they would deserve no special comment in this work.

The traditional misconception regarding the notion of scarcity concerning natural resources has recently been compounded by the presumed consequences for economic growth deriving from the Law of Entropy. This law expresses the irreversible process of heat passing from a "free" or available state to a "bound" or unavailable state: coal turns to ashes and releases its heat into the atmosphere. The discovery of this law occurred in the nineteenth century; but the process has gone on since time immemorial and will no doubt proceed on its course. From the observation of this natural phenomenon, the conclusion is drawn that men and women had better use natural resources sparingly if they do not want to exhaust them prematurely.

If the law of entropy were understood as the latest in a long series of warnings against waste, the widespread knowledge of this law should be highly welcomed. It states what every moralist, political scientist, or economist worth his or her salt has always stressed. However, to transform the entropy law into a pall over man's life is a totally different affair. There are serious objections to this attempt that must be brought forward.

The law of entropy does not, and cannot, distinguish between heat and energy. Heat is one form of energy; it is not energy. Moreover, the sun—our ultimate source of heat—has been here for a few billion years, and by all reckoning it is going to remain with us for a few more billion years. By the same reckoning, there is an infinite number of solar systems—a condition which, were it not for other terrestrial considerations, would totally justify the efforts involved in the exploration of space. Between these considerations, there is the other that the entropy law works its way through the coal and the sun, whether human beings use that heat for their own purposes or not. Furthermore, no one really knows what the final outcome of bound energy is. To maintain otherwise is to assert that we know everything about black holes, what presumably remains from the collapse of stars like our sun; and, at the same time, it is to deny the very law of entropy, which is the law of physical change.

Finally, the entropy law seems to foster at present a self-centered, anthropomorphic view of life. Human life is one manifestation of life. Whoever determined that human life is the only form of life that counts?

To repeat, if the entropy law helps to stir people against any form of uneconomic, anti-social, impolitic, ugly, and immoral waste; if it helps us to find the right dosage for the use of natural resources, that law should be welcomed. However, if that law is used to atrophy the energy and creativity of vast numbers of people, then the misconceptions deriving from it must be strenuously fought.

Just as we should not be overwhelmed by the unknown future of "energy" and natural resources, so we should not be overly impressed by the history of past shortages. Shortages have occurred in the past. But was it not sooner or later discovered that, taking into account the existence of a wide range of substitutes, such shortages were not due to natural causes? Was it not sooner or later—at least implicitly—admitted that shortages were due to human mismanagement? The work of Professor Amartya Sen is forcing these discussions right into the open. Current dire predictions about the future availability of energy and natural resources are built on a combination of these two factors: misconceptions regarding the law of entropy and the assumption that mismanagement will occur again and again in the future. Rather than wasting energy on the formulation of these dire predictions, would it not be more rational to husband those resources to avoid future occurrences of mismanagement?

Whatever happens on this account, just as one should strive to achieve the right dosage of natural resources in order to obtain normal economic growth, so one should strive to obtain the right dosage of stocks of physical capital. There is little to say in relation to those stocks that already exist: those that can be used should be used. But certainly recent experience should warn us against the misconception that the method to achieve economic development is to build steel plants, industrial parks, and airport terminals—whether they are located in developed or underdeveloped economies of the world.

It is vain to use capital-intensive, or fully automated equipment, and then have its ownership concentrated in a few hands or in the hands of the state, and at the same time to tolerate high unemployment. The practice is not only uneconomic and inhuman; it is highly explosive. But neither should one conceive of economic growth as a means of creating employment—or, worse, as a means of creating "busy" work.

Human beings were not created to work; certainly, not to work for others. Men and women are not slaves. Rather, human beings live to create—and to enjoy the benefits of their creation. At this point the discussion goes much beyond the prerequisites of economic growth. We had better stop here and talk instead of a related issue: we must find a substitute for the function that has traditionally been assumed to be performed by saving.

A Substitute for Saving: Conspicuous Consumption

The essential characteristic of organic processes is that either all ingredients are present and function smoothly, or the entire process breaks down. Economic theory has to reflect this reality. The decision of many writers, at least from the time of Adam Smith onward, to include savings as an essential prerequisite of economic growth was not an arbitrary one. Therefore, to put it briefly and directly, if we take that ingredient away we must find a substitute for it.

More explicitly, that prerequisite can be formulated as follows: what is the role of the rich in the process of economic growth? It is undeniable that their role is an important one; but what is it precisely? Mainstream economics has consistently insisted that their role is to accumulate wealth or to accumulate savings in order to finance the process of growth.

This is a hypothesis that, since it gave a plausible explanation of the role of the rich, was soon embodied in a tightly constructed system of thought. However, no one verified whether or not it was appropriate to the facts. Having gone beyond mainstream economics, we can now clearly see that it is not only a theory, but also a rough examination of economic facts that undermines that position.

Running through the gamut of enterprises flourishing today, one is hard put to find any justification for that hypothesis. The initial risk in establishing the enterprise was rarely, if ever, underwritten by the rich. Nine times out of ten, it was a fellow who really believed in the enterprise who, against great odds, took the risk to start it. The rich generally came in when the risk was taken out of the venture. They came in when the enterprise had proved its "financial worth"—namely, as soon as it began to earn a profit. Even though the situation seems at last to be changing, what is euphemistically called venture capital does not become available unless there is a near-certainty of eventual profits. And then the real question concerns the horrendous costs involved in the provision of such capital. Ten times out of ten, the real cost involves surrender of control and ownership of the venture.

Capitalists love money; they do not love risk. Whenever they advance capital, they do it not for the love of risk; but for the sake of increasing their capital. Certainly, if the rich were to invest in risky ventures, they would no longer be rich. By definition, many risky ventures are destined to fail. The issue can also be observed from another point of view. A new enterprise undermines the established order. Why would the rich who, by definition benefit from the established order, contribute to the undermining of their own position? Only to please a comfortable, rational explanation of their presumed behavior which has for so long been advanced by economists?

The reality is different. Wealthy people do perform an important role in the process of economic growth; but this role has not yet been incorporated into economic theory. Indeed, reasoning through abstract principles, economists and especially sociologists, whenever they could not resist or oppose that role, have blatantly belittled it. The role performed by the rich in the process of economic growth is through their conspicuous consumption. Since many economists and sociologists are—by definition—excluded from participating, to use Hemingway's felicitous phrase, in the "moveable feast" of conspicuous consumption, one is inclined to conclude that it was envy and not reason that led them to withdraw recognition from the important role performed by conspicuous consumption in the process of economic growth.

The facts are clear. Without the possibility of conspicuous consumption, risky ventures would not only be that much riskier; they would be well nigh impossible. A risky venture, by definition, means that there is no certainty of a market for its output. And the uncertainty is not related to the lack of a need for that output, but to the lack of money to buy it. Any entrepreneur with a modicum of self-respect engages in a venture only if the proposed output promises somehow to satisfy a real need. And it is here that the role of the rich manifests itself. The rich can afford to buy a new product—no matter the cost and no matter the uncertainties involved in any such product. If the product or service does not perform as expected, they have risked but an infinitesimal fraction of their wealth.

The risk of a new venture is thus partially assumed by the rich, not by assuming the front-end risk, but by the propensity to experiment with new tools, gadgets, and services. That is truly risky—and not "conspicuous" consumption. (And yet, since the expenditure involves only an infinitesimal portion of their income, it offers no danger of eroding their capital base—a danger against which, quite properly, economists of the caliber of Adam Smith have sternly warned their pupils.)

In any case, it is the habit of conspicuous consumption that allows the existence of risky ventures. It is conspicuous consumption that transfers financial resources from consumers to producers and allows the latter to improve the product, to lower its cost through economies of scale, and to make it "popular" in the mass market. At that point, the rich lose interest in the product or service and they are ready to experiment with a new idea.

Does conspicuous consumption perform only an economic function? Does it involve no waste? Do all products follow that route? Do all products made viable by conspicuous consumption eventually enter the mass consumption market? To these and many similar questions only a curt answer is allowed in this context: of course not. (To dispel doubts on this point, the reader is invited to read Veblen. He, after all, coined the phrase "conspicuous consumption.") Our concern is limited to one simple point. Conspicuous consumption performs a vital role in the process of economic growth. It performs the role that for so long has been mistakenly attributed to saving and to the accumulation of wealth per se.

Proofs? The proofs are scattered all around us: it is sufficient to look at the telephone, radio, and television; computers and computer programs; soap and the bathtub; fads, fashions, and foods; indeed, even medicinal drugs. Is there any need to continue? We must stop. To repeat, the ingredients in the process of economic growth are many, and they cannot be satisfactorily explored in this work. it is preferable to make explicit another broad implication of the discussion held so far: the prerequisite of economic freedom.

Economic Freedom

If there is a single prerequisite of economic growth that overshadows all others, this is the need for economic freedom. The economic system must be kept as free of unnecessary obstacles as humanly possible. The prescription is easy to formulate. But how is it carried into reality? The first immediate answer is well known and self-evident. That street cleaning function is a major, proper function of the state in the economic field. As Nobel laureate Professor Hayek never tires of repeating, including many things in his prescription, planning must be "planning for competition" and not "planning against competition."[82]

The government, alone, can in fact oversee and care for the interests of all concerns existing in the economic process. And yet, even this function should be undertaken by the government as a last resort—only when private concerns have failed to spontaneously perform that self-policing function. Were the government immediately to step in, what assurances would there be of its ability to distinguish between a pile of debris and a beautiful hill? What assurances are there of the government's ability not to shift the debris from one corner to another, thus creating perhaps a bigger obstacle than the one existing before? What assurances are there of the government's ability to avoid the creation of its own unseemly pile of debris?

Not to constantly raise these questions is tantamount to shutting one's eyes to reality; it is tantamount to shutting one's memory to the repeated warnings of Louis D. Brandeis, no less than Friedrich A. Hayek or Milton Friedman—to mention only three outstanding names. Not to raise these questions is tantamount to shutting one's mind off, thus interrupting the thinking processes concerning the need for always extending the area of freedom for the individual person that have been carried on, in particular, in the long Judeo-Greek-Christian tradition.

The continuation of such thinking processes, in fact, leads to one inescapable conclusion. The aim of a modern government ought to be the creation and preservation of economic freedom—for all. This task shall be more enthusiastically undertaken by society as a whole if it is widely realized: (a) that economic freedom is the logical extension of political freedom; and (b) that wealth is created by economic freedom—and by nothing else.

But what about justice? From Aristotle, through the Scholastic Doctors, to Adam Smith and Hayek, it has been recognized that the existence of a just society is another precondition of economic growth. This reality is not denied; rather it is incorporated into the present framework of analysis. Economic freedom is proof positive of justice in action. It is the role of justice to insure freedom for all.

But there is a division of labor here. Justice by itself will not do; we can have justice and still no economic development. More directly, wealth is created by free men and women—not by governments. Governments, which alone can create a system of justice, cannot create wealth; they can only stunt its growth or even destroy it, by failing to recognize that freedom is an indivisible and infinite, although not absolute, entity. As Norman G. Kurland emphasizes, justice outlines the limits of freedom and it is absolute: you can never have too much justice.

This is neither to imply that governments have no role to play in the pursuit of economic growth, nor that it is an easy matter to insure justice and to avoid privilege. This is only to state that the role of justice is too often neglected. Those who have understood the lessons taught by Adam Smith do not need any more words of explanation. A simple reminder, however, might still prove useful. The unprecedented world-wide growth which has occurred since 1776 has been due in no small measure to the efforts of Adam Smith to lower the barriers erected by Mercantilism in the field of international trade. What better way to celebrate that masterwork than to make a firm resolution not only to extend free trade among nations, but especially to lower internal barriers in order to allow free internal trade? This is the only—"complex"—economic policy that will give us steady, widespread, and deep-rooted economic growth. This indeed is the only policy that will extend the wave of political freedom to encompass economic freedom.

The alternative, as we shall see in the next chapter, is a continuous state of economic inflation—and worse. This particular task, however, has to wait. We must now attend to a final task. To provide a synthesis of what has been said in this chapter, we will develop a "model" of economic growth.

A Model of Economic Growth

If saving—or hoarding—is not an essential prerequisite for economic growth; if indeed saving or hoarding is wholly detrimental to the process of economic growth; if saving or hoarding tends to reduce the level of investment by its full amount, then it follows that we shall have maximum economic growth when and if the level of hoarding is zero.

On the assumption that the level of hoarding is at zero, the Flows model reads:

$$\text{Income} = 0 + \text{Consumption}$$
$$\text{Investment} = \text{Income} - 0$$
$$\text{Investment} = \text{Consumption.}$$

This is not simply another model of the economic system. This is *the* model of economic growth. Before we analyze this model to the extent feasible in this study, it is time to consolidate some of the positions already occupied. In the context of this model, we can dispel more gray area that might still surround the pseudo-concept of hoarding. Hoarding includes not only that wealth which has passed through the production process and might otherwise be used either as an investment-asset or a consumer item; it also includes wealth that has only nominally been allowed to enter that process. Much such wealth is composed of land or natural resources that are hoarded.

The inclusion of much existing land in the pseudo-concept of hoarding deserves further clarification. As repeatedly emphasized, wealth does not exist "in nature." Wealth is always the result of human activity. And yet, much unused land must be included in the concept of hoarding, even though men and women do not produce the land. "Production" in this case refers to land that has been explored, possibly surveyed, and a title of ownership has been issued for it. To insist on this point, this is land that—with full respect for proper limitations due to conservation and preservation requirements—can potentially become an integral part of the production process and thus create economic wealth. The same is true for natural resources. Another important point. When we speak of vacant land, we tend to envisage green pastures and woodlands. We ought to train ourselves to see the vacant lots that exist in the ghettos and are filled with weeds and rubbish. These are lands that are also hoarded and cause much economic damage.

As Henry George so beautifully and forcefully pointed out, and as many Nobel laureates in economics concur, to have full and normal economic development this barrier must somehow be lowered. This is what our model suggests; this is what our model requires.

This is the model of economic growth that we ought to aspire to implement. It describes a situation of maximum economic growth that would result from the reduction of the amount of hoarding to zero. Through the prism of this model, it can immediately be seen that economic growth can certainly be forced through an exogenous influx of public investment or consumption—which, however, must still be organically assimilated by the economic system. Yet, "normal" economic growth can only occur through the avoidance of private—as well as, indeed, public and corporate—hoarding. The production process, if left unhindered, does the rest. Is not this the "radical cure" that Keynes was searching for?

In the context of Concordian economics, what does an unhindered production process mean? It does not only mean that the process is free of internal, but also of external obstacles. The latter obstacles exist, in particular, in the distribution and consumption process. Without repeating what has been said in the previous chapters, it bears stressing that the distribution process has to facilitate, not hinder, the flow of money from the monetary authority to the consumer; and the consumption process has to facilitate the exchange of money for the available supply of goods and services. In brief, people have to be made ready to spend their money. And they will be so ready if they are secure in their receipt of both high quality for their expenditures and the renewal of their income. Only then will they not hoard wealth.

It might seem that it is difficult to implement the dictates of these theoretical implications. This is not the case. A socio-political system which works properly will produce as much and of as high quality as necessary; it will automatically distribute the wealth thus created in accordance with the simple principle of justice inherent in the right of property: the wealth belongs to the person who has contributed—whether directly or through the machines— to create it. And the persons who have not only created that wealth, but enjoy its untrammeled right of ownership (which among other things safely insures the procurement of future wealth), will happily enjoy the use of their wealth. They will consume it. In this way, men and women automatically meet the requirements of the production process, the distribution process, and the consumption process. This is what the newly found model of economic growth tells us.

To put it more directly, when there is no hoarding, all income is spent—i.e., it is consumed, it is used. Part of that income is spent on consumer goods that satisfy immediate needs. Part of that income is spent on capital goods that insure that the needs of the future will be met with relative ease. And, incidentally, it is to be stressed that equilibrium between the production of consumer and capital goods is assured neither by the wild dreams of the individual consumer nor by the empty preaching of the economist. It is rather the stern command of the equalization of profit rates that insures that balance. If this expression sounds so impersonal and mechanical, let us rephrase it in these terms. That command is issued by the majority of consumers and producers.

In any case, two conditions must be fulfilled. First, through a properly functioning distribution process, sufficient money satisfying material, psychological, and moral needs is placed at the disposal of consumers; and, second, through a properly functioning production process, sufficient goods and services satisfying material, psychological, and esthetic needs are made available on the market. Then the mechanisms of the consumption process are automatically triggered. Consumers will buy the entire output. In this way, an exchange of goods and services for money takes place: goods and services flow from producers to consumers; money flows from consumers to producers. The continuation of the economic process is thus insured.

It must also be pointed out that the implications of this model of economic growth appear to be valid not only in time, but also in space. Is it not true that in the urban "ghetto" and in "underdeveloped" economies there is plenty of hoarding, plenty of nonproductive wealth? Perhaps more than in developed areas; and certainly more than investment. Of course, the underutilized resources are not only human, but also physical. How many boarded-up buildings exist in the ghettos? How much gold—and land—is hoarded in underdeveloped countries?

Certainly the implementation of these theoretical conclusions must be aided by an appropriate set of economic policies that expands the current range of fiscal and monetary measures to include the vision of economic rights and responsibilities. Certainly, these issues ought to be explored at much greater depth. They cannot, because they belong to economic dynamics and economic policy and, as such, remain outside the realm of this work. In fact, it is now time to summarize what has been said so far.

A Summary in the Form of an Exhortation

From a more general point of view, the newly found model of economic growth urges us to say to those who engage in these practices: make full use of your wealth; enjoy it. But do not hoard it. Do not hoard wealth because there are many people on earth who would not only make use of it, they would also derive thorough enjoyment from it. Do not hoard wealth—because there are many people on earth who need it. In no uncertain terms, do not hoard wealth—because there are people dying for the lack of the privilege to use those resources that you keep idle. And they are dying not only—through a long chain reaction—in the Gulag Archipelago of tyrannical states. They are dying not only in Latin America or in India or in Africa. They are spiritually and physically dying right in the backyards of homes built in the wealthiest cities and suburbs of the world.

This appeal is not vain moralism. As we shall see, this policy recommendation makes supreme economic sense. In fact, this policy recommendation can be put more directly and simply still: do not hoard wealth, because it is contrary to your own best interests.

It is only in a world of scarcity, a world incorrigibly persisting in the fertile imagination of too many people and a world at times actually created by hoarding wealth, that one might benefit in the short run by that sort of action. But that benefit is only economic, and it is always lost in the long run. Besides, that short-run benefit is acquired at the sacrifice of a great many other values. And the collapse of these values will sooner or later engulf even the person who has been brought up to believe that individual safety lies in hoarding wealth. Finally, even that short run economic benefit might be deceptive. One also needs to take into account the loss of value inflicted upon all productive wealth as well as the loss of income implicit in holding nonproductive wealth.

A brief counterproof of the validity of this position can be provided. Every boom following a bust is the most convincing evidence that the previous downfall was due, not to scarcity or even specific bottlenecks, nor to strong unionism or to government meddling, but to a failure of nerve. Each succeeding boom proves that new and profitable opportunities for investment had been there all along; indeed, it proves that such opportunities are constantly there. One simply needs to look at the work that is still to be done.

Even assuming that opportunities for growth in quantity are at times slack, opportunities for growth in quality are always infinite.

In retrospect, it is easy to see that all explanations for hoarding wealth were rationalizations. There never was any objective reason to stop devoting energies to the maintenance, care, and development of productive resources. In retrospect, it is easy to see that the crisis was generated by the fear of losing one's riches, and hence by devoting energies to the acquisition of all forms of nonproductive wealth. Without this diversion of energies away from investment and into hoarding, the pattern of growth would have been steady.

Indeed in retrospect it becomes easy to see that, had the investment activities not been undertaken anew and with renewed vigor, the pattern of decline would have not been reversed. Perhaps the occasional lack of reversal of this pattern goes a long way to explain why civilizations decline and fall.

If the diversion of energies away from productive activities is potentially that important, a closer look at this phenomenon is fully warranted. This is our next major task. But first it is useful to deal with two minor issues that have been left pending so far. The treatment of these issues provides an opportunity to present a different type of summary of the argument.

A Summary in the Form of a Historical Review

Two minor issues can be adequately dealt with now that the argument has almost run its full course. First, at this point, we can clearly see the conceptual identity between the component elements of Keynes' model and the three major theories studied by classical economists. Indeed, in this context we can quickly summarize what was lacking in both types of analysis.

Income. As Keynes repeatedly pointed out, classical economists insisted on studying this concept mainly from the point of view of the theory of distribution. If one considers Keynes' analysis not as a revolution but as the apex of classical economic thought, one realizes that income is implicitly observed by Keynes from the point of view of distribution as well.

Consumption. In name, the concept remains the same for Keynes as for classical economists; in fact, Keynes freed the concept of consumption from its attachment to the physical world. But he succeeded only in part. With Keynes, one is presented with a theory of consumption of consumer goods.

Saving and Investment. If one considers them as a system, no matter which system—namely, the rational, the imaginary or the real system—saving and investment contain all that is required to build a theory of production. The structural identity between Keynes' model and classical economics is complete.

But we can go further. Through the understanding of hoarding, we can clearly see the basic deficiency that exists in classical economics as well as in Keynes' theory of production. In general, economic analysis uses the expressions "saving" and "accumulation of wealth" almost interchangeably. The last expression does much harm to the clarity of the economic discourse. "Accumulation of wealth" is a vague expression. To eliminate confusion, one ought to distinguish between the accumulation of passive or nonproductive wealth on one hand, and the accumulation of active or productive wealth on the other.

The first is an intensely private, exclusive, and deleterious phenomenon. The second is the opposite: it is a public, inclusive, beneficent affair. Active wealth, i.e., wealth that is accumulated in the form of investment, is in reality put at the disposal of large numbers of people, who commensurably derive as much benefit from that use as the legal owner of the wealth. Instead, passive wealth, i.e., wealth that is accumulated in the form of hoarding, in the long run does not provide benefit to anyone, not even to the owner. It should not have been, but it was a great surprise for me to find at the end of my research precisely this meaning in the Parable of the Talents given to us by the economic wisdom of Jesus.

It is better to explore this issue further within the context of another major economic problem: inflation. But first, let us provide a summary of this chapter from still another point of view.

A Summary in the Form of a Geometric Representation

The content of this chapter, and much of what has been said earlier, can be made graphically evident through the following Lorenz diagram—a diagram on which Time is put on the horizontal axis and the Quantity of both hoarding and investment are put on the vertical axis as seen below:

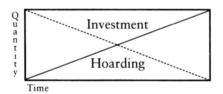

This, of course, is a stylized representation of reality. Actual figures would produce much more erratic patterns. This figure is obtained not only through the model of growth but also, directly, through the real saving (or hoarding)/investment system. At any one instant, if investment is at ninety percent (of yearly income minus expenditures on consumer goods), hoarding is at ten percent. And so with all other combinations of percentages between these two terms. Thus each point is the shadow of the other; and the diagram itself might be called the Shadow diagram.

Is it necessary to make it explicit that the future is determined by investment and not by hoarding?

XXII

Inflation:
The Outcome of the
Economic Process Gone Awry

Inflation is monetary regression.

———

IT IS OFTEN ASKED, and not always in jest, what did the Scholastic Doctors teach the world besides counting "how many angels can dance on the head of a pin"? The answer was once given by Benedetto Croce through a broad historical sweep. In essence, what Croce said was that the Scholastic Doctors—with St. Thomas Aquinas at the head of the procession—taught us to distinguish among issues which must be kept separate. (Thomas Aquinas, incidentally, studied at the University of Naples soon after it was founded in 1224 and taught there during the last years of his life. It is no great wonder, then, that this institution was the first university in Europe to recognize the need to separate "political economy" from all other moral sciences. The first chair in political economy was instituted there in 1764, twelve years before the publication of the *Wealth of Nations.*)

The disrespect of the past never goes unpunished. We are unable today to understand the phenomenon of inflation because we do not make a considerable number of not-so-subtle distinctions. The first distinction, introduced at the suggestion of Professor Franco Modigliani, is between price (or absolute) inflation and relative inflation. The former occupies the realm within which the prevailing economic discourse on the topic is generally held: as the words imply, price inflation describes a phenomenon of prices increasing from one level to another. The latter occupies the realm within which the discussion is held here: as the words imply, relative inflation describes a phenomenon of prices increasing in relation to other elements which we shall discover as we proceed.

If we devote undivided attention first to the mental process through which the existence of relative inflation is unearthed, and then to a brief examination of its characteristics, we shall find that we are not presented with two theories of inflation at all. Since one merges into the other, we shall find ourselves in possession of only one theory: a comprehensive theory of inflation.

Premises for the Discovery of Relative Inflation

With hindsight, the process of discovery of relative inflation is a simple one. We only need to wade through—and to keep separate—a number of rather familiar topics. The central set of distinctions emerges from a careful examination of the consequences implicit in a question upon which we have already spent some time. This is the question of the perspective through which the economic process is observed. When the economy is observed from the point of view of the "rim," one does not only lose sight of the distinction among production, distribution, and consumption. One even loses sight of the distinction between such fundamentally different issues as supply and demand. The reason is simple. When the economy is observed through a series of snapshots, supply and demand become one thing. At any instant, the supply of one transactor is "effectively" the same as the demand of the other.

How can one distinguish demand from supply when the exchange takes place? This is how a brilliant young economist, eventually Nobel laureate Professor Lawrence R. Klein, explained the issue: "Where is the supply?... Once we know the *demand* by business firms for factors of production, we know how much business firms will *supply* to the market because there is a technical relation connecting the output of business firms to their input of productive factors. The technical relationship, the production function, has been, so to speak, solved out of the system in constructing the models, but it has not been neglected."[83]

For certain purposes, this is not only a legitimate, but also quite fruitful an approach. If we want to understand inflation, however, this no longer is the case. Not surprisingly, the question "Where is the supply?" has been uttered again with a certain insistence ever since the 1970s. And, while remaining within the confines of contemporary economic theory, no better answer can perhaps be found for it than the one given above by Professor Klein. Since we have here been freed from those strictures, we can go forward with our discourse.

Every exchange is, of course, one act—and not two. But this act or, even better, this process is the resultant of two actions: the action of the buyer and the action of the seller. When this important distinction—together with the distinction between production, distribution, and consumption—is firmly kept in mind, only then can we begin to discover the missing link in our understanding of inflation.

This missing link is indeed included, as so much is included, in the *General Theory*. But it is included in a passage whose major thrust is directed elsewhere. That missing link can be found in this sentence: ". . . the conclusion that the *costs* of output are always covered in the aggregate by the sale-proceeds resulting from demand, has great plausibility, because it is difficult to distinguish it from another, similar-looking proposition which is indubitable, namely, that the income derived in the aggregate by all the elements in the community concerned in a productive activity necessarily has a value exactly equal to the *value* of the output."[84]

This is the clue to understanding inflation: costs of output are, or at least can be, "plausibly" confused with the value of output. And what is the value of output, if not its total market price? That is the clue, then. Costs represent a different economic phenomenon from prices. Observed from the point of view of the producer, costs are outflows of money and prices are inflows.

This distinction is clearly related to the distinction between production (or supply) and consumption (or demand). If the economy is observed from the point of view of the "rim," there is no distinction between prices and costs. What is cost for one transactor must be price for the other. However, if we do not shift our point of observation but remain fixed in our position, costs become clearly distinguishable from prices. Then it becomes clear that, as Keynes implied, "the costs of output are [not] always covered in the aggregate by the sale-proceeds [i.e., prices] resulting from demand."

The reasons for this difference between costs and prices are ingrained in the very economic process. If costs were always "covered" by prices, there would be no risk. But then an unforeseen consequence might also take place. At the limit, if costs were constantly equal to prices, the very basis of the economic process would be destroyed: there would be no economic effort—because there would be no possibility of profit. As nearly everyone knows, or should know, "it is better to play for nothing than to work for nothing"—or even to work always for the same amount of money, a likely consequence if prices were always equal to costs. For simplicity sake, we are assuming a constant purchasing power as well as no changes in technology that might reduce costs. And if costs are hypothesized as being constantly—or even just once—lower or higher than prices, then the entire case is given up. Costs become clearly different from prices—which is the only point at issue here. More specifically, the validity of this distinction must be preserved when we pass from microeconomics to macroeconomics.

The integration of this distinction in macroeconomic analysis was fully accomplished by Keynes in his analysis of the principle of effective demand. There, Keynes established that costs + profits = prices. In this volume, the theoretical implications of that principle cannot be explored at any greater depth than they have already been. Let us therefore confine our observation to the practical implications of that formula; but let us not fall from the frying pan of theory into the fire of practice.

Before proceeding any further, it is necessary to try to understand what is a profit —otherwise we might attribute inflation, and much more, to "excessive" profits. Profit is the scarecrow of economics and political science. It cannot be understood unless it is seen as a compensation—fair or unfair, depending upon the conditions of the market and the system of prevailing practical justice; a compensation which, through the entrepreneur, is sooner or later distributed to all factors of production. Thus interest or dividend is the profit received by the owner of capital; rent is the profit received by the landowner; and wages or salaries are nothing but the profit received by all employees. Without this element, i.e., the profit, all factors of production—including labor—would either shift to other ventures or, if possible, would withdraw from the market. As far as mobility is concerned, capital and land can be just as much "stuck" in a bad venture as labor so often is.

The issue is quite important. Let us remain with it a little longer. Let us see it in these terms. Let us imagine a joint venture in which no participant "advances" or is advanced any outlay of funds. This is a venture in which the three factors of production—namely, land, labor, and capital—wait to receive their compensation until one productive cycle is closed. Then "profit" disappears from sight. What remains is an amount of income that somehow has to be distributed among the owners of the three factors of production. All too succinctly, the issue is not with the existence of profits. The issue is with the distribution of profits. Were this a work on political economy, we would undoubtedly need to expand greatly upon the issue. Due to the different nature of this work, we can leave it at that. At any rate, with the idea of profit seen in this light, we can resume our major line of reasoning.

When the distinction between costs and prices is firmly established, and it is joined with the distinction between demand and supply as well as consumption and production, then we have some of the major intellectual tools to understand inflation. The clincher is as follows: there is a time gap between the producer buying his supplies, transforming them into finished products and then selling them to consumers, thus recovering his initial investment—plus, hopefully, a compensation for his efforts, i.e., a profit.

Our central concern here is the time gap between buying and selling. Without seeing that time gap, we can never understand inflation. That gap will shortly let us peer into the mechanics of inflation. That gap also makes it impossible to lose the distinction between costs and prices any longer. Even if profit, from a theoretical point of view, were to be lumped together with costs, that gap would remain there as a wedge to separate aggregate costs from aggregate prices. At any instant, aggregate costs (plus profits) of Group A remain of course identical to aggregate prices of Group B. Yet, there is no assurance that aggregate costs (plus profits) of Group A today will be identical to the aggregate prices which the same group will receive tomorrow. And not to distinguish between buyers and sellers would make national income figures comparable to the black night, of Hegelian memory, in which all cows are black.

Statisticians will simply have to do some additional work. They have to stop assuming, as they implicitly do today, that costs and prices instantaneously relate to the same group of people. By doing that, besides running the risk of never penetrating the understanding of the phenomenon of inflation, they reject the potential benefits to be derived from the integration into mainstream theory of Leontief's input-output analysis. In any case, the framework of analysis developed in this work should allay some of the worst fears. Empirical data will have to be gathered on the distribution of ownership over real as well as monetary wealth. Once that is done, numbers will attach themselves to people, and the distinction between costs and prices will become self-evident.

Let us pause on the general aspects of inflation for a while to observe two of its fundamental characteristics. First, inflation is a monetary phenomenon par excellence. It is all related to costs and prices—or, as we shall see, expenditures and income. (One can, of course, reduce that purely monetary phenomenon to the observance of the exchange of goods with goods as Professor Sraffa prefers to do. But this is too severe a mental exercise. We shall take the easier road.) Second, one must try to fix one's eyes solely on either the production process or the consumption process—not both at once.

With these bare minimum premises, we can now begin to look at the apparently intractable phenomenon of inflation—first in the world of production and then in that of consumption. Let us start at the beginning.

No Definition of Inflation

What is inflation? The common expression "inflation is too much money chasing too few goods" is not a definition. It is not an operational definition: what is too much; what is too few? Indeed, what is money? And who controls its creation? With these facts properly assessed, we are left with a firm but perhaps surprising point: there is no definition of inflation.

The expression about too much money chasing too few goods contains a kernel of truth that makes it useful in extreme cases. This is not denied. Nor is it denied that once it is placed in the context of the present work, namely, the equivalence of $P = D = M$, that expression can be transformed into an operational definition. What is undeniable is that at present no operational definition of inflation exists in economic analysis.

Any wonder, then, that we seem unable to find a cure for this phenomenon? Not that there is a dearth of attempts to solve the problem; but of cures, none. None that is workable. The economic system has always cured itself; but no cure has actually been administered to it. The fundamental reason for this state of affairs, to insist on the point, is that there is no definition of inflation. And without a definition one cannot develop a theory of inflation; and without a theory, one cannot design a cure. Not that there is a dearth of theories, either. As Professor John Sheahan testifies, "Theories of inflation are legion."[85] Decoded, this expression confirms that there is no theory and no definition of inflation.

It must be admitted, there is no definition of inflation—"unless," as Keynes cryptically and parenthetically pointed out, "we mean by *inflationary* merely that prices are rising."[86] Prices are rising, it is in fact often said; but it is never asked: in relation to what? To say that inflation is "rising prices," is the same as saying that the "moon moves." It moves in relation to what? Not even Ptolemy (of course) would have uttered a sentence like that.

To overcome this evident shortcoming, it has been assumed that prices move from one level to another. Contemporary economics, therefore, speaks of price inflation. Yet, logically, the expression "prices rise from one level to another" is empty of content, just as the expression "the moon moves from one point to another" is empty of content. Both expressions are tautologies; they leave the observer locked within the confines of one and the same entity.

Quite apart from the consideration that "to rise" is a synonym for "to inflate"—and, as we know, synonyms are not definitions—after Einstein (if not Keynes himself of the *Treatise on Probability*) it ought to be clear that the entity "price" has to be put in relation to something else in order to acquire meaning.

This reasoning receives economic validation as soon as it is realized that a movement in the general price index from one hundred to one hundred ten would have no economic effect if all other values were to rise by ten percent. This lack of content is the ultimate reason why all efforts to explain the theory of price inflation have proved fruitless.

Put in other terms, the theory of price inflation suffers from the same basic deficiency as contemporary economics as a whole. It makes a tremendous intellectual effort to observe phenomena in isolation. Thus, no matter how well analyzed is the phenomenon in itself, its understanding remains insufficient because things exist only in relation to other things—and what is left outside one's conveniently restricted field of observation is, by definition, bigger than the phenomenon which is being analyzed. Besides, by themselves, individual affairs are mere abstractions; they are mere intellectual rationalizations. Briefly and directly, the theory of price (or absolute) inflation must fade into the understanding of relative inflation.

Two Points and a Conclusion

There is one major point to bring forward. The cry of inflation is overly abused. Not all price increases cause inflation. An otherwise long story can be cut short by recalling the fabled cry: "wolf."

This is also an appropriate place to settle an issue left open in the previous chapter. We only need to remark that we have found the major shortcoming in the second element of the presumed trade-off between "inflation" and unemployment. Price inflation has the semblance of being an important phenomenon; in reality, by itself, it is meaningless. Rising prices can either increase or decrease employment. The outcome depends on the way in which other circumstances react upon the increase in prices.

Instead of pursuing price inflation one step further, let us pursue the train of thought that centers around the theory of relative inflation. If we do this we find, first of all, the definition of inflation. Let us observe the issues first in relation to the world of production.

Inflation in the World of Production

The starting point for our analysis is the question: in relation to what do prices increase? The answer is that prices rise in relation to costs. Indeed, the reverse is what actually happens in the world of production: costs rise in relation to prices. When producers' costs rise faster than the prices that they are able to exact from consumers, then they are experiencing a state of inflation. That is inflation in the world of production, then: inflation is costs becoming higher than prices.

Alternatively, using contemporary terminology, this definition can be formulated as follows: a state of true inflation in the world of production arises when production costs grow faster than consumer expenditures. This form has the advantage of providing a direct link with the discussion of inflation in the world of consumption that is presented below. However, this formulation is offered as the second best choice because of a major implicit drawback. In contemporary economics one is liable to automatically translate the expression "consumer expenditures" as expenditures on consumer goods. In this book, that expression includes also expenditures on capital goods and goods to be hoarded.

Either definition achieves numerous objectives. First of all, it clarifies what inflation is: a monetary phenomenon par excellence that directly and immediately affects concrete, but scattered, human beings. For a nation as a whole, in fact, a state of true inflation is approached when prices increase faster than the prices of its trading partners. And that takes a while to develop. Besides, even in this condition, a sizeable number of people can still make sizeable profits.

This definition also clarifies the understanding of the *General Theory*. It pulls together the various clues that Keynes left scattered throughout his work and eliminates the cryptic element in the parenthetical expression quoted above that not all price increases are inflationary. Indeed, our definition even clarifies Keynes' own definition of inflation, a definition which preceded that parenthetical expression and a definition which is recalled here for the benefit of the reader: "When a further increase in the quantity of effective demand produces no further increase in output and entirely spends itself on an increase in the cost-unit fully proportionate to the increase in effective demand, we have reached a condition which might be appropriately designated as one of true inflation."

When one observes the situation from a dynamic point of view; when one relates the discussion to the producer; when one translates the expression effective demand as "expenditure," then one can interpret Keynes' definition as follows. A state of true inflation arises at the point in which expenditures—i.e., costs—increase without creating a proportionate amount of output, namely, without creating the possibility of obtaining prices to cover those costs. But the discussion does not need to be overly theoretical either. There is one empirical test that has consistently been advocated in a variety of forms by the highest authorities in economics, from Alfred Marshall to Wassily Leontief. Any doubts as to the validity of this definition cannot be dispelled through theoretical argumen tation. Inflation is an empirical fact. Doubts have to be spelled out to the producers. They would be happy to say that they really do not care that much about rising costs (which are the prices they pay). Their concern in this regard is limited to the observation of their national and foreign competition; if their competitors also raise the prices they charge, their concern is limited. A real concern is aroused when costs become higher than the prices at which they are able to sell their goods or services. When this happens, they really worry. They are then experiencing a state of true inflation.

As long as costs rise and prices rise too, producers do not worry. They should, because they are shifting the burden onto the shoulders of the consumer—and even onto their own shoulders as consumers. But this is another story, a much larger story that can only be hinted at in this work. Later on, we shall in fact see only a small part of that story: the other half of the problem, inflation in the world of consumption. But the reader shall have to join the two halves together; and all needs to be integrated into the understanding of the economic process as a whole. The issue is one of economic dynamics and not one of economic statics.

When costs rise, prices must rise—otherwise the entrepreneur is not able to pay a fair compensation to all factors of production. The entrepreneur would sooner or later go bankrupt, thus being forced to get out of the market and by definition restricting the size of the total economic system. Instead of growth, there would be a contraction in the economy. This in fact is the ultimate result of inflation: first a stasis in the growth of output and then, likely, a decrease. Indeed, it is through this mechanism that a purely monetary phenomenon such as inflation is transformed into a "real" one. It is at this juncture that the monetary and the "real" world merge into one entity, which, for short, we call the economic world. (Other steps in this linkage can be found in the previous discussion of the law of increasing prices and decreasing performance.)

Whatever formulation is used, the mechanism of inflation is clear. The profit margin—for all factors of production—is at first restricted. Then, it is annulled. Thereafter, if the business operation is continued, one incurs a loss. And the losses can be covered either by digging into past reserves, i.e., profits, or by selling part of one's capital (to foreigners, for instance), or by recurring to debt financing. It is evident that these alternatives do not remain open for long. If prices—or consumer expenditures—do not soon begin to cover costs again, the ultimate result is a restriction of business activities. In any case, a thorough analysis of these alternatives belongs to the field of economic dynamics.

A reduction in output is the real danger—indeed, the real characteristic—of true or relative inflation. And this characteristic explains why the Keynes of *How to Pay for the War* (1940) was no longer concerned with it. During the war, there was no economic fear of a fall in output. In fact, Keynes assumed the civilian output to be constant; and he could then devote his attention solely to the "inflation of prices" or price inflation, by putting it in relation to the attendant dangers of unequal distribution of income and excessive profits by profiteers. (Is it necessary to stress that price inflation, by itself, cannot produce even these effects? These effects are caused by the combination of rising prices with innumerable other factors: not all prices rise in the same proportion; all prices, when "effective," imply income distribution; not all income is distributed through the price mechanism; many people live on fixed income, etc.)

But let us abandon price inflation to its destiny. If the essential characteristic of true or relative inflation is a stasis, and then a reduction in output, it becomes evident that the issue must also be observed from the point of view of the consumer. Let us do that.

Inflation in the World of Consumption

If inflation in the world of production is costs rising faster than prices, then inflation in the world of consumption is the reverse. It is its mirror image. Here, inflation is expenditure becoming higher than money income.

This definition ought to be self-explanatory: the gap between expenditures and income is filled by dis-hoarding, debt, fewer expenditures, starvation, and suicides. (Entrepreneurs, too—as businessmen—can get into a situation in which expenditures run ahead of income. And they have exactly the same alternatives to get out of it as any other consumer.) We shall see below some of the causes of this condition. But is it necessary to emphasize that inflation is not a problem of national accounts? Indeed, is it necessary to emphasize that inflation is not a "national," but an intensely human and personal affair?

Only a dynamic analysis can follow inflation in its course, from start to finish. Only a dynamic analysis can suggest remedies to curb inflation. We cannot go that far; we have to respect the limitations of this book. Our attention must be shifted to the avoidance of a different type of danger. Lest the reader be left with the impression that we are building a dual theory of inflation, one in the world of production and one in the world of consumption; or worse, lest the reader be left with the impression that there is no such thing as a general theory of inflation at all, let us hasten to see how the two definitions given so far merge into one.

A Unified Definition of Inflation

To eliminate the impression that there might be two definitions, and hence two theories of inflation, it is not sufficient to stress that every producer is also a consumer—and, conversely, within certain limits, that every consumer is also a producer. Nor is it sufficient to stress that, with certain time lags (to be empirically ascertained when statistics are collected in accordance with the categories of thought developed in this book), what happens in the field of production is soon transferred to that of consumption—and vice versa. To avoid that impression it is necessary that we truly understand the nature of inflation.

Inflation is a relative phenomenon par excellence. Inflation does not affect all groups in a society, nor does it affect all groups at once. In the scramble between prices and costs, expenditures and income, one group gains at the expense of the other. This condition is the opposite of that which prevails during periods of normal economic growth when all groups gain something, while none lose anything. And inflation is such an abnormal condition that when the situation degenerates and a large reduction in output occurs, even though some groups might lose less than others in relative terms, we all lose something in absolute terms.

Hence, it is rare that inflation is transformed into a national problem. It is this characteristic which compounds the difficulty of fighting inflation. Indeed, as we have seen, apart from periods of large reductions in output, something approaching a national problem arises when the rise in prices for one nation is far ahead of the rise in prices for the rest of the world. But, even then, certain prices increase while others decrease or at least increase less rapidly than others. As noted, the nature of inflation is that of being a relative phenomenon par excellence.

And yet, should one conclude that there is no hope of building a unified theory—and eventually a unified cure—for inflation? Perhaps there is no reason to be that pessimistic. The thread of hope lies in the fact that inflation does show a common characteristic after all. Whether costs become higher than prices or expenditures become higher than income, what is the net effect? With constant quantity of money, static income distribution patterns, and constant quantity and quality of goods traded, the net effect, it is submitted, is a reduction in purchasing power of money. Purchasing power is in fact the relation that links together costs and prices or outflows and inflows of money.

That is inflation, then, wherever it occurs: a personal no less than a national reduction in purchasing power. This is a true definition. Indeed, this is a unified definition of inflation. This definition, in turn, holds the hope that we might eventually build a full-fledged theory of inflation—and thereafter discover a cure for it.

This task cannot be performed in these pages. To proceed one more step along this road, however, it might be useful to give a new designation to the phenomenon we are observing—even though, to facilitate understanding of the issues in the balance of this work we shall not impose this new terminology upon the reader. The theory we are enunciating might be called monetary regression. It is a phenomenon very much related to the fallacy of composition. If only one entrepreneur were to raise prices, it would be lovely for this one person. But when everyone (sooner or later) raises prices, the advantage is illusory and temporary at best. In substance, this designation implies a reduction in purchasing power that results from costs becoming higher than prices, or expenditures becoming higher than incomes.

Since this work is devoted to a static analysis, it is impossible to see inflation as it actually is: a tortuous process which, when rationalized and smoothed out, can be expressed in this fashion. It results from the interplay of those forces that we call costs and prices on one side, and expenditures and income on the other. These four sets of forces gradually create relative inflation in the monetary world. This effect, in turn, reacts upon the "real" world to create first a reduction in the "normal" growth rate of output, then a stasis in the absolute level of output, and finally a reduction in that level—a reduction that we call either recession or depression in accordance with the severity of the final outcome.

Rather than insisting on the new designation, or remaining any longer on the general characteristics of the phenomenon we are observing, let us instead inquire about the causes of inflation—meaning, of course, relative inflation.

The Causes of Inflation

As it can be seen, inflation is like a deadly virus in the process of economic growth. But this characterization is not sufficient to guide us in search for the causes of inflation. We also have to realize that inflation is an organic process that sooner or later affects the entire body economic.

The search for the causes of inflation, therefore, has to span each and every aspect of the economic system. There is no item that is more important than any other. There is no "first" item. We simply have to start somewhere. The following starting point is arbitrary; other researchers might start somewhere else.

The key question that must be asked in order to understand the phenomenon of inflation is: why do costs rise? Upon reflection, it becomes evident that this is not a theoretical, but an empirical question—a question of political economy and, as such, very little can be said on it here. One can simply recite part of the litany: costs rise because wage demands rise; interest rates rise; rents rise. The litany passes through the recitation of government rules and regulations; and it does not stop there. Supplies do get exhausted. Thus one needs to look for different or farther away sources, and even for changes in science and technology. But science and technology—as well as new supplies—not only contribute to the increase in costs; quite often they contribute to a reduction in costs. Thus trends are never unidirectional, they do change; and, at times, they are even reversed. This, to repeat, is an empirical and not a theoretical area. It also falls into the realm of political economy.

It is in fact within the realm of political economy and economic dynamics that people who are seriously interested in the notion of profit can explore why costs, and therefore prices, rise. They are likely to find some of the reasons not only in the time differential between the producers' buying and selling, whereby transactions do not occur continuously and costs are not continuously "equal" to prices. They will also find that prices rise because costs or "profits" are paid out to different factors of production in different proportions. And more important, as we shall briefly see, is the issue of what people do with their profits.

Thus with this type of analysis concerning the reasons why specific costs increase—when completed and fully understood, and when not made circular by saying that costs rise because prices do—one begins to acquire a rather in-depth knowledge of the causes of inflation. But that is only a beginning. There are many other causes that cannot be adequately and consistently treated in these pages. In certain cases far too little, and in others far too much, research has been done on these topics. Besides, one should separate those causes that affect the world of consumption from those which affect the world of production, and then one should study the interrelationships that exist among these causes and their effects. We have to be less ambitious than that; we can only skim the surface of the issues. In fact, we shall not even mention a not-too-infrequent illness: the tendency for certain people to spend more than their income—no matter their level of income.

Certainly, if the monetary authority interjects "too much" money into the economic system, and if many other conditions stipulated in this text obtain, inflation results. This is such a well-known point that there is no need to insist on it. And the same is true for that part of the inflationary process that is created by the government borrowing and spending far in excess, not only of its tax revenue, but especially in imbalance with the available supply of goods and services. Furthermore, to limit our observation to the major issues, there is the existence of the concentration of the available supply of money in far too few hands: this is an inflationary development as well on which far too little research exists. Finally, there is the issue of that psychological law discovered by Keynes: the tendency, or propensity, for people to spend always a little less than the income they receive. They tend to hoard part of it. (One brief comment: money deposited in a bank is not hoarded; it is invested, just as money lent to a business corporation or exchanged for the stock of a business corporation is invested.)

In that psychological "law" discovered by Keynes—once it is adapted to the framework of analysis developed in this book—one finds a major clue for the solution to the problem of inflation. The issue is: why do people tend to hoard part of their wealth? And, perhaps much more important: what are the consequences of people hoarding part of their wealth? The converse of these questions is: why do certain people spend more than their income? What is the effect of this habit?

The first set of questions could not be addressed prior to the development of the Flows model. In mainstream economics, let us recall, hoarding—or saving—is considered "equal" to investment. If, however, the limitations of mainstream economics start there, they do not end there. So far, in fact, we have essentially repeated the traditional analysis. We have absorbed nearly all that can be learned from the theory of price inflation. Indeed, we have done something more. The "legion" of theories on this topic has been transformed into one theory; and this one theory, the theory of relative inflation, has been given a sense of direction by hitching it to the understanding of the economic process as a whole. And yet, what have we really learned? The lesson, it is submitted, is that traditional theory does not go, nor can it go, to the bottom of things. Were we to break off the analysis at this juncture, would we have any deeper understanding of the causes of inflation than we had before?

Hardly so. A final distinction still needs to be kept in mind. One must distinguish between short- and long-range causes. It is this distinction that eliminates the circular reasoning between cost and price increases. After all, even though inflation appears to surge in the public consciousness when it is especially acute, it is evident that its innermost causes smolder under the ashes for a long while. Remember when economists used to say that a one to two percent annual rate of increase in prices was a "normal" phenomenon? It takes a long time, but that rate of increase gradually rises to double- and, in certain countries, even to triple-digit figures. It is then that the economic process has gone awry.

But, then, one no longer speaks of inflation. One begins to talk of "recession" and even "depression." Should we not see these phenomena as symptoms of the same causes; should we not see them as a progression?

Indeed, we must. At least at the level of hypothesis. The hypothesis suggested here is that we see all those phenomena as part of the business cycle. After all, in this most imprecise of worlds, Kondratieff did discover cycles that tend to run over fifty to sixty years. Incidentally, perhaps there is here a cause-effect relationship not only between inflation and the Kondratieff cycles, but even between the business cycle and the "revolutions" in economic theory. Major innovations in economic theory have tended to occur at the bottom of the cycle or the depth of depressions. It is then that the sensitivity of economists is heightened; it is then that the major premises in accepted economic theory are more easily questioned again.

But let us neglect the cycle in economic theory, and concentrate our attention on the business cycle. If the identity between Kondratieff cycles and the "inflation cycle" proves to be correct; and if the Flows model developed in this book has any validity, then we might have some of the major tools for the discovery of the long-range causes of inflation—meaning, to repeat, relative inflation. It might also be stressed that our field of observation is that of inflation from the point of view of the consumer. Since this perspective is not firmly kept in mind by the theory of price inflation, one is presented with an additional reason why this theory cannot produce results. It looks in the wrong direction to find the root cause of the trouble. It looks at producers, and even the government, for clues.

The Long-Range Causes of Inflation

The hypothesis is that, if periods of maximum economic growth occur when hoarding expenditures are at zero or near zero level as we have seen earlier, then the height of inflation must occur when expenditures on hoarding are at one hundred or near one hundred percent of the total income minus expenditures on consumer goods. Let us look at this hypothesis by placing it in a historical context. Experts might be helped by picturing a Lorenz diagram, or the Shadow Diagram given in the previous chapter.

It is evident that during the years between, let us say, 1931 and 1937, few people could afford to hoard wealth—and to hoard it in any significant amount. There was a good reason for this. The production of goods and services had been steadily declining. Whatever production existed, served to satisfy needs of immediate consumption. But what happened between, let us say, 1938 and 1945? All energies were devoted to production, and little wealth was hoarded. From then on, it is safe to assume, an increasingly greater margin of income, for those who could, was devoted to hoarding. As the proportion of hoarding increased, that of investment decreased—until the years, let us say, 1973-81 when the greatest amount of resources was taken, by those who could, out of the production process. It was hoarded. It was hoarded as a hedge against inflation—and it was not realized that such an action created exactly what was most feared: inflation.

Why? The reasons are obviously numerous. Let us observe a few of them.

To simplify the issues, we shall be mainly concerned with the case of the expenditure of money. If money itself is hoarded then, depending upon the stage of the business cycle, the net result might not only be a restriction of the business activity, but even a deflationary effect. On the contrary, if the money spent does not come from active funds, but from reserves previously hoarded, the effect is going to be more inflationary. Yet, in a sense, these are details.

What is essential to realize are the basic consequences of any purchase of nonproductive wealth. Any such purchase—even at the bottom of the depression—is by definition inflationary. An amount of money is injected into the economy for which there is no correspondent increase of goods and services. The $M = P$ equivalence is disturbed. As the early monetarists of the seventeenth and eighteenth centuries realized, through "saving" or through a purchase of nonproductive wealth, the flow of the economic process is cut in two—with one half left frozen, or unproductive of further income and/or goods and services; and the second half fluctuating. As a direct consequence of the existence of that frozen wealth, we have "too much money chasing too few goods"—hence prices rise. The consequences of that fluctuating wealth vary. This second half might be directed toward the purchase of more nonproductive wealth; then the negative effects of the action of the first marginal operator might become cumulative.

This chain of actions and reactions is better analyzed when it is at its peak. With this short-cut, to say the least, we eliminate the need to repeat and to expand upon all that has been said so far whenever the issue of hoarding has come up for discussion. What happens then? A large number of phenomena occur—and occur at once. Here are a few of them:

- Some money is directly hoarded. Thus money becomes scarce and "the" interest rate rises. Even more importantly, apart from indispensable consumer items, what type of wealth is bought with the money actually spent? (Money sent abroad is neglected here.)

- The largest part of the flow of money reverses its "normal" course from investment-assets into comparatively scarce nonproductive wealth. This is indeed a world of "scarcity." And the flow reverses itself because nonproductive wealth—no matter its cost—is supposed to be "secure" wealth, secure from the ills of inflation;

- Financial fortunes are lost in the bear market. Hence stocks and bonds which represent productive wealth become "scarce"—stocks more so than bonds;

- The above two points are better seen if joined together, in this fashion: the value of nonproductive wealth increases as the value of productive wealth decreases. Furthermore, the rate of increase in value for nonproductive wealth is generally faster and its rate of decrease slower than the correspondent rates for the value of productive wealth, because downturns in business activity are generally faster than upturns. (Downturns are at first purely monetary affairs);

- The financial needs of the productive process must somehow be satisfied and are satisfied through borrowing. Hence money becomes scarcer;

- Interest rates rise even further. Hence the level of borrowing is reduced or borrowing becomes scarce;

- The financial (and perhaps labor) cost of investment-assets increases while their production decreases. Hence investment-assets become scarce;

- The price of consumer goods increases. With ongoing dis-investment and high interest rates, the productive process begins to provide less than the peak flow of such goods and services. Hence consumer goods become scarce;

- Indeed, even nonproductive wealth—which is by nature scarce—becomes scarcer, because its demand rises and its production cannot keep up with the demand. Hence its cost, reflecting increasing production costs, rises;

- Due to these efforts, the relative share of production, employment, and income involved in the field of nonproductive wealth increases. But the total gross national product tends to decrease;

- Less money-income, in the form of labor—as well as rent—and capital-income, is created and distributed. Hence the propensity to consume is lowered;

• Less revenue is received by the production process because of a lower consumption rate.

These are some of the manifestations—and the immediate causes—of what Keynes termed the collapse of the marginal efficiency of capital, which remains collapsed until actual prices and the expectation of future prices begin to outrun costs.

It should also be noted that soon after the "peak" of frantic but negative economic activity, and throughout the entire phase of the collapse of the marginal efficiency of capital, relative prices as well as the absolute price level might even be falling. And yet, due to their "stickiness," costs—whether costs of labor, or land, or capital, including taxes—do not immediately fall behind prices.

This is deflation, of course. Deflation is the reverse image of inflation. And the normal outcome of deflation is depression.

This is what happened in the world during the 1930s. This is what is happening at this writing in Japan. A near-depression occurred in the United States in the early 1980s, but it was neither as long nor as acute as the Great Depression. This result elicited the hope that the business cycle had been abolished.

Has the Business Cycle Been Abolished?

Has the business cycle been abolished? The answer to this very important and urgent question is nuanced. Can the business cycle be abolished? The reasoning followed in this book yields a decisively positive answer—provided one takes steps to avoid hoarding throughout the cycle. Has the business cycle already been abolished? Wisdom calls for caution about uttering definitive judgments and begs for much more empirical data.

The facts under observation for the United States ever since the 1980s seem to indicate the existence of a new—or perhaps very old—phenomenon: a split-level economy. Artificially infusing inordinate amounts of money into the economy, the monetary authority (of many countries) managed to sustain exorbitant values of financial assets; and the trickle-down effect created real growth for certain industries and certain segments of the population. Upstairs, all was fluffy. Yet, what happened to the majority of the people in the majority of industries who lived downstairs in the economic system? While the number of jobs grew, since wages did not grow, the purchasing power of most labor income remained stable or declined. A number of factors contributed to this outcome. Mountains of debt engulfed everyone; labor unions were disempowered; new jobs were mostly in low-paying service jobs, while the real work of production of goods was done abroad, as reflected in the surging deficit in the balance of payments; women entered the labor market en masse and received lower wages than men for comparable work; long hours and part-time work dominated the labor market; two jobs were necessary to sustain a person, and two incomes were necessary to sustain a family; and, as some convincing research done by Juliet Schor, a professor of economics at Harvard, revealed, much of the weight of the overall poor status of the real economy was shifted onto the shoulders of children.

This is not news. It is not an original analysis. Everyone knew about it, but it was mostly shunted aside in the polite conversation controlled by popular news media and elite financial analysis. Presumably no one wanted to learn about the sappy stories of the real world; everyone only wanted to know about phantasmagoric rises in the stock market and fast cars and fast women.

So much for the observation of the past. What can be said about the general case? Seen over a time curve, inflation is the ascending portion of the cycle and deflation its descending portion. In either case, unless equilibrium between costs and prices is restored, the marginal efficiency of capital remains collapsed and the net effect is identical: a reduction of output or, at least, less output than possible. These processes are never smooth; they proceed by fits and starts and tend to reinforce each other. Where does it all stop? To insist on the point, the process can be interrupted at any moment. But it rarely is.

Quite apart from the case of Japan, now that the stock market bubble has burst, it seems that the economy of the United States is also in free fall. In Paul Krugman's phrase, we are experiencing a "return of depression economics"—if not in fact at least as a set of theoretical issues at the center of our attention. Where will it end?

The "normal" resting place is at the bottom of the depression. Then money is no longer available for the purchase of nonproductive wealth. Then opportunities of greater and, hopefully, more secure income begin to become evident again. Then consumer confidence rises, and so does the confidence of the producer.

A Few Reflective Questions

The closer one looks at the head of a pin, the bigger it becomes; at the limit, it becomes so big as to be blinding. The phenomenon of hoarding is certainly not like the head of a pin. Nonetheless it is safer to put some distance between ourselves and our topic by asking a few relevant questions. First of all, how certain is the description of the chain of events outlined above?

Those mechanisms have been reconstructed through the observation of fragmentary and vastly uncoordinated data—a situation that will not change so long as we continue to collect information and analyze it on the basis of current categories of economic thought. Due to their character and their ready availability, it would be redundant to reproduce those figures in this work. In any case, the question of reliability of the above description cannot be answered otherwise than by saying that it relies on the power of logic and the force of naked observation. This is not to say that there is no need for further work. Indeed, as encouragement for the eventual performance of the necessary empirical and statistical tests, a brief examination of another question might be of help. How intrinsically important is the phenomenon of hoarding?

If the above analysis turns out to have any validity, the quantitative importance of hoarding will be found to vary with the business cycle. But that is not the crux of the matter. The crux of the matter lies in the "absolute" economic importance of hoarding; it lies in the economic function constantly performed by hoarding, whatever its quantitative value. In the current absence of hoarding as a separate category of thought and with the prevailing models of economic growth, hoarding—when it is mentioned at all—is assumed to perform the function of equalizing present and future demand for specific goods. The present work has hopefully altered this intellectual framework of analysis. Hence it can be said that hoarding which performs that important function from a technological point of view (i.e., that part of necessarily but temporarily physically inactive wealth), more accurately, ought to be defined as investment. This is not a verbal manipulation of the reality. It respects the reality fully.

The question in fact remains in relation to that wealth which is kept inactive beyond mere technological requirements. This wealth must be classified as hoarding. This wealth, far from equalizing present and future demand, performs an enormously destabilizing function in the economic system. In brief, it creates either oversupply or underconsumption—or both. A detailed analysis of these conditions belongs to the fields of econometrics and economic dynamics. Indeed, it belongs even to the field of sociology: it is likely in fact that many of the forces which are generally assumed to foster "conspicuous" consumption will also be found to foster hoarding.

In any case, the analysis of the importance of hoarding will be completed when a full answer is given to the question: what price does society pay for this practice? The tentative answer found in this chapter is that the price of hoarding is inflation. And deflation is the cost of bringing inflated prices down toward "normalcy" of alignment of costs and prices both in the real and the monetary economy.

A Larger Truth

It would appear that we have thus reached the end of our research. And yet, that is too convenient—one is tempted to say, too rational—an answer, not to be suspect. It is sufficient to recall the narrowness of our scope of observation to realize that we are not truly entitled to draw final conclusions. Still another question must be asked: why do people hoard wealth?

The answer to this question appears to be that people hoard wealth for fear of future costs running ahead of prices and/or future expenditures running ahead of income. Is not this a near-universal fear? If this is true, then it becomes necessary to conclude that the fundamental cause of inflation is—not hoarding—but the fear of future events and the insecurity concerning the future behavior of the economy. (A much deeper analysis than can possibly be performed in these pages would reveal that this fear is also the ultimate reason why certain people have a tendency to spend more than their income.)

As it can be seen, we are presented here with what at first glance appears to be a vicious circle. For fear of the future, people hoard wealth; and the more wealth is hoarded, the more inflation—and the more fear of the future—is created. The situation is circular—or better, as we shall see later on, the situation is a complementary one. It cannot be resolved in theory. Only in practice, through economic policies which foster economic security, we can break that mutually reinforcing pattern.

The Power of Economic Policies

There is one basic reason why economic policies alone have the tremendous power of breaking that complementary pattern. It is mainly other people's costs that run ahead of prices, and other people's expenditures that run ahead of income, because of personal incontinence and improvidence. Personal incontinence and improvidence do not always explain why our costs run ahead of prices and our expenditures run ahead of income. One can ascribe this reasoning to self-deceit and self-conceit. But much of this reasoning is sound. There are periods—by definition, inflationary periods—in which personal continence and providence are so powerless that they are swept under by forces which are bigger than our power of decision: forces which are external to us. These are the forces that are largely generated by too many existing economic policies. That is the reason why economic policies can break that vicious circle: they largely create it.

The Work Ahead

This conclusion brings into focus the whole impact of economic policies upon the subjects treated in this work. This is an area we have conveniently shunted aside. But here, more than in other fields, it presses forth for recognition. Indeed, it carries along with it the vast horizons of psychology and politics, esthetics and morality. Were we to deal with all this baggage at this juncture, we would run the risk of being overwhelmed by its weight.

To proceed as smoothly as we can, we shall beg for time—promising a somewhat fuller treatment of these issues at a later moment. The opportunity will be offered by the observation of the relationships between poverty and the economic process as a whole. But a partial recognition of the impact of economic policies upon inflation can hardly be avoided at this point.

If people hoard wealth (or spend more than their income) not for the sake of hoarding (or spending) but to allay the fear of future events, then the burden must be shifted from hoarding (or spending) upon economic policies. Contrary to general expectations, hard observation reveals that it is those policies that create too large a share of that fear. Should one recite the litany? Taxes, taxes, and taxes. Rules, rules, and regulations. The intentions are certainly good. But what are the effects? Does ninety percent of the population today not depend for its livelihood on other people's will? Does this condition not engender economic insecurity? No matter how unintentional it might be, is not economic insecurity the result of too many policies being implemented today?

Certainly, much more empirical work remains to be done on these issues. And the Flows model ought to be of assistance in this research. But are we not entitled to reach the conclusion that the root cause of inflation (observed from the point of view of the consumer, and ultimately affecting the world of production) can be found in the existence of a long string of economic policies which foster economic *insecurity* for all? If there were economic security in the land, the calculations of the monetary authority would be more apt to be accurate. If there were economic security in the land, the government would be more apt to spend less. If there were economic security abroad, people would be more apt to spend more (but not more than their income)—or at least to spend more on consumer and capital goods than on wealth which can be hoarded as a hedge against inflation, thus fostering inflation.

We cannot dwell on these issues. Only one observation is necessary. Who is in a constant state of inflation? The poor, of course, are. What the majority of people perhaps experience for ten percent of their lives, the poor experience continuously. Theirs is a losing struggle against expenses that run ahead of income.

We shall have something to say on this issue in a few concluding comments at the end of the book. Here let us ask one final question: are the harrowing experiences of a depression—or even those of a "mild" recession— really necessary? The reader shall be the judge. But before rushing to conclusions, let us issue a warning.

A Warning

Do not think that it is easy to fight inflation. Even though a "radical cure" for the ills which afflict the contemporary world, as Keynes anticipated, has eventually to be found in a set of economic policies which create economic security for all and would eliminate the need for the attainment of security through the purchase of nonproductive wealth—do not think that these policies are easy to design and then to implement. If, through exorbitant taxes or other penalties, we should try to ban the purchase of items of wealth which can be and are commonly hoarded, some "uncommon" items will become so desired and so scarce that they will perform the same functions which today are performed by those items which are generally hoarded. Specifically, if a tax or a ban should ever be placed upon the production or sale of unused diamonds, gold, and dollar bills in a safe deposit box—then black beans may end up being produced and hoarded.

Inflation is too important an issue to be left on a flippant note and with a negative warning. Let us re-cast the warning in a positive light. Even though the original cause of inflation can be found in the action of the first person who after a depression—if not during a depression—starts accumulating nonproductive wealth, we are all, or nearly all, responsible for inflation. Some of us follow the lead of that "first" person; others simply go on asking for increasingly higher profits or rents or wages. Some of us give in to these "cost-push" pressures and raise prices; others give in to the "demand-pull" pressures and buy an article or a service which clearly is overpriced—instead of looking for an equally good, if not better, product or service which is available at a lower price. How to put it? We are all responsible for inflation. Some more, some less, but we are all responsible for it—rich and poor alike, producers and consumers, private citizens and public officials.

If this is the case, then there is no simple cure—no "radical cure"—for inflation. The only cure, short of a catastrophic depression, is a slow, long-term, relentless activity that guards against every possible sign of inflation. We must use the broom, rather than the bulldozer (of fiscal and monetary policy). We must all become involved in this fight. We must make it a common fight, a general fight; and not an individualized fight which finds only one outlet to create economic security: the acquisition of nonproductive wealth. Such a remedy is worse than the illness. It is actually its ultimate cause.

And what is the essential prerequisite for this capillary, strenuous, continuous fight against inflation? The prerequisite is that we all, or nearly all, learn about the inner workings of the economic process.

If the issue of inflation is seen in this light, it becomes self-evident how important it is to keep the economic discourse as clear and as simple as possible. Since we all create inflation, since we are all potential treasurers of the only "radical" remedy, we must all try to understand as much as we can about that which is involved in our own economic actions. The emphasis must be shifted from the government onto the people.

Hence to keep the economic discourse in a highly specialized, and at times secretive, fashion is comparable to the action of chemists who badly want certain reactions from their elements in the laboratory but fail to give to those elements clear and precise "instructions." Or worse, they give the wrong instructions. Or worse yet, they give such ambivalent instructions that are liable to be misunderstood by those elements. The latter approach does not only prevent the achievement of the desired results; it even confuses the chemists. Was the reaction caused by some structural problem, or was it caused by the misunderstanding of the instructions?

A Counter-warning

If the reader is left with the impression that to fight inflation is the sole responsibility of the individual person, the reader is left with the wrong impression. But such a faulty impression is not due to a deficiency in the reader, nor perhaps to a deficiency in the writer. It rather is a deficiency in our language; a deficiency in our culture. Our language and our culture have not yet come to full terms with the social reality. Nurtured as we are by the powerful imagination of an uninterrupted string of writers who perhaps go from Daniel Defoe to Ayn Rand, our language and our culture tend to perpetuate the myth of the "individual person." And each reader—so palpably flattered—never seems able to distinguish literary fiction from reality. Robinson Crusoe did not find society only when he discovered the "good" Friday; he carried society with him. The knowledge he brought with him was not a product of his doing; it was society's doing. It was the result of accumulated millennia. It was the result of a great many people's effort. (In truth, it must be said that unlike many of his commentators, and imitators, Defoe often tried to convey exactly this message.)

Technically, as we have seen, society perforce enters into half of the economic process. It enters at three stages in a particularly forceful way: the creation of money, its distribution, and the delivery of so much and so widespread economic security that the individual person feels free to spend money on consumer and capital goods instead of hoarding it. Without the enlightened intervention from the public, the state, or society upon at least these three facets of the economic process, the fight against inflation is a lost cause. Society alone can insure the smooth creation of as large a supply of money as necessary; a fair distribution of such a supply; and the existence of economic security. These are the bare essentials.

But these essentials are of extreme importance. It cannot be stressed too highly: unlike persons who spend more than their income to soothe their fear of future events, persons who hoard wealth are not irrational. That is the only course left open to them, and they logically pursue it in the hope of acquiring economic security. This hope is not unjustified either. When prices of items that can be hoarded fall, they tend to fall to a level higher than that reached in the previous bottom or trough. Of course, this is not to say that all hoarding is rational. Some of it is due to ignorance of better opportunities; some is due to carelessness—and some is due to pure meanness. But these are aberrations. Far more important is the case of "rational" hoarding.

It is society that at is highly irrational. Instead of exploring the myriad of opportunities open to society as a whole, opportunities to build economic security for all, in a thousand subtle ways many notable groups of people—led by flamboyant characters—have for a few centuries now been intensely involved in pursuing exactly the opposite policy. Driven by a series of misguided and clearly unrealizable ideas, these groups seem to take particular delight in building economic insecurity for all.

Toward the Civilized Society

In the present context, no more can be said on these topics. Only one thought that spills over into political science is in order. Is it not clear why all efforts directed at the improvement of either man alone or society alone are generally destined to fail rather miserably? The reality is such that the individual person does not exist without society, nor does society exist without man. These two poles of the reality exist only as a unity: separated, they are non-existing abstractions. Translating this reality into the field of economics, it means that the individual person shall be engaged in a quixotic battle if he or she struggles against inflation alone. The individual person must join with other people in this fight. It has to become society's struggle, just as much as the individual's struggle.

All these cumbersome expressions can be avoided if and when Somism—meaning the study of the social man, the civilized person—becomes an accepted and widely recognized cultural expression, whose meaning I have fitfully explored during the last forty years. Then the solution to many of our socio-political dilemmas becomes much simpler than it appears at first sight. We do not need to create men and women who are "better" in relation to some abstract world. We need to create the social man, the civilized person—the person who recognizes and respects the rights of others—because they are the same as one's own rights.

The goal is to work toward the achievement of a set of economic rights and responsibilities that are shared by all, and thus lead to economic security, indeed, economic serenity for all.

It is hoped that these chapters have opened new avenues of research and new vistas upon lines of action in the pursuit of that elusive and ancient dream: the building of a Civilized Society.

A Complementary Theory of Inflation

If the issues treated in this chapter have such a fundamental importance not only in relation to purely economic affairs but for civilization itself, they deserve to be clarified to the maximum extent possible. A final characterization might achieve this aim. What has been so sketchily outlined above can be generically named a complementary theory of inflation.

Since the social reality is composed of two entities—man and society—at each step of the way we have been confronted with two aspects of the situation, and not one. For the definition of the problem, we had to look first at the world of production and then at that of consumption. (Under different circumstances, the order would have been reversed.) For the identification of its causes, we had to look first at the individual person's propensity to hoard wealth and then—however briefly—at those economic policies which create economic insecurity. For the solution of the problem, we had to look first at what the individual person can do and then at what society must do.

Certainly, all these issues deserve to be scrutinized much more closely than they have been. But this scrutiny will be successfully accomplished only if it is pursued with a great sense of balance. No single aspect of each pair is more important than the other: they have a fully complementary value.

By the same token, issues of inflation have neither more nor less importance than the issues of economic growth. These two sets of complementary issues had to be physically and mentally separated in these pages. But in reality they are intertwined: the seeds of inflation exist within the process of economic growth. Certain prices have a tendency to rise. This is an unavoidable consequence of the dynamics of the economic process—a consequence that, under "normal" circumstances, is offset by other prices falling. But when the majority of prices rise; and, above all, when the majority of costs run ahead of prices, then many things go awry. Equally, it is perhaps unavoidable that certain people's expenditures show a tendency to run ahead of their incomes; but when the majority of people's (or certain economic sectors) expenditures run ahead of their incomes, then many things go awry. Then, instead of the process of economic growth, we are faced with the process of economic decline. It is this pattern that, if protracted, largely explains why civilizations decline and fall.

And the issue is even more subtle than that. The issue is not so much the long-term destiny of civilizations. The issue is the quality of the civilization at each stage of its life. The issue is whether or not we live our entire lives in a civilized society, in a civilized manner.

Rather than exploring these fascinating issues at any greater depth, we must bring this chapter to a close by returning pretty much to our starting point. We now have all the intellectual tools to settle an issue that has been fitfully touched upon and which must still trouble the inquisitive reader.

The Cost-Price Spiral: *a Double Helix*

Were this a work on economic dynamics, we would now follow "the cost-price spiral" step by step in its development. We would then see that such a spiral is more complex than it appears at first sight. Its structure is actually a double helix—just like the DNA structure, as depicted in the attached graph.

Costs rise for their own independent reasons in the world of production, just as prices rise for their own independent reasons in the world of consumption. But they do not remain independent for long. In their rise, costs and prices meet each other at various junctures—and, instead of neutralizing each other, reinforce each other.

In this work, no more can be said on this topic, except emphasizing that clarity of vision is obtained by following first the development of the one and then the development of the other—but never forgetting that they are complementary issues. Only in this way can we avoid the circular thinking involved in the assumption that costs rise because prices rise—or vice versa. Both these statements are correct. But it is only by combining both statements through the mechanism of the double helix that one captures the whole truth concerning inflation.

A final word. The title of this section, as well as the title of the enclosed graph, represents a concession to the history of economic analysis. That title could have just as properly been "The Expenditure-Income Spiral." A dynamic analysis of inflation, in fact, will not be complete unless both sides of the issue are explored in depth.

A Final Warning

It would be wrong to conclude that, since the DNA structure is a natural one, the cost-price double helix is also a "natural" structure and therefore that it is either impossible or unwise to change it.

While the results of the DNA structure are beneficent, the effects of the cost-price structure are maleficent. It is this basic difference between the two that should indeed spur us to break the prevailing structure assumed by the relationship between costs and prices—or expenditures and incomes.

The Cost-Price Spiral
as a DNA double helix

> The cost-price spiral can also be seen as a relationship between production costs and consumer expenditures — including expenditures on consumer goods as well as expenditures on capital goods.

1. A ladder

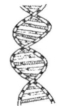

2. DNA: a twisted ladder (a double helix)

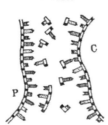

3. Many forces contribute to the formation of Prices (P) as well as Costs (C).

4. Costs and Prices merge into one structure — a structure which is *much more* complex than the one depicted here as representing the DNA structure.

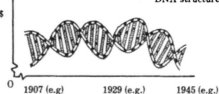

$

0   1907 (e.g)   1929 (e.g.)   1945 (e.g.)

5. Even a simplified reproduction of the cost-price structure has to be seen developing over time and representing the "inflation cycle."

Credits:

Drawings have been reproduced and adapted from *DNA — Ladder of Life*, by Edward Frankel and illustrated by Anne Marie Jauss (New York: McGraw-Hill Company, 1964), pp. 45 and 57.

To break that structure means first of all to discover what is a truly natural relationship between the two. This is easy to define. At least in the aggregate, costs must be constantly kept below the level of prices; expenditures must be constantly kept below the level of incomes. Time must be allowed to run its natural course. This prescription is valid for individual persons as well as for corporations and governments. This is the only road which, to borrow Eric Fromm's happy phrase, will lead us to the Sane Society—to the sane society at least in the economic world; and, from there, gradually and hopefully to the sane society in so many other spheres of life.

Conceding that we do not and perhaps we shall not ever live in an economic world of perfect calculations and foresight; conceding that the forces of the business cycle are too powerful and undisciplined to be ever completely mastered, the most we should tolerate is a mildly undulating set of near parallel lines. The relationship to be assumed by costs and prices or expenditures and incomes that would prevail in a sane economic society, then, can be visually expressed as in the following diagram:

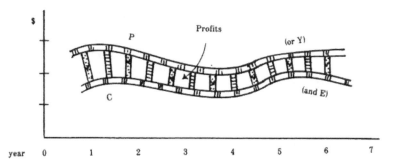

where P stands for Prices; C for Costs; Y for Income; and E for Expenditure.

The implications of this structure are too vast to be tackled in these pages. But a brief answer to one key question can hardly be avoided: how do we get there?

How Do We Get There: *Need for a Dynamic Analysis*

How do we get to the Serene Economic Society? The road will certainly be long—but not necessarily painful. We have to remember that the present prevailing economic condition is the result of perhaps eight thousand years of recorded history. And we have to remember that we have reached this stage, not through malicious planning, but essentially through lack of understanding of the economic process. Economic analysis is a very young discipline indeed.

There is much to be done. The bare outline of the work ahead can be visualized if the reader recalls to mind three illustrations given above and entitled respectively: (1) A Few Verbal Contradictions in the Current Economic Discourse; (2) A Simplified Flow of Income Distribution; and, (3) The Cost-Price Spiral as a DNA Double Helix.

What do these illustrations have in common? Their basic structure is identical. They represent a series of twists and turns. Once we unsnarl those knots, we shall obtain the serene economic society. We have to eliminate internal contradictions from the economic discourse; we have to create a smooth flow in the distribution of income and wealth; we have to keep costs and expenditures constantly in balance with prices and incomes. (Of course, one is fully aware that this line of argument is going to be attacked by that small band of vociferous, short sighted, self-flagellating people who will describe this as the "dull" society.)

Let us gratifyingly assume that the knots in the prevailing economic discourse have all been unsnarled in this book. What remains to be done is to clearly see that verbal contradictions in theory actually lead to economic policies that create twists and turns in the distribution of income. What remains to be done is to clearly see that twists and turns in the distribution of income lead to the cost-price double helix. It is submitted that to clearly observe this chain of causation it is necessary to conduct a detailed, dynamic analysis of the issues: a dynamic analysis that cuts across the artificial barrier between economic theory and economic policy.

The hour is early. This is work that must be left undone. Many more tasks lie immediately ahead of us.

PART IV

Foundations of Economics

HARVEST TIME. What has the reader gathered from this investigation? What has the economist gathered from it?

Whatever personal answer is given to these questions, some readers may be concerned that the investigation of the economic process has led us farther and farther away from the interests of modern economic theory. That is a superficial—and wrong—impression. The investigation has been involved with the foundations of economic analysis.

This section, then, has to be seen, rather than as an ending, as a new beginning in its own right. It lays bare the seeds of a new comprehensive form of economic analysis, an analysis—to repeat—whose reasoning can be followed by any interested reader. And it issues a plea for the application of the most up-to-date tools of mathematics to economic reasoning. Once econometricians take hold of the "new analytic engine," some readers might want to take a breath of fresh air: it is really not necessary for every participant in a feast to be in the kitchen. But the dawn of that day is not on the time horizon yet.

XXIII

Toward Econometrics:
Closing the Gap Between
Micro and Macro Economics

*The econometric investigation can start
from the models presented below.*

———

FROM MY GENERAL KNOWLEDGE of the field, I have the impression
that few any longer read Professor Samuelson's widely acknowledged masterpiece, *Foundations of Economic Analysis* (1947).
While there are reasons for this neglect, I consider it to be a strategic mistake. As the following suggests, even though the book does
not contain all the answers, as if any book ever could, the framework of the book contains the right question.

As Professor Samuelson later acknowledged, relying on pure
mathematical reasoning, the book, which was conceived and written primarily in 1937, reduced economic thinking to a rather repetitive and mechanical process.[87] However, its weakness emerged
when, in 1948, Professor Samuelson presented his popular text-
book entitled *Economics*. This work was built on two foundations:
micro foundations, as in one form of traditional analysis, and the
foundations of economics as a whole about which he had written
in his basic theoretical book and which had become obligatory after
the publication of Keynes' General Theory. All twelve editions of
Economics, the latest of which was published in 1985 with
Professor William D. Nordhaus of Yale University, remained split
into two sections, one relating to microeconomics and the other to
macroeconomics. The linkage between the two has been called the
neoclassical synthesis. But this expression refers, not so much to an
accomplished meshing of the two segments, as to a program of
research that still needs to be brought to fruition. The split between
micro and macroeconomic analysis persists to this very day.

The persistence of the split is fully evident in the research jour-
nals, and is confirmed in the textbooks. In one of the most

acclaimed economics textbooks issued of late, a book entitled *Principles of Economics* (1998), the author, N. Gregory Mankiw, a professor of economics at Harvard, writes: "The field of economics is traditionally divided into two broad subfields. Microeconomics is the study of how households and firms make decisions and how they interact in specific markets. Macroeconomics is the study of economy-wide phenomena." Professor Mankiw lists inflation, unemployment, and economic growth among the latter phenomena; and he continues "...because microeconomics and macroeconomics address different questions, they sometimes take quite different approaches and are often taught in separate courses."[88]

On the surface, the economics profession seems to be at peace with the assumption that it is proper to have such a split in the very nature of their discipline. But this representation does not accurately reflect the issues. Professional economists are clearly dissatisfied with the split. This is what Barbara Petrongolo and Christopher A. Pissarides have concluded in a survey article published in the current issue of the *Journal of Economic Literature*: "Like most aggregate functions in the macroeconomist's tool kit, the matching function [between jobs and workers] is a black box: we have good intuition about its existence and properties but only some tentative ideas about its microfoundations."[89]

At the core of the discipline there is an intense effort to unify the two strands through a field of research that goes under the banner of microfoundations of economics. The assumption in this field of study is that the analysis has to be painstakingly built step by step from microeconomics to macroeconomics.

Years of meticulous effort have yielded a wealth of hypotheses, but not a coherent program of research. The approach runs against insurmountable problems of aggregation. Once data are collected and analyzed in accordance with one methodology, the data cannot be consistently put together again to fit the requirements of other methodologies. The data cannot be unscrambled and reorganized at will. But this is an explanation that is concerned with mathematics and statistics. A more fundamental issue concerns the assumption that, as put by Professor Mankiw, "microeconomics and macroeconomics address different questions."

Is this not a fundamentally weak assumption?

A Call for Reconsideration

Might this be an opportune moment to reconsider the issues? What are the foundations of the microfoundations of economics?

Is not the issue, as in the original Samuelson's program, with the foundations of economics as a whole?

Once one studies the economic process as a process, all questions seem to fall into the same framework of analysis. In the previous chapters we have been able to address questions of macroeconomics as well as questions of microeconomics without ever feeling the need to change methodology. And yet, the issue is so important that surely the present investigation is not going to be the last word on the topic.

Certainly, it was not in the intention of this study to resolve that split, nor did the split directly enter into any consideration whatsoever during the investigation. The split seems to have vanished simply because every model that has been presented in this volume is equally applicable to the micro and the macro economic world. The assumption here is that each model applies equally fittingly to the "economy" of the individual person, the firm or the family, the city or the state, the nation, or the world as a whole. What changes is not the structure of the investigation or even the complexity of the analysis; what changes is simply the scale of the analysis. The pattern of the analysis, to use a term from non-linear mathematics, is self-similar.

Toward a Renewed Econometrics

It is not the intention of this writer to try to convince the reader of the validity of the assumption that with the new models the split between microeconomics and macroeconomics has been healed. The intention is only to convince the reader to take this possibility under serious advisement. Indeed, this is only a call to both microeconomists and macroeconomists to investigate whether they can use the new models in their own researches. It is eventually the use of the "new analytic engine" that will dispel doubts about the soundness of the hypothesis that the distinction between the two fields has disappeared.

And the models presented so far are not ready for immediate use by econometricians. There is much work to be done to bridge the gap between the analysis contained in the previous chapters and empirical research. In particular, data have to be gathered and organized in accordance with the categories of thought proposed in this study. And the models themselves need some other adjustments.

To bring this task a step closer to fruition we will hereafter first introduce money into the economic system by presenting the Flows model in a monetary garb. Then we will transform both the Stocks model and the Flows model into three new models in which (a) money is an integral part of the system and (b) stocks and flows merge into one another. We will thus obtain a model of production, a model of distribution, and a model of consumption. The reader is then left alone to see how these three models flow one into the other. Since the issues are clearly of economic dynamics, this study must stop there. It is in a subsequent investigation that I will present a model that fuses all three models into one.

The econometric investigation can start from the models presented below. They were copyrighted in 2001 and might be patented. The purpose of the use of these legal mechanisms is not to stifle scientific research, but to share in the benefits of their commercial exploitation.

The Interjection of Money Into the System

Perhaps the best way to start on the road toward a renewed field of econometrics is, not to recapitulate all that has been said in the previous chapters, but to present the Flows model in a new attire, the monetary garb. After all, flows of "goods and services" are analyzed by physicists, engineers, and other natural scientists. Economists analyze exclusively flows of funds. The distinction that underlies this discussion is between monetary (or financial) values measured, e.g., in dollar bills and the value of real goods and services measured in any *numeraire* such as beans, energy units, or even dollar bills themselves. In the latter case, the essential caveat concerns the inclusion of a series of statistical devices such as the use of stable or "real" currency, namely, currency that is unaffected by inflation or deflation. Other devices for the differentiation between monetary and real values are implicit in the very conceptual apparatus we are developing in these pages, namely,

- Since values are measured from three viewpoints—production, distribution, and consumption—there is a continuous triple-check on our reasoning and calculations;

- The objects being measured are clearly distinct from each other. They are: real goods and services; ownership rights over goods, services, and money; and financial instruments;

- Each category within the three broad categories is clear and distinct from all other categories of economic thought.

Therefore, when numbers pass from one category to another, values increase in one and decrease in the other;

• The numbers in each category are not foot-loose. Through the category of distribution of ownership rights, numbers are continuously attached to specific human beings and institutions that perform specific economic functions. For instance, an "x" value of producer goods remains in the category of producer goods until bought by consumers. Therefore, numbers pass from one category to another only if owners are different and/or perform a different economic function.

These technical difficulties aside, the following formulation of the Flows model in purely monetary terms does not only avoid a schematic, largely meaningless, and potentially misleading summary of what has been presented so far. The monetary formulation of the Flows model confirms the validity of the revision of Keynes' model. It allows us to introduce a grand overview of the material presented so far; and, through the open interjection of money into the system, grants us a more realistic picture of the economic process.

Monetary Formulation of the Flows Model

The Monetary model is the Flows model expressed in purely monetary terms. The structure is identical. It is only its outer attire that is different. Needless to say, the need for these distinctions manifested itself through the probing questioning of Professor Modigliani.

The Monetary model reads as follows:

$$MY = E + E_h$$
$$E_k = MY - E_h$$
$$E_k = E$$

where MY is monetary income, E expenditure, E_h hoarding-expenditure, namely, money directly hoarded and/or spent on goods hoarded, and E_k investment-expenditure.

The Monetary model becomes more easily intelligible if one breaks down the general category of expenditure (E) into money directly hoarded and/or spent on goods hoarded (E_h), expenditure on consumer goods (E_g), and expenditure on capital goods (E_k).

Thus the first equation can also be written:

$$MY = E_k + E_g + E_h.$$

If one observes monetary income, as is in reality, through this last specification, namely, divided among expenditure on goods hoarded, expenditure on consumer goods, and expenditure on capital goods, the second equation of the Monetary model—namely,

$$E_k = MY - E_h$$

becomes immediately intelligible: investment-expenditure cannot be but the difference between monetary income and money which is hoarded in a safe deposit box or kept "under the mattress." Quantitatively, the category of hoarding can be better evaluated if it is seen to include not only money which for any number of reasons is kept in nonproductive forms, but especially money which is spent for the purchase of such "nonproductive" wealth as unused land (land which is kept unused for a period of time longer than necessary for productive cycles), empty buildings, objects of art held in a safe, and the like. Then it becomes clear why such wealth cannot be considered an investment-expenditure: it does not, nor can it, produce goods and services—as the word investment must, and does, mean in economics. Hence investment-expenditure cannot be but the difference between monetary income and hoarding-expenditure or money directly hoarded. This relationship becomes more easily recognizable if one restricts the observation to pure hoarding of money and neglects expenditures on wealth that can be hoarded.

The third equation of the Monetary model, namely,

$$E_k = E$$

becomes intelligible as soon as it is realized that the term "consumer goods" is a spurious economic concept. Qualitatively, if the "sole end and purpose" of all production is consumption, as Adam Smith stated and Keynes repeated almost verbatim, one cannot observe any difference between expenditure on consumer goods and expenditure on capital goods. The former satisfies needs in a direct and immediate way; the latter satisfies those same needs in a delayed and, as the Austrians would say, "roundabout" fashion. There is no difference between them from an economic point of view: the producer calls both the purchaser of consumer goods and the purchaser of capital goods "consumers." Money is exchanged for goods in either case, and it is this money that keeps the economic process in movement. In particular, money spent on capital goods is clearly an investment; but equally an economic investment is money spent on consumer goods—so much so that this money flows directly back into the productive process.

Further clarification of the Monetary model is brought by the breakdown of investment-expenditure (E_k) into expenditure on fixed capital (I_f) and expenditure on liquid or working capital (I_w), and E into expenditure by the consumer-buyer to purchase capital goods (C_k) and consumer goods (C_g). It then becomes possible to write the third equation in this fashion:

$$I_f + I_w = C_k + C_g.$$

The identity of I_f and C_k is of immediate evidence: these symbols represent the same expenditure looked at from two different points of view: the point of view of the producer-seller and that of the consumer-buyer. The (consumer-) buyer acquires capital goods. The identity of I_w and C_g becomes immediately intelligible as soon as one observes the economic process over time: expenditure on working capital (I_w) is eventually to be turned into traditional consumer goods expenditure (C_g). Indeed, even from a static viewpoint, this statement indicates that one is observing the same reality first from the viewpoint of the producer-seller and then from the viewpoint of the consumer-buyer. The time of observation thus becomes the precise instant in which an exchange takes place.

What are the advantages of the new formulations? Two advantages can be quickly highlighted. First, as opposed to the inherently static structure of contemporary economic theory, the new models are organic and dynamic. Hence, even when the economy is observed at one (static) instant in time, the need to establish a relation of equivalence out of a relation of equality allows us to return automatically to the first equation. Thus we can write:

$$E = E_k + E_g + E_h = MY.$$

The second advantage is that the new formulations may heal many ills that afflict contemporary economic theory. For instance, the newly formulated equivalence, in plain English, reads: out of last year's monetary income, one (person or country) saved—or, better, hoarded—so much, spent so much on consumer goods, and invested so much. Hence, the new equivalence does not only allow us to be in close touch with the daily economic reality. As pointed out above, this equivalence also seems to allow us the opportunity to heal the otherwise unbridgeable gap between microeconomics and macroeconomics that exists in contemporary economic theory. The new models describe the economy of the individual person or the individual firm, as microeconomics does, as well as the economy of the nation or even the world, as macroeconomics does. The structure remains the same; what changes is the scale of the specific economic system that is under investigation.

All these models will be fused into one synthetic model in another study.

Now that we have introduced, even though so sketchily, the monetary formulation of the Flows model, we can proceed to present an overview of the work that has been done so far. We will get one step closer to the economic reality. Without going into too much depth, we will see how stocks evolve into flows.

An Overview

An overview of the content of this book can be provided by briefly elaborating upon one characteristic of both the Flows and the Stocks model which has only vaguely been mentioned so far in order to keep the discourse as simple, and to make its progression as gradual as possible. Mentally, we have kept stocks strictly separated from flows, and real values strictly separated from monetary or financial values. The reality, of course, does not allow for such neat separations. We must overcome these barriers.

There are two operational solutions to this great difficulty of economic analysis. First, once a comprehensive system of national accounts is built, what needs to be calculated is only the net change of values of stocks (concerning both the real and the monetary economy—even though stocks of monetary values are passed under complete silence in this volume). Net changes to the value of stocks of real and monetary wealth will be continuously calculated with the help of the useful assumption that at the moment of calculation the Flows model becomes an automatically static tool of analysis.

The second solution is provided combining the three formulations presented so far, namely, the Stocks model, the Flows model, and the Monetary model, and transforming them into three new models in which there is an intermingling of real and monetary values.

This operation yields three additional formulations of the same structural model that has been obtained from the revision of Keynes' model. This operation becomes a final testimony to the complexity of that model and to the fecundity of the operation of its revision. The three new models are the model of distribution, the model of consumption, and the model of production.

Instead of attempting to describe these three final formulations at this point, let us write them down in symbols that are apt to convey their meaning in a clear and more direct fashion. To clarify the movements described by these models, the reader is spurred to give a look at the diagram entitled "Flows of Values in the Economic Process" that has been given earlier on page 145. Needless to say, these formulations are also due to the probing questioning of Professor Modigliani.

The Model of Production

The production of goods and services unfolds in accordance with the principles discovered in the earlier chapter on the production process. Since econometricians are likely to remain unconvinced by those formulations, in an attempt to make them more amenable to eventual econometric analysis and a little more clear to the reader who has carefully followed the argument so far, here follows a restatement of the production process.

$$P = CG + KG + GH$$
$$KG = P - (GH + CG)$$
$$KG = ?$$

where P stands for Production or Real Income observed from the point of view of production, CG stands for consumer goods, KG for capital goods, GH for goods hoarded, and "?" stands for a puzzlement in economic science that will be clarified forthwith.

The puzzlement can be resolved only by stepping outside of the confines of economic science. It can be solved by substituting the

The Economic Process
A Visual Sythesis

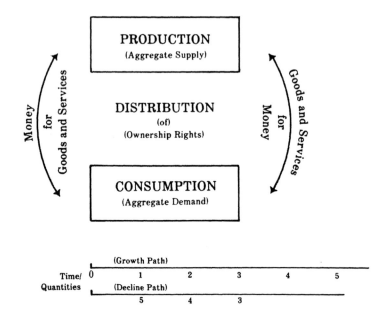

Notes:

— Clockwise, *starting with Production* one observes either the exchange of goods and services for money or the entire flow of such goods and services — or both entities. (See related graph given at page 145 entitled "Flow of Values in the Economic Process.")

— Clockwise, *starting with Consumption* one observes either the exchange of money for goods and services or the entire flow of money — or both entities.

— Counterclockwise, one can observe the same patterns in reverse.

question mark with OKG, which stands for ownership rights over capital goods. The model of production, in brief, captures the reality from a dynamic point of view; and the third equation relates information about the instant in which the exchange of goods and services for ownership rights occurs.

This is what, in a slightly more extended form, the model of production describes. Having economic rights, namely, access to economic resources, Mr. Ego the Producer decides to create economic wealth. The first equation of the production model tells us that he is producing consumer goods, capital goods, and goods to be hoarded. The second equation tells us that he has instantaneously decided to use consumer goods for his immediate enjoyment and he reserves goods to be hoarded for his future enjoyment. The left-hand side of the third equation tells us that he is now left with a certain quantity of capital goods.

Being of an extrovert bent, Mr. Ego rushes to his lawyer and says: "Please, Marc, draw me a document I can show the entire world that I am indeed the proud owner of the capital goods I have produced." Marc is happy to comply. (As we know, lawyers have the magic power to make the reality real.) And he soon starts outlining his conditions.

Marc the Lawyer, being of a cautious bent, says: "You are my friend, Mr. Ego, and I can draw you any document you want. But I need to have a number. Go to my friend, Howard the Accountant, and he will give you the number." (As we know, accountants alone can make the reality more real.)

Howard the Accountant says, "Mr. Ego, your capital goods are worth $1.00. Happy about that? If you are, I would like to make you even happier. (Accountants are like that. They do try to make the harsh reality a happy reality.) Wait, Mr. Ego, don't go just yet. I have an idea that will save you some money. Now that you are here, I want to save you the sole of your shoes. Rather than you coming back to me tomorrow, why don't we calculate today the worth of your consumer goods and the goods you have hoarded?" Mr. Ego: "And what will I do with that information?" Howard: "Don't ask. You never know what you can do with information." Mr. Ego agrees and he goes home with three documents bearing three numbers, each stating: Mr. Ego's capital goods are worth $1.00, his consumer goods are worth $2.00, and his goods hoarded are worth $3.00. Mr. Ego promises to send along to Howard the Accountant 15 cents for services rendered. (Accountants are like that. They work with very small figures, therefore they have to be very precise—and very patient because, *à la* Senator Everett

Dirksen, they know that a cent here and a cent there will some day amount to something worth talking about.)

Happy go lucky, Mr. Ego turns toward home, bumps into a friend, Mario, who is accustomed to roaming the highways and byways of the world to collect ideas and to plant the seed of future action, and engages in idle conversation with him. Actually, Mr. Ego thinks he is engaged in idle conversation. But Mario never rests. Mario always thinks and asks more and more pointed questions of Mr. Ego. He is especially intrigued about all that idle information that Mr. Ego has accumulated about the value of his wealth.

Mario goes home, and thinks, and thinks harder. Mario, you know, is a magician. He is an economist. He is the guy who, unbeknownst to the audience, is putting all the pieces of information in the hat, and *Voilá*, the dove flies toward you. Here is the model of distribution he has come up with.

The Model of Distribution

$$D = OCG + OKG + OGH$$
$$OKG = D - (OGH + OCG)$$
$$OKG = \,??$$

where D stands for Distribution or Real Income observed from the point of view of distribution of ownership rights, OCG Ownership of Consumer Goods, OKG stands for Ownership of Capital Goods, OGH for Ownership of Goods Hoarded, and the two question marks stand for another great puzzlement in economic science.

This formulation describes the distribution of ownership rights from a static point of view, or the point of view of stocks observed at one instant in time. Since it is on these two formulations essentially that we have spent much time, nothing will be added to them at this point. All that we have to do is to solve the second puzzlement. The way to the solution is as follows.

While Mario the Economist is puzzled, Mr. Ego is elated. Having produced something and having a document showing that he owns a certain amount of capital goods, he realizes that his accountant and his lawyer have done him a great service. They have doubled his choices: he can now keep the capital goods and engage in the next production cycle, or he can sell them.

While in search of a buyer, Mr. Ego decides to retire to Florida.

But first, he has to solve his problem of liquidity. He does not want to part with his consumer goods, and he does not want to part with his goods hoarded. Neither does he want to have a fire sale for his capital goods. How can he compensate Howard the Accountant for 15 cents and Marc the Lawyer for an undisclosed sum of money due him? (Lawyers are like that. They love secrecy).

His dearest friend, Martha the Matchmaker, comes to his rescue: "Listen, Mr. Ego, I have a plan that can help you and can help me. And it can help a few more people I know—people who trust me. For quite some time now, I have been looking for something to do with my time. I always had an idea in mind. I always wanted to become a banker."

"A banker? What is a banker," says Mr. Ego. Martha says: "I'll show you what a banker does. You give me the document that says you are the owner of $1.00 worth of capital goods. I will discount it. I will give you 98 cents." Mr. Ego is so happy to have solved his liquidity problem that he does not ask any question.

How does Martha perform that task? Don't ask. And yet, the reader ought to ask those questions. Where does Martha get the 98 cents? Hint: she creates them. On which power? Mainly on the expectation of selling Mr. Ego's ownership document to one of her friends for $1.03. Why does she make this transaction is clear. Martha expects to earn the combined sum of 5 cents on the exchanges. The hard question is how can she convince other people to buy that piece of paper for $1.03? The quick answer is this simple. By putting her signature to it, or by some other outward visible sign of identification, Martha has transformed the private contract created by Mr. Ego's lawyer into a public contract between Martha and the rest of society. A harder still question is: how does Martha expect her friends to have any money at all? Remember, this is economic science, not magic. Again the quick answer is simple. Martha expects to lend money to her willing customers, again by creating money.

With these tools in mind and hand, Mr. Ego has the prospect of solving a bunch of practical problems. He is so relaxed that he finally goes to Florida. Yet, no sooner has he arrived there, than Mr. Ego starts to feel lonely. He searches the horizon, and, with his usual luck, there on the golden sand, against the clear hazel sky and the deep blue of the ocean, he spots a gorgeous blonde. Instinctively curious, Mr. Ego strikes a conversation: "What do you do here?" And the blonde says: "You cannot imagine my plight. I live up in the cold North. I come down here to rest. I am exhausted. There, I shop and shop. I shop until I drop. But then what do I do when I am here? I soon become restless. I have lots of money and lots of ideas, but down here I find only sun and sand, and no one wants to sell them to me."

Mr. Ego starts rubbing his hands and licking his chops, he thinks to himself: "I've found a live one!"

He proposes: "I, too, live up North. I, too, am lonely down here. Would you want to buy my capital goods?"

Her eyes flicker: a deal is struck.

Mr. Ego and Alterego, the Consumer, live happily thereafter.

Martha smiles. Gotten old and tired herself, this is likely to be her last business affair. She is rocking on the porch from which, with eyes half closed, tall glass in hand, she takes the world in. The entire world is wrapped in a golden hue.

And that is the story of the second half of the third equation of the model of distribution. There is no puzzlement in economics. There is no puzzlement in the land, that is—except for economists. Mario has not yet solved the theoretical problem of how things hang together in economics.

But Mario never gives up. Mario has a plethora of information at hand. Remember, he knows that Mr. Ego also has documents stating the value of consumer goods and goods that he has hoarded. At one point, the incorrigible optimist that he is, he starts to feel he has gathered all the information he needs—and there, something explodes in his brain: *eureka!* Mario is so happy that he starts talking to anyone who wants to listen. Mario tells people that he has created the model of consumption.

The Model of Consumption

$$C = E_h + E$$
$$I = C - E_h$$
$$I = E$$

where C stands for Consumption or Monetary Income observed from the point of view of consumption, E_h stands for money reserved for Hoarding-Expenditure, E for money reserved for Expenditure (on consumer goods and capital goods), and I for Investment.

This formulation describes the economic reality from a dynamic point of view, or the point of view of flows over time. In particular, the equation $I = E$ indicates that an exchange is taking place— an exchange of money for (capital) goods and services.

As Keynes repeatedly emphasized, demand—and supply—are

"two-sided" affairs. Any exchange is an exchange of two entities: goods for money or money for goods. The last three formulations of the Flows model make this simple fact palpably evident; and each formulation also stresses that the observer must have in mind a clear and undisturbed vision of the flow that is being followed. If one starts observing the exchange of money for goods, one must not be distracted by the vision of the flow of goods: one must see where the flow of money starts and where it ends. The same applies for the flow of goods and services.

———•———

All is pink. All is rosy. All is good for everyone, or nearly everyone. The major exception is Mario. At this point, Mario says: "God, my God, what have I created? Three more models on top of the three earlier ones? Where does it all end? What does this all mean?"

Then and there he runs into Benoit, who, being accustomed to the multiplication of the good, says: "I saw you from up, up there and I immediately knew what was going on: you have created three—or better six—self-similar structures."

Mario and Benoit the Good start talking. The conversation becomes more and more animated, more and more technical, more and more enlightening. They fade into the sunset and leave what happens next in the field of economics to the imagination of the econometrician.

———•———

The econometrician who is no longer faced with insoluble problems of aggregation, steps up to conquer the world. Before he runs, however, the econometrician has to realize that the three final formulations of the Flows model must be joined together in order to have a continuous vision of the entire economic process. This, of course, is a task that belongs to the realm of economic dynamics. And it is only the first of a multiplicity of tasks to be performed. We cannot go an inch farther. We have to bring this work to a close. And we can bring it nearer to a close by observing that we have met once again our basic equivalence: P = D = C, or the equivalence of the three processes which compose the economic process. They are the production process, the distribution process, and the consumption process.

From this overview it can clearly be seen how correct Professor Hicks was in developing the IS-LM curve apparatus. There must be a point in which money markets are cleared and vanish into the goods markets—and vice versa. Our work has simply expanded that point into a sphere: a sphere which incorporates the essence of Keynes' Principle of Effective Demand, and goes beyond it; a sphere which can now more comprehensively be represented with the attached diagram given at page 145 entitled "The Economic Process: A Visual Synthesis."

The three final formulations of the Flows model and the attached diagram bring into focus the essential characteristic of the economic process. The economic process is a dynamic and organic process. During its analysis, even though performed only from a static point of view, it is indispensable to keep its three major component elements separate. Production, distribution, and consumption are three distinct operations; and during the analysis they have to be kept separate. It is now, during this overview, that we can truly grasp their complexity. There is no production without distribution and without consumption—just as, in brief, there is no consumption without distribution and without production.

Jean-Baptiste Say, his predecessors, and his followers were correct after all. Every consumer depends on the existence of a producer somewhere. But they were right only by half, not so much because every producer depends on a consumer somewhere—as because every producer is himself a consumer, just as every consumer is himself a producer. (This chain is logically, but not economically, broken by transfer payments.)

This organic characteristic of the economic process should be self-evident now thanks to the assistance of the three final formulations of the Flows model and the attached diagram. Certainly, producers provide goods and services in exchange for money. But do they not, at the same time, also consume and distribute wealth? Similarly, certainly consumers—or more specifically, workers—consume wealth; but do they not at the same time also produce goods and services? And do they not receive part of the wealth they have contributed to produce? This essential characteristic of the economic process will become analytically clearer in future studies. The reader can receive but little further assistance through this work. More than analysis, in fact, it is now time for testing.

A Series of Tests

The reader is left undisturbed to pursue a social, a psychological, a moral, and even an esthetic test on the model. Namely, does the Flows model make better social, psychological, moral, and esthetic sense than Keynes' model? But some assistance might still be given for the accurate performance of a battery of other tests. And this writer would fail to pay due homage to Vico and Croce were he not to suggest a test of history first.

The Test of History

This is a test that might also be called the test of continuity. The reader, in other words, is invited to observe the linkages that exist between the Flows model and the tradition of economic analysis. The reader who performs this test will find that:

- By differentiating between streams of consumption- and streams of investment-expenditure, Keynes' model—as well as the fundamental equations in his *Treatise on Money*—allowed us to obtain a more intimate look into the dynamics of the Equation of Exchange. (Through this equation, one obtains a very undifferentiated view of the economic reality; here, Supply of Money x Velocity of Circulation = Prices x Quantity of Goods and Services.) The Flows model allows us to bring economics a step closer to reality: it allows us to differentiate the monetary reality into hoarding-expenditure, consumer-goods-expenditure, and capital-goods-expenditure. This test will connect the reader with discussions which were prevalent during the first half of the twentieth century;

- By writing the Equation of Income in a more synthetic form than $MY = E_h + E_g + E_k$, by writing it as $Y = E$, the Flows model affords a direct link with Walrasian analysis. This test will connect the reader with discussions which were prevalent during the second half of the nineteenth century;

- By separating investment-expenditure from all other types of expenditure, the Flows model recaptures the distinction which classical economists used to make between "unproductive" $(E_h + E_g)$ and "productive" (E_k) consumption. This test will connect the reader with discussions that were prevalent during the eighteenth and nineteenth century.

In other words, with the assistance of the Flows model one can read again the writers of the past—a habit nearly lost with the con-

centration on Keynes' model as a mathematical tool of analysis—
and, with profit, learn about the solutions they proposed for practical no less than theoretical problems (of today, of course).
Included here among the writers of the past is Keynes himself. By
using the Flows model as a tool of exegesis, one eliminates nearly
all obscurity from the understanding of the General Theory.

The Test of Usefulness

To allow us to read what the writers of the past, no less than the
writers of the present, have to say to us in relation to the solution
of economic problems is already one use to which the Flows model
can be put. But it is not necessarily the most important. The most
important use of it is as a tool of analysis to design economic policies that do indeed solve current problems—as opposed to postponing the day of reckoning, or shifting the burden for their solution onto a revolving group of people.

This task cannot be performed here. Within the present context,
only a warning can be issued. Let us not rush to design economic
policies before we fully master economic theory; indeed, let us
make absolutely certain that there is nothing subtly but fundamentally wrong in any aspect of the economic "theory" as outlined
in these pages. Since the Flows model brings the language of economics a few steps closer to the language of the non-economist,
this scrutiny ought to be exercised by as many minds as possible.
To insist on the point, economics is too important a matter to be
left to economists alone.

Yet, "pure" reasoning can lead the mind along some beautifully
stray paths—which then become labyrinths. Let us not trust reason alone. It was Goya, the painter, who issued this warning in the
strongest possible language. As René Dubos reminds us, Goya
said: "The dreams of reason produce monsters."[90] Let us not trust
reason alone. Let us—at least—make use of the rules of "correct
reasoning" which have been elaborated through centuries of
effort. Let us, in other words, subject what has been said in this
book to stringent tests of logic. The mere beginning of such tests is
outlined below.

The Test of Logic

The test of logic that has been fitfully applied in these chapters as
we went farther along in the discussion, can now be applied in a
more thorough and uninterrupted fashion. We shall see that both

the Flows model as a whole and each one of its component elements are built upon the rules of identity and of equivalence. It might be useful to recall that the relation of identity allows us to look at any one entity from the outside in or inward, and the relation of equivalence allows us to look at that same entity from the inside out or outward. And in both perspectives man—just as in the conception of the Renaissance man—remains at the center of the economic universe. Let us start this test from an examination of each component element of the Flows model. (It might be pointed out that, while formally new, this test is a shortened version of the verification of the criteria for the validity of a concept that, as mentioned earlier, were set by Immanuel Kant.)

Real Income. We have often seen real income as an equivalence: either $P = C = Y$ or $P = C$ (or EX) $= D$. In either case, Production $\leftrightarrow$ Consumption (or Exchange) $\leftrightarrow$ Distribution. The concept can now be construed as an identity, thus: Income = Machinery, Consumer Goods, etc. = All Wealth which is Produced, Exchanged, or Distributed. The concept of real income is a complex and complete concept from a logical point of view.

Monetary Income. Monetary income can equally be construed both as an equivalence and an identity relation. To perform this test, it is necessary to break down the overall flow of income into the component elements that determine actual expenditure for consumer goods, capital goods, and goods to be hoarded. Then these expenditures can be observed from the viewpoint of producers, consumers, and owners of wealth. The test is a mirror image of the test performed concerning real income.

Investment. We have already seen it both as an identity and an equivalence relation. As an identity, it reads: Investment = Machinery, Supplies, etc. = Productive Wealth. As an equivalence, it reads: Investment $\leftrightarrow$ Consumption $\leftrightarrow$ Economic Process (or Principle of Effective Demand). Investment also is a formally correct concept.

Consumption. We have just seen once more the concept of consumption in the form of an equivalence ($I = C = EP$). Is it an identity? As an identity it can be formulated this way: Consumption = Exchange of Items which can be Hoarded, of Consumer Goods, and of Capital Goods = Spending. Consumption is a formally correct concept.

Distribution. We have often seen distribution as an equivalence ($P = C = D$). Let us now formulate it as an identity: Distribution = Ownership of Machinery, Supplies, Consumer Goods, etc. = Acquisition of Wealth or all wealth which is received by people.

Distribution is an equally valid concept.

Hoarding. It can be given as an identity, but not as an equivalence. As we have seen in the context of the discussion on economic growth, hoarding is a spurious economic concept. Instead of repeating any of what has already been said on this pseudo-concept, let us apply to it a test of an even higher order than logic. If this entity has traditionally caused so such disturbance, it is because economic analysis has observed it from a false perspective. It has been assumed that saving must be some activity, or the result of some activity, which has occurred in the past. Economic analysis thus has failed to apply to it the highest possible test of validity, a test which for lack of more elaborate terms can be called the test of reality or the test of being. Economic analysis has failed to realize that, if it is to be considered a science, it cannot be concerned with anything which occurred in the past or which is supposed to occur in the future. Science is interested only in what is— thus science, in its purest form, is philosophy. In fact, if one has discovered what truly is, one can rest reasonably assured that such an entity existed in the past and is likely to exist in the future as well. If one applies this test to hoarding, one is confirmed in the conclusion that hoarding is a spurious economic concept. Did hoarding always exist in the past? Certainly, hoarding will not necessarily exist in the future—or at least exist in any significant and effective amounts. As observed in a previous chapter, one can build a pure model of economic growth that does not contain hoarding as one of its component elements.

Consumer goods. We can find in the realm of logic the reason why the expression "consumer goods" has in this work been classified as a partially useful, but essentially spurious economic concept. No equivalence has been given for it because none can be obtained. There is no other point of view—except from the viewpoint of itself—from which it can be studied. The impression is therefore left that it is an identity; and yet, if one tries to present it as an identity, one discovers that not even this is possible. The only likely identity is: Consumer Goods = Bread, Diamonds, etc. = Perishable Wealth. But then, if we analyze those items one by one, we find that some of them (diamonds, for instance) are—nearly— not "perishable" at all. Perishability ought to be a characteristic of every consumer good. The expression "consumer goods" is not a formally valid concept; it is a spurious economic concept.

Of course, the fact that consumer goods and hoarding or hoarding-expenditure are spurious concepts does not mean that they can be excluded from the analysis. It only means that they have to be kept at bay; it only means that the proper place must be found for them. After all, the function of theory is not to build a perfect theoretical world, but to reflect and interpret the reality—and still keep the secret hope that some day the reality will be so "perfect" that it reflects an "ideal" theory: that someday the gap between theory and reality will vanish.

Thus we have completed a brief examination of the logical validity of each element of the Flows model. There are in it three perfectly valid concepts and two spurious ones. This "fault" does not lie with the model, but with the reality—and our description of that reality. If there were no hoarding in the daily reality, and if the description of that reality would eliminate the use of "consumer goods" from its range of expressions, we would have a perfectly homogeneous model a model composed not only of three full-fledged concepts, but also of three identities and three equivalences. We have found such model within the context of the theory of growth—i.e., the description of the process of economic growth. It reads:

$$Y = C$$
$$I = Y$$
$$I = C.$$

To translate this model of growth into practice is a task of economic policy, not a task of economic theory. We must therefore stop here. We have completed our test of logic. But, is there not some other test that ought to be applied? One can call it the test of mathematics. By all means, let us consider the issue.

The Test of Mathematics

So much of economics—and sociology, and politics—is today described in mathematical terms, that the reader is entitled to inquire whether or not the models presented in this work can pass this test.

The question is premature. The economic data is collected and analyzed on the basis of different categories of thought, different from those outlined here. Therefore, no such test can yet be applied—except to verify the validity of the reasoning from a theoretical point of view. Do the equations expressed here respect the basic rules of algebra? But this is only a formal test. Indeed, this test would still be formal if not just the basic models but all or nearly all propositions advanced above were expressed through mathematical symbols and operations.

A substantive test will come when data are collected and analyzed in accordance with the categories of thought outlined here.
This test must wait. But its performance is not only suggested. It is
urged. Indeed, the plea is for the application of the latest tools of
non-linear mathematics and fractal geometry to economics.

The application of mathematics and statistics to the Flows model
is urged because—unlike Keynes' model—this model and other
models presented in these pages are finished products that have the
capacity to withstand such a test. To underline the importance of
this issue it must be recalled that Keynes opposed the application
of this test to his original model rather vehemently. He based his
reasoning on pure logic and intuition. Therefore, although he was
an accomplished mathematician, he left the impression that he
himself preferred "the mazes of logic" to "the mazes of arith-
metic."[91] And he lost this battle. His repeated warnings were not
heeded. Keynes' arguments were weakened because he had little
time for basing his reasoning on experience. Today, we are at an
advantage. Today we do have the facts that history has developed.
And today we can categorically state that Keynes lost the entire
battle that he had been ready to wage with the publication of the
General Theory. Those young economists who, as Professor
Johnson recalled, were ready "to jump on and drive the bandwagon," were left with no choice: in order to apply mathematics to
economics, they had to accept Keynes' model at face value. The
model was assumed to represent faithfully the content of the
General Theory. But if the model, as a literal expression and indeed
as a syllogism, could, through long and delicate elucidations, be
made to express that content—the model as a mathematical
expression could not perform this function. How could one
express, through numbers, such modulations as are included in
Keynes' understanding of the relationship between saving and
investment? The expression $3 = 3$ cannot be made to carry such
subtleties as: "Thus the old-fashioned view that saving always
involves investment, though incomplete and misleading, is formally sounder than the new-fangled view that there can be saving
without investment or investment without 'genuine' saving. The
error lies in proceeding to the plausible inference that . . . "
Etcetera. Etcetera.

This is only one example. There are many others. Indeed, what
is rarely realized is that when the model was transformed into a
mathematical expression it *ipso facto* lost all contact with the
General Theory. The two entities became irreconcilable. Thus the

acceptance of the model necessarily implied the rejection of the General Theory. This rejection was largely unconscious—but a rejection it was. The pull of mathematics was too strong; it had been exercised on people's minds ever since the spectacular successes of Descartes, Leibniz, and Newton. Who could resist it? Who could resist the splendor involved in finally transforming economics into a "science"?

The reader is not likely to be struck by these observations until a commonly held assumption is called to mind. The assumption is that all science is "mathematical"—as if before taking the measurements, one would not first need to resolve a host of such non-mathematical issues as: which object to measure? From which side? When? In relation to which other object? Indeed, one must first resolve logically, mentally, economically, aesthetically, and of course morally many more issues which relate to "pure"—i.e., non-experimental—mathematics and statistics, such as the following ones. What set of measures to use? How to organize the numbers collected? What type of mathematical and statistical operation is the most appropriate for the elaboration of the data? In what form ought one to present the results of the analysis? When to release these results? To whom? The list is endless.

Stated more succinctly, in the hope of becoming a "mathematical" science, mainstream economics has focused great attention on numbers and it has neglected people: people who stand behind the classification, collection, and elaboration of numbers; people who, indeed, create those numbers. These are important and intriguing issues; but unfortunately we cannot remain any longer on them. We have to return to our immediate concern.

The models presented above are a finished product. They express exactly what the economic theory that stands behind them wants to express. The test of mathematics will be welcomed. Indeed, it is urged. And it will be welcomed not only because the suggested models can withstand the test; but also because in the twentieth century we developed a tool, the computer, which seems to be a true "extension" of our mind. Minds like those of Jay Forrester, Lawrence Klein, and Wassily Leontief—to mention three outstanding authorities who have spearheaded the use the computer in economic analysis—should especially welcome the revision of Keynes' model as sketched so far. They will immediately recognize that many of the diagrams presented here are "flow-charts"—integrated flow-charts—which after being accompanied by many other charts wait only to be put on a longer sheet of paper, and to be "fed" with numbers, in order to become alive.

There is an even more important reason why, as soon as the numbers are collected in accordance with the categories of thought suggested in this book, the test of mathematics can be applied to economics. The precise language of mathematics can now be superimposed upon the language of economics, because the latter has become equally precise. In Concordian economics there is no longer the discrepancy between the two languages that exists in mainstream economics.

Finally, the test of mathematics is urged because—rightly or wrongly—only if the Flows model and the other models built on it pass this test, only then will possible remaining doubts concerning the validity of what has been outlined in this work be completely dispelled. The collection and analysis of data is a task to be performed by many minds and many organizations. It is only this "hands-on" experience—and not "theory"—that, rightly, is convincing. (The only minor reservation on this account, which must still be expressed, is that one ought to be able to "experience" a theory no less than a simple addition or a complex equation—just as, for that matter, one ought to be able to experience a dip in the ocean through a beautiful literary rendition of the event.)

The case is rested. What remains to be seen is only the direction toward which the economic process ought, in the opinion of this writer, to be led.

PART V

Consciousness and Conscience of Economics

AT THIS POINT WE HAVE ANALYZED as much as possible of the economic process at one instant in time and one discovery seems to be most prominent. The process is not ruled by mechanical and impersonal forces; rather, it is ruled by very human forces: decisions to consume, decisions to invest, decisions to hoard are very human decisions indeed. The focus of our attention can therefore shift from the tools of economic analysis to the problems of economics.

Once the process is recognized for being a conscious process, the issue becomes: what is the conscience of economics?

This writer finds a simple and direct answer to this question. The conscience of economics calls for the elimination of absolute poverty from our midst.

XXIV

Poverty and the Economic Process

"Justice will not come to Athens until those who are not injured are as indignant as those who are."

Thucydides, 455 BC

———

LEST THIS CHAPTER BE JUDGED as an extraneous appendage to the central body of this work, or even as an arbitrary view of economic theory and the economic process, let us ask one crucial question: what is the fundamental cause of the uncertainty in economics? An economic theory conceived not as a conglomerate of abstract notions but, rather, as a theory that tends to represent and interpret the economic behavior of concrete human beings meets no difficulty in finding the answer.

The essential reason for all existing uncertainty in the world of economics is the fear of poverty. The linkage between the description of the economic process and these concluding comments is quite intimate. People try to amass indestructible wealth, try to hoard wealth, ultimately as insurance against poverty.

To establish the link between poverty and economic theory in no uncertain terms, it might be useful to review the main findings of this work. By hoarding wealth, people immediately hamper potential economic growth and, in the long run, sow the seeds for the explosion of a state of true inflation: that state during which the size of the economic system begins to be reduced; then the system enters the stage of deflation. And deflation leads to recessions and depressions. Thus a world of scarcity is created. Thus poverty is fostered. Thus the fear of poverty is increased. This is neither the first nor the last case in which people destroy what they love most—thereby unwittingly realizing their worst fears; and reinforcing these fears through a least suspect vehicle, through economic policies which foster economic insecurity for all.

In the face of so many utterances stating the contrary, namely, stating that scarcity creates poverty, these ideas may sound too vague or too esoteric. Let us express them again using irrefutable, if banal, terms. Even assuming that we had used or we were soon going to use all natural resources and all "energy" available on earth, an assumption which is far from being realistic, we still have to realize that our planet is only one grain of sand in the entire universe. Therefore, natural resources and energy potentially available to us are infinite. In addition, the exploration of space—toward the infinitely small as the infinitely large—is making those resources and that energy available to us. A further fear, the fear of the population explosion, is being allayed by the reduced birth rate for rich families and rich countries.

Whence the persistent fear of scarcity of energy and natural resources? It is submitted that the fear comes from lack of sufficient attention paid to a basic truth. The amount of energy and natural resources actually available to us at any time is inextricably related to three human factors: technology, management, and economics. The dismal projections about the future of energy and natural resources are based on the rather dismal performance of present day technology, management, and economics—and on the assumption that this condition will not change in the future.

The fear does not stem from any objective evaluation of the amount of resources. It comes from deficiencies in the human factors that relate to their actual availability and use. In other words, there is no scarcity.

And the relationship between scarcity and poverty is the other way around. It is the fear of poverty that creates scarcity. How? Through the many interferences with the normal process of economic growth.

The absence of absolute poverty would therefore allay the fears that lead to misuse of technologies, mismanagement of natural resources, and misguided economic policies: namely, the factors that lead to economic insecurity.

———

With the prevailing lack of understanding of the chain of causation from poverty to scarcity, it is no surprise that we should lack even the conception of possible solutions for the many problems of poverty. What are, in fact, the solutions that are commonly suggested?

The first, all-encompassing solution is supposed to be education.

But education for what? Certainly not to learn about the cultures of the past, so that one may be better able to develop one's own culture. No. That is supposed to be elitist education—as if "culture" did not ultimately mean "what everybody produces"; as if what we find in libraries, museums, and archeological digs were "cultures" and not the harvest of past cultures. The education called for as a solution to the problems of poverty is not that kind of education. Rather, it is education "to hold a job" and education "to acquire socialization habits." Translated into economic terms and properly understood, what else do these expressions mean if not the learning of skills on how to earn money and how to spend the money once earned? This teaching is not only "cheap." It is easy. Earning to spend is habit forming. But not for the poor. Earning to spend is the "rat race"—for the majority of people who enter it. This type of education is not the solution to the problems of poverty.

In fact, since it is secretly admitted that this type of education has no impact on the conditions of poverty, other solutions are lightly suggested. And when one goes beneath the surface of these further suggestions, one readily discovers their militaristic origin. These solutions, as is well-known, are: a vague hope, following evacuation from the so-called pockets of poverty; and, for those who insist on remaining attached to their native soil, the soup kitchen of concentration camps. David Wise, wisely, recommends: do not confuse the issues; call them neighborhoods of neglect—be they the "open" neighborhoods in rural areas and the suburbs, or the closed ones in urban ghettos.

What can one say about policies that rely on vague hopes and soup kitchens? The Great God of Mercy must somehow have pity on those who execute these policies—and even on those who contribute to their design. They simply seem to stumble through life. Those He seems to allow to torment themselves are different people. These are the people who commit the ultimate crime: by not going to the root cause of things, they kill morality, and then they provide rationalizations for compromised actions and compromised policies through pseudo-morality—the most recent expressions of which are "triage," "benign neglect," and "lifeboat ethic." Of course, when it is too late, it is better to have triage than not to have it.

The moral struggle is different. The moral struggle requires work on the causes of war, the causes of violence, the causes of poverty. And let us not bring God's will into these discussions, as Voltaire did after the Lisbon earthquake of 1755. We know nothing of God's will, except that it must be love. What we know about human affairs is that, if we build near volcanoes and along fault lines, our house is likely to be buried someday.

Once dissected, pseudo-morality is always found composed of fallacious reasoning, lies, repressed envy, racial slurs, group supremacy,
nationalistic chauvinism, suicidal tendencies, and similar sentiments.
Who are the people who foster pseudo-morality? I do not know who
they are, and I do not wish to know them. They know. This is neither a witch-hunt nor an argument *ad hominem*. This is only a call
to think deeper and harder.

These are words. And words have traditionally been unable to
combat policies and practices. A contest of words vs. policies and
practices is an uneven affair. A ray of hope begins to flicker when
words are themselves translated into policies and practices. Then
you have policies and practices vs. policies and practices. Policies
and practices to combat the policies and practices generated according to principles of "triage," "benign neglect," and "lifeboat ethic"
might be inaugurated only if the irony involved in the prevailing
solutions to the many problems of poverty is realized. The irony is
that those solutions are meant to imply—what? The existence of a
"democratic choice," of course: the choice between empty education
and unemployment; the choice between toiling for others and leaving one's homeland; the choice between accepting the offerings of
soup kitchens and starving.

Policies and practices to combat the policies and practices generated according to principles of "triage," "benign neglect," and
"lifeboat ethic" might be inaugurated only if the potentially explosive content of those policies and practices is realized. They have set
a time bomb ticking. Their most dangerous aspect, which is becoming more and more evident, is to let young people suspect that
democracy involves choosing between two negatives. Is this a
choice?

The apex of the irony—or is it insanity—is reached when, with a
straight face, a final choice is offered by the political right as well as
the political left. And what is this final choice? The final choice is
supposed to exist between this democratic choice and totalitarianism.

The choice suggested by this work takes its lead from the attempt
to impart a definite sense of direction to the economic system. To
achieve this aim, ultimately it is not sufficient to be puzzled by what
Lord Keynes, among others, has termed the paradox of poverty
amid plenty. Much more is required. A reversal must take place in
what has traditionally been assumed to be the final aim of economic theory and, consequently, the final aim of the economic process.
The aim must not be, as Adam Smith put it, an inquiry into the caus-

es of the wealth—of nations. Rather, the aim must be the elimination of absolute poverty—of individuals.

Wealth is the "normal" case; it presents no challenge to the serious student of human affairs. And nations are an abstraction, just as individuals are. The final aim of the economic process ought to be reformulated so to become: the elimination of absolute poverty for people operating within a society.

The goal of Concordians is to create Somists: civilized people living in a civilized society.

The General Question

Would anyone buy an expensive fur coat, if ten percent of it were frayed and patched? Would anyone buy a sports car if ten percent of its parts were missing—or worse, if there were the absolute certainty that it would abruptly break down ten percent of the time?

The questions are, on their face, preposterous. And yet, we do buy the most expensive machinery on earth—the economic system, for which we pay not only in hard currency but even in lives—notwithstanding its proven record of being broken down one hundred percent of the time for at least ten percent of the people, and for one hundred percent of the people at least ten percent of the time.

On the face of it, the situation is preposterous. In this situation we can find—among many, very many other things—the immediate, perennial origin of the conditions of poverty. Graphically, the situation can be represented as a sphere within a sphere, where the smaller sphere stands for poverty (PV) and the larger one stands for the economic system (ES).

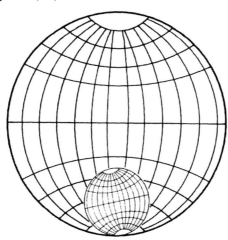

Two Angles of Observation

Then it becomes evident that there are two points of view from which the situation can be observed. One looks at poverty as an entity in itself; we may call it "the narrow point of view." The other looks at the same condition, but looks at it as an integral part of the economic system; we may call it "the broad point of view." Poverty vs. poverty within the economic system, is the question.

The Legitimacy of Both Angles of Observation

The legitimacy of the narrow point of view does not need to be established. It is the general and common practice. It might only be added that poverty is indeed a world in itself. Those who work directly and frontally on that condition know how complete, comprehensive, and organic it is: to emphasize the point, poverty is a world in itself; a world which, strictly speaking, can be observed from a "narrower"—but never a narrow—point of view. Those who work on the conditions of poverty know how vast that world is.

What needs to be legitimatised is the broad point of view. We shall devote a good portion of these concluding comments to this task. At this moment, let us point out the essential reason for its legitimacy. As stated before, the economic system does not work for one hundred percent of the people at least ten percent of the time. How to express this point graphically? Only computer animation can do that. Visually, we have to picture the smaller sphere (PV) gradually growing to encompass the larger one (ES). Intellectually, this transition is represented by the perennial condition of poverty which—through economic pauses, recessions, and depressions—gradually grows to envelop an increasingly larger percentage of people: near one hundred percent during the worst depressions.

The second point of view—the broad point of view—through which the condition of poverty can be observed, then, is legitimate. The attentive reader, moreover, will notice that this search for legitimacy has implicitly performed also another function. It has provided *prima facie* evidence for the validity of the thesis held in these concluding comments: the final aim of the economic process is—and, indeed, ought to be—the elimination of absolute poverty. If the economic system fails to achieve this goal, it fails miserably and totally. The system does not work as it should; indeed, the system does not work at all.

This might appear to be too strong a commitment. However, it is

based on a fundamental reason. Poverty is not an economic problem. Poverty is the economic problem. And not only because all
other economic problems are of a technological nature, while the
problem of poverty is a quintessential human problem. No, not
only because of that. But because no matter which economic problem we may select, we find that the poor suffer from it—perennially and totally. Take unemployment. The poor are perennially and
totally without a "job." High prices. That is a total and perennial
affliction for the poor. Low income. Is it necessary to mention the
size of the flow of income that reaches the poor? Provision of services, from health delivery systems to trash collection. Is it necessary
to emphasize the quantity or the quality of such services, if and
when they reach the poor? The list is endless.

Definitely, if the economic system does not eliminate the most
abject forms of poverty, the economic system performs no function
whatsoever. Certainly no one is prepared to suggest that the function of the economic system is to provide goods and services to
those who do not need them. And no one should suggest that the
function of the economic system is to provide goods and services.
Per se, this is a totally mechanical and worthless function: goods
and services in this case become useless gadgets and boring pas-
times. No. Even goods and services have a much more noble function to perform. Goods and services have value insofar as they satisfy human needs; insofar as, in the inimitable expression of
Marshall McLuhan, they become an extension of man—thus forming an inseparable, coherent, organic unit.

That is the function of goods and services. To provide them is one
of the functions of the economic system. To eliminate absolute
poverty is the function of the economic process; its final and deeply
respectable function.

Having established the legitimacy of the broad point of view, and
having established the legitimacy of the point of view that to eliminate absolute poverty is the final aim of the economic process, let
us proceed step by step. Let us first observe poverty through the
lenses of the narrow point of view.

The Narrow Point of View

Poverty observed through the lenses of the narrow point of view is
such an extensive, detailed, and delicate topic that it cannot in any
way, shape, or form be described here. Fortunately, the literature—
if not personal knowledge—on it is so vast and readily available
that the reader who needs further information can easily acquire it.

What we can be concerned with here is the much more modest, and still overwhelming, task of passing a judgment on existing efforts to eliminate absolute poverty, namely, those efforts which are undertaken while considering poverty as an entity in itself, an entity separate from the rest of the economic system.

If one discards all traditional forms of individual charity and all forms of institutional public assistance as expressions of guilt-appeasing tokenism of the comfortable and as activities which, however praiseworthy in themselves, have never been presented as the final solution to the problem of absolute poverty, what is one left with?

To its credit, the United States during the1960s made a substantial, frontal, and direct effort to eliminate absolute poverty. At the urging of President Lyndon B. Johnson, an Act of Congress in 1964 even established an office with a proper name—the Office of Economic Opportunity (OEO)—and endowed it with a certain amount of funds. But does this effort qualify as a serious attempt to wage what was commonly labeled as a "war on poverty"? By its "fruits" shall you know the tree: that official effort, literally, was working—to the extent that it could—only on ten percent of the problem; and it could, at best, obtain only ten percent of the needed results.

Indeed, since every tree is a product of its seeds, in the limited scope of that effort we can find explanations for the eventual lack of real success of the official War on Poverty. For reasons that shall momentarily become at least dimly apparent, absolute poverty will not be eliminated through the services of any "office." Absolute poverty will not be eliminated through the expenditure of any amount of funds—especially when the funds are meager, and they are applied to conditions which have a great deal to do with social necessities and very little with economic affairs.

The judgment must be quick, drastic, and pitiless: all efforts to eliminate absolute poverty by attacking the problem frontally and directly have not yet met with success. And, as we shall cursorily see, they could not succeed. The harshness of this judgment vanishes when it is realized that the judgment is directed not at those efforts but at the rhetoric surrounding those efforts. Deprived of rhetoric, it appears evident that those efforts were never really intended to eliminate absolute poverty; they were intended to ameliorate the conditions of poverty. As such, those efforts were not only rather successful; they were even praiseworthy.

Begging the Question

The position reached above begs the question as to the conditions of absolute poverty. This is a question that can be settled only on another level of analysis. And the analysis has to start from this firm point. When the veil of words is pierced, one can immediately grasp the naked truth: no nation on earth has yet tried to make a concerted effort to solve the many problems of absolute poverty. There is no exception. Communist countries, of course, think and say that they do; but in reality they have made a concerted effort to create—unwittingly—economic exploitation for all. And economic exploitation, it must soon be added, is the condition that for too many people prevails in capitalist countries as well.

The discourse would be greatly clarified if it were openly admitted that capitalism is a social and economic order that might prevail in the future, if and when all available productive capital is owned by one hundred percent of the people, not as a group but as individual human beings. To state that capitalism exists at this time is to confuse the issues. At best, we have Five-Percent-Capitalism. The proper name for this system is monopolism—just as the proper name for Communism is bureaucratism. The use of proper names is essential if we do not want to be confused by rhetoric.

Another warning. Political classifications have become tools of propaganda: empty labels on empty containers. To return them to their status of tools of analysis, we must not jump national boundaries. Then we come to realize not only that the modes of thought, but also the practices, which stand behind those classifications can be found within each national boundary. Greatly simplifying things and neglecting all the political shades between the two extremes, today Communism is to be found in the capitalist countries and—perhaps to the same degree—capitalism is to be found in Communist countries.

To insist on the central point, in "capitalist" countries there has never been a concerted effort to eliminate absolute poverty: whoever reads Michael Harrington's *The Other America* or more recent literature issuing from the think tanks on the ideological right will become convinced that the various efforts to eliminate absolute poverty, which have been undertaken under the banner of the welfare state, reach the exact opposite of their stated purpose. They unwittingly create poverty. And, certainly, it must be admitted that the policy of "full" employment, the only radical cure of absolute poverty that exists today in the economist's diagnostic book, is a mirage. This much is clear. Near zero unemployment—of all economic resources—is not a goal to be reached by approaching the task frontally. Full employment is a reality that either is there, as a result of the "normal" unfolding of the economic process, or it is not there, i.e., it is a mirage. Admittedly, what is harder to realize is that in search for this mirage humanity makes a desert out of the landscape.

As for Communist countries, one does not need to think of China to pierce the veil of words. But one perhaps needed to visit Russia at the height of the Communist Party's power. The striving and the pride were deeply moving; but if eyes were kept open, one could see on the icy streets of Kalinin a dried-out elderly woman carrying a heavy burden on her shoulders and stopping every three steps to catch her breath.

No. It is safe to say that no nation on earth has yet made a concerted effort to eradicate absolute poverty from its gardens. (Is there any need to emphasize that all energies so far have been expended on unsatisfactory and unworkable solutions?) And no nation will really attempt to make such an effort as long as all sorts of rationalizations are allowed to envelop the field. The list is long and many-sided: poverty is the work of God, or the work of greed; poverty is "their" fault, the fault of the poor—because they are lazy, spendthrift, and full of vices; they "want" to be poor; poverty existed in the past and not in the present; poverty exists abroad; poverty is ineradicable.

The list of rationalizations could easily be extended. What is important to realize is that the existence of such rationalizations is the ultimate cause of the failure of whatever attempts are made to eliminate absolute poverty: "Every kingdom divided against itself is laid waste." What is even more important to realize is that those rationalizations will not disappear through airtight argumentation to prove the contrary of that which is held as sacred; those rationalizations will disappear only if they are vanquished by concrete actions.

Such actions will not be the result of happenstance; they can only be the result of a comprehensive and well-coordinated program of action.

The Need for a Concerted Effort

A comprehensive and well-coordinated program of action cannot, by definition, be drawn by any single person. And yet the economist is uniquely endowed to become the central figure in drawing up such a program. He or she receives such endowment not only from training but from the more or less openly admitted aspiration of the profession to bring a decisive contribution to the solution of the many problems of absolute poverty. There is more than one moving page in the economic literature on this account. A single sentence by Alfred Marshall will suffice: ". . . the study of the causes of poverty is the study of the causes of the degradation of a large part of mankind."[92]

By training, aspiration, and moral commitment the economist knows in his or her bones what must be the central element of that plan: a sense of direction to be imparted to the economic process. Unless the economic process is led in the direction of the elimination of absolute poverty, the economic system will act as a pitiful giant. It will move in all directions, which will mostly turn out to be fraught with danger. It is not the fault of the giant that he smashes everything which happens to be in his way. It is his sheer size that does that. But think of the case in which a road is opened and kept clear of obstacles; think of the case in which the giant is given a clear-cut task to perform. Think how much faster and more efficiently the heavy burden is pulled by the giant than by a whole crowd of pitiful people. Our giant is the economic system as a whole. Think of directing it to solve the problems of absolute poverty. This is the only approach that will eventually lead to satisfactory results; and it has to pass through a broad understanding of the overall condition of poverty.

The Broad Point of View

To describe poverty from the broad point of view in a satisfactory manner, we would need to describe not only the conditions of the poor but also those of the middle classes and the rich. And then we would need to tie the three descriptions together by highlighting contrasts, as well as similarities, in those modes of existence. We would need to analyze the shades through which one condition gradually vanishes into the other; we would need to analyze that spark of humanity that persists in all conditions. Fortunately, this task can be skipped.

Rather, let us take a few steps toward solutions whose design and implementation have not been attempted yet. Satisfactory solutions can be searched for, eventually found, and implemented if the analysis of the problem is placed in its proper context. Conditions of abject poverty for at least ten percent of the people, and breakdowns of the economic system for at least ten percent of the time, are to be seen in their true light: as manifestations of a subtle malady of the world's social, economic, legal, and political system.

More than this, economics has to be seen as an esthetic and moral problem rather than a scientific and technological problem. This analysis, which is not new, is generally presented as a tall order. It is not. It can be reduced to a simple statement: our judgments have to be reversed and then expanded.

We have, for the most part, been looking for symptoms, and not for real causes. Therefore, we have not even been able to agree on the list of symptoms or their seat of priority. The list has been too long and too personal: inflation, unemployment, pauses, recessions, depressions, collapse of the work ethic, collapse of community values, collapse of cultural values, collapse of esthetic values, collapse of moral values. The list is much more detailed than this. Our judgment has to be reversed. We have to search for causes and not for symptoms. If such an inquiry is made, it shall be found that the primary cause of many contemporary ills is a persistent, capillary, continuous lack of economic security for all—rich, middle classes, and poor.

A line of inquiry that cannot be explored much more than it has already been, leads to the conclusions that through lack of economic security we have inflation; through lack of economic security, we have unemployment—as well as many other contemporary ills. Not vice versa. Lack of economic security is the ultimate cause of the instability of the economic system.

Only when our judgment is thus reversed, only then can it be expanded. Then the issue becomes clear-cut. The issue is:

- Either we have economic growth through which a few people think that they become rich—while their comfort is actually lessened by lack of security in the streets and in the home, vandalism, harassment, envy, and hatred, despoiling of open spaces and decaying of public places, deficient workmanship and inefficient as well as ill-mannered delivery of services, bankruptcies, inflation and depressions, and worse things yet;

- Or we have economic growth which creates economic security for all.

And what would the achievement of economic security for all bring about? The answer might come as a surprise to those who have not given much thought to what poverty is. The answer is that economic security for all would—necessarily gradually—bring about the final elimination of absolute poverty. There is, in fact it can be easily demonstrated, no other tenable definition of poverty but this: poverty is lack of economic security.

And what would the achievement of economic security for all—automatically—also bring about? Those who have followed the relevant line of argument will not be surprised. The achievement of economic security for all would also automatically bring about the only reasonable, workable, and logical "radical cure" for inflation.

And there is still something else. The achievement of economic security for all would also—automatically—bring about the only reasonable and workable cure for the many ecological problems that afflict our age.

An Organic Argument

The argument is not circular. It is organic. There is a world of difference between the two. When a living organism is broken down, by treating symptoms, we make the overall condition worse. The repair of a symptom generally causes much unforeseen damage. The cure comes only by attacking the cause of the malady: in our case, lack of economic security.

The argument is organic. Let us look at the economic system as a whole. Let us look at it as a living organism, or even as a machine. Once we have solved the moral problem of making the right choice between economic growth for the benefit of the few and economic growth for the benefit of everyone, we can see how simple the rest of the economic problem really is. It is a technological problem in the strictest sense of the word; it is a mechanical problem. It encompasses the delivery of goods and services, as well as the delivery of the financial means to acquire those goods and services, to one hundred percent of the people one hundred percent of the time. People go to the four corners of the earth, they go to deserts and to glaciers, to deliver goods and services to people who pay for them.

This is economic security. To give this assurance is just as much a task of the businessman as it is the task of the economist, and the accountant, and the lawyer, and the political scientist, and the physical scientist, and the moralist. In short, it is a task of society as a whole.

Because the economic problem—when fully understood in its myriad of details—is that simple, it must be solved. It must be solved because only if we put our economic house in order can we tackle the more interesting and challenging psychological, social, political, esthetic, moral—in short, human—problems which we face today and which undoubtedly we shall face perhaps for ever and ever. And it will be easier to solve all these human problems within the context of economic security for all.

An Organic Solution

The solution is organic. And it must be organic—because the problem is indivisible. It concerns and affects all of us: rich and poor
alike. It concerns and affects our total human and natural environment—our "eco": that unity which has lately been rediscovered by
the study of ecology; that unity which has not yet been discovered
by the study of economics.

Amidst many doubts, what economics has found so far is the
"trade-off" between inflation and unemployment. The next discovery for economics in this specific area has been a puzzlement—the
puzzlement arising from not seeing that mechanical theory translated into practice, neither in the ascending part of the business
cycle nor in the descending one. In practice, we have seen an
increase in both inflation (i.e., prices) and unemployment as well as
an increase in employment and stable prices.

The next stage on the road to self-discovery for economics ought
to pass through a detailed inquiry into the following questions concerning the presumed trade-off between "inflation" and unemployment: what choice is this? What a choice is this. Is this a choice? Is
this a choice to present to the people? Is this a choice to present to
the politician? Indeed, is this a choice to present to the mind?

This line of inquiry, it is pleasing to predict, will lead to these firm
conclusions and their eventual widespread acceptance. The trade-
off is not between inflation and unemployment. The trade-off is
between inflation + poverty + pollution *and* wealth for everybody.
Wealth in varying degrees, to be sure, but wealth for everyone: i.e.,
economic security for all. This is a choice.

The Missing Link

Coming one step down from this "lofty" atmosphere to that of the
prerequisites for the translation of the above truly general theory
into a concrete program of action, only one—but extremely important—"missing link" can be provided. Namely, for the design of the
type of economic policy that leads to economic security for all,
there is no need—no need whatsoever—for the rich to grow poor.
Were that the case, we would not be building economic security for
all. We would only, arbitrarily and simplistically, use economic policy as a revolving door.

No. There is no need for the rich to grow poor. There is no need at all for the redistribution of income. With the traditional rates of growth prevailing in the economy, and with the benefit of hindsight, it generally becomes clear that the total yearly income, if not a pittance, has traditionally been insufficient to meet the needs of all the people; and the division of such a pittance cannot but produce meager results. At any time, an equal distribution of income would yield a paltry sum per person on a one-shot deal. For those who do not have it, this sum looks like an enormous amount of money. But this is not the real test. The test is the judgment of those who do have this amount of money at their disposal: almost to a person, they are ready to confess that such an amount is a pittance. And then there are other serious tests that such a policy ought to pass. A test of realism, first: is a policy of equal redistribution of income ever going to be implemented? Leaving the answer to itself, let us consider other issues. Let us think of the inflationary boost this operation would generate: the money would immediately go up in the smoke of higher prices. And then, let us think of the disruption in the next year's production patterns: should the producers plan on a repetition of that action? On the basis of which price level and purchasing power should they plan to deliver goods and services? Certainly, next year's income would be less than the amount distributed this year: at a paltry level of income, no one can afford to set resources aside to create capital goods. Therefore, next year's production level will be lower and, the following year, lower still.

That is the road to reach levels of production that were prevalent in the Stone Age. And what about levels of justice? No matter how unjustly wealth was ever acquired, a policy of forcible redistribution of income unavoidably involves much injustice. Or is this policy going to be implemented on a voluntary basis?

People accustomed to receiving and to taking do not realize that perhaps the most difficult act in life is the act of giving. Thus, a continuation of this discussion becomes idle talk. So much for the redistribution of income, then. But what about the redistribution of wealth? From an economic standpoint, the only useful function of wealth is to produce income—either immediately and directly through an exchange, or gradually and indirectly through the production process. From all other points of view, the function of wealth is to produce "enjoyment." But enjoyment is an intensely personal affair. Hence this wealth, when redistributed, automatically becomes almost entirely worthless.

This is the reason why, when revolutionaries and conquerors enter the palaces of the vanquished, they destroy—what? Wealth? No. They are not so unobservant and careless as to destroy "wealth." They destroy material things that can give enjoyment only to their possessors.

The Alternative

If absolute poverty has never been—and never will be—eliminated through the redistribution of income or even existing wealth, what is one left with? The best is left.

Poverty will be eliminated through the right to create, and to acquire possession of all the new wealth which our visible hands are capable of creating and holding; machines, it must not be forgotten, are an extension of our hands and our brains.

This—as the real poor people know—is the only dignified and certain policy through which the poor can ever hope to get out of poverty. This is the only policy through which the poor—and the middle classes, and the rich themselves—can ever hope to grow slowly, but steadily and securely, richer. This is a certainty—because, without any waste, we shall then experience balanced rates of economic growth that have so far been deemed impossible of attainment.

This is a certainty because the spring of man's action is not equality. Equality is a truly monstrous intellectual construction; it is not only impossible of implementation; it even confuses dignity with wealth. People know in their bones that, while potentially we are all equal, actually we are all infinitely different from one another. What we care about is to be treated with dignity.

This is a certainty because the spring of man's action is justice. It is no disrespect toward Professor Galbraith, who coined the phrase, to point out that his best hopes of "fine tuning" the economy have not materialized. It is high time to hope that we will eventually run the economy to the tune of justice.

With economic freedom as concrete evidence of justice in the land, we will create all the wealth that we need. And we will not create more than we need, because we will immediately realize that there are costs associated with the production of wealth. The dissociation between costs and results exists only when our wants are associated with other people's wealth.

But what happens to people who cannot take care of themselves in the economic world? Clearly, charity has to intervene. And, by calling on the offerings of charity as a last resort, we give charity a possible task.

A Few Pragmatic Questions

Can the struggle against poverty, inflation, and pollution be won? We know that without the active participation of everyone, the poor included, this struggle becomes a rush into a bottomless abyss. By the same token, we should also know that, provided people fully acquire the wealth they create, there is no question that the struggle can be won. Too many people stand ready to help. To help themselves and others in the process.

The real question is not whether we can win the struggle. The real question is: will the struggle ever be waged? Perhaps it will never be waged. Perhaps, the poor will always be with us. But if we are ready to accept this as an immutable condition, we must also be ready to accept its ineluctable consequence. If we do not wage that struggle, life becomes a scramble for riches—a scramble for power over things and over people. Then the theater of the absurd becomes the real condition of life; and the exhilaration of living is destroyed by the feeling of guilt.

The point is that, although the poor will always be with us in a relative sense, they do not need to be with us in an absolute sense. Wealth and poverty are relative things. If we were all equally rich or equally poor, we would not know, we would not enjoy, we would not appreciate either condition. And, to enjoy poverty, to recognize its innumerable advantages—indeed, its possible nobility—we do not need the sanctity of Francis of Assisi. We only need clear thinking.

We must recognize that we cannot and need not eliminate relative poverty: this is an absurdity, this is an impossibility which saps all our energies. It is the most abject forms of poverty that we need to eliminate.

And we do not need to eliminate these forms of absolute poverty for "them," the poor; or, if we are poor, for "them," the rich, in order to appease their sense of guilt, to soothe their esthetic exigencies. No. It is for us that we need to eliminate the most abject forms of poverty—for us, whether we are rich or poor. It is the laws of heaven and earth that command us to wage this struggle.

How to make it indisputably clear that it is for us that we have to wage this struggle? If the statistics of economic insecurity were kept, we would find that we all suffer from this malady. The poor, undoubtedly, live an insecure economic existence. They have to rely on the will and the largesse of other people—a will and largesse that automatically becomes narrower at the moment of greatest need: during periods of general hard times. But do not most rich people suffer from that malady as well? Too many of them seem to be so insecure that, no matter how much they possess, they feel the need to have more.

This much might ultimately be agreed upon: at present, we are all economically insecure; we are all poor. The issue remains: how to wage the struggle for economic security? Clear thinking again suggests the solution.

We need to recognize that all forms of abject poverty are the symptoms of poverty. Poverty is lack of economic security. In act, it is lack of economic security that makes it impossible to define what is "enough"—what is a reasonable amount of wealth that one needs to accumulate for a "rainy day." Since rainy days are not only certain to occur, but are also totally unpredictable in their virulence, a prudent person must accumulate as much wealth as possible for oneself and for one's family.

Nor is this accumulation of wealth the worst that can happen to society. The worst occurs when much of that wealth is kept in unproductive uses: hoarded as a possible hedge against the vicissitudes of the economic system. A vicious circle is then set in motion. The hoarding of wealth reduces the potential for healthy economic growth, it increases the pressures for ecologically unsound projects and, in the long run, it creates inflation. Inflation ultimately means recession and depression. Thus the most abject forms of poverty engulf an increasingly larger number of people.

It is up to the economist to break this vicious circle—first by pointing out the mechanisms of its existence, and then by devising economic policies that build economic security in people. This is our only hope.

When economic security has been acquired by all, many changes will occur naturally within the soul of each person; but many other changes will have to be fostered by every agent of society. To put it briefly, we have to stop downgrading people who are not as wealthy as we are—or as wealthy as we think they should be. Conversely, we have to stop dreaming that we can ever eliminate the phenomenon of relative poverty.

When these changes take place, compulsory poverty will be transformed into voluntary poverty. It will not matter any longer that other people have more than we do. Whatever we have is enough for us.

Then we shall find what we have been searching for all along: Absolute Wealth. We cannot be any richer.

XXV

The Elimination of Absolute Poverty
Through the Right to Create
All the Wealth One Needs

*"Every man is a consumer, and ought to be
a producer. He fails to make his place good
in the world, unless he not only pays his
debts, but also adds something to the
common wealth."*

Ralph Waldo Emerson

———•———

IF POVERTY MEANS LACK OF ECONOMIC security, the question becomes:
How can we all acquire economic security?

The answer is simple and straightforward: through the right to
create all the wealth we feel we need.

Why are rights so magical? They stir the deepest chords in man's
souls because they cut through the chains of illusion and are powerful teachers of realism. It is a cruel illusion to blame the poor for
being poor. Realism suggests otherwise.

The Reality of the Present

Shocking as it may seem at first sight, no one today has the economic
right to create wealth. Indeed, the theory of economic justice has no
understanding of economic rights. Economic rights are not distinguished from property rights and entitlements.[93]

Whatever wealth is created today, it is created under a regimen of
property rights—not economic rights. And there is a very strong,
well meaning, but deeply misguided political movement afoot to
weaken traditional property rights. That is the road that creates economic insecurity for all.

Whatever wealth is created today, it is created under a regimen of privilege. Economic rights are exercised by the few as facts of life, but they are not recognized by the many. This is the fundamental reason why no one has economic security today. Economic rights have to be extended to all human beings.

This reality is not recognized for varied and sundry reasons, yet at the bottom of a deep pool there is this simple intellectual chain reaction. We live in a dysfunctional intellectual age. The economist stays aloof from issues of law and society. And the lawyer is prevented from touching the realm of economics. The barrier of mathematics is sufficient enough to enforce this mutual understanding about the division of labor and protection of turf.

The Reality of the Past

From time immemorial, society and each individual component of society reserved to every other human being the right of access to property that was held in common. Hence the name "commons." No one was poor then. And no one is really poor in a fishing community in most of the world today where most of the ocean is still legally held as common property. It is in this culture, indeed, that the most important lesson of the war on poverty was learned anew in the 1960s: "Give someone a fish, and you create a slave; teach a person how to fish and you create a free citizen."

The right of access to the commons was never cast in stone. It was held from time immemorial, and certainly from Biblical times, until it was disemboweled with the enclosure of the commons in the sixteenth century Europe (with deep apologies for my deep ignorance of the history of the East). And just in these days it is drawing its last breath under the assault of a form of legal trickery that is no longer affecting the steep mountains but the open seas: the invention and the crafty implementation of Individual Transferable Quotas (ITQs). This proposed management system of the oceans has gathered steam on the basis of a fallacious analysis concerning "the tragedy of the commons," namely, the collapse of the economy of the commons.

Astonishingly, only a few are recalling the facts of history: the collapse of the commons occurred after, not before, the establishment of the enclosures: the commons had been there, healthy, ever since time immemorial. The economic sustainability of those lands collapsed after they were enclosed. Astonishingly, only a few are paying much attention to a deep constitutional issue these days: the government is issuing these ITQs; and yet the government has no rights to that property. That is common property.

The right of access to the commons was never codified in a set of legal laws. It was only codified in a set of moral laws. And these laws fell apart as one consequence of the belief in apotheosis of the individual. This entity, heretofore unknown to history, began to be exalted after the benefits of the Renaissance produced Leonardo, Michelangelo, and Raphael. We thought we could all become like them. We supposed that if we only had infinite freedom, we would all become like them. But the conditions for the flowering of those giants were not quickly extended to all members of society. And the dream of the Renaissance collapsed.

The dream collapsed when the moral fuel was choked off the social compact. What fueled the social compact in all those millennia was an understated intellectual and practical reality: ever since Biblical time, through Jesus, to Locke everyone knew of hoarding and tried to keep it in check through private and public means. The existence of the commons was one of the outstanding manifestations of this deep understanding of the moral basis of the social compact. There were many others.

The social compact imploded when it was caught and mangled in the pincer movement of the economic abstractions of Adam Smith in England and the forced vacuity of Thomas Jefferson in the United States. Jefferson had to forge a united nation out of thirteen weak and divided colonies—an unprecedented immense effort that was taking place in the presence of a horrible human tragedy. Human beings whose color was black were considered property in the South. Jefferson, therefore, could not adopt the formula used by George Mason in the Virginia Declaration of Rights, a document unanimously adopted on June 12, 1776. He could not herald that our country would be engaged in the pursuit of the "Enjoyment of Life and Liberty, with the Means of acquiring and possessing Property." The Puritan North would not have gathered around this formula.

Since Jefferson did not have the political power to wipe the moral sin of slavery off the face of America, he had to draw a veil over it. Since he could not talk of property, he ingeniously focused on one of the end results of property: happiness. He promised that our country would stand for the right to "Life, Liberty and the pursuit of Happiness."

Ever since 1776 the world has plunged into the lala-land of entitlements. We all feel entitled to happiness. And since, as the Greeks knew, happiness can be achieved only on the deathbed, the subtext of entitlements is this: I am entitled, not to my happiness, but to your happiness—meaning your property.

The Reality of History

The above paragraphs are too fast. Let us catch our breath by reviewing the major steps in the history of these issues. If John Locke still casts such a shadow over political science, it is because his framework of analysis—distilled in the formula of the right to life, liberty, and property—summarized the wisdom of the ages from at least Aristotle to the Scholastic Doctors.

Notwithstanding glaring abuses, such as the tolerance of slavery, the rights of property were held in check by a capillary theory of economic justice. From Aristotle to the Scholastic Doctors the economic discourse was carried out within the context of economic justice, specifically distributive and commutative justice. All wealth that was created had to be distributed in accordance with rules of justice; all wealth that was exchanged had to be exchanged in accordance with rules of justice. (Thus two aspects of the economic process, the distribution and the consumption process, had a corresponding treatment in the field of law and morality.)

Since the audience of these thinkers and writers, up to Adam Smith with his own Duke of Buccleuch, was mostly the landed gentry, no need was felt to investigate a third necessary plank to the field of economic justice: participative justice. The landed gentry had access to all the resources that were necessary to create wealth, as a fact and as an unchallenged privilege. And the landed gentry exercised this privilege.

This privilege has now to be turned into a right for everyone.

A Moral Issue

Property is so entwined with issues of life and liberty that at its core it is a moral issue.

All indications point to this conclusion. And the strongest set of evidence is that when human beings were included in the right of property, there gradually grew such a revulsion in the soul of many human beings that it is lasting to this very day and manifests itself in a hundred different forms as a revulsion against the very right of property.

This is the mental impasse in which our civilization is caught. How to break the impasse? How to re-establish the linkage between property rights and the sacredness of life and liberty?

A False Start out of a Moral Dilemma

Jefferson was keenly aware of the dissolution of the social bonds and the perversion of morality once human beings become slaves of other human beings. He did not have the political power to face the dilemma frontally. And he thought he could find an escape from it that would satisfy most people: he simply expunged the right of property from the political discourse.

The substance of the compromise could not last forever: the nation was born; the North was appeased; and the South went on in its merry ways. The compromise lasted about eighty years and the nation needed to be purified with the blood of the Civil War.

As a price we are still paying, the compromise plunged the political discourse into the lala-land of "right" to entitlements.

A New Start, A Right Start

"Rights" are in the air. No matter to which page of the political discourse one turns, one is likely to meet the enunciation of a new right. Surely the world can bring the discussion of one more right to the table: the right to create all the wealth that one needs.

No. This is not a plea for the illusions of plenty or a call for the wreckage of the earth. As soon as one creates one's own property, one automatically discovers that there are costs involved in the creation of wealth. It is this reality that will curb people's illusions. It is this reality that will curb all the excesses of consumerism.

Once costs are firmly associated with prices or earnings and profits, then one discovers a corresponding reality in the fields of the law. Economic rights, if they are indeed rights, are automatically and indissolubly tied to a corresponding set of responsibilities.

This is the proposal that is offered for most careful consideration, then. The proposal that issues forth from the present work is that, after a hiatus of a couple of centuries, we earnestly start the discussion on the institution of economic rights. Economic rights, not property rights—specific rights indissolubly related to specific responsibilities.

This is a new start. This is the right start. Economic rights and responsibilities will function as "tipping points." In the every course of implementation, the application of economic rights and responsibilities will lead to a renewal of our economic life.

Epilogue

THIS BOOK WILL LOSE MOST OF ITS MEANING if it is not inserted into the broadest possible trends in history. There have been three major waves of liberty so far: the wave of religious liberty, the wave of political liberty, and the wave of intellectual liberty. The book has to be inserted into the need for a fourth wave: Economic Liberty.

Come to Concord

*Concord is a magic place in which words
become action.*

WHILE SAYING GOODBYE AND ISSUING MY LAST PERORATION, I would
like to formally introduce myself and my work to the reader. My
name is Carmine Gorga; my third order Carmelite name is
Carmelo; I was born in the deep South of Southern Italy,
Roccadaspide, Salerno, in 1935; I received a Ph.D. in Political
Science from the University of Naples, Italy, and my highest academic honor has been a Fulbright Scholarship. It has been my good
fortune to study at the feet of a long series of tough teachers,
including two Nobel laureates in economics, Robert A. Mundell
and Franco Modigliani.

Currently, I am the executive director of the Gloucester
Community Development Corporation, the president of Polis-tics,
Inc., and a scholar at the Center for American Studies at Concord,
Massachusetts.

My publications are cited and in part reproduced on my web
sites, which can be accessed at <www.polis-tics.com>.

This is my first volume in Concordian economics. Concordian
economics is a new paradigm that spans the arc from economic
theory to economic practice, through the transmission belt of economic rights and responsibilities.

Powerfully assisted by Professor Franco Modigliani and
Professor M.L. Burstein, a professor of economics at York
University, I have developed this integrated structure over the
course of forty years of interdisciplinary studies and practices.

This is my peroration. The participation of the reader in the evaluation, further development, and implementation of Concordian

economics is essential. There are many things the reader can do. The most important is to "Come to Concord"—mentally, if not physically.

Concord is a magic place in which words become action. It is here that our Founding Fathers exploded the seed of our political freedom, and the shot was heard around the world. It is here that our Transcendentalist authors dispersed the seed of our intellectual freedom (freedom from the intellectual enclosures of Europe), and we have been and we will all be gathering its fruits for a long time to come.

Is Concordian economics the seed that will give us economic justice and, with it, economic freedom for all? President Franklin Delano Roosevelt called for a bill of economic rights. Dr. Martin Luther King called for a bill of economic rights. The issue is not whether, but when and where we will obtain economic justice. Is Concord the place? Is the time now?

———

Well, if not in Concord, will this fourth wave arise in Gloucester, Massachusetts? Gloucester is the place where the land meets the sea and the sky; it is the place where fishermen live; it is the place where religious liberty, the inner core of intellectual freedom, was born—at the other end of Middle Street, the street where I live.

Appendix 1

Symbols, Meanings, and Definitions

Symbols in Concordian economics

H	=	hoarding
P	=	production of all real goods and services
D	=	distribution of ownership rights over real and monetary wealth
CG	=	consumer goods
KG	=	capital goods
GH	=	goods hoarded
OCG	=	ownership of consumer goods
OKG	=	ownership of capital goods
OGH	=	ownership of goods hoarded
EP	=	economic process
PED	=	principle of effective demand
npW	=	nonproductive wealth
pW	=	productive wealth
MY	=	monetary income
E	=	expenditure
E_h	=	expenditure to purchase goods to be hoarded
E_k	=	expenditure to purchase capital goods
E_g	=	expenditure to purchase consumer goods
I_f	=	expenditure on fixed capital
I_w	=	expenditure on working capital
C_k	=	expenditure on capital goods
C_g	=	expenditure on consumer goods

Meanings in Concordian economics and mainstream economics

Y	=	income produced and consumed in mainstream economics
Y	=	income produced, *distributed,* and consumed in Concordian economics

C = consumption or expenditure to buy consumer goods in mainstream economics

C = consumption or *any* type of expenditure in Concordian economics

S = saving means literally 100,000 things in mainstream economics as calculated by Professor W. R. Goldsmith

S = saving means *financial savings* in Concordian economics

I = investment is equal to saving in mainstream economics

I = investment is *all productive wealth* in Concordian economics

Definitions in Concordian economics and mainstream economics

	Concordian Economics	Mainstream Economics
Hoarding	Nonproductive wealth, distinguished between real wealth and monetary wealth	Does not exist
Saving	Financial savings, accounted as a form of money	100,000 possible definitions, as calculated by Professor W. R. Goldsmith
Investment	Productive wealth	Identified through synonyms
Consumption	Spending	Spending on consumer goods
Production Process	Creative activity applied to combination of financial and physical assets (result of division of labor as well as added activity)	For an analog, see Aggregate supply derived from production function (function of various combinations of capital and labor; result of division of labor)

Definitions in Concordian economics and mainstream economics

	Concordian Economics	Mainstream Economics
Consumption Process	The matching of availability of goods and services with readiness to spend that results in an exchange	For an analog, see Aggregate demand (at times considered as automatic response to aggregate supply)
Distribution Process	Availability of money supply matched with ability to obtain part of that supply	Not identified
Economic Process	Resultant of production process, consumption process, and distribution process	For an analog, see Market exchange
Income	Value of goods and services produced (real income, measured in any stable *numeraire*), distributed, and sold (monetary income)	Monetary value of goods and services produced and sold
Personal Income	Sum of proceeds from rent, dividends, principal and/or interest, labor, borrowing, sale of goods, transfers	For an analog, see National Income, in which borrowing cannot exist (just as borrowing exists between nations, but not in total world economy)
Wealth	Monetary wealth is distinguished from real wealth	Monetary wealth is NOT distinguished from real wealth
Real Wealth	Sum of consumer goods, capital goods, and goods hoarded, measured in any stable *numeraire*	Generally understood as sum of real wealth and monetary wealth measured in stable money

Definitions in Concordian economics and mainstream economics

	Concordian Economics	Mainstream Economics
Monetary Wealth	Sum of all financial instruments	Generally understood as sum of all forms of money
Money	Sum of values of all financial instruments	Changing definitions of M1, M2... depending on the category into which one puts currency and various forms of bank balances
Flows	Flows of monetary wealth are distinguished from flows of real wealth	Flows of monetary wealth are NOT distinguished from flows of real wealth
Stocks	Stocks of monetary wealth are distinguished from stocks of real wealth	There are no models of stocks
Models	Mathematical models of flows are distinguished from models of stocks. There are models of stocks and flows of production, distribution, and consumption. In Appendices 2 and 3, there is also a model of the economic system as a whole.	There is an enormous variety of mathematical models, each attempting to represent a specific human activity. Lately, economic models of non-economic activities have also been produced.

Appendix 2

Concordian Economics
Tools to Return Relevance to Economics

Carmine Gorga

—·—

Reprinted by permission of *Forum for Social Economics*
(http://www.springerlink.com/content/1w885686112kt7r//),
May 2008.
For Soc Econ (2009) 38:53-69
The original publication is available at www.springerlink.com.

Abstract   With the help of planes and solids, this paper presents an enlargement of the field of observation of economic theory. Through this transformation, the distribution of ownership rights to money and wealth assumes a central position in economic analysis. Thus social relevance is returned to economics. The validity of this operation is confirmed by the return of the millenarian field of economic justice to its traditional function as guidance to economic policy. The paper then presents four sets of economic rights and responsibilities that offer the potential of translating principles of economic justice into the complexities of the modern world.

Keywords   Economic theory · Economic policy · Economic practice · Economic justice · Economic rights and economic responsibilities · Social relevance

As problems of human and natural ecology mount up, there is growing in mainstream economics the conception of economics for economics sake. The tendency is to see economics as an autonomous discipline isolated from other sciences, and yet dominating all other social sciences. No matter what concerned people within and without the economics profession maintain, the tendency is to neglect those concerns, because mainstream economics has an unstoppable inner force of its own that makes it impossible to change course. This paper assumes that this tendency is due not to the will of any individual economist but to the sheer power of their tools of economic analysis. The action is involuntary. The process is mechanical (cf. *PAER*).

The process is not without consequences. Economic theory has lost control of itself. Perhaps no one has made the case stronger than Alan Blinder (1999: A17, A19), who has said: "...too much of what young scholars write these days is 'theoretical drivel, mathematically elegant but not about anything real.'" As a direct consequence, economic theory has become splintered into various schools, which vie for their own preferred policies. Because of the current disarray, monetary policy has largely been left to the bankers; fiscal policy to the politicians, and hardly anyone speaks of labor or land or industrial policy any longer. In a word, by becoming detached from reality, both economic theory and policy risk becoming socially ineffective—which does not mean that economic practices are not causing social consequences of their own.

This paper offers a set of new tools that is capable of changing this course of action. Through these tools social relevance reveals itself as an integral part of the constitution of economic theory, policy, and practice. To be specified at the outset, the new tools do not reject but incorporate the old tools of analysis. Using planes and solids in space, in addition to points and lines, economic theory automatically encompasses a larger social reality and returns to the fold of socially relevant sciences with authority to suggest desirable policies and practices.

While the proposed tools in economic theory are the result of forty years of analysis published in Gorga (1982, 2002), desirable policies and practices are distilled from a program of action presented in Gorga (1959, 1964, 1991a, 1994, 1999, 2002, and 2007), Gorga and Kurland (1987), and Gorga and Weeks (1997). More extensive treatments can be found in the writings of Benjamin Franklin, Henry George, Louis D. Brandeis, and Louis O. Kelso—with their works, necessarily all their works, read in rapid succession and not any of them as a stand-alone effort. Standing alone, these works are open to debilitating objections. Together, they become an impregnable fortress.

Tools to Control Economic Theory

Mainstream economic theory is an impressive intellectual construction with its own internal logic. Its structure is a bastion impervious to any external influence; it has become a mathematical science, and as such it is autonomous of any influence that does not enter into its logical structure. The intellectual apparatus of mainstream economic theory, once deconstructed, revolves around the following tool kit, which we propose to preserve and to build upon.

Existing Tool Kit

As everyone knows, economics is built on the theory of supply and demand. The demand of most everything increases as its price decreases; and the supply of everything increases as its price increases. This is the bare structure of most theories in economics, from the theory of growth to the theory of money. To appreciate the full force of this method of analysis one needs to realize that the lines of supply and demand represent sets of numbers—in turn derived from functions of two variables, prices and costs—and then one must see those schedules in movement. As they move up or down, right or left, they meet each other at different points on the Cartesian grid and determine a specific equilibrium of prices and quantities offered and accepted of any item of wealth in the market, from bread to gold. The basic characteristics of this framework of analysis become evident upon reflection. The focus of attention is on the market exchange; all that goes on before or after the exchange rests outside the purview of the analyst. The mainstream economist qua economist can only analyze, forecast, and report on present or likely future tendencies toward equilibrium of items of wealth that are offered in the market in exchange for other items of wealth, be they currency or pet rocks. The consequences that follow from market exchanges fall mostly outside the purview this framework of analysis. Is the production of items being exchanged in the market causing physical damage, or moral depravation? Is the distribution of ownership rights over items being exchanged causing a concentration of wealth into too few hands? Is the consumption of items being exchanged causing ecological disaster? These are all familiar questions that are at the heart of the economist's concern. Yet, they can at best be acknowledged by the economist, but they will unavoidably be dismissed as belonging to other fields of analysis such as politics, ecology, morality, and the law, fields that are outside the expertise and control of the economist.

The analysis becomes more complex daily by the sheer weight of accumulated data; hence equations multiply, econometric applications become more sophisticated, and theorems concerning the characteristics of economic relationships become more and more subtle; indeed, there now seems to be a model for every economic activity—and, lately, for many non-economic activities as well; and if the information is missing or it does not quite fit the case, there is the stand-by option of "as if" assumptions. Impressive as these techniques are, beyond all refinements in the state of the art of mainstream economic analysis, most economists admit to its basic limitations; not only that, they also admit that economic theory has been in a state of crisis at least since the publication of Keynes' *General Theory* in 1936. (What did Keynes say is a question that has plagued the profession ever since). Three of the most recent recognitions of the crisis span the arc from acknowledgment of the limits of mainstream economics (Mankiw 2006) to criticism about the relevance of mainstream economic theory (Manicas 2007) to the belief that economic theory has improved and that it is expected to improve over time (Warsh 2006).

As the history of minor and major theoretical revolutions and counterrevolutions proves, economists are ready to try nearly any stop-gap measure to resolve the crisis—provided the proposed measure does not affect the structure of the theory. This position is non-negotiable; and it is not the purpose of this paper to negotiate it. What is presented for discussion is a far simpler proposition: if we want more comprehensive and more accurate results, we need different tools of analysis. In addition to points and lines, we shall be using planes and solids in space: at first, only rectangles and spheres.

The consequences of this transformation are far-reaching. Rather than attempting to create an improved mainstream theory, we shall incorporate its vital and functioning core into a new framework of analysis which, for a number of consilient reasons, this writer likes to call Concordian economics: as we will see below, the structure makes room for the perspective of each one of the various schools dominating today's economic analysis; it opens its doors to inputs from various other intellectual disciplines; and it extends itself in a seamless web to cover economic policies and economic practices.

New Tools in Economic Theory

Through laborious logico-mathematical steps (Gorga 2002: 41-158), one obtains a restructure of mainstream economic theory (Gorga 1982) and its gradual transformation into Concordian economics. While the book presents a description of that transformation with its resultant new mathematical models (Gorga 2002: 25, 38, 71, 74-6, 121-25, 129-37, 153-58, 168-70, 264, 303-20), the present paper reproduces the core of that ground with primary assistance from geometry; thereafter, it extends the analysis to cover economic policy as well as economic practices for implementation of selected economic policies.

The key results of Concordian economic analysis are these. In order to eliminate a set of innate logical contradictions at the very foundation of economic analysis, the nexus between saving and investment is broken and it is replaced by the complementary relation between Investment defined as all productive wealth and Saving defined as all nonproductive wealth—a term that is better replaced with Hoarding.[1] The analysis starts anew on the basis of the proposition that Investment is Income minus Hoarding. Furthermore, since money and financial instruments are not wealth, but only represent wealth, in macro, as distinguished from microeconomics, one cannot add money to real wealth.[2] The two entities have to be kept separate. And then the question arises: What is the relationship between the two? From Aristotle to the late Scholastics such as Ludovicus Molina (1535-1600), Leonhardus Lessius (1554-1623), and Iohannes de Lugo (1583-1660), there was no doubt as to the answer to this question. During this long stretch of time, much economic analysis was built on the equivalence of money and goods in the exchange. It was the distinction between the two and their linkage in the relation of equivalence that provided the objective base for the determination of conditions of justice in the exchange of wealth. If we accept this answer, to satisfy well-known requirements of the principle of equivalence, we search for a third element to link monetary and real wealth together and we find it in the set of rules and regulations that in every society governs the distribution of ownership rights over real and monetary wealth—and we do not stray away from pure economic theory, because we are presented with the monetary value of those rights. The following diagram (Gorga 2002: 36, 163, 314) incorporates these results; it represents the integration of these values on one plane, in this fashion:

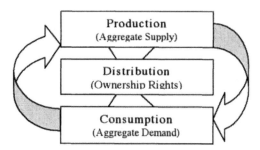

Figure 1. The Economic Process

In this figure, the values of "production", namely the values of all real wealth produced over a specified unit of time are assembled into one category of thought that is recognized as aggregate supply. (It is to be noticed that this unit is "pure" because it contains only stocks of real wealth and no monetary wealth. It is also to be noted that in a more complete treatment this value ought to be observed from the point of view of demand as well as supply: thus we ought to have an analysis of the demand and supply of the production of all real wealth). We follow the same procedure for the values of monetary wealth, thus firmly separating real wealth from monetary wealth, and we call the result "consumption" or aggregate demand. (Ditto for the treatment of all monetary values, which here are not observed from the point of view of supply: The question of the quantity of monetary values created is outside the scope of this presentation). We finally repeat the procedure for the aggregate values of ownership rights over real and monetary wealth, and we call the result "distribution" of ownership rights. (At this juncture we assume that the values of ownership rights over real wealth are identical to the values over monetary wealth). In sum, we have enlarged our field of observation from points and lines to planes and interactions among planes; and, rather than leaving the question of the interaction between demand and supply open (cf. Klein 1970: 143), we have continuously specified—and distinguished one from the other—the demand and supply of (a) real goods, (b) monetary instruments, and (c) values of ownership rights over real and monetary wealth.

Figure 1 reads as follows. When real goods and services pass from producers to consumers, monetary instruments of a corresponding value pass from consumers to producers. Then one cycle of the economic process is completed—and it is accompanied by the silent exchange of values of ownership rights over monetary and real wealth. Both money and goods change hands. The unit of account can be the economy of one person, one nation, or the world. In macroeconomics, the exchange occurs neither between two insignificant commodities as in microeconomics (cf. Schumpeter 1936) nor between any two forms of financial instruments as in the economics of Wall Street. In macroeconomics, fully respecting the laws of supply and demand the total production of real wealth is exchanged for the total availability of financial resources—as in Keynes' principle of effective demand (see Brady 1996). Finally, in this figure the exchange visibly occurs under a regimen of social and legal relationships: ownership is apportioned at the moment of creation of wealth; and only owners can legally exchange wealth.

An effective way to analyze the instantaneous relationships cap-
tured by Figure 1 is to reduce it all to the economics of only one
person. A person who snaps the apple from a tree, vs. gathering
seeds, for instance, while respecting as always the rules of supply
and demand commits an act of production. This person automatically apportions the ownership of the apple to the self, which
means that this person is legally empowered, as it were, to sell the
apple to the self. Thereafter, this person is free to eat the apple—
or sell it to others. One of the merits of Figure 1 is that it describes
the economic process as a whole. Everything is instantaneously
related to everything else. Thus we run away from the shattered
world of the schools and go back to the world of Classical economists who knew that economics is composed of the integration of
Production, Distribution, and Consumption of wealth. This inte
gration can be made more specific by a more extensive and updat-
ed reading of the terms, along these lines: The Theory of
Production—namely a pure and robust production function—is
concerned with the production of real goods and services (as might
be studied by Supply-Side economists); the Theory of Distribution
is concerned with the distribution of the value of ownership rights
over real and monetary wealth (as might be studied by
Institutionalists); and the Theory of Consumption is concerned
with the consumption—or expenditure—of monetary, *i.e.*, financial instruments (as might be studied by Demand-Side economists).
More importantly, by recognizing that Figure 1 is the flat image of
a sphere we bring the mathematics and geometry of economics up
to the standards that prevail among modern engineers and scientists (see, e.g., Thompson 1986: 36), namely:

Synthetic Model of the Economic System as a Whole
(From Gorga 1991b)

$$p\cdot = fp(p,d,c)$$
$$d\cdot = fd(p,d,c)$$
$$c\cdot = fc(p,d,c)$$

where
p· stands for rate of change in total production
d· for rate of change in the values of distribution of ownership
   rights
c· for rate of change in total expenditure.

Most important for our immediate purposes, we can see that the theory of distribution of income and wealth now occupies a very central position in economics. All that relates to the distribution of ownership of income and wealth becomes an immediate and integral concern of economic theory—no longer an afterthought or an issue placed at the margins of economic science. Related issues of social relevance of economics can no longer be shunned aside by the economist on the assumption that they are external to economic theory. These are indeed issues that live at the very core of economic theory; and one does not stray away either from mathematical and quantifiable theory. What is to be measured and evaluated is the economic value of ownership rights over income and wealth—and the different economic effects of different patterns of distribution of income and wealth. Decisions relative to these issues are taken during the very process of production and exchange of wealth; they are not something to be concerned with only after the more impellent problems of production and exchange are resolved, as assumed in Keynesian economics and, mutatis mutandis, in mainstream economics, see, e.g., Klein ([1947] 1968: 187). The concern about the social relevance of economics—as all Institutionalists have devoutly wished—is now brought within the purview of the economist.

Issues of distribution of economic values of income and wealth are not external givens; they exist at the very core of the economic process and are determined by the inner workings of this process. On Mars the situation might be different; on earth, people create not only real or physical wealth—they also assign values to this wealth. Indeed, it is economists (and accountants) who, assisted by the laws of supply and demand, assign these values as best they can. Lawyers only validate these statements by transforming them in negotiable legal instruments that are called ownership rights. These rights might belong to an individual person, to a corporation, or to the state; but they legally belong to someone. And an exchange of real wealth for monetary wealth involves at the same time an exchange of the value of ownership rights over real and monetary wealth. It is thus that, no matter the disclaimer by many economists, economic values are created and are created at the very core of the economic process.

Tools to Control Economic Policy

Having discovered that the distribution of ownership rights over income and wealth is an integral part of economic theory, the question becomes: What are the tools to obtain the desired pattern of distribution of income and wealth? This is the eminent question of economic policy. Economic theory tells us that, once this pattern is set, most other questions of economic policy are automatically settled. The answer to the question is well known.

Existing Tool Kit

Even though the historic roots of economics lie in moral philosophy, economists have lately assumed that they have nothing to contribute to the discussion concerning the selection of patterns of distribution of income and wealth. They have left the field to lawyers, ethicists, philosophers, sociologists, and political scientists. Mainstream economists believe that they do not have—and, what is more important, they ought not to have—any tools to control the pattern of distribution of income and wealth. Mainstream economists assume that this is a given, namely a determination that is and ought to be left to society as a whole. Economics, as pure science, as an autonomous mathematical science, is supposed to analyze the effects of various societal decisions, but not to intervene in those decisions. It is a direct consequence of this assumption that economic theory is fast becoming socially irrelevant. Under these conditions, the discussion on economic policy falls into a trap. The discussion becomes the property of various schools of economics, each purporting the benefits of its own dictates and none being able to convince the other schools of the validity of its positions.

We do not need to put a step on this slippery slope. Once it is established that the pattern of distribution of income and wealth is an integral part of economic theory, the analysis is restricted to this question: How can we translate economic theory into economic policy? In the paragraphs below we will offer a set of new/old tools for consideration. This set calls for the construction of the theory of *economic* justice, and therefore economists will discover that they have much to contribute to it. This is the high road to re-establish social relevance to economics.

Proposed Tools to Control Economic Policy

A mere glance at the history of economic thought makes us glean this proposition: The transmission belt that for millennia carried economic theory into economic policy is the doctrine of economic justice. While remaining astonishingly constant from Aristotle to the late, or early modern, Scholastics (see, e.g., Wood 2002: 83), this understanding allowed for continuous adaptations to the circumstances of the moment.[3] The doctrine of economic justice was divided into two planks: distributive and commutative justice. Distributive justice guided rules and regulations that govern the division of wealth as it is created; commutative justice guided rules and regulations that govern the transferal of wealth between buyers and sellers at the moment of the exchange. While the Doctors of the Church, most notably St. Thomas Aquinas, left much room for discretion in the determination of distributive justice to the parties involved in the economic process, they reached a firm and revolutionary conclusion about the dictates of commutative justice. The commutation of wealth, namely the exchange, occurs in accordance with principles of justice, they discovered, only if it reflects a free market price: a price determined in a market that is not dominated by either governmental or private monopolistic forces (see, e.g., Schumpeter 1954: 98-99).

While this formula appears simple, it envelops great complexities. With it, the Doctors of the Church unified the social requirements of freedom with those of morality in economics; and it was the exercise of morality that yielded freedom. The application of this formula created the essential conditions for the enterprise system to be as free as it could be at the time. Over time, this ordered set of priorities was twisted around and its power dissolved. Through insistence on unfettered economic freedom (cf. Fanfani 2003), the unity of freedom and morality—with its inherent social relevance—was shattered and the doctrine of economic justice was lost in the fog of time.

Truth to tell, the dissolution of the doctrine of economic justice was facilitated by the fact that it was never presented with a visible head. People with direct or indirect access to land and natural resources participated in the economic process as a matter of fact through well-established privileges and as a consequence of unspoken sets of rights (indirectly, access to land and natural resources was secured through the commons: for millennia the safety valve to preserve the dignity of the poor). Hence, it never occurred to Aristotle or any of the Doctors of the Church to make explicit the requirements of a third plank that might be called participative justice (Gorga 1999, 2007). For a great variety of reasons, those conditions are no longer in existence. Today, one has to beg in order to participate in the economic process. And if one does not take part in it, one is marginalized; one is shunted to the margins of society. Hence the plank of participative justice, as it is increasingly recognized from many quarters, must be explicitly formulated. When participative justice is added to the other two planks, the doctrine is completed and transformed into the theory of economic justice. Once that is done, one is presented with a framework of analysis that can be represented in this fashion:

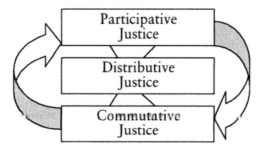

Figure 2. Economic Justice

Figure 2 reads as follows. Participation in the economic process is a matter of justice, because only men and women who participate in the production of wealth are entitled to the distribution of ownership of a share of the wealth created through their participation.[4] A just commutation of wealth, a just exchange, is implicit in the very distribution of wealth in accordance with one's participation; but, of course, the principle of commutative justice extends itself to cover the exchange of wealth just created for other wealth existing on the market. It is in accordance with these objective principles that the pattern of distribution of current income and wealth is and ought to be determined. Economists can render these calculations very precise.

But economists have much broader tasks than these. Figure 2 is a mirror image of Figure 1. If the distribution of ownership rights is an inherent part of the economic process, as we have seen in the previous section, economic justice becomes a natural extension of economic theory. Indeed, one can just as soon separate economic theory from economic justice as one can separate a person from her shadow. (The forced separation of these two entities has ineluctable consequences of its own that ought to be of great interest to the investigative powers of the economist). Given this condition, a minimum set of questions to be asked by economists in the formulation and evaluation of any economic policy might be: Does the proposed policy favor participation in the creation of wealth? Does it allow for a fair distribution of the wealth thus created? Does it allow for a fair transfer of wealth from one person or group to another? Much could be said on these issues, but since much is already well known, we shall shun away from broad and elaborate discussions of these issues.

The wisdom of staying away from broad and elaborate discussions, however, does not necessarily require staying away from the specifics of the case. The specific question is: How can we transfer the principles of economic justice into the complexities of the modern economy? Needless to say, this is a question that is not formally and comprehensively raised in mainstream theory. This is a question that arises naturally and forcefully within the context of the structure of Concordian economics.

Tools to Control Economic Practices

In the section on economic theory we have seen how does the economic system create wealth, how its value is determined by economists and accountants, and how its value is then transformed in ownership rights by lawyers. In the section on economic policy we have observed how economic justice determines the apportionment of those ownership rights. In this section we shall observe how the economic system operates in practice.

Lack of an Existing Tool Kit

"High" mainstream theory is silent on the practices of economics. This neglect is not due to chance; rather, it is due to the assumption that, since economic practices are determined by society at large and are supposedly controlled by allied social disciplines, they lie outside the economist's field of expertise. Indeed, having abandoned the field to lawyers, and ethicists, and philosophers, and sociologists, and political scientists, mainstream economists have become passive takers of a proposition that exists at the very core of the issue. This is the proposition that present ownership rights provide practical rules for the distribution of future ownership rights. The proposition has long legs, because it determines the pattern of future distribution of income and wealth. Economists observe every day the manifold negative consequences of this belief, but feel powerless to even address the issues. This is another juncture at which, by taking themselves out of the discussion, economists are threatening to make economics a socially irrelevant discipline.

To regain their power, economists have only to look at it as an economic, rather than a legal, political, or moral issue. If they do that, they discover that their assumptions are faulty. The error is elementary. The reasoning is circular. In order to enter and to break this circular form of argumentation, namely that present property rights determine future property rights, economists need to remember that property rights are pieces of paper: a piece of paper does not—and cannot—create real wealth. It is not even the *exercise* of property rights that creates real wealth. Property rights are a bundle of rights that link human beings to things. Their current owners may wish as hard as they can, it is not in the nature of property rights to create wealth.

It is not the use of property rights, but the use of property—namely, the use of real goods and services that creates new wealth. The distinction is fundamental. The discussion is shifted away from the abstract legal field on to a concrete field. The discussion is focused on the observation of the economic reality. The use of real goods and services to create new wealth is infused, not by property rights, but by the exercise of economic power. To an economic power corresponds an economic right. As specified below, temporally, logically, economically, and legally, economic rights precede property rights. Economic rights are the generators, the fathers and the mothers, of property rights. The nature of economic rights becomes clear when the two rights, economic rights and property rights, are observed as separate and distinct entities, and then both rights are placed in contraposition with entitlements. The three terms are often used as synonyms. They are not. As specified in Gorga (1999),

> First, the content of these three entities is different. The object of property rights are *marketable things,* tangible or intangible things such as material goods and services. The object of entitlements are *human needs,* from food to shelter to health. The object of economic rights are *economic needs.* Second, the legal form of these three entities is different. Property rights are *concrete legal* titles over existing wealth; economic rights are *abstract legal* claims over future wealth; and entitlements are *moral* claims on wealth that legally belong to others. Finally, the quantity that they measure is variable. While both property rights and entitlements relate to existing wealth, and therefore a necessarily finite quantity, economic rights relate to future wealth, an unknown and elastic—if not a potentially infinite—quantity.

Economically, and consequently legally, real wealth is created by the exercise of economic rights—indeed, economic rights and economic responsibilities, as we shall see. Hence economists are fully entitled to extend their competence to the field of economic rights and economic responsibilities. Economists will discover that the field is wholly within their range of expertise and responsibility. At the end of this journey, economists shall be able to offer to lawyers, ethicists, and philosophers, as well as political scientists and politicians, this proposition: Future ownership rights are determined, not by property rights, but by economic rights—indeed, they are determined by economic rights and economic responsibilities. Thus the closed circuit that at present imprisons economic theory, the proposition that property rights beget property rights, is broken. Economists are in charge of economic issues.

New Tools to Control Economic Practices

The transmission belt that carries principles of economic justice into the complexity of modern economic life, and shapes objective guidelines for the formulation and evaluation of just economic policies is the presence of economic rights and economic responsibilities (ERs&ERs), both lodged in the same person at the same time. These two conditions need to be clarified. Economic rights and responsibilities need to be lodged into the same person, otherwise one does not follow an economic discourse in which everything is strictly related to everything else; rather, one follows escapism: if my father, my uncle, or the state is responsible for my welfare, we are lost, as Keynes used to say, "in a haze where nothing is clear and everything is possible" (Keynes 1936: 292). The second condition is equally important. Economic rights are rooted, not in abstract morality, but in our own concrete economic responsibilities (cf. Gorga 1999).

ERs&ERs come forward in response to the well-known requirements of the factors of production identified by Classical economists as land, capital, and labor—with the addition of a modern distinction between financial and physical capital. Guided by these economic needs, placing ourselves in a Schumpeterian world our focus of attention is on the satisfaction of the plank of participative justice; successive iterations that are mostly skipped in this presentation would reveal that the same rights and responsibilities satisfy also the requirements of the planks of distributive justice and commutative justice. A minimal set of economic rights and corresponding responsibilities is as follows:

1. *We all have the right of access to land and natural resources.* This is a natural right. It belongs to us just in virtue of our human-

ness. Land and natural resources are our original commons. They belong to us all. This is an essential right, because without the possibility of exercising it, we are deprived of the possibility of participating in the economic process. And without this participation, we are marginalized; we are made dependent on the good will of others. The most direct way of securing this right in the complexity of the modern world is neither through squatting nor through expropriation; rather, it is through the exercise of *the responsibility to pay taxes* for the exclusive use of those resources that are under our command—with a corresponding reduction of taxes on buildings and improvements on the land. The exercise of the responsibility to pay taxes on land has a double function: It secures our right to the use of the resources that are under our command and it also makes room for others to access land and natural resources that they need. Land taxation is the economic bridge between hoarding, namely the accumulation of idle land, and the right of access to that land with its natural resources. Paying taxes on the value of land and natural resources gradually encourages dis-hoarding, hence it lowers the price of the land, and correspondingly opens up the resources of that land to all those who need them and can make use of them. Worrisome hoarding is especially that which occurs both downtown and in the belt surrounding major cities and towns. It is to leapfrog over this belt that people go to the suburbs in search for affordable land, thus creating overstretched lines of communication and protection and overlong commuting lines—with consequent waste of fuel that overtaxes nonrenewable resources, the ozone layer, the pocketbook, and the nervous system. Paying taxes on land value is a most fair form of taxation, because it implies returning to the community part of the value that is created, not by the individual owner, but by the community. Land that sits idle does not produce income, true; yet, it produces capital appreciation over time: Rare is the case of capital loss; and even when that occurs, the relative loss tends to be smaller than the loss on other assets. (To see how this pair of ERs&ERs meets also the requirements of distributive and commutative justice, let us simply consider that, if one avoids taxes, the total tax load is not going to be distributed fairly among the population. And if one avoids taxes, one obtains something—*i.e.*, private control over a quantity of resources—for which one does not offer proportionate compensation to the rest of the community.)

2. *We all have the right of access to national credit.* Since national credit is the power of a nation to create money, and since the value of money is given by the value of wealth left over by past

generations and the creativity of every person in a nation, national credit is the last frontier, the last commons. Without access to credit today one is made economically impotent. Worse, since this advantage is granted to the privileged few, it is automatically denied to the majority of the population who are henceforth condemned to pay a higher rate of interest, if they obtain credit at all. Of course, such a loan should be extended only on the basis of *the responsibility to repay the loan*. And these loans will have a high chance of being repaid because they ought to be issued at cost and issued exclusively to individually owned enterprises, Employee Stock Ownership Plans (ESOPs), and cooperatives, as well as states and municipalities, and issued exclusively for capital formation, namely for the creation of new wealth—not to buy financial paper, consumer goods or goods to be hoarded or to cover administrative expenses of states and municipalities. Capital credit liberates people, while consumer credit enslaves them.

3.   *We all have the right to the fruits of our labor.* This right should not be limited to the right to obtain only a wage. It should be extended to cover the other major fruit of economic growth over time: capital appreciation—as well as being subject to capital loss, of course. The only justification for reserving capital appreciation for stockholders, the owners of a corporation, and excluding workers from it, can be found in the fact that loans are given only to owners of past wealth (the Catch-22 of today's economic reasoning: "save and invest and you too can become rich"—as if this proposition were either economically feasible or ecologically sustainable). But from now on this right can be extended to people who do not have prior wealth through the right of access to national credit—especially by legally transforming workers into owners through individually owned enterprises, Employee Stock Ownership Plans (ESOPs), and cooperatives. Of course, this full right should be extended only in correspondence with *the responsibility to offer services* of value equivalent to projected compensation. And there will be an outpouring of such services because, while in a command and control economy workers are requested to check their brain at the factory gates, in a socially responsible economy—an economy in which rights are exercised on the basis of responsibilities—workers/owners are legally, socially, and psychologically empowered to exercise their brain fully at their work post.

4.   *We all have the right to protect our wealth.* This right seems to be universally accepted, except in one case that matters most: in the case of the trustification process, the process used especially

after the Civil War in the United States to create corporate trusts and repeated in a hundred subtle variations ever since. (People feel free, not only to acquire shares of the stock of one corporation, but free to use that stock to acquire another whole corporation by all forms of trusts, mergers, and acquisition. The very idea of the corporation, forever a public entity, has thus been privatized and monetized). There are two ways in which corporations grow: one is through internal growth, and this approach ought to be protected in no uncertain terms; the other is through external purchase and, with limits, this manifestation ought to be prohibited in no uncertain terms. Why? Because this prohibition is the only certain way to protect the wealth of present owners. And if it is assumed that most stockholders of the modern corporation are happy to have their shares bought and sold on the market, it must be granted that growth-by-purchase takes wealth away from workers who have contributed to create that value—and many times, in the trustification process, lose their work site as well. All in the name of efficiency—a misnomer that stands for private financial gain generated at the expense of shifting costs onto the shoulders of the community at large. Of course, this right ought to be purchased only at the cost of *the responsibility to respect the wealth of others*. These are two-way streets. We cannot even attempt to restrain the Pac-Man economy, while we use Pac-Man instruments.

These economic rights and responsibilities can be exercised by anyone who does not only want to receive economic justice, but also wants to grant economic justice to others. Indeed, these are the essential conditions for the establishment of economic justice, as well as the establishment of a free enterprise system, in the modern world. As a consequence of the dynamics of the implementation of these four marginal changes in our current practices, economic freedom will be expanded to embrace all who want to subject themselves to the rigors of the economic process—and then the few remaining hard cases can be easily taken care of by charity. No. There is no compulsion in any of the above suggestions. The landowner can pay more taxes and control more land or can escape the tax levy altogether by reducing land ownership to zero; the applicant for a national loan can escape the constraints suggested for access to national credit by tapping into private capital markets; the worker can escape the responsibilities of ownership by vying for a job rather than an equity position; and the owner of physical capital can escape the constraints implicit in the proposed anti-trust policy by remaining below the trigger of an agreed-upon threshold for growth-by-purchase prohibition. This prohibition should apply to the largest corporations first and be gradually expanded to include eventually all except, let us say, corporations engaged in intrastate or regional commerce.

Intellectually, the proposed economic rights and economic responsibilities perform functions outlined in the conception of "general abstract rules" by Hayek (1960: 153), the "original position" by Rawls (1971: 12, 72, 136, 538), the "reverse theory" by Nozick (1974: 238), and the "Principle of Generic Consistency" by Gewirth (1985: 19); practically, they will function as Gladwell's (2000) "tipping points". Ultimately, it was a poet, Vincent Ferrini (2002), who caught the essence of economic rights and economic responsibilities by identifying their ability to provide "the answers to universal poverty and the anxieties of the affluent."

Operating as tipping points in our *modus vivendi*, ERs&ERs will set in motion a process of interdependence that respects the reality of economic affairs, and the reality of human relationships. Recognizing that most people and most businesses always act morally, the increasing number of "bad apples" that at times seem to receive all the attention (and envious support) of a superficial intellectual world will be recognized as dangerous exceptions, perhaps ostracized, but certainly no longer applauded. Once the tendencies of these people are kept in check, all wealth will be distributed, not equally—that is meaningless utopianism—but fairly. The assurance for this result resides in the transformation of the current social contract into a legal contract: when landowners pay their share of land taxes, they will sell their hoards and access to land and natural resources will automatically be opened up for most people; when people will get access to national credit, many will become independent entrepreneurs; when workers are transformed into owners, they will have the legal tools to demand a fair distribution of income; when growth-by-purchase will mostly become a forbidden activity, most corporations and most employee/owners will preserve their independence. These measures, by consistently curbing the excesses of the few for a period of at least ten years, will cumulatively lead to a fair distribution of income and wealth. To reassure ourselves of this outcome, let us comprehensively look at the issues from another point of view. If land owners were to use their possessions of land and natural resources efficiently (with efficiency measured through lower private capitalization and higher effective demand), would there be such wanting in the world? If national credit were made available to all entrepreneurs at cost, would we not translate the immanent reservoir of creative powers into economically profitable ventures? If workers were transformed into worker/owners, would we not increase our extant productive capacity incommensurably? If corporate growth-by-purchase—with accompanying translation of that economic power into corruption of our political system—were curbed, would we not obtain less concentration of economic power into a few hands?

All four ERs&ERs naturally lead to a fairer distribution of income than prevails today. Eventually, with a fair distribution of income and wealth, there will no longer be any need for redistributive programs, which are an expression of double utopianism (first, people as if living in la-la land are allowed to accumulate much, no matter how; and then they are expected to peacefully discharge their ill-gotten wealth). Preserving their current wealth, the rich will grow richer at a steady but slower pace; and the poor will no longer be poor, because they will have all they need. Lacking fuel at both ends, violent oscillations in the business cycle will be abated.

We will thus recover the essential truth of economics. This is the truth that there are two conditions of growth: economic freedom and economic justice, as concrete expressions of freedom and morality. Both are essential. The relationship between the two is quite clear: While freedom does not necessarily bring justice with it, justice unavoidably brings freedom. One can abuse freedom by denying freedom to others, one can never abuse justice. Hence, the initial condition of freedom for all is proof positive of the existence of economic justice in the land. This is economics that is socially relevant. And the relevance is not an afterthought. The relevance is implicit. The social import of economic theory is realized when the distribution of ownership rights is seen as an integral part of its constitution; and the social import of economic justice and economic rights and responsibilities is simply stated: We must prevent all foreseeable injustices from occurring. Once an injustice has occurred, there is nothing that can be done to undo the dastard deed. This is the bosom of realism.

One last question: Is the proposed program of action the latest expression of utopianism? The curt answer is: No. Utopianism has consistently been based on the wishful thinking of a single person. The proposed program of action results from filling in the gaps of a millenarian train of thought that, in a seamless web, extends itself at least from morality to economic theory and from there—through economic justice—to economic policy and practice. Utopianism promises immediate results, as if by magic. This proposed program of action asks for concerted, protracted effort.

Whatever life Utopianism has, it is based on the fanatical following of a small group of people who try to force it upon the will of
the multitudes. The proposed program of action is expected to be
readily understood and spontaneously implemented by the multitudes.

Conclusion

The lament that economics lacks social relevance assumes many
forms, but these are mostly centered on the treatment of issues of
distribution of income and wealth. We have found that these issues
are not even investigated by economists today because they assume
that they lie beyond the field of economics. Hence, by placing this
issue at the very core of economics, we have given back social relevance first to economic theory, then to economic policy, and finally to economic practices. Without ever abandoning the field of economics, we have established a continuity of discourse between
three stepping stones in economic analysis. We have followed this
line of reasoning. Since money and financial instruments are not
wealth, but only represent wealth, in macroeconomics one cannot
add money to real wealth. The two have to be kept separate. This
condition raises the question about the relation between money
and real wealth. As in the economics tradition from Aristotle to the
Doctors of the Church, we have recognized that money and real
wealth must be equivalent in value. But equivalence is a formal
relation among three terms. What is the third term? The third term
that links money to real wealth is the economic value of ownership
rights; hence, we have presented a restructure of economic theory
that reflects the need to study not only the monetary economy but
also the real and the legal economy at the same time. From this
new framework of analysis, novel answers are given to the question: How is the distribution of ownership rights achieved today,
and how "should" it be achieved? An investigation of the economic, rather than the legal, moral, or philosophical aspects of this
question leads to the transformation of an age-old doctrine into
the theory of economic justice and to the discovery that the creation of wealth is achieved, not through the exercise of property
rights, which are static, but through the exercise of well-defined
economic rights and economic responsibilities, which take care of
the dynamic needs of the economic world.

Footnotes

1. Every step of the way in Concordian economics, decisions are taken following relentlessly the dictates of fundamental rules of logic. For instance, analysis reveals that since current definitions of saving and investment contain items that are productive (farmed land) and items that are nonproductive (fallow land) of further wealth, both saving and investment respect neither the principle of identity nor the principle of non-contradiction and therefore they cannot be equivalent to each other, as they ought to be for their relation of equality to be formally valid (see, e.g., Allen 1970: 748).

2. The separation of real wealth from monetary wealth is an integral part of the transformation of Keynes' model into the series of mathematical models that provide structure to Concordian economics. This is a procedure that, outlined with the help of geometry (Gorga 2002: 32-37), starts with the enlargement of the definition of consumption from expenditure on consumer goods to spending in all its manifestations (*ibid.*, 139-50), passes through the definition of money (*ibid.*, 222) and the monetary formulation of the Flows Model (*ibid.*, 309-12), and ends with the establishment of the equivalence of the processes of production, distribution, and consumption (*ibid.*, 312-19). The description of these three processes and the economic process as a whole form the substance of Concordian economic theory (*ibid.*, 159-234).

3. To fully appreciate the work of the Scholastics and the Doctors of the Church, we have to remember that "Life, liberty, and property" is the powerful formula that separates modern from ancient political philosophy. It was used by Locke to synthesize the great tradition that goes from Greek philosophers to the late Scholastics in which the concept of property — unlike modern economics — was fully integrated into a system of thought that incorporated all aspects of human knowledge, from theology and metaphysics to law and the physical sciences.

4. What to do with the widow, the orphan, and the handicapped is a moral issue. Economics does not do anything for them. Indeed, as proved by the history of the world, even in the richest of the communities at the height of the business cycle, economics cannot do anything for them. Their number can become so overwhelming, their needs so vast, that even charity becomes powerless.

Economics cannot do anything for the widow, the orphan, and the handicapped—unless, of course, they own stocks and bonds. But then they are not poor; they do not need any assistance through morality. They are capitalists and by the virtue of being capitalists, by the virtue of owning the machines, they participate—through remote control of the machines—by right in the economic process.

Acknowledgments   This paper is uniquely due to several maieutic interventions, truly beyond the call of duty, by Dr. Wilfred Dolfsma. I also would like to acknowledge a clarification brought to this paper by Godfrey Dunkley. If this paper has become a cogent presentation less exposed to potential debilitating criticism of single points, it is due to innumerable constructive suggestions by two referees of *Forum*. A more detailed background for this paper is contained in "The Economics of Jubilation", an unpublished monograph that has been well received by such a diverse audience as Dr. Michael E. Brady, Dr. John C. Rao, Professor William J. Baumol, and Professor Roger H. Gordon. That work, in turn, is based on a framework of analysis which was greatly assisted for 27 years by Professor Franco Modigliani and 21 years by Professor Meyer L. Burstein, among others.

References

Allen, R. G. D. (1970). *Mathematical economics* (2nd ed.). London: Macmillan.

Blinder, A. (1999). Quoted in "Students Seek Some Reality Amid the Math Of Economics," by Michael M. Weinstein, *The New York Times*, September 18, 1999, pp. A17, A19.

Brady, M.E. (1996). A comparison - Contrast of J.M. Keynes' mathematical modeling approach in *The General Theory* with some of his *General Theory* interpreters, especially J.E. Meade. *History of Economics Review*, 25, 129-158.

Fanfani, A. (2003). *Catholicism, protestantism, and capitalism*. Norfolk, VA: IHS Press.

Ferrini, V. (2002). Gorga worthy of note. *Gloucester Daily Times*. December 11, A6.

Gewirth, A. (1985). Economic justice: Concepts and criteria. In K. Kipnis & D. T. Meyers (Eds.), *Economic justice: Private rights and public responsibilities*. Totowa, N.J.: Rowman & Allanheld.

Gladwell, M. (2000). *The tipping point: How little things can make a big difference*. NY: Little, Brown & Company.

Gorga, C. (1959). *A synthesis of the political thought of Louis D. Brandeis*. Graduation Dissertation, University of Naples.

Gorga, C. (1964). Not simply a national fund, but a stabilization and development fund. *Mondo Economico*, 19(14), 14-16.

[Gorga, C. (1982). The revised Keynes' model (an Abstract). *Atlantic Economic Journal*, 10(3): 52.

Gorga, C. (1991a). Bold new directions in politics and economics. *The Human Economy Newsletter*, 12(1), 3-6, 12.

Gorga, C. (1991b). The Dynamics of the Economic System, unpublished manuscript.

Gorga, C. 1994. Four economic rights: Social renewal through economic justice for all *Social Justice Reiew*, 85(1-2), 3-6.

Gorga, C. (1999). Toward the definition of economic rights. *Journal of Markets and Morality*, 2(1), 88-101.

Gorga, C. (2002). *The economic process: An instantaneous non-newtonian picture*, Lanham, MD: University Press of America.

Gorga, C. (2007). Economic justice. In *Catholic social thought, social science, and social policy: An Encyclopedia*. Lanham, MD: Scarecrow Press.

Gorga, C. & Kurland, N. G. (1987). The productivity standard: A true golden standard. In D. M. Kurland (Ed.) *Every worker an owner. A revolutionary free enterprise challenge to Marxism*. Washington, DC: Center for Economic and Social Justice.

Gorga, C. & Weeks, S. B. (1997). Fisheries renewal: A renewal of the soul of business. *Catholic Social Science Review*, 2, 145-161.

Hayek, F. A. (1960). *The constitution of liberty*, Chicago: University of Chicago Press.

Keynes, J. M. (1936). *The general theory of employment, interest, and money*. New York: Harcourt.

Klein, L. R. (1968 [1947]). *The Keynesian Revolution* (2nd ed.). New York: Macmillan.

Klein, L. R. (1970). The use of econometric models as a guide to economic policy. In *Selected Readings in Econometrics*. Cambridge: MIT Press.

Manicas, P. T. (2007). Endogenous growth theory: The most recent 'revolution' in economics. *Post-autistic economics review* 41, 39-53.

Mankiw, N. G. (2006). The macroeconomist as scientist and engineer. *Journal of Economic Perspectives* 20, 29-46.

Nozick, R. (1974). *Anarchy, state, and utopia*, New York: Basic Books.

PAER (Post-autistic economics review) (2000-2008). Available at http://www.paecon.net/PAEReview/index.htm.

Rawls, J. (1971). *A theory of justice*, Cambridge, MA: Harvard University Press.

Schumpeter, J. A. (1936). The general theory of employment, interest and money. *Journal of American Statistical Association*, 31, 791-95.

Schumpeter, J. A. (1954). *History of Economic Analysis*. New York: Oxford University Press.

Thompson, J. M. T. (1986). *Nonlinear dynamics and chaos, geometric methods for engineers and scientists*, New York: Wiley.

Warsh, D. (2006). *Knowledge and the wealth of nations: A story of economic discovery*, New York: Norton.

Wood, D. (2002). *Medieval Economic Thought*. UK: Cambridge University Press.

Carmine Gorga is a former Fulbright scholar and the recipient of a Council of Europe Scholarship for his dissertation on "The Political Thought of Louis D. Brandeis." Dr. Gorga has transformed the linear world of economic theory into a relational discipline in which everything is related to everything else—internally as well as externally. He was assisted in this endeavor by many people, notably for twenty-seven years by Professor Franco Modigliani, a Nobel laureate in economics from MIT. The resulting work, *The Economic Process: An Instantaneous Non-Newtonian Picture,* was published in 2002. During the last few years, Mr. Gorga has concentrated his attention on the requirements for the unification of economic theory and policy. For details, see www.carmine-gorga.us.

Economics for Physicists and Ecologists

Reprinted by permission of *Transactions on Advanced Research* (January 2008 Volume 4 Number 1): pp. 6-9. This paper is also available at
http://internetjournals.net/journals/tar/TAR2007july.pdf

Gorga, Carmine

C. Gorga is with Concordians.org Inc. (e-mail: cgorga@jhu.edu)

Abstract The lack of communication among physicists, ecologists, and economists can be mostly attributed to the type of mathematics economists use as well as their study of flows of money rather than stocks of real wealth. This paper presents the essential characteristics of a new framework of economic analysis, Concordian economics, which uses standard mathematics and geometry and observes stocks as well as flows of real and monetary wealth. This paper thus attempts to build bridges among the relative disciplines, because it is becoming increasingly clear that vexing problems of human and natural ecology can be solved only through collaboration among economists, physicists, and ecologists.

1. INTRODUCTION

There is a well-known lack of communication among physicists, ecologists, and economists. Using a new framework of economic analysis, Concordian economics [1], a system of thought that results from the relentless application of age-old tools of logic and epistemology to mainstream economic theory, this paper attempts to build bridges among the various disciplines so that lines of communication can be opened and solutions can be found to today's vexing problems of economics and ecology. Physicists, being practical problem solvers, and ecologists, being deeply concerned about the status quo, might join together in this mission to let economics reach the splendor of its full potential.

2. PROBLEM STATEMENT

Lack of communication among physicists, ecologists, and economists is rooted in the practice of economists, who have developed
their own specialized form of mathematics to analyze economic
problems; and have reduced the number of admissible problems to
those that exist in the market at the moment of the exchange. Thus
they analyze only flows, not stocks of wealth; and they observe only
money, not real resources. In particular, physicists have long
remarked that modern economic theory cannot possibly be a fit
description of the reality because, among other reasons, it is a closed
system without inlets and outlets [2]. Ecologists, on their part, never
seem to engage economists because, among other reasons, while
they are mainly concerned with stocks of real wealth, economists are
mainly concerned with flows of money [3].

3. FINDINGS

Three essential findings of Concordian economics are reported here
with the assistance of modern mathematics and geometry: stocks are
separated from flows of wealth; the real economy is separated from
the monetary economy; these two parts of the economic process are
then joined together through the introduction of the legal and institutional economy into the equations.
Through painstaking analysis (Gorga 2002, 23-158) [4], real wealth
(RW) is defined as stocks of consumer goods (CG), plus capital
goods (KG) and goods hoarded (GH). The fundamental model of
production (P) is formulated as follows (*Ibid.*, 38, 313):

$$P = CG + KG + GH$$
$$IA = P - GH$$
$$IA = (CG + KG)$$

where IA = Investment Assets (until sold).

Monetary wealth (MW) is defined as the sum of all financial instruments used to purchase CG, KG, and GH as well as other financial
instruments: corresponding equations form the model of consumption (*Ibid.*, 318). The legal economy is defined as the value of all
rights of ownership over real and monetary wealth: corresponding
equations form the model of distribution (*Ibid.*, 316). Since the structure of these models is self-similar, they are omitted here.

The three systems of equations form an equivalence [5], the equivalence of production to distribution and to consumption. They
describe the same entity, the economic process, from three strictly
interconnected points of view. In more detail, this equivalence refers

to the production of all real wealth; the distribution of ownership rights over both monetary and real wealth; and consumption (or expenditure) of monetary instruments to purchase real wealth. This equivalence can be more easily observed with the assistance of geometry. Thus, using established protocols, it is possible to synthesize the above three systems of equations into one unit represented by the following diagram:

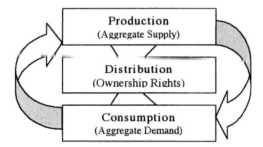

Figure 1. The Economic Process

Figure 1 represents the economic process at the moment of the exchange—as in mainstream economics, but with an enlarged focus. The unit of account can be the economy of an individual person, an individual firm, the local, the national, or the world economy. Figure 1 reads as follows: When goods and services pass from producers to consumers, monetary instruments of a corresponding value pass from consumers to producers. For the exchange to occur, the transactors must be the owners of both money and real wealth. Then, one cycle of the economic process is completed. As can be seen, Concordian economics is wholly relational and inherently dynamic. This second characteristic becomes more explicit if one sees each rectangle of Figure 1 as a Poincaré section. In Figure 1 the economic process is observed at one static moment in time.

There are three approaches for a comprehensive study of the dynamics of the economic process. One is the analytical/mathematical approach. It yields the following generalized system of equations:

$$p^{\cdot} = fp(p,d,c)$$
$$d^{\cdot} = fd(p,d,c)$$
$$c^{\cdot} = fc(p,d,c),$$

where $p\cdot$ = rate of change in the production of real wealth, $d\cdot$ = rate of change in the pattern of distribution of ownership rights over real and monetary wealth, and $c\cdot$ = rate of change in the consumption or expenditure of monetary wealth.

The second approach for the study of the dynamics of the economic process is the historical/latitudinal one. This study calls for following the dynamic transformation of the system, ideally from the beginning of time till today. Starting from flows of real and monetary wealth one obtains a result that is very familiar to modern physicists, a strange attractor or a Lorenz attractor, see, e.g., Thompson (1986, 228) [6]. A few cycles are reproduced here:

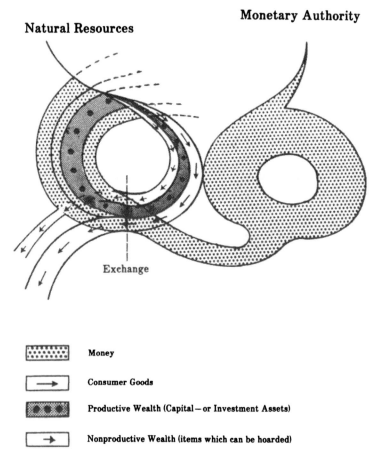

Natural Resources

Monetary Authority

Exchange

Money

Consumer Goods

Productive Wealth (Capital – or Investment Assets)

Nonproductive Wealth (items which can be hoarded)

Figure 2. Flow of Values

With Figure 2, we are not only within the economic process—an area that is a black box to mainstream economics [7]; we have also found the inlets and outlets requested by physicists. The inlets are flows of real and monetary wealth; the outlets are consumer goods, goods hoarded, and money hoarded. It is only capital goods and money to purchase real wealth that remain permanently within the system. The flows of the legal/institutional economy are fully inserted in this construction: They are invisibly present at the moment of the exchange. In order to buy and sell wealth one has forever had to have ownership of that wealth. Indeed, to think of the extreme complexity of the reactions that occur within the economic system, the reader is encouraged to mentally close the two halves of Figure 2 thus creating the image of a torus or a cyclotron. In the reality of daily life, stocks and flows of real and monetary values do not organize themselves into neat patterns, but tend to intermingle and interact with each other.

The third approach is the longitudinal/programmatic one, through which one obtains an external view of the economic system as a whole. This is a new perspective that yields a simplified understanding of other characteristics of the economic system. This mode of analysis can be briefly described as follows: If the economic system were composed of three identical, synchronous, and compenetrating spheres (obtained by rotating each rectangle of Figure 1 at ever increasing speed and in all directions about their geometric center), the system would leave behind only one trajectory as an indication of its dynamics. This line—whatever its pattern—would indicate that the three spheres were in continuous equilibrium with each other. This is not the case in economics: As Mandelbrot (1983, 1) [8] is fond of saying, "Clouds are not spheres, mountains are not cones, coastlines are not circles, and bark is not smooth, nor does lightning travel in straight lines." Can economic systems be expected to be represented by perfect solids? To say the least, the trajectory of aggregate values of monetary wealth (MW) can be expected to soon leave the initial condition of equilibrium (0,0,0) and, spurred by the facility with which monetary instruments can be produced, grow at a faster rate than the trajectory of values of real wealth (RW). Also, the spheres representing the pattern of distribution of values of ownership rights over real *and* monetary wealth, which are known to remain rather static over time, can be conflated into two overlapping straight lines to be identified as DO. Then, over time, eliminating all short and long term, cyclical, random, or aperiodic loops, breaks, and turns, the system as a whole can be expected to leave behind idealized traces of motion as in the following figure:

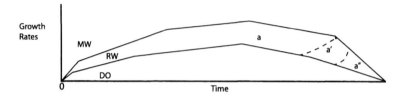

Figure 3. Trajectories of the System as a Whole.

The distance between RW and MW will eventually yield the mathematical measurement of the "bubble". Current efforts to identify the bubble are especially intense [9]; physicists adept at chaos theory have been investigating this issue for quite some time [10]. Area "a"—with its alternative sub-areas a' and a"—attempts to describe the condition of disequilibrium (the bubble) that so often develops between monetary and real wealth and suggests that the smaller this area, the smaller the loss of real income over time. How to close the gap between the real and the monetary economy in the shortest possible time is clearly a problem of control, namely, a problem of economic policy—the problem of creating a just and sustainable economy.

4. CONCLUSION

There is much work to be done. As can be seen, the intellectual framework is mostly done; it is the practical work that is all to be done. This is the work of organizing the data in accordance with the categories of thought specified above; this is the work of analyzing the data with the assistance of modern tools of scientific research. The tempi for the performance of this work can be enormously speeded up if physicists, ecologists, and economists assiduously work together [11].

REFERENCES

[1] Gorga, C. (forthcoming), "Concordian economics: Tools to return relevance to economics" *Forum on Social Economics*.

[2] Nadeau, R. (2008). "Brother, Can You Spare Me a Planet? (Extended version) Mainstream Economics and the Environmental Crisis." *Scientific American,* March.

[3] Daly, H. E. (2008). "Frugality First." In *Frugality: Rebalancing Material and Spiritual Values in Economic Life,* Bouckaert, L., Opdebeeck, H., and Zsolnai, L. (eds.), Oxford, Bern, Berlin, Bruxelles, Frankfurt am Main, New York, Wien: Peter Lang; pp. 207-226.

[4] Gorga, C. (2002). *The Economic Process: An Instantaneous Non-Newtonian Picture.* University Press of America, Lanham, Md., and Oxford.

[5] Gorga, C. (2007). "On the Equivalence of Matter to Energy and to Spirit," *Transactions on Advanced Research* Vol. 3, N. 2: 40-45.

[6] Thompson, J. M. T. (1986). *Nonlinear Dynamics and Chaos, Geometric Methods for Engineers and Scientists.* New York: Wiley.

[7] Petrongolo, B. and Pissarides, C. A. (2001) "Looking into the Black Box: A Survey of the Matching Function," *Journal of Economic Literature,* Vol. XXXIX: 424.

[8] Mandelbrot, B. B. (1983). *The Fractal Geometry of Nature.* New York: W. H. Freeman.

[9] Because of its guidance from Ben Bernanke, most notable today is the work done at the Bendheim Center for Finance at Princeton (*Princeton Weekly Bulletin,* May 26, 1997 and ff.).

[10] See much work done at the Santa Fe Institute.

[11] Matthews, E. (2000). *The Weight of Nations: Material Outflows from Industrial Economies.* Washington, D.C.: World Resources Institute.

Brief Biographical Sketch of the Author

Carmine Gorga is a former Fulbright scholar and the recipient of a Council of Europe Scholarship for his dissertation on "The Political Thought of Louis D. Brandeis." Using age-old principles of logic and epistemology, in a book and a series of papers Dr. Gorga has transformed the linear world of economic theory into a relational discipline in which everything is related to everything else—internally as well as externally. He was assisted in this endeavor by many people, notably for twenty-seven years by Professor Franco Modigliani, a Nobel laureate in economics at MIT. The resulting work, *The Economic Process: An Instantaneous Non-Newtonian Picture,* was published in 2002. For reviews, see http://www.carmine-gorga.us/id18.htm. During the last few years, Mr. Gorga has concentrated his attention on matters of methodology for the reunification of the sciences.

Endnotes

Prolegomena

1. Quoted in "A Third Way for the Third World," by Akash Kapur, *The Atlantic Monthly* Vol. 284, No. 6, December 1999, pp. 124-129.
2. Quoted in "New Millennium Economics: How Did It Get This Way, and What Way is It?" by David Colander, *The Journal of Economic Perspectives* Vol. 14, Number 1, Winter 2000, p. 131.
3. Quoted in "Students Seek Some Reality Amid the Math Of Economics," by Michael M. Weinstein, *The New York Times*, September 18, 1999, pp. A17, A19.
4. See, e.g., Arnold C. Harberger, "A Vision of the Growth Process, *American Economic Review*, March 1998, pp. 1-32.
5. Alvin H. Hansen, "The General Theory," in *The New Economics*, S. E. Harris, ed., (New York: Knopf, 1947), p. 136.
6. John Maynard Keynes, *The Collected Writings of John Maynard Keynes*, D. E. Moggridge, ed., Vol. XIV (London, New York and Toronto: Macmillan, St. Martin's, 1973), pp. 47, 150.

Chapter 1

7. John Maynard Keynes, *The General Theory of Employment, Interest, and Money* (New York: Harcourt, 1936), p. 183.
8. *Ibid.*, p. 52.
9. *Ibid.*, p. 31.

Chapter 2

10. Mandelbrot, Benoit B., *The Fractal Nature of Geometry* (New York: W. H. Freeman, 1983, p. 62.

Chapter 3

11. Keynes, *A Treatise on Probability*, (London: Macmillan, 1921), pp. 3-4.

Chapter 4

12. *General Theory, op. cit.*, p. 74.

Chapter 5

13. *Introduction to Logic* (Princeton: van Nostrand, 1957), p. 218.
14. *General Theory, op. cit.*, pp. 63, 84.
15. *Ibid.*, p. 83.
16. *Ibid.*, pp. 211-12. Cf. also pp. 83-5.
17. *Price Theory* (Chicago: Aldine, 1968), pp. 244-63.
18. *Mathematical Economics* (2nd ed.; London and New York: Macmillan, St. Martin's, 1970), p. 748.

Chapter 6

19. *On Keynesian Economics and the Economics of Keynes* (New York: Oxford University Press, 1968), pp. 28-31, 215-16. Cf. also *General Theory, op. cit.*, pp. 20-1.
20. *Wealth of Nations* (New York: Collier, 1909), Book II, Chapter iii, pp. 277-5.
21. *Elements of Political Economy* (3rd ed.; New York: Kelley, 1963), p. 20. Italics added.
22. Cf., e.g., Henry W. Spiegel, *The Growth of Economic Thought* (Englewood

Cliffs, N. J.: Prentice-Hall, 1971), pp. 260-64. Of course, see Jean-Baptiste Say, e.g., *A Treatise on Political Economy*, trans. C. R. Prinsep (Philadelphia: Lippincott, 1867), Book I, Chapter xv, esp. pp. 132-46.

23. *Chapters in Biography* (New York: Norton, 1963), pp. 102-3, 112-23. Also *General Theory, op. cit.*, pp. 3n, 4n, 5n, 13-18, 32-34.

24. Quoted by R. F. Harrod, "Keynes, the Economist," in *The New Economics, op. cit.*, p. 66.

25. For the influence of the marginalist analysis on Keynes, cf. M. F. Timlin, *Keynesian Economics* (Toronto: The University of Toronto Press, 1942), esp. p. 92n; or Harry G. Johnson, "The General Theory after Twenty-five Years," *American Economic Review*, Vol. LI, No. 2 (May, 1961), esp. p. 5.

26. *A Treatise on Money* (2 vols.; New York: Harcourt, 1930), esp. Vol. I, pp. 123-26.

27. Cf. R. W. Clower, "The Keynesian Counter-Revolution: A Theoretical Appraisal," in *Monetary Theory*, R. W. Clower, ed. (Harmondsworth, Baltimore and Ringwood: Penguin, 1973), pp. 270-97. Cf. also footnote 30 below.

28. *On Keynesian Economics and the Economics of Keynes, op. cit.*, p. 327. For the substantive portion of Leijonhufvud' s analysis, see Chapter III:2.

29. "Lessons from the Current Economic Expansion," *American Economic Review Proceedings*, Vol. LXIV, No. 2 (May, 1974), p. 77. (Lesson 11).

30. "Revolution & Counter-Revolution in Economics: From Lord Keynes to Milton Friedman," *Encounter*, Vol. XXXVI, No. 4, (April, 1971), p. 26.

31. *Essays in Persuasion* (New York: Norton, 1963), p. 373.

32. Joseph A. Schumpeter, *History of Economic Analysis* (New York: Oxford University Press, 1954), p. 280.

Chapter 8

33. *Wealth of Nations, op. cit.*, Book II, Chapter iii, pp. 277-78.

34. Cf. Marian Bowley, *Nassau Senior and Classical Economics* (New York: Octagon Books, 1967), pp. 137-66.

35. Alfred Marshall, *Principles of Economics* (9th ed.; London and New York: Macmillan, 1961), pp. 230-35.

36. Gustav Cassel, *The Nature and Necessity of Interest* (London: Macmillan, 1903), esp. pp. 48, 66-69.

37. Cf. Milton Friedman, *Price Theory, op. cit.*, pp. 257-63.

38. Cf. Lawrence R. Klein, *The Keynesian Revolution* (2nd ed.; New York: Macmillan, 1968), esp. p. 76.

39. *General Theory, op. cit.*, p. 64.

40. "The Savings Problem: A Survey," in *Savings in the Modern Economy*, W. H. Heller, ed. (Minneapolis: University of Minnesota Press, 1953), p.12.

41. *A Study of Saving in the United States* (3 vols.; Princeton: Princeton University Press, 1955-1956), Vol. II, pp. 68, 69n.

Chapter 9

42. *The Nature and Necessity of Interest, op. cit.*, p. 1.

43. *General Theory, op. cit.*, p. 325.

44. *Wealth of Nations, op. cit.*, Book IV, Chapter viii, p. 444.

Chapter 10

45. *General Theory, op. cit.*, p. 161.

47. "The General Theory of Employment," *Quarterly Journal of Economics,* Vol. LI (February, 1937), pp. 211-12.

48. *General Theory, op. cit.,* p. 75.

Chapter 11

46. Immanuel Kant, *Critique of Pure Reason,* trans. F. M. Muller (Garden City, N.Y.: Doubleday, 1966), pp. 66-7.

Chapter 14

49. Thomas Robert Malthus, *Definitions in Political Economy* (London: Murray, 1827), p. 247.

50. J. B. Say, *A Treatise on Political Economy, op. cit.,* Book III, Chapter I, pp. 387-91. John Stuart Mill, *Principles of Political Economy* (2 vols.; 5th ed.; New York: Appleton, 1888), Vol. I, Book I, Chapter iii, esp. p. 72.

51. *Principles of Economics, op. cit.,* p. 64

52. *General Theory, op. cit.,* p. 62.

53. *op. cit.,* p. vi.

54. *General Theory,* op. *cit.,* p. 61.

55. *Ibid., p.* 104.

Chapter 16

56. James Steuart, *Principles of Political Oeconomy,* in *The Works of Sir James Steuart* (New York: Kelley, 1967), Vol. I, pp. 153-54.

57. See E. G. West, *Adam Smith, op. cit.,* p. 168.

58. See *General Theory, op. cit.,* pp. 23-34. Cf. also footnote 23 above.

59. In *American Bar Association Journal,* Vol. XLIII, No. 3 (March, 1957).

60. *General Theory, op. cit.,* p. 25.

61. Paul A. Samuelson, "The General Theory," in *Keynes' General Theory: Reports of Three Decades,* R. Lekachman, ed. (New York and London: St. Martin's, Macmillan, 1964), p. 319.

62. *General Theory, op. cit.,* p. 25.

Chapter 17

63. *Wealth of Nations, op. cit.,* Book II, Chapter iii, pp. 277-8.

64. *Ibid.,* Book II, Chapter viii, p. 444.

65. *General Theory,* op. *cit.,* p. 31.

66. *Ibid.,* p. 85. Italics added.

67. "The General Theory," *op. cit.,* p. 318.

Chapter 18

68. "Keynes and the Classics: A Dynamical Perspective," *Quarterly Journal of Economics,* Vol. 74, No. 2 (May, 1960), p. 323.

69. *Wealth of Nations, op. cit.,* Book II, Chapter iii, p. 275.

Chapter 19

70. Milton Friedman, *A Theory of the Consumption Function* (Princeton: Princeton University Press, 1957), p. 220.

71. Nicholas Kaldor, *Essays on Value and Distribution* (London: Duck-worth, 1960), p. 230. The phrase was originally used by Kalecki.

72. Cf. esp. Joan Robinson, "Prelude to *a* Critique of Economic Theory," in *A Critique of Economic Theory: Selected Readings,* E. K. Hunt and J. G. Schwartz, eds. (Harmondsworth, Baltimore and Ringwood: Penguin, 1972),

pp. 197-204.

73. *Risk, Uncertainty and Profit* (New York: Kelley, 1964), p. xx.

Chapter 20

74. *General Theory, op. cit.,* p. 292.

75. *Ibid.,* p. 305.

76. Cf. footnote 9 above.

77. Robert Clower, "A Reconsideration of the Microfoundations of Monetary Theory," *Western Economic Journal,* Vol. VI, No. 1 (December, [967), p. 5.

Chapter 21

78. *General Theory, op. cit.,* p. 213.

79. *Wealth of Nations, op. cit.,* Book II, Chapter iii, p. 270.

80. *Introduction to Contemporary Microeconomics* (New York: McGraw, 1970), p. 262.

81. *General Theory, op. cit.,* pp. 166-7, 174. Also p.182,

82. Friedrich A. Hayek, *The Road to Serfdom* (Chicago: University of Chicago Press, 1944), p. 42.

Chapter 22

83. "The Use of Econometric Models as a Guide to Economic Policy," in *Selected Readings in Econometrics,* (Cambridge, Massachusetts and London: The M.I.T. Press, 197O), p 143.

84. *General Theory, op. cit.,* p. 20.

85. John Sheahan, *The Wage-Price Guideposts* (Washington: Brookings, 1967), p. 123.

86. *General Theory, op. cit.,* p. 304.

Chapter 23

87. Paul Anthony Samuelson, *Foundations of Economic Analysis* (Cambridge: Harvard University Press, 1947,1966), see, e.g., pp. vii and 167.

88. N. Gregory Mankiw, *Principles of Economics* (The Dryden Press, Orlando, Fl., 1998), p. 25.

89. Barbara Petrongolo and Christopher A. Pissarides, "Looking into the Black Box: A Survey of the Matching Function," *Journal of Economic Literature,* Vol. XXXIX (June 2001), p. 424.

90. René Dubos, *The Dreams of Reason: Science and Utopias* (New York and London: Columbia University Press, 1961), p. 12ff.

91. "Professor Tinbergen's Method," *The Economic Journal,* Vol. XLIX, No. 195 (September, 1939), p. 559.

Chapter 24

92. *Principles of Economics, op. cit.,* p. 3.

Chapter 25

93. See Carmine Gorga, "Toward the Definition of Economic Rights," *The Journal of Markets and Morality,* Spring 1999, II (1) 88-101.

Index

Index

162, 169, 172, 176, 178, 192, 195,
221, 224, 231, 237, 239-242, 245,
255-257, 262, 264-265, 276, 279,
283-284, 289, 291, 307, 312, 331,
334-338, 341-343, 348
system, saving-investment, 7, 19, 72-
79, 86, 100-102, 117-119, 121-125,
132-134, 153
Tables, Penn World, 227
technology, 35, 37, 187, 213, 237,
251, 274, 283, 332
The Capitalist Manifesto (Adler and
Kelso), 166
The New Pioneers (Petzinger), 37
theory, consumption, 200
theory, economic, 3, 5-8, 11-14, 18,
22-24, 27, 29-33, 39-50, 53, 55-56,
59, 63, 69-75, 81, 85-90, 92-93, 98,
100-101, 103, 108, 115-117, 125,
132-133, 137, 139, 142-143, 147,
173, 178-180, 184, 200, 209, 211-
214, 227, 239, 243, 248, 251, 255,
260-261, 272, 285-286, 302-303,
311-312, 322, 325, 327, 331, 334,
357, 361-362
Theory, Journal of Economic, *xx*
theory, law of increasing prices and
decreasing performance. See consumption
Theory of Moral Sentiments (Smith),
164
theory of value, economic value of
wealth, 98
theory of value, market theory of
value, 215
theory of value, market value, 215
theory of value, value in exchange, 215
Thoreau, Henry David, 8
Thucydides, 331
Torto, Raymond G., *xi*, 27
totalitarianism, 334
trade, free internal, 264
Treatise on Money, A (Keynes), 321
Treatise on Probability (Keynes), 10,
42, 277
triage, 333-334
triplespeak, 89, 116
trough, See bottom

tune, 346
tune, of justice, 346
Turgot, Anne Robert Jacques, Baron
de Turgot, 25
underconsumption, 108-109, 291
unemployment, 4, 118, 255-257, 277,
306, 334, 337, 339, 342, 344
unified definition, inflation, 281-282
usefulness, test of, 322
utility, 204, 215
validity, test of, 74-76, 324
value, 43-44, 60, 62, 64, 70, 75, 80,
95, 98, 106-108, 110-111, 118,
121-122, 132, 137, 142-144, 147,
149, 151, 154, 168, 175, 181, 190-
191, 200, 202, 205, 208, 210, 212-
215, 217, 219, 225-230, 245, 247,
268, 273, 288, 291, 298, 308-309,
312, 316, 318, 326, 337, 361
value, economic, 111, 118, 214
value, financial, 107, 111
value, market, 106-107, 219, 228-230
value, monetary, 144
value, theory of, 60, 208, 213-215
Veblen, Thornstein, 165, 262
velocity of circulation (of money), 321
Vico, Giambattista, 251
Voltaire, (Arouet, François Marie), 333
von Neumann's model, 74, 77
wage, 256, 283, 326, 338, 347-348
Walras, M. E. Leon, 33, 166, 321
Walsh, Vivian Charles, 250
wealth, 4, 8, 11-12, 15, 18, 26, 29, 32,
37-39, 43, 45-46, 48-50, 54, 64-65,
67, 85, 90, 97-99, 102, 105-115,
118, 120-123, 127, 130-131, 136-
137, 139, 143-144, 146-148, 151-
152, 154-155, 157, 164, 183, 186-
188, 190, 192-193, 195-196, 200,
211-216, 222, 225-227, 231-232,
237, 246, 249, 251-253, 257, 260-
271, 275, 284, 286-288, 290-296,
298, 302, 306, 310, 312, 315-316,
320, 323-324, 331, 335, 344-349,
352-353, 361-362, 363-375, 377-
383, 387-392
wealth, monetary, *xvi*, *xvii*, 11, 37,
114, 144, 211, 216, 275, 312, 360-